THE ANTISLAVERY VANGUARD:

NEW ESSAYS ON THE ABOLITIONISTS

THE
ANTISLAVERY
VANGUARD:

NEW ESSAYS ON THE
ABOLITIONISTS

EDITED BY

MARTIN DUBERMAN

✳

PRINCETON, NEW JERSEY
PRINCETON UNIVERSITY PRESS
1965

CONTENTS

INTRODUCTION*

FOR a long while the historical verdict on the abolitionists seemed settled. It had been widely agreed that they were meddlesome fanatics, men blind to their own motives, to the needs of the country, and even to the welfare of the slave. It was these men, wrapped in their self-righteous fury, who did so much to bring on a needless war.

Recently, re-examination of the abolitionist movement has begun, and it is already clear that the old portrait no longer satisfies; its dictums are too categorical, its sympathies too restricted. It is still too early for a new synthesis of abolitionist history—itself but part of that broader antislavery movement which also needs re-evaluation—and this volume of essays makes no such claim. Its aim will have been accomplished if it offers enough new data and new insights to demonstrate that a reevaluation is both possible and necessary.**

The history of this collection is itself a revealing commentary on current attitudes toward abolitionism. In conceiving the volume, I had two objectives in mind: first, to excavate and encourage the recent tendency toward a more sympathetic appraisal of the movement,

* Robert Lowell, *For the Union Dead* (New York, Farrar, Straus and Giroux, Inc.; copyright © 1964 by Robert Lowell). Reprinted by permission of the publishers.

** All the essays in this volume, except two, were written especially for it. Mr. McPherson's essay is a revised version of a chapter in his recent book, *The Struggle for Equality*; Mr. Zinn's contribution is part of a study he is currently working on. The authors of two or three other essays will later use them in longer works.

A special word is due Silvan S. Tomkins, Director of the Center for Research in Cognition and Affect, City University of New York. In an effort to broaden the context of discussion by adding insights from a related discipline, I prevailed upon Professor Tomkins to undertake an essay. To do so, he has had to research deeply in historical materials, and I am grateful for this unusual expenditure

but second, to include all scholarly points of view, so
that disagreements in interpretation might be further
clarified, even if not resolved.

This second objective has been difficult to meet, largely
because one end of the spectrum of opinion—that holding to the traditional view of the abolitionists—has
shrunk considerably. This is not to say that historians
critical of the abolitionist position no longer exist. They
do, and include some of the most distinguished scholars
of the older generation. But when I invited several of
these men to contribute essays, they replied that they had
long since "had their say," that their views were already
well known and in any case had recently changed but
little, and that their presence in a volume aimed even in
part at re-evaluation would thus be of dubious fitness.

Still aiming at inclusiveness, I then searched for like-
minded replacements among the younger generation of
historians—but with little result. The younger generation, it seems—and I was surprised at the degree of consensus—is not "like-minded." As one historian wrote
when I asked him to join the search for critics: "as for
'anti-abolitionists,' you are right—they are hard to find.
Naturally, I think. The attitudes which underlay the historical assault on abolitionism of thirty or forty years
ago are now decaying."

Though most of the contributors to this volume may
be said to be sympathetic to the abolitionists, they
have not seen their function as one of vindication or
special pleading. One or two of the essayists have chosen
to make explicit defenses of abolitionism, but the
large majority have dealt in neutral terms of analysis.
Yet the cumulative weight of their analysis points in the
same direction as that of the overt defenders—toward

---

of time and energy. He insists that he has gained from the experience as many new insights into his own field as historians may
have gained from him—which should cheer believers in inter-
disciplinary cooperation.

a more sympathetic evaluation of the motives, tactics, and effects of the movement. In this regard, the volume accurately reflects, I believe, the dominant view of the younger generation of historians.

It would be naïve to ignore the connection between this "new view" and the current civil rights struggle. Committed as they are to that struggle, many historians are now predisposed to look kindly on an earlier move-ment of roughly analogous outlines: the scholarship of this generation is no more immune to contemporary pressures than scholarship has ever been. But historians have, needless to say, a responsibility to resist those pres-sures. If historical study is to preserve any claim to ob-jectivity, or to remain differentiated from propaganda, scholars must make every effort to separate past and pres-ent. Yet the separation can never be complete, and in one sense, it is well that it is not. For while the past should never be distorted to meet present needs, the focus of historical investigation will always reflect those needs; that is, inquiry will be directed, consciously or otherwise, toward those areas of past experience which seem to have most pertinence for our own. Thus the continuously shifting focus of historical study, paralleling the shifting needs of historical generations.

An historian's deep engagement in contemporary af-fairs, moreover, is not presumptive proof that his histor-ical interpretations will be distorted. His involvement may, on the contrary, allow him to share, and thereby understand more fully, the comparable commitment of an earlier generation. He may see aspects of their experi-ence previously closed off to historians who lacked the needed points of identification. Thus it is possible that our generation, again absorbed by the "Negro Question," may for the first time be able to appreciate certain quali-ties of the mid-nineteenth century experience. But this identification carries potential dangers along with po-tential gains. Our vision can be clouded as well as sharpened by present concerns, our wish to see certain patterns in the past can lead us to new inventions rather than to new perceptions—dangers the contributors have been aware of and have tried to avoid, but which they know they cannot hope to have wholly escaped.

In one sense this volume bears depressing testimony. Time and again it offers excerpts from past writings and speeches which repeat almost word for word arguments and attitudes still current today. On a variety of questions—the quality of the African past, the utility of social protest, the meaning of race—we hear not echoes but what are almost literal transcripts of contemporary debates. After a hundred years—or would a thousand be more accurate?—there are still the same shibboleths, the same fears, the same denunciations. Perhaps men cannot learn from past experience; it may be that each generation must always repeat the errors of preceding ones. But perhaps we repeat the past only because we have never really learned it. If we once understood, for example, how much of the debate on the "Negro Question" has already been rehearsed, we might not endlessly restage it. The essayists in this volume will feel rewarded beyond expectation if, by presenting the past debate, they make any small contribution toward its present foreshortening.

MARTIN DUBERMAN

May 19, 1964
Princeton University

PART I: BACKGROUND

Colonel Shaw

is riding on his bubble,

he waits

for the blesséd break.

*Robert Lowell, "For the Union Dead"**

CHAPTER I

SLAVERY AND SIN:

THE CULTURAL BACKGROUND

BY DAVID BRION DAVIS

I

THE inherent contradiction of slavery lies not in its cruelty or economic exploitation, but in the underlying conception of a man as a conveyable possession with no more autonomy of will and consciousness than a domestic animal. This conception has always raised a host of problems and has never been held without compromise. From the ancient world we find no assertion that slavery was an intolerable evil that should be eradicated by any civilized nation.[1] But this does not mean that the Bible and classical literature had no bearing on the later antislavery movements. From the earliest times slavery was taken as a model for certain religious, philosophic, and political dualisms, and was thus implicitly connected with some of the greatest problems in the history of human thought. As a result of these associations and precedents, embodied in holy Scripture, in the works of philoso-

[1] Isaac Mendelsohn, *Slavery in the Ancient Near East: a Comparative Study of Slavery in Babylonia, Assyria, Syria, and Palestine from the Middle of the Third Millennium to the End of the First Millennium* (New York, 1949), p. 123; William L. Westermann, "Between Slavery and Freedom," *American Historical Review*, L (January 1945), 213-16; Westermann, *The Slave Systems of Greek and Roman Antiquity* (Philadelphia, 1955), pp. 1, 26; Moses I. Finley, "Was Greek Civilization Based on Slave Labor?" reprinted in *Slavery in Classical Antiquity: Views and Controversies*, ed. Moses I. Finley (Cambridge, Eng., 1960), pp. 61, 63-64. For a different view, see Gerhard Kehnscherper, *Die Stellung der Bibel und der alten christlichen Kirche zur Sklaverei* (Halle, 1957), *passim.*

phers and divines, in the corpora of Jewish and Roman law, any future attack on slavery would be bound to produce reverberations through the vast range of Western culture. Slavery could never be isolated as an objective issue of public policy.

The word "slave," as applied to the American Negro, had connotations different from those of *'ebed, doulos,* or *servus.* Yet the English translators of the Bible, who rendered the two former words as "servant" or "bond-servant," evoked meanings associated with an essentially medieval or early modern concept of "service." The ancient words were closer in meaning to "slave" than to "servant," and were derived from such concepts as labor, burden, and bonds.[2] In their adjectival form they were used loosely to suggest servile, slavish, and lowly.

The Hebrew word was used in one sense to refer to a righteous punishment sanctioned by the Lord. "Cursed be Canaan," cried Noah, "a servant of servants shall he be unto his brethren." The phrase "a servant of servants," we are told, meant "the meanest slave," and the descendants of Canaan were thus condemned to perpet-

---

[2] *Doulos* may have come from a root meaning to bind. Romans thought that *servus* came from *servo,* to save or preserve, thus deriving from the sparing of captives; but modern authorities find the root in *svar,* a weight or burden, or *sero,* which would have referred to the binding of the slave. The Hebrew *'ebed,* "slave," and *'abādīm,* "slaves," are probably related to words meaning work or labor. A similar connection can be seen between the Russian *rob,* "slave," and *robotati,* "to work," although by the eleventh century the word *kholop* was frequently used for "slave," and as in many languages, there was anything but clarity in the precise meaning of the various words for slave and servant (see B. Grekov, *Kiev Rus,* tr. Y. Sdobnikov, Moscow, 1959, pp. 207-15, 226-49). For the changing meaning of such words as *servus, Knecht,* and *vassus,* see Marc Bloch, "Comment et pourquoi finit l'Esclavage antique," reprinted in *Slavery in Classical Antiquity,* pp. 219-21, and the discussion of *servus* in Polydore Vergil, *De Inventoribus Rerum* (Paris, 1528), *lib.* v, *cap.* 2. Confusion is increased further by the fact that some English writers of the 17th century, such as Hobbes, used the word "servant" for the most absolute type of slave (*Leviathan,* ii, xx).

ual bondage.[3] But slavery was also the clearest example of the total subordination of one individual to another, of the negation of personal choice and desire. It was associated in the Old Testament with religious humility and self-surrender, as when Abraham, Lot, Moses, Job, and David were referred to as slaves of the Lord. That their Master gave them protection and guidance hardly altered the essential meaning of this relationship. Moses used the same word to refer both to Israel's slavery in Egypt and, after deliverance, to their bondage to Yahweh. And he repeatedly reminded his people of their former slavery and of their new obligations: "And thou shalt remember that thou wast a servant in the land of Egypt."[4] Hence liberation and purposeful mission were conceived as a transfer of dependence from worldly masters to the Lord. The promise of God revealing himself to mankind through a chosen people was associated with emancipation from physical slavery and the voluntary acceptance of a higher form of service.

These religious connotations of slavery had profound consequences. On Sinai Moses was told that the Hebrews should buy their slaves from neighboring nations, "And ye shall make them an inheritance for your children after you, to hold for a possession . . . but over your brethren

---

[3] Gen. 9:25; John Skinner, *A Critical and Exegetical Commentary on Genesis* (New York, 1900), p. 184. In view of the significance attached to Noah's curse by later apologists for Negro slavery, we might note that the passage is filled with complexities. According to Gerhard Von Rad, the original Yahwistic narrative had nothing to do with Shem, Ham, and Japheth, and the ecumenical scheme of nations which follows. It was rather an older story, limited to the Palestinian Shem, Japheth, and Canaan, and connected with the horror felt by newly arrived Israel at the sexual depravity of the Canaanites. Later on, a redacter inserted the name of Ham as the father of Canaan, in an effort to harmonize the narrative with the later table of nations (*Genesis, a Commentary*, tr. John H. Marks, Philadelphia, 1961, pp. 131-33). Apparently because of this accident, Negroes, who were early associated with Ham, were stigmatized with the curse of Canaan.

[4] Exod. 2:23; 6:6,9; 13:3,4; Deut. 5:15; 15:15.

the children of Israel ye shall not rule, one over another, with rigor."[5] As Josephus later noted, explaining Jewish history to the Hellenistic world, it was not reasonable for Hebrews to make slaves from their own people when God had made so many nations subject to Israel.[6] The careful regulations concerning Jewish servants were justified by the memory of bondage in Egypt—by the recognition of a common dependence on Yahweh the emancipator. But while Jeremiah condemned his people for re-enslaving Hebrew bondsmen who had been released from service, and while Job tried to prove his righteousness by acknowledging that God would have had reason to punish him if he had despised the cause of his servants, the Old Testament contains no explicit protest against slavery.[7] Yet religious mission was closely linked with liberation from bondage to men and with a new bondage to a higher authority. This central conception would ultimately have special meaning for American colonists who thought of their own mission as a deliverance from spiritual slavery in Europe, and as adherence to divine law in a New Jerusalem.

II

Plato's view of slavery was related to his general philosophy in certain ways that were of importance for the future. By the fifth century B.C. many Greeks had come to believe that the inferiority of barbarians could be seen in their willingness to submit to despotic and absolutist rulers. According to Herodotus, when two brave Spartans were told by a Persian commander that they might expect great rewards if they submitted to Xerxes, they said in defiance: "A slave's life you understand, but never having tasted liberty, you can not tell whether it be sweet or no."[8] For certain Greek writers, including

---

[5] Lev. 25:44-46.

[6] Josephus *Jewish Antiq.* viii. 160.   [7] Jer. 34:8-20; Job 31:13-15.

[8] *Pers. Wars* vii. 135 (Mod. Lib. edn., tr. George Rawlinson, New York, 1942).

Plato, two consequences followed from this popular distinction between Hellene and barbarian.[9] Firstly, bondage was closely associated with tyrannical government and arbitrary power; a people with a capacity and ardent desire for freedom, as evidenced by their political institutions, could not legitimately be slaves. Secondly, a "slavish people" lacked the capacity not only for self-government but also for the higher pursuits of virtue and culture. Thus for Plato a slave might hold a true belief but could never know the truth of his belief, since he was inherently deficient in reason.

Plato also saw the relation of slave to master as a kind of microcosm of the hierarchical pattern that pervaded society and the entire universe.[10] This is not to say that he derived his cosmology or political theory from the model of slavery; yet his reference to the body as the slave of the soul, as Gregory Vlastos has pointed out, was meant as a serious philosophic truth.[11] The relations of body and soul, of sovereign and subjects, of master and slave Plato subsumed under a single theory of authority and obedience. Moreover, in his cosmology he perceived a similar dualism of primary cause, which was intelligent and divine, and mechanical or slave cause, which was irrational, disorderly, and lacking in both freedom and conscious purpose. Like a wise master, the Demiurge guided the *ananke* of the material universe toward the

[9] For the development of the Greek concept of barbarian inferiority, see Robert Schlaifer, "Greek Theories of Slavery from Homer to Aristotle," *Harvard Studies in Classical Philology*, XLVII (1936), 166-70.

[10] See *ibid.*, p. 190, for a passage from Philemon "where the entire universe is viewed as a hierarchy of slavery, in which one's place on the scale mattered but little." For Plato's suggested slave laws, which were more severe than any American slave code, see *Laws*, vi. 776E, 777D, 778A; ix. 865, 868, 872, 882; xi. 914, 936, and Glenn R. Morrow, *Plato's Law of Slavery in its Relation to Greek Law* (Urbana, Ill., 1939), pp. 122-31.

[11] Gregory Vlastos, "Slavery in Plato's Republic," *The Philosophical Review*, L (1941), 289-304.

good.[12] It is of the utmost significance that Plato associated slavery with both the unruly multitude and with
the chaotic material world devoid of Logos. In effect, he
rationalized the contradiction of slavery within a vast
cosmic scheme in which irrational nature was ordered
and controlled by a divine, intelligent authority. Future
apologists for slavery were no doubt indebted to Plato
for linking the authority of masters to the cosmic principle of order. On the other hand, when we note that the
Abbé Raynal pictured a slave revolt as Nature vindi-
cating herself against the perversions of society, it is clear
that the terms of the dualism could be reversed when
"nature" acquired new meanings.

In one sense Plato's doctrine of ideas was a source for
future social criticism, since it implied that the imperfections of this world could be judged in the light of
eternal ideals of perfection. This potentiality was largely
nullified, however, by what Arthur Lovejoy has termed
the "principle of plenitude."[13] If God's goodness depended on his unlimited fecundity and the completeness
of his creation, then the world was a full replica of the
realm of ideas or essences; every link in the great chain
of being had a valid and necessary function. Evil, which
was simply the privation of some good, had a sufficient
reason for existence, and could not be eliminated without
destroying the beauty and balance of the whole. While
few thinkers accepted this principle of plenitude in its
extreme form, which could easily become a kind of pan-
theism, it was to exercise an enormous influence on Western thought. Thus slavery could be seen not only as

[12] *Ibid.* According to Vlastos, *ananke* was used in Greek to denote
both the state of slavery and the constraint and torture to which
slaves were subjected.

[13] Arthur O. Lovejoy, *The Great Chain of Being: a Study of the
History of an Idea* (Harper Torchbook edn., New York, 1960), p. 53.
The abolitionist potentiality in Plato is exaggerated, I think, by
Alfred North Whitehead, *Adventures of Ideas* (New York, 1933),
p. 30.

exemplifying a cosmic principle of authority and subordination, but as having a necessary place in the ordered
structure of being. Like other contradictions, it could
be absorbed in higher unities.[14]

According to Plato, Aristotle noted, the same principle
governed the rule of slaves, of a household, or of a nation.
Yet "others affirm that the rule of a master over slaves is
contrary to nature, and that the distinction between
slave and freeman exists by law only, and not by nature;
and being an interference with nature is therefore unjust."[15] This is the first definite indication that some philosophers had taken the momentous step of associating
the contradiction of slavery with the dualism of nature
and conventional society, rather than that of rational
order and brute chaos. Aristotle felt the force of this
argument, but like Plato he wished to rationalize slavery
by showing its relation to the structure and purposes of
being. It had emerged, he thought, from the primitive
household, or *oikia*, and was as natural as other relationships of superior and inferior, such as soul and body, man
and wife, or father and child. By considering slavery as
an essentially domestic relationship, Aristotle endowed
it with the sanction of paternal authority, and helped to
establish a precedent that would govern discussions of
political philosophers as late as the eighteenth century.

On one crucial point, however, he disagreed with Plato.
Each type of rule had its own characteristics, and one
could not say that the master's government of his slaves
was the same as the constitutional government of subjects who by nature were free.[16] In fact, if a free people

[14] For examples of this tendency with respect to slavery, see
Aquinas, *Sum. theol.* Part III (Supplement), Q. 52; Grotius,
De Jure Belli et Pacis (3 vols., London, 1853), III, 148-56;
[Malachy Postlethwayt] *The National and Private Advantages of the
African Trade Considered . . .* (London, 1746), pp. 1-7, 20-39; Jean-
François Melon, "Essai politique sur le Commerce," printed in
Economistes Financiers du XVIIIᵉ Siècle (Paris, 1851), pp. 680-82.
[15] *Pol.* i. 1253ᵇ (W. D. Ross, tr. and ed., New York, 1942).
[16] *Ibid.* i. 1255ᵇ.

were subjected to the absolute rule of a sovereign who was responsible to no one but himself, they would be the victims of tyranny and would have reason to be the enemies of their government.[17] By drawing this distinction between the authority of masters and the authority of constitutional rulers, Aristotle narrowed the ground on which slavery could be justified. He was certain that the institution had a rational basis that differentiated it from tyranny. Yet the Greeks had long used the term "slavery" to describe the tyrannical governments of their neighbors; and a desire for political liberty might easily develop into a hostility to slavery in any form. To reinforce the separation of political freedom and domestic servitude, Aristotle built his entire argument around Plato's theory of natural inferiority. Later apologists for slavery would adopt a similar strategy to meet a similar problem.

Aristotle was obviously attracted by the idea of a social relationship founded on natural differences, analogous to the subordination of body to soul, or of animals to men.[18] Living in a society that increasingly dissociated culture and public service from the slightest taint of manual labor, he saw slavery as an expedient and even necessary means of supplying the wants of life. In an apparent admission, seized upon by nineteenth-century reformers, he said that if the shuttle would weave and the plectrum touch the lyre without a hand to guide them, "chief workmen would not want servants, nor masters slaves."[19] We may doubt, however, whether he yearned for the industrial revolution. The illustration was meant to show the complex nature of the slave as both an instrument of action and a conscious agent who must obey and anticipate his master's will.

This ambiguous conception raised many problems and did little more than magnify the basic contradiction of

17 *Ibid.* iv. 1295ᵃ.
18 *Ibid.* i. 1254ᵃ, 1254ᵇ; *Ethics* i. xiii.
19 *Pol.* i. 1253ᵇ.

human bondage. For Aristotle true slavery derived from an innate deficiency in the beauty and inner virtue of the soul. The natural slave lacked the moral and intellectual freedom to make decisions in the light of deliberative judgment. But just as later Calvinists were to deny that the sinner was capable of righteous action, and yet allow that certain restraining graces enabled him to approximate virtue, so Aristotle admitted that the slave had a partial soul and might at least participate in reason. The bondsman was even capable of a lower form of moral virtue, which arose from the proper fulfillment of his function. Aristotle had no sympathy with Plato's view that masters should only command their slaves and never converse with them in a friendly manner; and yet true friendship was impossible, for the slave was incapable of reciprocating genuine goodwill or benevolence. His true interests could never be other than those of his master. Indeed, one could scarcely speak of his having interests, since as a tool or possession he was only an extension of his master's physical nature.[20] The best slave, it would appear, was the one whose humanity had been most nearly effaced.

The difficulties raised by this conception, even in the Hellenic world, can be illustrated by several passages from the plays of Euripides, which of course were written in the previous century. In *Helen* a slave finds his moral freedom and human identity precisely where Aristotle would obliterate them. Sympathizing with his master's joys and sorrows, this bondsman says that he would not want to suffer the two evils of physical slavery and a corrupt heart.[21] Thus even a born slave could assert his inner freedom by identifying himself with his master. And while Euripides raised no protest against the injustice of

[20] *Ibid.* i. 1254^a, 1259^b–1260^b; *Ethics* vii. v; viii. ii; x. vi. For a discussion of the inconsistencies in Aristotle's position, see Schlaifer, "Greek Theories of Slavery," pp. 192-98.

[21] *Hel.* lines 727-34.

slavery, he sensed that its origins were filled with dramatic pathos. Any Greek could admire the spirit of Polyxena, sister of Hector, who was marked, as she said, to be a bride for kings, and who preferred death to degrading slavery.[22] She and Andromache were shadowy prototypes of the royal African slaves of eighteenth-century verse and drama.

It is clear that even Aristotle was bothered by the origin of slavery and by the messiness and ambiguity of social, as opposed to natural, distinctions. The natural slave, having no deliberative faculty, could not be happy with freedom. But obviously some men who by nature were free and virtuous had been enslaved as a result of war. Aristotle acknowledged that such slaves, held by force and mere social convention, could have no common interest with their masters.[23] Presumably, the authority of their masters was no more legitimate than that of political tyrants. Though he was confident that nature would like to make sharp distinctions in the bodies of men, equipping some for a docile acceptance of hard labor, others for politics and the arts of war and peace, he admitted that physical differences were no clear indication of natural status. This admission opened a significant gap between the actual and theoretical slave—a gap that would be widened by Stoics and Christians and not fully closed until later generations invented the theory of racial inferiority.

[22] *Hec.* lines 352-78. In the early 17th century Alonso de Sandoval called slavery "una junta de todos los males," and to reinforce his point, cited Euripides and Philo of Alexandria, whom we shall discuss shortly (José Antonio Saco, *Historia de la Esclavitud, desde los Tiempos mas remotos hasta nuestos Dias*, segunda edición, 6 vols., Havana, 1937, IV, 254-57). But while Sandoval attacked the abuses of the African slave trade, he can hardly be classed as an antislavery writer (Georges Scelle, *La Traite négrière aux Indes de Castille*, 2 vols., Paris, 1906, I, 712, 718-19).

[23] *Pol.* i. 1255ᵃ, 1255ᵇ.

III

We do not know the identity of Aristotle's opponents who believed that slavery was a violation of nature. Along with the Hebrew concept of deliverance, the doctrine was one of the cultural sources of antislavery thought, though this potentiality was limited by the fact that it was the product of a developing trend in philosophy which exhibited a profound indifference to worldly problems.[24] Only fragments survive from the writings of Cynics and early Stoics, whose influence for some five centuries was nevertheless greater than that of the Peripatetics. We know that instead of rationalizing the diverse elements of society into a coherent system, in which such institutions as slavery were securely connected to natural principles or to an ideal realm of essences, they perceived a sharp division between objective truth and human conventions. Virtue they conceived as action in accord with nature, as revealed to man through uncorrupted reason. This meant that instead of subordinating himself to an ordered system of social relationships, the individual must liberate himself from the constraint of both institutions and the ideology that supported them. He could work out the meaning of truth only in independent and practical conduct. While such a quest for individual freedom could easily lead to a challenge of accepted norms and institutions, the dissident philosophers were largely unconcerned with questions of social

[24] A good example of the mixing of these sources can be seen in the sermons of the 17th century Portuguese Jesuit, Antonio Vieira, who compared the calamities of Brazil to the punishments of Pharaoh for refusing to release the Israelites, and who denounced the slaveholders of Maranham for violating the law of nature by keeping in bondage men who had a right to freedom; yet Vieira also told Negro slaves that if they endured their sufferings with patience, following the example of the blessed Redeemer, they would have the merit as well as the torment of martyrdom (Serafim Leite, *Historia da Companhia de Jesus no Brasil*, 10 vols., Rio de Janeiro and Lisbon, 1938-50, VII, 81, 351; Robert Southey, *History of Brazil*, 3 vols., London, 1817-22, I, 663; II, 474-78, 675-76).

justice; their brave skepticism arose from a desire for truth and inner purity.

The Sophists appear to have been the first to reject the distinction between Greek and barbarian, and to conclude that since slavery was a product of human convention, it had no basis in the objective and unchanging law of nature. Alcidamas, when defending the emancipation of the Messenians by the Thebans, argued that the distinction of slave and freeman was unknown to nature. It is impossible to tell how far he would have carried the point. Antisthenes, who was the crucial link between Socrates and the Stoics, was said to have written a treatise, "Of Freedom and Slavery," which may have been a source of later Stoic doctrine.[25] Believing that virtue was a matter of individual commitment and independence, this founder of the Cynic school also strove to shock public opinion in a way that anticipated later reformers. The pattern of demonstrative contempt for accepted values was most pronounced in Antisthenes' famous pupil, Diogenes of Sinope. Striving for a life of perfect simplicity, he lived in a tub, walked barefoot in snow, and threw his cup away in shame after seeing a child drink from its hands. Though he favored abolishing marriage and holding wives in common, there is no report of his having denounced slavery. Yet a defiant disregard for the conventional distinction between slave and freeman was part of his quest for virtue as an inner freedom and independence. "It would be absurd," he said, when his own slave had run away, "if Manes can live without Diogenes, but Diogenes cannot get on without Manes." When he was captured by pirates on a voyage to Aegina and taken to a slave market in Crete, he pointed to a spectator wearing purple robes, and said, "sell me to this man; he needs a master." He called the friends who wished to re-

[25] Eduard Zeller, *A History of Greek Philosophy from the Earliest Period to the Time of Socrates*, tr. S. F. Alleyne (2 vols., London, 1881), II, 476-77; Diog. Laer. vi. 16.

deem him simpletons. Lions, he said, were not the slaves of those who fed them, "for fear is the mark of the slave, whereas wild beasts make men afraid of them."[26] These tales illustrate a pattern of thought that gave rise to the first explicit questioning of slavery. For if freedom is conceived as a liberation of the individual from the norms and institutions of society, as well as from the desires of the flesh, external distinctions lose all importance. According to Bion, a pupil of Crates, "Good slaves are free, but evil men are slaves, desiring many things."[27]

But we must not read too much into these isolated statements. Zeno, who was also a pupil of Crates, is supposed to have said that it was as great a crime to strike a slave as to strike one's father. Yet Diogenes Laertius tells us that when Zeno was chastising a slave who said that it was his fate to steal, the philosopher replied, "Yes, and to be beaten, too."[28] It has been claimed that Onesicritus, a Cynic philosopher and pupil of Diogenes of Sinope, advocated the abolition of slavery and was even a forerunner of William Lloyd Garrison. Onesicritus was sent to India by Alexander, and his account of his travels was one of the first combinations of historical narrative and utopian fantasy. The land of Musicanus he described as a kind of ideal society in which the people refrained from the use of gold and silver and ate publicly at a common mess. One might assume that a Cynic philosopher would exclude slavery from such a primitivistic utopia. Yet the passage in Strabo which has been taken as evidence of Onesicritus' hostility to slavery has precisely the opposite meaning: "Onesicritus declares that slavery is peculiar to the Indians in the country of Musicanus, and

[26] Diog. Laer. vi. 20-75 (Loeb Classical Library edn., tr. R. D. Hicks, London, 1925).

[27] Ferrand Sayre, *The Greek Cynics* (Baltimore, 1948), p. 33. The quotation is from Stobaeus; the idea, which was expanded by Philo of Alexandria, may have come from Crates. A fragment from the comic poet, Philemon, also anticipates the Stoic view of slavery.

[28] Diog. Laer. vii. 23.

tells what a success it is there, just as he mentions many other successes of this country, speaking of it as a country excellently governed."[29]

Whereas Aristotle held that a slave was actually part of his master's physical being, Zeno and Chrysippus saw his soul as part of the total substance of a universal reason. External distinctions between Greek and barbarian, male and female, or slave and freeman were thus mere accidents that had no relevance to nature. But as these early Stoics attempted to work out the practical meaning of virtue, they qualified their belief in the universal brotherhood of man with the principle that the majority of men were slaves to desire and prejudice. Only the philosopher, who achieved the power of independent action in the cold light of reason, could be termed truly free.[30] There is a rough analogy between the Stoic and Hebrew conceptions of liberation from human authorities and conformity to the laws of a higher power. From both points of view true freedom was a privilege to be enjoyed by an elite group, and there could be no gradations of relative improvement between the slavish multitude and the Children of Virtue. The Stoics' ethical world was one of stark antithesis. All sins were equally sinful, and from moral slavery there could be no gradual emancipation.[31]

[29] Strabo *Geog.*, xv. i. 54 (Loeb Classical Library edn., tr. Horace Leonard Jones, London, 1923). This is the passage referred to by Schlaifer ("Greek Theories of Slavery," p. 200), who says that Onesicritus favored the abolition of slavery. Schlaifer has been followed by other writers who have expanded upon the error. Strabo, Plutarch, Lucian, Pliny, Diogenes Laertius, and Arrian all provide material on Onesicritus, but none of them mentions his being opposed to slavery. See also, Pauly-Wissowa, *Realencyclopädie*, XXXV, 460-67.

[30] Diog. Laer. vii. 187-88; Epictetus *Discourses* iii. xxiv. 66-69; iv. i. 114-15; Eduard Zeller, *The Stoics, Epicureans and Sceptics*, tr. Oswald J. Reichel (London, 1880), p. 211.

[31] Diog. Laer. vii. 121-22, 127-28; C. J. de Vogel, *Greek Philosophy, a Collection of Texts with Notes and Explanations* (Leiden, 1959), p. 140. For a critical but perceptive view of the Stoic response to

And while the Stoics measured the evils of society against the absolute standard of nature, and held that the philosopher-saint must persevere in exercising his virtue, they found no difficulty in accepting as inevitable the many imperfections of the world. The wise man's virtue lay not in good works but in decisions that revealed an inner purity and self-control. Since the world had fallen irretrievably from a former Golden Age, he could not regard poverty, slavery, or even death as evils in themselves, any more than he could consider their opposites as intrinsic goods. The only thing that mattered was the way that one responded to the vicissitudes of fortune. True freedom meant self-transcendence, a disengagement of the ego from one's surroundings; and thus the environment of the slave was no more dangerous than any other to the well-being of the soul.[32] It might, indeed, afford greater security against distracting stimuli. Epictetus, who had been a slave himself in his early life, used the bondsman's desire for immediate liberty as an example of the illusions of worldly expectations. After describing the plight of the hungry, homeless freedman, Epictetus observed that even if the ex-slave should ultimately enjoy material success, he would have no knowledge of virtue, and would only become a slave to love, to desire, or to political faction. The philosopher pictured the disenchanted freedman looking back with nostalgia to a time when his physical needs were limited and cared for by a master.[33]

---

slavery, see E. Ciccotti, *Il Tramonto della Schiavitù nel Mondo antico* (Torino, 1899). Eleuterio Elorduy has modified and extended Ciccotti's analysis, and has provided a theoretical framework for interpreting the positions of Old, Middle, and New Stoa (*Die Sozialphilosophie der Stoa, Philologus,* Supplementband, XXVIII, Heft 3, Leipzig, 1936, 203-6).

[32] Zeller, *Stoics*, pp. 228-32. It should be noted that Aristotle placed more emphasis on the environment and recognized that men would be perverted if subjected to gross indignities from childhood (*Ethics* vii. v).

[33] *Discourses* iv. i.

But the Stoics' indifference to society and history should not blind us to the fact that they associated slavery with the imperfections of the world, and sin with a particular kind of slavery. These associations would have a different meaning if combined with the belief that a particular time or place was marked for the redemption of humanity. Even in the Roman world of the first and second centuries A.D. the Stoic doctrines led to what William Westermann has aptly termed a "frigid sympathy" for the slave. Though Cicero believed that subjection was beneficial for some men, he saw slavery as the result of greed and ignorance.[34] Epictetus suggested that slaveholders could not attain true freedom and virtue, since the owner of a slave could not help but become a slave himself.[35] And Seneca developed the theory that only the body of the slave was at the mercy of his master, for "that inner part cannot be delivered into bondage." Because the slave's soul was untouched by his condition, he had the capacity to do more for his master than required. Such beneficent service might provide the basis for a relationship transcending external condition.[36] The same

[34] It might be said that Juvenal anticipated Jefferson on the effect of slavery on free children: "What is a young man taught by a sire who delights in the clanking of the iron chains, the branded slaves, and the dungeons?" (*Satires*, tr. Rolfe Humphries, Bloomington, Ind., 1958, p. 162).

[35] *Fragmenta* xlii-xliii. Doubt has been expressed concerning the authenticity of some of these selections, which appeared first in Stobaeus. Though Epictetus may have been one of the first to say that a man who desires freedom should be careful not to enslave others, I think that it is incorrect to read this as a moral protest against slavery (see Kehnscherper, *Die Stellung der Bibel*, pp. 53-54). Epictetus is clearly concerned about the effect of slaveholding on the master; he likens the free man being served by slaves to the healthy man being ministered to by the sick. In his *Discourses*, however, he plainly states that the physical slave is far better off than many types of freemen, and anticipates some of the favorite arguments of proslavery theorists. Like other Stoics, he probably regarded physical slavery as a matter of small importance so long as it did not corrupt the soul of a particular master.

[36] *De Benef.* III. xvii-xxviii (Loeb Classical Library edn., tr. John W. Basore, London, 1935); *Epist. Mor.* xlvii. 1-5.

idea had been rejected by Aristotle but affirmed long before by Euripides.

Seneca's eloquent defense of the freedom of the slave's soul has often been contrasted with Aristotle's doctrine of total inferiority. The difference, while significant, can easily be exaggerated. Aristotle had admitted that some slaves had the souls of free men, though of course he had assumed a closer correspondence between inner slavishness and external condition than did Seneca. Yet Seneca had no doubt that some men, as the result of sin and corruption, had the souls of slaves. Moreover, he was far more concerned with the pride of masters than with the sufferings of slaves. Discussion of slavery was a vehicle for preaching simplicity and humility, and for reminding the well-to-do of how much they owed to fortune. When Seneca wanted to give evidence of his own simplicity of life, he told of taking only a few personal slaves on one of his trips.[37]

In the Hellenistic period two of the most significant attempts to relate slavery to the progress of the human spirit were those of Philo of Alexandria and Dio Chrysostom, a wandering Greek Sophist who was known for denouncing the immorality of cities and for his idealization of the simple life of the herdsmen of Euboea. Both philosophers endeavored to distinguish the true from the literal meaning of "slave." They agreed that men naturally loved liberty and looked on slavery as shameful and degrading. The difficulty was that ordinary men had no understanding of what the words really meant.[38]

Two lines of argument exposed the ambiguities of common usage. What do we mean, asked Dio, in the tan-

[37] *Epist. Mor.* lxxxvii. 2.

[38] Hellenistic Jews, especially Philo, had been influenced by the Stoic doctrine that if one truly understood a name, apart from the accidents of convention, he could understand the nature of the thing named; this led to an allegorical interpretation of the Pentateuch. See Robert M. Grant, *The Letter and the Spirit* (London, 1957), pp. 6-7.

talizing spirit of all philosophers, when we say that a
man is a slave? It cannot be a lack of freedom to act on
his own judgment, for soldiers and sick men are not
slaves. It cannot be that money has been paid for a man,
since this is done in a ransom. It cannot be a negation
of all personal benefit, since wise masters will always
look out for the well-being of their property. It cannot
be dependence upon another for one's life, since pirates
and judges may execute those who come within their
power. And is it not possible, Philo asked, for a man to
be a slave to vices and passions, to the fear of death or
to the opinions of the multitude?[39]

After showing the difficulties in arriving at a satisfactory definition, both philosophers used the traditional
Stoic argument that slavery of the body is the result of
mere chance and convention. Since this condition had
no basis in objective nature, Philo concluded that it was
not a proper subject for philosophy, the implication being that the vicissitudes of fortune could not raise moral
issues.[40] Apparently Dio would have agreed with this
judgment, but in order to show that true slavery and
freedom had nothing to do with external conditions, he
went on to undermine the entire legal basis of the institution. Prisoners of war, he said, could not be true slaves;
held only by force, there was no reason why, if given the
power, they should not escape or retaliate by capturing
their former masters. If this were true, masters had no
better title to the descendants of captives: "Consequently,
if this method of gaining possession, from which all the

[39] Dio Chrysostom, "The Fourteenth Discourse: On Slavery and
Freedom, I" (Loeb Classical Library edn., *Dio Chrysostom*, tr. J. W.
Cohoon, Cambridge, Mass., 1939, II), 1-12; Philo Judaeus *Quod
Omnis Probus Liber Sit* 11, 17, 23. The argument was a Stoic com-
monplace; see Epictetus *Discourses* iv. i. 6-10, 128-31; Seneca *Epist.
Mor.* xlvii. 17. The thought continually reappears in Western cul-
ture, as in *Hamlet* (III, ii, 77): "Give me that man that is not
passion's slave."

[40] *Quod Omnis Probus* 17-19.

others take their beginning, is not just, it is likely that no other one is either, and that the term 'slave' does not in reality correspond to the truth."[41] This argument would seem to come close to the position of later abolitionists who held that slavery had no legal basis whatsoever. The abolitionist would assume that if the term "slave" did not correspond to the truth, then freeborn men were being subjected to an oppressive environment and should in all justice be released from illegal coercion. Dio Chrysostom, however, lived in a different intellectual world, and the fact that physical slavery lacked any legitimate basis suggested to him only that one must look beyond the literal meanings to understand the true nature of slavery and freedom. He utterly rejected, of course, the Aristotelian distinction between Greek and barbarian, and pointed out that any race would have countless ancestors who were both slaves and freemen. Yet in one sense he and Philo simply reframed the Aristotelian distinction on Stoic principles.

The true slave was a man ignorant of what was allowed and forbidden by natural law. A great king might be a slave, a man in bonds a freeman. For Philo and Dio Chrysostom this was not figurative language but a statement of reality.[42] Every good man was free. But "he who with a mean and slavish spirit puts his hand to mean and slavish actions contrary to his own proper judgment is a slave indeed." Philo said he agreed with Zeno that a true slave had no right to speak to a good man as an equal.[43] The slave was, in short, a sinner.

And despite his indifference to social condition, Philo slipped back into the significant inconsistency of identifying spiritual with physical slavery. To show that good

[41] Dio Chrysostom, "The Fifteenth Discourse: On Slavery and Freedom, II," 25-26.
[42] Dio Chrysostom, "Fourteenth Discourse," 18; "Fifteenth Discourse," 31-32.
[43] Philo Judaeus *Quod Omnis Probus* 24, 53-54 (Loeb Classical Library edn., tr. F. H. Colson, London, 1941).

men love freedom and detest slaves, he cited the examples of Athenians excluding bondsmen from the celebrations of the Venerable Goddesses, and of the Argonauts barring slaves from their crew. Apparently forgetting his distinction between true and apparent slaves, he wrote: "We may well deride the folly of those who think that when they are released from the ownership of their masters they become free. Servants, indeed, they are no longer now that they have been dismissed, but slaves they are and of the vilest kind. . . . For as the proclamation cannot make them men of knowledge, so neither can it make them free, for that is a state of blessedness."[44] Philo did not see that a man released from physical bondage might have a greater chance of acquiring spiritual freedom. Environment, he believed, had no bearing on morality. Yet he still thought of the "slavish character" as that exhibited by physical slaves, and this was a defect that no deed of manumission could remedy.

But when Philo had given examples of groups of men dedicated to a life of virtue, he had allowed himself a long digression on the Essenes of Palestinian Syria. There is no evidence that he had firsthand knowledge of the Essenes, and his picture bears a resemblance in tone to the idealizations of American Quakers by French *philosophes*. He presented these "athletes of virtue" as proof of the possibility of a life of true freedom and perfection. Refraining from any association with war or weapons, or from any employment that stimulated vice, they led a frugal and simple existence, sharing houses and property, providing for the sick and aged, and contributing their earnings to a common fund. Moreover, "not a single slave is to be found among them, but all are free . . . and they denounce the owners of slaves, not merely for their injustice in outraging the law of equality, but also for their impiety in annulling the statute of Nature,

[44] *Ibid.*, 139-42, 156-57.

who mother-like has born and reared all men alike, and created them genuine brothers. . . ."[45]

We should not need to stress that such an unqualified condemnation of slaveholding was unusual, even unprecedented, in antiquity.[46] It was associated, let us note, with a combination of three elements: first, the primitivistic ideal of liberating the individual from the corrupting influences of society; second, the perfectionist ideal of working out in concrete terms the social meaning of moral freedom; third, the expectation of an apocalyptic fulfillment and judgment in history. In the sense that they sought freedom from sin, from society, and from history as mere repetition, the Essenes anticipated the more radical sects of Protestantism, which were the first groups in the modern world to denounce the holding of slaves. From the little that we know, we can only surmise that with the Essenes the Hebraic sense of place and promise gave a forward momentum to the Stoic belief that mankind was united through a common reason unaffected by the accidents of time.

I V

According to the jurists Florentinus and Ulpian, slavery was a manifest departure from the *jus naturale*, but

[45] *Ibid.*, 79. In his *Hypothetica* 11.14, Philo said that the Essenes avoided marriage. Josephus, the other principal source on the Essenes, claimed to have lived with the association. His account in the *Jewish War* (ii. viii. 2-14) says nothing of slavery; among the several references to the Essenes in his *Jewish Antiquities*, the only relevant one is a statement that they neither married nor were "desirous" to keep servants, since servants tempted men to be unjust (xviii. 1. 5). This hardly confirms the strong antislavery attitude mentioned by Philo. The problem is further complicated by the relation between the Essenes and the famous Qumran documents. The only certainty is that antislavery was part of Philo's probably idealized picture of the brotherhood.

[46] Glenn Morrow says that slaveholding was forbidden in Locris and Phocis, but that these were remote areas that never would have had many slaves (*Plato's Law of Slavery*, p. 130n.).

was sanctioned by the *jus gentium*. It was the single instance, Ulpian said, of a conflict between the principles of nature and the common law of nations.[47] This sense of tension, inherited from the Stoics, was passed on to the Institutes of Justinian, and thence to the jurisprudence of Western civilization. But if slavery was unknown to nature and yet was so universal as to be part of the *jus gentium*, how could one account for the degeneration? And if all good men were free and all bad men slaves, could the bad men become good and so escape their slavery? What would prevent the original causes of slavery from reducing them to their former bondage? These questions the Stoics raised but could not answer. They associated true slavery with a kind of sin, but it was a sin that could be conquered only by man's inner resources.

For Christians, Jesus gave the answer when he spoke to the Pharisees:

> If ye abide in my word, then are ye truly my disciples; and ye shall know the truth, and the truth shall make you free. They answered unto him, We are Abraham's seed, and have never yet been in bondage to any man: how sayest thou, Ye shall be made free? Jesus answered them, Verily, verily, I say unto you, Every one that committeth sin is the bondservant [*doulos*] of sin. And the bondservant abideth not in the house for ever: the son abideth for ever.[48]

At first sight this passage resembles the Stoic paradox that true liberty can come only from an inner change in man's nature—that most men who think of themselves as free are really slaves. Yet Jesus preached a profounder conception of man's need for redemption from his slavery

---

[47] R. W. Carlyle and A. J. Carlyle, *A History of Medieval Political Theory in the West* (6 vols., London and Edinburgh, 1927), I, 46, 50.
[48] John 8: 31-35.

to sin. It may be objected (as the Pharisees might well have done) that the word "slave" was only figuratively applied to the sinner. But as early Christians repeatedly conceived of sin and salvation in terms of slavery and freedom, the words acquired complex layers of meaning that necessarily affected men's response to the institution of slavery. Thus St. John Chrysostom, commenting on the above passage in the fourth century, complained that many people would still prefer to be the slaves of sin rather than the slaves of men.[49] And whereas Plato associated the disorder of the material world with slavery, and the Stoics thought of conventional society as irretrievably fallen, Paul spoke of all creation being delivered from the *douleia* of corruption into the liberty of the children of God. Both he and Jude referred to themselves as the slaves of Jesus Christ. And since no servant (*oiketes*) could have two masters, men were told that they must choose between God and mammon.[50] The concept of slavery is further widened when we learn that the story of Abraham's sons was an allegory of Christ's liberating mankind from bondage to Mosaic law. This meant that Christians had been called for a life of freedom, not of the flesh, but as willing slaves to one another.[51]

In the eyes of Christians the independent, natural man, idealized by primitivists in all ages, was a sinner who, lacking the essential capacity for virtue, bore a certain resemblance to Aristotle's natural slave. Even Aristotle had implied that the natural slave, bereft though he was of the highest faculties, had at least the freedom to accept the gift of emancipation. So under Christianity the most hardened sinner could accept the gift of grace. In a rather extravagant analogy, Tertullian said that just

[49] St. John Chrysostom, *Commentary on Saint John the Apostle and Evangelist*, Homily 54 (tr. Sister Thomas Aquinas Goggin "The Fathers of the Church Series," New York, 1960, XLI, 66).
[50] Rom. 1:1; 8:20; Jude 1; Luke 16:13.
[51] Gal. 3:23-29; 4:1-4.

as a slave girl who was espoused but not yet married, because not yet freed, should be excused if she committed adultery with another man, so a pagan who was a slave to sin, though pledged to Christ, would be forgiven for his sins.[52] But freedom from the slavery of sin was not freedom from the principle of bondage. If the sinner was free from righteousness, the saint was the slave of righteousness.[53] Perfect liberty, as theologians were long to maintain, lay in absolute conformity to God's will. The result, as Lecky acutely observed, was that Christianity gave a certain moral dignity to servitude. And Lecky concluded, with perhaps too much zeal, that Christianity inevitably equalized men and thus led to the abolition of slavery.[54]

It is true that upon conversion, early Christians sometimes gave up their property and manumitted their slaves.[55] As a priest, the ex-slave saw the greatest nobles kneeling humbly at his feet. The author of Ephesians said that God, no respecter of persons, was the master of masters as well as of slaves. But he also told slaves to be obedient "unto them that according to the flesh are your masters, with fear and trembling, in a singleness of your heart, as unto Christ."[56] We thus come to a fundamental duality in the New Testament. As men gathered to prepare for the imminent Kingdom, temporal distinctions were of little importance. Christ's message was universal; all men were brothers in union with God. But for this very reason if a man were called to be a slave, he

[52] Tertullian, *Treatises on Penance: On Penitence and On Purity* (tr. William P. Le Saint, "Ancient Christian Writers Series," Westminster, Md., 1959), p. 280. For other associations of sin and slavery, see pp. 25, 77, 118, 160.

[53] Rom. 6:15-23.

[54] William E. H. Lecky, *History of European Morals from Augustine to Charlemagne*, 3d ed. (2 vols., New York, 1890), II, 66-68.

[55] Frederick van der Meer, *Augustine the Bishop; the Life and Work of a Father of the Church*, tr. Brian Battershaw and G. R. Lamb (London, 1962), p. 136.

[56] Eph. 6:5-9.

should not try to become free: "For he that was called in the Lord being a bondservant, is the Lord's freeman: likewise he that was called being free, is Christ's bondservant."[57] In the blinding light of the Gospel message, men could both accept and disregard social distinctions.[58] There is reason to assume that the early Christian attitude was correctly summarized by Ignatius, Bishop of Antioch, in his Epistle to Polycarp: "Despise not men or women slaves. Yet let them not be puffed up, but rather bear their slavery for the glory of God, that they may win from Him thereby a better liberty. Let them not seek to be emancipated at the expense of the common fund, that they may not be found the slaves of desire."[59]

Theologians, it is true, continued to insist on a theoretical distinction between spiritual and physical slaves. Like the earlier Stoics, St. Ambrose and Ambrosiaster maintained that a slave may in reality be freer than his master. Augustine agreed with Philo of Alexandria that good men were free and evil men slaves, irrespective of

[57] I Cor. 7:20-22; 12:13.

[58] It is only with this attitude in mind that we can understand the meaning of Paul's Epistle to Philemon, which aroused such wearisome debates during the 19th century. The letter would seem to prove no more than that early Christians were allowed to hold even fellow Christians as slaves, though they were urged to treat such bondsmen as spiritual brethren. For a contrary view see Paul Robinson Coleman-Norton, *Studies in Roman Economic and Social History, in Honor of Allan Chester Johnson* (Princeton, 1951), pp. 164-69. It is true that St. John Chrysostom wrote three homilies on the Epistle to Philemon in which he stated that while slavery was the consequence of sin, masters should treat their bondsmen as brothers in Christ and manumit them if at all possible (Johannes Quasten, *Patrology*, Utrecht and Westminster, Md., 1960, II, 450). But in the 4th century St. Basil saw in the Epistle no implication that Christian slaves should be freed; on the contrary, he thought that Paul had set a precedent for admonishing and returning fugitives to their masters (*The Ascetic Works of Saint Basil*, tr. W.K.L. Clarke ["Translations of Christian Literature, Series I, Greek Texts," London, 1925], pp. 172-73).

[59] Ernest Barker, *From Alexander to Constantine: Passages and Documents Illustrating the History of Social and Political Ideas, 336 B.C.–A.D. 337* (Oxford, 1956), pp. 406-7.

their stations in life.[60] Masters were often charged with the sins of pride and sensuality. Clement of Alexandria saw a connection between slavery and sexual perversion.[61] Gregory of Nyssa accused the arrogant slave owner of condemning a man who by nature was free, and thus of setting himself up in rivalry to God.[62] But since the entire drama of sin and salvation was conceived as a spiritual analogy to slavery and emancipation, even to the point of imagining sin as an inherited but deserved defect that one could not escape on his own volition, it was only natural that physical slavery should increasingly be seen as the consequence of sin.

St. Ambrose, St. Isidore of Seville, and especially St. Augustine thought of slavery as part of the punishment for man's fall from grace. They recognized, as had Aristotle and the Stoics, that the chances of fortune did not always correspond to the inner condition of an individual's soul. It was inconceivable, however, that injustice should darken God's omnipotent rule of the world. According to Augustine, slavery was a remedy as well as a penalty for sin, and it was God who bore the direct responsibility for appointing both masters and slaves. Though man had originally been free and had been given dominion over only the beasts, his presumptuous violation of the natural order had made bondage a necessary check on the excesses of his own evil will.[63] Thus as Plato had intimated, slavery was part of the grand scheme of divine order and government, a disciplining force restraining subterranean currents of evil and rebellion. If it were objected that military victories were sometimes won by wicked men who enslaved their innocent

[60] *City of God* iv. iii. See also *Conf.* vi. xv.

[61] *Christ the Educator* (tr. Simon P. Wood, "Fathers of the Church Series," New York, 1954, XXIII), 216-17, 226.

[62] Westermann, *Slave Systems*, p. 160.

[63] *City of God* xix. xv. He noted that the word "slave" was not mentioned in Scripture until Noah branded his son's sin with this name.

victims, Augustine's reply was that no men were innocent; even such an apparent injustice should be seen as a divine judgment. All slaves thus deserved to be slaves, and their only comfort might be in the thought that if they served with faithful affection, they might at least make their bondage in some sense free. The only true slave, after all, was the slave to sin.[64] The Christian household should be a sanctuary for the cultivation of piety and discipline; the *paterfamilias* was enjoined to treat his dependents with charity, but he was also obliged to enforce the domestic peace.[65]

As Christians looked less to an imminent millennium and more to the need of accommodating themselves to the world, they tended to accept the institutions of state and society as a necessary framework for controlling sin and allowing the Church to perform its sacramental functions. Slavery was increasingly justified under what Ernst Troeltsch has termed "das relative Naturrecht," which was a natural law adapted and modified for sinful man.[66] The Church not only accepted the institution, but made every effort to ensure the security of masters in controlling their property. Thus the Canons of the Church re-

[64] *Ibid.* See also the discussion in Carlyle, *History*, I, 113-21.

[65] *City of God* xix. xvi. In his *Sermones*, Augustine preached that kindness to slaves was a Christian duty. His view that the power of masters should be limited by charity and by a recognition that God was no respecter of ranks and worldly condition, but that slaves could achieve spiritual liberty only through meekness, obedience, and resignation, was accepted with little change by British Protestants of the 17th and early 18th centuries (Robert Sanderson, *XXXIV Sermons*, 6th ed., London, 1674, pp. 289-92; William Perkins, *The Works of that Famous and Worthy Minister of Christ in the Universitie of Cambridge, Mr. W. Perkins*, 3 vols., Cambridge, 1618, III, 697-98; Samuel Willard, *A Compleat Body of Divinity* . . . Boston, 1726, pp. 613-16, 643; Richard Baxter, *Chapters from a Christian Directory* . . . , selec. by Jeannette Tawney, London, 1925, pp. 15, 27-30; Morgan Godwyn, *The Negro's & Indians Advocate* . . . London, 1680, p. 112).

[66] Ernst Troeltsch, *Die Soziallehren der christlichen Kirchen und Gruppen* (*Gesammelte Schriften*, Erster Band, n.p., 1961), pp. 53-54, 132-34, 144-74, 264.

inforced civil law in protecting owners against the loss
of slaves to the Church; no slave could be ordained unless he had first been emancipated.[67] The Fathers exhorted slaves to obey even the harshest masters, and in
A.D. 362 the Council of Gangrae laid anathema on "anyone who under the pretence of godliness should teach a
slave to despise his master, or to withdraw himself from
his service."[68]

On the other hand, the Church embodied the principle that all men were equal, not as a positive right but
as the dependent children of God. It upheld the ideal of
a spiritual world in which all men might be free. We
cannot discuss here the complex question of Christianity's role in ameliorating the condition of European
slaves. Despite the Church's unquestioning acceptance of
slavery as an institution made necessary by original sin,
there can be little doubt that it often lightened the burden of the individual slave. But if Christians preached
religious equality and expected pious masters to be kind
to their slaves, the same would later be true of the Mos-
lems. In neither instance is there any reason to believe
that religion promoted the outright abolition of slavery.
The fact that Christians accepted the institution until
the late eighteenth century without marked protest suggests a high degree of toleration.

Many historians have exaggerated the antithesis between slavery and Christian doctrine. The contradiction,
we have tried to suggest, lay more within the idea of
slavery itself. Christianity provided one way of responding to this contradiction, and contained both rational-
izations for slavery and ideals that were potentially
abolitionist. The significant point, however, is that attitudes toward slavery were interwoven with central religious concepts. This amalgam, which had developed

[67] Carlyle, *History*, I, 205-6, 122; Westermann, *Slave Systems*, p.
158.
[68] Carlyle, *History*, I, 120-21.

through antiquity, was foreshadowed in Judaism and in Greek philosophy.

In one sense slavery was seen as a punishment resulting from sin or from a natural defect of soul that precluded virtuous conduct. The slave was a Canaanite, a man devoid of Logos, or a sinner who scorned the truth. Stoics and Christians endeavored to distinguish the true from the apparent slave, but physical bondage always suffered from the guilt of association.

In a second sense slavery was seen as a model of dependence and self-surrender. For Plato, Aristotle, and Augustine this meant that it was a necessary part of a world that required moral order and discipline; it was the base on which rested an intricate and hierarchical pattern of authority. Yet Jews called themselves the slaves of Yahweh, Christians called themselves the slaves of Christ. No other word so well expressed an ultimate in willing devotion and self-sacrifice.

In a third sense slavery stood as the starting point for a divine quest. It was from slavery that Hebrews were delivered and from which they acquired their unique mission. It was slavery to desire and social convention that Cynics and Stoics sought to overcome by self-discipline and indifference to the world. And it was from slavery to the corrupted flesh of Adam that Christ redeemed mankind.

For some two thousand years men thought of sin as a kind of slavery. One day they would come to think of slavery as sin.

CHAPTER 2

WHO WAS AN ABOLITIONIST?*

BY LARRY GARA

FIVE years after the close of the Civil War William Lloyd Garrison spoke at the funeral of Samuel B. Chace, his friend and co-worker in the abolition movement. "It is an easy matter to be an abolitionist at the present day," he remarked, "because it is to be on the winning side." Ten years earlier it had been a different matter. "Yet, not ten, but thirty-five years since," continued Garrison, "our departed friend, in the darkest and stormiest period of the Anti-Slavery conflicts, gave his adhesion to the cause."[1] Samuel B. Chace's antislavery credentials were of the highest order. Very few veterans of the reform cause could boast the personal endorsement of America's best known abolitionist.

Indeed, as the pre-Civil War events became further removed from human memory it became increasingly difficult to distinguish between those who had participated in the crusade against slavery and those who had not. The abolition of slavery was only the most significant of a number of events that worked to modify the contemporary definition of an abolitionist. The term's meaning not only changed with the passage of time, but it was always highly subjective, carrying different connotations with different groups and even individuals. To some,

* This essay is based, in part, upon research made possible by a grant from the Penrose Fund of the American Philosophical Society.

[1] Quotation from *Representative Men and Old Families of Rhode Island* included in letter from Marion LaMere to Wilbur H. Siebert, April 26, 1935, in scrapbook "The Underground Railroad in Rhode Island" in the Wilbur H. Siebert Papers, Houghton Library, Harvard University.

abolitionists were God's chosen people; to others, they were the devil's disciples. Further complications arose because of the varieties of means to end slavery which antislavery groups had embraced, and the many degrees of commitment which their adherents had exhibited.

Scholars have correctly distinguished between those who were opposed to slavery in an abstract sort of way and those who were actually involved in the abolition movement. According to this distinction even a slaveholder such as Thomas Jefferson, because of his dislike for the institution and his recognition that the slaves would eventually be emancipated, could be considered antislavery in his point of view, but he could not be considered an abolitionist. The people of the pre-Civil War era made similar distinctions in their thinking, though they were by no means so precise in their use of terms. Nearly all of the abolitionist organizations were called antislavery societies and more often than not their members used the words antislavery and abolition interchangeably.

The antislavery crusade, combining religious enthusiasm and radical social thought, was plagued by the sectarianism that so often weakens religious and reform groups. Each faction became convinced that its approach was the only right, and hence the only effective, one. As early as 1844 Jonathan B. Turner of Jacksonville, Illinois, commented in his newspaper, the *Illinois Statesman,* on "Protestant Abolition." "There has already arisen so many various [abolition] sects . . . ," he wrote, "that the term 'abolition' like the term 'orthodox' really means nothing more than that a man may believe 'some things as well as others,' provided he sticks hard to the name." Several years later a New Jersey Quaker sent a letter to the *National Anti-Slavery Standard* which underscored the truth of Turner's earlier comment. "I am an Abolitionist in the full meaning of the word," he wrote, "but do not approve of the operations of the Anti-Slavery

Society." He objected to such activities as publishing incendiary material on slavery which excited the slaves' minds, "causing them to rise against their masters, . . . and commit bloodshed and murder," and working on weak minds "to induce them to go south, for the purpose of running Slaves to the north," which irritated the owner and closed his ears against all abolitionist arguments. By his definition an abolitionist was one who used lawful means to ameliorate the slaves' condition and to obtain state laws for abolishing slavery, and who attempted to change the South by convincing the slave-owners through persuasion. The *Standard's* editor published the letter under the heading "Pro-Slavery"![2]

While few abolitionists would have accepted the very cautious point of view of the New Jersey Quaker, there were a great variety of abolitionist positions on nearly every question growing out of their concern for reform. "The abolitionists are split to pieces," lamented one of their number in 1849, with "each piece imagining itself holier than the others." And the passage of time brought greater divisiveness rather than unity growing out of a common effort. On the eve of the Civil War Frederick Douglass commented that the abolitionists' "fratricidal conduct has continued, bringing new divisions and parties into the field, till at length there is little of associated effort left to carry on the work of popular antislavery agitation." Indeed, antislavery factionalism did not disappear even with the triumph of the cause. As late as 1892 Douglass lamented: "the time has not come when a true and impartial history of the Anti-slavery movement can be written or reasonably be expected. The preferences for modes of action and partialities" had descended "from sires to sons" and "made the task of writing a true history hard if not impossible. . . . 'New Or-

[2] Jacksonville *Illinois Statesman*, February 26, 1844; New York *National Anti-Slavery Standard*, January 11, 1849.

ganization,' 'Old Organization,' 'Liberty Party,' 'Non Voters,' 'Come Outers,' 'Moral suasionists' and political abolitionists, all did their work . . . ," but Douglass doubted if any one of the various sects could "do full justice to the services rendered by the others."[3]

One of the events that affected the defining of abolitionism and reaction to it was the emergence of William Lloyd Garrison as a leader in the movement, beginning with the publication of *The Liberator* in 1831 and culminating with his taking control of the American Anti-Slavery Society in 1840. Perhaps more than any.other leader, Garrison shifted the emphasis of the crusade from gradualism to immediatism, and with others he led a devastating attack against colonization as a solution to the race problem which would become more acute with emancipation. Garrison's uncompromising language, his rejection of political action, his criticism of the churches, and his espousal of such causes as women's rights and nonresistance made him unacceptable as a leader to many who were active in the cause, and led to several factional divisions. His egotism and his demand for unflagging obedience from his followers also alienated many of the reformers. Yet he remained a significant symbol of the antislavery crusade and continued to influence a small but highly vocal segment of the reformer population.

Garrison's emphasis on immediatism influenced numerous antislavery advocates beyond the realm of his personal following. To some, this doctrine of refusal to countenance any delay in dealing with the slavery problem became a test of abolitionism itself. In 1834 St. Louis reform editor Elijah Lovejoy, whose strong antislavery editorials and anti-Catholicism evoked violent reaction from the local citizenry, insisted that he was not an aboli-

[3] Salem (Ohio) *Anti-Slavery Bugle*, July 6, 1849; Philip S. Foner, *Life and Writings of Frederick Douglass* (4 vols., New York, 1950-55), II, 524; Frederick Douglass to Marshall Pierce, February 18, 1892 in the Nathaniel P. Rogers Collection, Haverford College.

tionist. Two years before he met a violent death at the hands of an Alton, Illinois, mob and became antislavery's first martyr, Lovejoy wrote, "Gradual Emancipation is the remedy we propose. This we look upon as the only feasible, and indeed, the only desirable way of affecting our release from the thraldom in which we are held."[4] After his martyrdom the "immediatists" tended to overlook Lovejoy's more moderate antislavery pronouncements as well as his opposition to Catholicism, and claim him as one of their own.[5]

Antislavery reformers attempted to use incidents and issues in such a way as to promote their ultimate objective, the complete abolition of slavery. The Garrisonians relied upon moral suasion and constant verbal attacks against the "sin" of slaveholding. Wendell Phillips said, "Our agitation is intended to stun the nation into sobriety, drunken as it is with prosperity, with triumph, with gainful indifference to justice and humanity. . . . We rely upon agitation." The Salem (Ohio) *Anti-Slavery Bugle*, organ of the Western Garrisonians, summarized "What Abolitionists Believe" by stating that "we believe slavery to be a sin, always, everywhere, and only, sin—sin, in itself, . . ." When critics accused abolitionists of using hard language Garrison cheerfully accepted the charge. "The whole scope of the English language is inadequate to describe the horrors and impieties of Slavery," he wrote, "and the transcendent wickedness of those who sustain this bloody system."[6]

[4] Extracts from Joseph C. and Owen Lovejoy, *Memoir of the Rev. Elijah P. Lovejoy* in scrapbook "The Underground Railroad in Illinois, vol. 3" in the Wilbur H. Siebert Papers in the Ohio Historical Society.

[5] Lovejoy's recent biographer maintains that even by the summer of 1835 he had become an abolitionist, perhaps without realizing it himself. Merton L. Dillon, *Elijah P. Lovejoy, Abolitionist Editor* (Urbana, Ill., 1961), p. 55.

[6] New York *National Anti-Slavery Standard*, June 2, 1860; Salem (Ohio) *Anti-Slavery Bugle*, September 24, 1847; William Lloyd Garrison, "Hard Language," in *The Liberty Bell* (1848), p. 284.

As early as 1844 Garrison stated that slavery had to be eliminated from American soil, "cost what it may." He was willing, if necessary, to bury slavery in the "grave of infamy," to see every party "torn by dissensions, every sect dashed into fragments, the national compact dissolved, [or] the land filled with the horrors of a civil or a servile war." And as far as Garrison was concerned, only "traitors and tyrants" would raise an outcry against his declaration. The test of character was as infallible as it was simple. "He that is with the slaveholder is against the slave! he that is with the slave is against the slaveholder." Instead of formulating a program and attempting to implement it the Garrisonian abolitionists merely repeated their objective. "The plan of the abolitionists," wrote one of them, "is immediate emancipation by every individual Slave-holder. Let no one deny its existence."[7]

Such single-mindedness inevitably brought strong reaction from antislavery sympathizers with a different approach as well as from those totally unsympathetic to the cause. William Ellery Channing deplored the "extremism" of the Garrisonians. "They have fallen into the common error of enthusiasts," he commented, "that of exaggerating their object, of feeling as if no evil existed but that which they opposed, and as if no guilt could be compared with that of countenancing or upholding it." Even former slave Frederick Douglass became the object of the wrath of Garrison and his followers after he broke with them. Douglass said they hated him because he had rejected "Garrisonism—an 'ism' which comprehends opposition to the Church, the ministry, the Sabbath and the government . . . apart from the question of slavery."[8]

[7] William Lloyd Garrison, "No Compromise With Slavery," in *The Liberty Bell* (1844), 215-20; Charles K. Whipple, "The Abolitionists' Plan," in *The Liberty Bell* (1845), p. 90.

[8] Frederick Von Raumer, *America and the American People* (New York, 1846), 122; Frederick Douglass to Secretary of the Edinburgh New Anti-Slavery Association, July 9, 1857 in Foner, *Life and Writings of Douglass*, II, 425-26.

Douglass was correct in assessing the Garrisonians' view of abolitionism. One had to accept their complete program in order to be included in their select group of abolitionists. In 1846 Samuel Brooke, an Ohio Garrisonian, disputed Samuel Lewis' claim to be an abolitionist, and Gamaliel Bailey challenged Brooke to defend his remarks. Brooke admitted that Lewis was clearly "in favor of the enfranchisement of the slave" but that his abolitionism amounted to no more than that. To meet Brooke's standard of abolitionism a man must refuse "to acknowledge as fellow Christians, those whose countenance and support is given ecclesiastically to the continuance of slavery," and he should also decline "by the political action of himself or agent, to uphold and support a slave-holding government." The Garrisonian path to righteousness was extremely narrow and it is little wonder that other antislavery leaders resented their criticism. Samuel Lewis, for example, was convinced that the Garrisonians stood "directly in the way of the advancement of the Anti-Slavery cause," and that without them, New England, at least, would have been quickly abolitionized.[9]

It was the question of political action which finally separated Garrison and his followers from the majority of those who considered themselves abolitionists. The organization of an antislavery party in 1840 was another event which worked to modify the concept of abolitionism.[10] To the Garrisonians, politics required the compromise of basic principle. Garrison was virtually a Christian anarchist who advocated seceding, if necessary, from a government which condoned slavery.[11] Furthermore, the Garrisonians did not believe it possible to deal with a moral problem by using political means. Com-

[9] *Anti-Slavery Bugle*, May 1, 1846.

[10] Dwight Lowell Dumond, *Antislavery: The Crusade for Freedom in America* (Ann Arbor, Mich., 1961), p. 297.

[11] John L. Thomas, *The Liberator: William Lloyd Garrison* (Boston and Toronto, 1963), pp. 324-37.

menting on the very light Free Soil party vote in the 1852 national election, Samuel May, Jr. said that "the Anti-Slavery men of this country must cease to rely upon human devices and deep-laid schemes," and "trust solely to the *moral power* inherent in their cause. Party organization, drill and machinery are worthless. God's truth is to be their shield, their helmet, their whole armor." Such sentiments, however, had little effect on those in the anti-slavery movement who were turning increasingly to political action. In 1855 an abolitionist wrote May enthusiastically predicting a large Free Soil vote in his town at the next election. As for the people in his area, "they don't think much of Garrisonism," he said, "because it don't do anything."[12]

Abolitionists were also divided on the matter of devoting time and energy to assisting fugitive slaves making their way to Canada. There were those who concentrated on this form of service and who carried on their work in a manner similar to that usually associated with the underground railroad of tradition.[13] Others had serious reservations concerning such activity. Sending fugitives to Canada, after all, was another form of colonization and as such it alienated a segment of the antislavery force even though it attracted many individuals who wished to avoid the implications of the race problem which would follow emancipation. The Garrisonians were quite willing to assist fugitive slaves when called upon but they considered such assistance, along with other peripheral antislavery activity, as diversionary rather than fundamental. At their 1857 meeting in Alliance, Ohio, members of the Western Anti-Slavery Society re-

[12] Samuel May, Jr., "A More Excellent Way," in *The Liberty Bell* (1853), pp. 239-42; Joseph A. Howland to May, September 9, 1855 in the William Lloyd Garrison Papers, Boston Public Library.

[13] For a discussion of the role that underground railroad activity played in the abolition movement, see Larry Gara, *The Liberty Line: The Legend of the Underground Railroad* (Lexington, Ky., 1961), pp. 93-114.

solved: "That it is of the highest importance to guard against the mistake of supposing opposition to extension of slavery, or to the Fugitive Slave law, or the Dred Scott decision, or any other incident of the Slave Institution, as necessarily opposition to the system itself." Abby Kelly was firmly convinced that real antislavery work did not consist of aiding fugitives in Canada, or fighting legal battles for imprisoned abolitionists. These, she said, "were not blows aimed directly at the Slave system—that though these things ought to be done, they are not the weightier matters of real Anti-Slavery." She urged co-workers in the cause to keep their eyes "steadily fixed on the polar star of principle, nor be turned either to the right or the left. Our work," she emphasized, "is to inculcate these great truths, the right of man to Freedom, the atrocious sin of Slavery, and the duty of ceasing to give it support, whether in Church or in State."[14]

While all abolitionists proclaimed "the right of man to Freedom," they did not always agree about the place of the Negro in a predominantly white society. On occasion, the question of admitting Negroes to membership in antislavery societies proved highly controversial to the reformers. One later recalled that there were some cases of persons opposed to slavery and willing to work for its abolition who "strongly objected to any association with colored · persons in their Anti-Slavery labors." On the other hand, there were abolitionists who recognized the need to combat race prejudice and further civil rights, a need urged upon them by the Negroes active in the cause. Speaking to a convention of the New York State Anti-Slavery Society in 1839, Theodore S. Wright, a colored minister, pointed out that where some years earlier abolitionists were few and everyone knew what

[14] Report of the fifteenth annual meeting in the Minute Book of the Western Anti-Slavery Society in the Library of Congress; Abby Kelly, "What is Real Anti-Slavery Work?" in *The Liberty Bell* (1845), pp. 203-8.

they stood for, "Now a man may call himself an Abolitionist and we know not where to find him." He emphasized the importance of human equality and brotherhood.
"It is an easy thing to ask about the vileness of slavery
at the South," he said, "but to call the dark man a
brother, . . . to treat all men according to their moral
worth, to treat the man of color in all circumstances as
a man and brother—that is the test." In 1854 another
Negro antislavery writer maintained that though "abolitionism" had formerly meant "antislavery," it had come
to have a "deeper significance and wider scope" and included not only bodily freedom but also the "collateral
issues connected with human enfranchisement, independent of race, complexion, or sex."[15]

Garrison and his followers were especially conscious
of the race issue. Many of the subscribers to *The Liberator* were free Negroes, and the Garrisonians cooperated with local groups of Negroes in several campaigns
against discrimination, including their successful opposition to segregated schools in Boston. Certain aspects of
their crusade, especially working with the fugitives from
slavery, brought them into frequent contact with Negro
crusaders and fellow workers. It was Frederick Douglass,
a former slave, who insisted upon making a distinction
between the abolitionists and those Negroes who worked
for the same cause. In 1874 Douglass sent a message to an
abolitionists' convention meeting in Chicago. He referred
to abolitionists in the third person, declining to class
himself with them. "The men who have a right to that
title were born free," he wrote, "and were as noble as

15 Leon F. Litwack, "The Abolitionist Dilemma: The Antislavery
Movement and the Northern Negro," in *The New England Quar-
terly*, 34 (March 1961), 51-59; Elizabeth Buffum Chace, "My Anti-
Slavery Reminiscences," in *Two Quaker Sisters* (New York, 1937),
p. 118; Herbert Aptheker, ed. *A Documentary History of the Negro
People in the United States* (New York, 1951), pp. 171-73; Charles
L. Reason's introduction to Julia Griffiths, ed. *Autographs For Free-
dom* (Boston, 1854), II, 11.

free. They were not struggling for their own freedom, as I was; but they were periling everything but honor for the freedom of others,—the noblest height to which men can rise."[16]

Disagreement over a definition of abolitionism was matched by a difference of opinion over the influence of the crusaders. There were those who viewed abolitionist propaganda and activity as clear proof that the whole North had fallen under the antislavery influence. In 1850 Congressman John McQueen of South Carolina maintained that the records of Congress showed only a meaningless distinction between those in the North who were called abolitionists and those who were not, unless it meant that "one party aim openly to accomplish their object, whilst the others disavow it, yet always vote with them when slavery is concerned." And, in 1851 Senator Robert Barnwell Rhett of the same state asked, "What has Congress for the last ten years been, but a grand abolition convention, preaching and inspiring insurrection among our slaves?"[17]

On the other hand a Richmond, Virginia, newspaper in 1850 published extracts from a letter in which a number of influential New Yorkers wrote that Southerners exaggerated the abolition sentiment of the North and offered assurance that, were the question put to a vote, a majority of Northerners would vote against emancipation. The agitation was the work of a very small proportion of the population and the agitators included "some of the most despicable wretches on God's earth." The editor of the *Cincinnati Enquirer* replied indignantly when a Nashville paper referred to "a State as strongly tinctured with abolition as Ohio." It was only "a few indefatigable ultras," making "a loud noise and

[16] Clipping in scrapbook "Abolitionists' Convention, 1874," in State Historical Society of Wisconsin.

[17] *Congressional Globe*, 31 Cong., 1 sess., app., 736, 32 Cong., 1 sess., app. 44.

din" in each section of Ohio which gave distant people the impression that the whole state was moving that way. "In truth," said the editor, "not one man in one thousand has any sympathy with them, much less connection or agency."[18]

Yet there was a germ of truth in the Southern editor's charges. The absence of slavery in the North played an important part in determining the section's outlook toward the institution, and as the feelings between the two sections became increasingly bitter, Northern antislavery sentiment waxed proportionately stronger. In 1848 Mrs. Eleanor J. W. Baker of Boston wrote to a Southern friend detailing some of the irresponsible acts of those she called "Crazy Abolitionists" with "ultra ideas." However, she added, *we are all Abolitionists— in principle—at the North,* but the national and religious part of the community have no fellowship with the class of people to whom I have alluded." An antislavery tract published in 1853 expressed similar sentiments: "the North, with no very important exceptions, although not enthusiastic in the matter, are abolitionists at heart."[19]

As the sectional rift deepened the abolitionists became aware of a climate of opinion more sympathetic to their message. They attributed the change to a growing popular awareness of the aggressive spirit of slavery. In 1849 a Western society reported that "the Anti-Slavery cause is still advancing; the number of those willing to be called abolitionists, and to act in a manner deserving the name, is continually and rapidly increasing." A decade later an abolitionist from Chautauqua County, New York, reported that in her locality there were individuals who five years earlier had been ashamed "to bear the ap-

[18] *Richmond Enquirer,* November 8, 1850; *Cincinnati Enquirer,* December 27, 1852.

[19] Mrs. Eleanor J. W. Baker to Anna Gurney, January 31, 1848 in the Eleanor J. W. Baker Papers, Duke University; Lysander Spooner, *The Unconstitutionality of Slavery* (Boston, 1853), p. 290.

pellation of 'Anti-slavery,' who can now manfully bear
the one then still more repellant of *Abolitionist.*"[20]

To those with proslavery sentiments the term "abolitionist" was virtually profane and occasionally it was
used as an execration. In 1836 a master whose slave
escaped while servant and master were staying at New
York's Astor House received little sympathy from the
hotel's manager. When the manager quickly withdrew
from the ensuing investigation the slaveholder "turned
upon his heel and cursed him for an *abolitionist!*" Frequently the more extremist Southern newspapers rivaled
the abolition press in the use of denunciatory language
and referred to their Northern neighbors as the "Abolition States of the North."[21]

Slaveowners often assumed that successful escapes were
the direct result of abolitionist interference. Though
most abolitionists disavowed any plan for running slaves
from the South, when an occasional abolitionist was
caught in such activity it tended to confirm the slave-
owners' suspicions. When escapes occurred the proslavery
element seldom made fine distinctions. After a series of
episodes involving runaway slaves, a group of Cass
County, Missouri, citizens accused a Methodist minister
of "having promulgated publicly, abolition sentiments."
The local citizenry appointed a special committee which,
after a thorough investigation, decided that the minister's
"sentiments savored too thoroughly of Abolitionism, . . .
and that it was necessary for the peace and harmony of
the county that he leave the State." The group raised a
fund to help defray his travel expenses and, it was re-

[20] New York *National Anti-Slavery Standard*, July 12, 1849; Mrs.
D. Brooks to William Still, December 7, 1859 in William Still, *The
Underground Rail Road* (Philadelphia, 1872), p. 590.

[21] Elizur Wright, Jr. to James G. Birney, October 12, 1836 in
Dwight L. Dumond, ed. *Letters of James Gillespie Birney, 1831-1857*
(2 vols., New York, 1938), I, 366; Louisville *Daily Courier*, August
22, 1859.

ported, "he acquiesced without a murmur in the wishes of the large concourse present."[22]

In calmer circumstances, critics of the reformers usually distinguished between different kinds of abolitionists. Garrison's visit to Cincinnati in 1854 brought an editorial in the Democratic *Cincinnati Enquirer* which commented, "among the notorious and ultra Abolitionists of the North, WILLIAM LLOYD GARRISON stands pre-eminent." He was a pioneer in the work who had made antislavery a hobby and had expressed such astonishingly "ultra" ideas that many sober and intelligent people considered him "but little better than a monomaniac upon his favorite topic." He was, however, a person of "much more than ordinary ability," and even those who detested his doctrines could "hardly withhold the tribute of respect for his courage in expressing them at the certain risk of unmeasured reproach." The editor contrasted Garrison's open advocacy of the dissolution of the Union with the hypocrisy of the antislavery politicians, especially "SUMNER, SEWARD, CHASE, HALE, and the rest of that kidney, who profess an attachment and devotion to the Union while endeavoring to render principles successful certain to lead to its overthrow and dismemberment."[23]

Other critics of the antislavery cause made similar distinctions. In 1857 Edmund Ruffin maintained that the "true abolitionist—an abolitionist for the sake of conscience and what he deems religion" would welcome any horror that might be necessary to accomplish his object. But such persons, "the only sincere and honest members of the great antislavery party," were few in number and they were tools of the more selfish and base "Sewards, and Sumners, and Greeleys, who know full well the folly and falsehood of their professed doctrines, and who advocate them merely to acquire political power

[22] St. Louis *Republican*, August 11, 1855.
[23] *Cincinnati Enquirer*, November 4, 1854.

or personal gain." Henry A. Wise of Virginia identified three classes of Northern enemies: the "honest minded, zealous fanatic" who was least to be feared; the more dangerous "cunning, heartless, reckless politician, who sought elevation and preferment, by agitating, inflaming and directing the popular mind on the slavery question"; and the most dangerous enemy of all, the "secret, silent, ever-active political manager, who strove, by all means, fair or foul, to increase the ascendancy of Northern power in the National Councils, and thus to bear down the South by the crushing weight of Northern votes."[24]

After antislavery became a thorny political issue it was indeed difficult to disassociate the political program against slavery from the sectional attack on the South itself. Criticism of the South had more appeal for Northern voters than abolition, and none of the antislavery political parties went so far as to embrace a clear-cut abolitionist program. Free soil, or the containment of slavery, was the common program basic to the Liberty party, the Free Soil party, and the Republican party. Such a moderate antislavery position enabled political leaders to attract the support of some abolitionists as well as many who would shrink at abolitionism but could accept the free soil idea.

So long as abolition was an unpopular doctrine in the North it was common for political opponents to use the term to discredit those with mild antislavery views. During the years that John Quincy Adams served as congressman from Massachusetts his supporters had to defend him from such charges. A pro-Adams newspaper in Kentucky admitted that Adams regarded slavery "abstractly as an evil institution" but denied that he was a political abolitionist or wished in any way to violate the "constitutional rights of slaveholders." In 1850 a Pitts-

[24] Edmund Ruffin, *Consequences of Abolition Agitation* (reprinted from *DeBow's Review*, Washington, 1857), p. 11; *Richmond Enquirer*, January 18, 1850.

burgh paper accused President Millard Fillmore of being an abolitionist, recalling his answers to some questions posed to him by an abolitionist society twelve years earlier. Fillmore's supporters gladly admitted that his views were antislavery but denied that he was "an abolitionist in the technical sense of the word," or that his opinions on any subject of national moment were "sectional, or narrow, or fanatical, or ultra. . . ."[25]

Some political personalities who emphasized the antislavery issue far more than Fillmore also found it necessary to deny that they were abolitionists. Congressmen supporting the Wilmot Proviso, including Jacob Brinkerhoff and David Wilmot, vehemently denied that their program to keep slavery out of territory acquired from Mexico had an abolition complexion. Brinkerhoff pointed out that he frequently denounced the abolitionists publicly and Wilmot told Congress that he proposed "nowhere to abolish slavery, or to interfere with it where it exists."[26] The best that William Seward's political friends could do was to point out that he had refused to support the Liberty and Free Soil candidates in 1844 and 1848.[27] When Ohio's Senator Salmon P. Chase objected to his inclusion in a list of "disunion abolitionists," Henry Clay justified the association. "Upon my word," said Clay, "if the Senator does not know what an abolitionist means, when he has practiced the doctrine for so many years, I am sure I am unable to instruct or inform him. All sorts of abolitionists seem to act together," he added.[28]

The Republicans were especially sensitive to the abolition question and for the most part took great trouble to distinguish between their program of opposition to slavery extension and the ideas of the antislavery extremists. Yet Southern spokesmen found ample opportunity

[25] *Frankfort* (Ky.) *Commonwealth*, November 14, 1843; *Pittsburgh Gazette*, July 15, 1850.

[26] *Congressional Globe*, 29 Cong., 2 sess., 353, 377.

[27] *Frankfort Commonwealth*, April 17, 1849.

[28] *Congressional Globe*, 31 Cong., 2 sess., app., 322.

to deny this distinction. A Mississippi senator alleged that there was "a sort of billing and cooing, a sort of caressing, a sort of old-fashioned courtship, between certain [Republican] gentlemen here and the ultra-Abolition party." And in 1860 when Republican Congressman John Sherman was candidate for Speaker of the House, one of his colleagues from Arkansas maintained that Sherman, by his record, had shown himself to be in the "very front rank of Republican ultraism." Among other things he had given "full scope and vent to his abolition zeal" by encouraging Negro-stealing and assisting the underground railroad.[29]

Those abolitionists who supported the Republican cause did so, according to the *Oberlin Evangelist*, despite the party's antislavery shortcomings and with the wish that its position on slavery were more to their liking. Frederick Douglass, however, took a more positive view of the Republican program. He readily admitted that those who opposed slavery did so for many different reasons, including a desire to keep Negroes from mingling with whites in the territories, yet he asserted that strong opposition to slavery was the "main and all-sustaining element of the Republican party" and that basically it was the genuine abolition element which formed the party's major support.[30]

Difficult as it was to identify abolitionists in the period preceding the Civil War when the label carried with it so many conflicting connotations, such identification became even less meaningful after Union victory settled the slavery question. Some abolitionists correctly predicted that when their cause triumphed, many newcomers would join the crusade. As early as 1835 William Lloyd Garrison had said that in the free states his cause

[29] *Congressional Globe*, 34 Cong., 3 sess., app., 93, 36 Cong., 1 sess., app., 83.
[30] *Oberlin Evangelist*, September 12, 1860; Foner, *Life and Writings*, II, 491-92.

was "sweeping every thing before it," and predicted that great men would come in "at the death of the monster slavery. . . . Let us beware how we trust or eulogise such men," he warned. In 1864 Lydia Maria Child wrote Garrison a letter which fulfilled his prediction. "New anti-slavery friends are becoming as plenty as roses in June," she reported. "Sometimes, when they tell me they have always been anti-slavery, I smile inwardly, but I do not contradict the assertion; I merely marvel at their power of keeping a secret so long!"[31] In 1869 Samuel May, Jr. found it difficult to make a list of antislavery ministers, "so different are the standards set up by different persons as to what constituted an abolitionist." Some thought that "a single sermon a year, and praying for the slave in moderate and unexciting phrase, and abstaining from abuse of the antislavery movement was enough." May, a Garrisonian veteran, believed "more than that was needful—a great deal."[32]

One thing was clear. While many felt it necessary before the Civil War to avoid the label "abolitionist," after the struggle many tried to make their support of the abolitionist crusade retroactive. The heroism which authentic antislavery veterans flaunted in their memoirs met a sympathetic response from thousands of readers. Men with even a remote connection with the crusade or one of its leaders became legendary figures in countless northern communities. The descendants of abolitionists glowed with pride over the courageous deeds of their forbears. Such second generation admirers seldom made distinctions between varieties of abolitionist thought nor did they give much concern to the type or degree of participation their heroes had rendered to the cause. "These men—these Abolitionists—did not fear

[31] William Lloyd Garrison to Lewis Tappan, December 17, 1835 in the Lewis Tappan Papers, Library of Congress; *Liberator*, February 19, 1864.

[32] Samuel May, Jr. to Samuel J. May, November 2, 1869 in the May Papers, Boston Public Library.

anything," said a son of one of them. "They believed it was their duty to help the slaves get their freedom, for to them life and liberty were the great things."[33]

Yet the oversimplified view of the abolitionists and their descendants was not acceptable to all Northerners. Eli Thayer, for instance, was convinced that his plan for colonizing Kansas with free state settlers contributed more to the success of the antislavery cause than all the activities of the abolitionists. Thayer considered them "a cabal, active, noisy, and pugnacious, but never effective." They erred in constantly attempting "to stimulate feeling upon the slavery question without suggesting any practical action," and as a substitute for action "they passed resolutions." Leonard Bacon, the son of a moderate antislavery minister, and others published similar criticism of Garrison and the more extreme abolitionists.[34]

Aging Garrisonians quickly rushed to their own defense, often impugning the motives of their challengers. Oliver Johnson was especially active in defending the Garrisonians and protecting their exalted place in history. "I wonder what ignoramus will next take up the cudgel in opposition to the Garrisonians!" he wrote a former co-worker in 1887. "I have demolished quite a crowd in the last seven years," he boasted, "but I am ready for more if there are others yet to come."[35]

In 1874 Zebina Eastman, a Chicago editor, organized an abolitionist convention in that city to which he invited veterans of the antislavery struggle whether they believed in "voting, or non-voting, and in moral suasion

[33] Wilbur H. Siebert interview with James C. McGrew, March 19, 1892 in scrapbook "Underground Railroad in Ohio, vol. 1" in the Siebert Papers, Ohio Historical Society.

[34] Eli Thayer, *A History of the Kansas Crusade: Its Friends and Foes* (New York, 1889), p. 139; Rev. Leonard Woolsey Bacon, "A Good Fight Finished," *Century Magazine*, 25 (March 1883), 658-59.

[35] Oliver Johnson to Samuel May, Jr., April 17, 1887 in the May Papers, Boston Public Library; Oliver Johnson, *The Abolitionists Vindicated in a Review of Eli Thayer's Paper on the New England Emigrant Aid Company* (Worcester, Mass., 1887), pp. 18-19.

or political or church action, gradualism or immediatism." In his introductory address, however, Eastman revealed his own point of view when he proclaimed, "Lincoln became the greatest abolitionist that ever lived, . . . for he set more men free from abject slavery than were ever before delivered from the chains of bondage by any one man." Oliver Johnson took exception to the overemphasis on political abolitionism in the entire gathering and sent a protest to Eastman who answered with a letter which satisfied Johnson that his suspicions had not been well founded.[36]

The different points of view reflected in the mild quarrel between Zebina Eastman and Oliver Johnson underscores the lack of unanimity among individuals who had unquestioned records in the antislavery cause. Each faction remained convinced that its own contribution overshadowed the others. Recent scholars have continued the argument, especially that phase of it involving the Garrisonians and the political abolitionists. With such a complex set of factors contributing to the antebellum picture it is little wonder that no scholar has yet brought finality to antislavery history.

The question "Who was an abolitionist?" may not have an answer, certainly not a simple one. Too much has been taken for granted in writing about the reform movement. To understand the complexities of such a crusade, historians must make careful distinctions. In evaluating the term "abolitionist" it is necessary to keep in mind who was affixing the label and when, for without taking such considerations into account historians are quite likely to find themselves unconsciously enlisting in one cause or another, injecting value judgments of a later time, or entering some other blind alley which obscures their view of the past and lessens the value of their labors.

[36] Clipping in scrapbook "Abolitionists' Convention, 1874" in the State Historical Society of Wisconsin; Oliver Johnson to Zebina Eastman, June 15, 25, 1874 in the Eastman Papers, Chicago Historical Society.

CHAPTER 3

WHO DEFENDS
THE ABOLITIONIST?

BY FAWN M. BRODIE

ONE of the most celebrated passages in the writings of Mark Twain describes the episode where Huckleberry Finn, in helping the runaway slave Jim to freedom, is suddenly seized with guilt and almost demoralized by the enormity of his behavior. "It got to troubling me so I couldn't rest," he says, ". . . it stayed with me, and scorched me more and more. . . . I got to feeling so mean and so miserable I most wished I was dead." And when Jim reveals his plans to earn money to buy his wife and children, plans which include getting "an Ab'litionist to go and steal them" if their master wouldn't sell them, Huck is horrified. "It most froze me to hear such talk," Huck says. "Here was this nigger, which I had as good as helped to run away, coming right out flatfooted and saying he would steal his children—children that belonged to a man I didn't even know: a man that hadn't ever done me no harm."

The irony implicit in this sequence is Mark Twain's; the guilt and ambivalence were, however, a reflection of widespread and astonishingly tenacious attitudes. One thing is certain: in *Huckleberry Finn* the abolitionist is no hero to the boy who is himself playing the role of abolitionist. And it is one of the paradoxes of American history that a nation that has for generations delighted in the complexities attending Jim's escape still looks upon the abolitionist with suspicion and occasional hatred. Except in the eyes of the Negro and a small minority of whites he has never been accepted as hero. Far from being applauded for his compassion and courage in combating a corrosive national blight, he is assailed for his fanaticism and "pertinacious meddling"; he is condemned for taking Puritanism into politics, and is accused of being a major cause of the Civil War.

Historians continue to use the scalpel on both the abolitionists and their political successors, the Radical Republicans, labeling them vindictive, laying bare their neuroses, equating their "fanaticism for freedom" with the fire-eaters' "fanaticism for slavery." As Avery Craven put it in his *Civil War in the Making*, "the Yanceys, the Rhetts, the Charles Sumners and the John Browns and their 'fellow-travelers' . . . made war inevitable."[1] And though the "plague on both your houses" attitude would seem to imply a certain detachment, actually it is the fanatics for freedom who get the lion's share of the blame.

South Carolina's Senator Andrew P. Butler, one of the authors of the mischievous Fugitive Slave Law of 1850, made thirty-six speeches defending slavery on the floor of the Senate, including some contemptuous personal references to his abolitionist colleague, Charles Sumner. Sumner made three speeches attacking slavery, in the third of which he also made some indelicate personal references. He was repaid by being beaten into insensibility by Congressman Brooks in the Senate Chamber. But in our recent histories it is Sumner's speech that is deplored for its "disregard of truth and sportsmanship," for its "deplorable taste" and "pure rant."[2] It is the incendiary paragraphs from Sumner's not Butler's speeches that are invariably quoted; it is Sumner's mo-

[1] Avery Craven, *The Civil War in the Making, 1815-1860* (Baton Rouge, La., 1959), p. 114.
[2] Avery Craven, *The Coming of the Civil War* (New York, 1942), p. 367; Allan Nevins, *Ordeal of the Union* (2 vols., New York, 1947), II, 440.

tives that are dissected in search of arrogance, or sexual impotence, or martyr hunger; the hidden motives of Senator Butler and Preston Brooks are left inviolate.

Thaddeus Stevens until recently had a reputation as low as any political figure in American history—described by George Fort Milton, for example, as "an apostle of proscription and hate," and by James Truslow Adams as "perhaps the most despicable, malevolent and morally deformed character who has ever risen to high power in America."[3] Such judgments are pronounced about a man who started out as an abolitionist lawyer defending fugitive slaves in Pennsylvania, and who climaxed his career by fathering that potentially great bulwark of individual liberty, the Fourteenth Amendment.

To compound the paradox, we have on the other hand the ever-accelerating glorification of moderate Southern leaders, notably Robert E. Lee, who, though he fought with devotion as well as skill for a government dedicated to slavery, has become a national hero only a step below Lincoln. Jefferson Davis in a recent biography by Hudson Strode emerges as "the most misunderstood man in history," a Southerner who all along was in favor of gradual emancipation. "When the time shall arrive at which emancipation is proper," Strode quotes Davis as saying, "those most interested will be most anxious to effect it." No one would guess in reading Strode's volumes that Davis argued hotly for slavery in California ("I hold that the pursuit of gold washing and mining is better adapted to slave labor than to any other"), that he fought to make slavery permanent in Kansas and encouraged conspiracies to annex Cuba and convert her to a slave state. In recounting Davis' reaction to Preston Brooks' beating of Sumner, Strode states that "Davis realized that Brooks had done the pro-slavery forces considerable

[3] James T. Adams, *Epic of America* (Boston, 1931), p. 275; George F. Milton, *The Age of Hate* (New York, 1930), p. 262.

harm," failing to note that Davis wrote a letter to Brooks praising his character and the deed.[4]

Many histories of the Confederacy are written with such skillful disregard of the ugly that slavery shrinks to an unpleasant anomaly of small consequence. It is treated as an essential transition from African savagery to enlightened citizenship, a labor system which would somehow easily have evolved into freedom without war. Some writers even try to replace the word slave by the word servant, as if expecting that the ancient, terrible curse could be exorcised by a simple, semantic trick.

A recent biography of Stonewall Jackson omits critical evidence of Jackson's fanaticism, like his first speech to his troops, in which he urged a war to the death with no prisoners taken. The distortion of history by omission is just as real as distortion by vituperation. But there is a certain honesty of attitude in the old vituperation, and one gets a much sharper picture of what the Civil War was all about by reading the violently partisan and proslavery biography of Jackson written by his chaplain, R. L. Dabney, published in 1866, than by the more seriously researched but still sentimentalized biography of Lenoir Chambers published in 1959.[5]

There was one period in our history when a substantial number of historians described the abolitionists as just and courageous fighters for freedom. This was shortly after the Civil War, when men like Henry Wilson, Horace Greeley, Alexander McClure, Joshua Giddings, John A. Logan, and George W. Julian, many of whom had themselves been either active abolitionists or Radical Repub-

---

[4] Hudson Strode, *Jefferson Davis, American Patriot, 1808-1861* (New York, 1955), pp. 204, 284. For Davis' statement advocating slavery in California see *Congressional Globe*, 31 Cong., 1 sess., app. vol. I, p. 154, February 14, 1850. The fact that Davis wrote an approving letter to Brooks is reported by Edward L. Pierce in his *Memoir and Letters of Charles Sumner* (4 vols., Boston, 1893), III, 496.

[5] See Robert L. Dabney, *Life and Campaigns of Lieut.-Gen. Thomas J. Jackson* (New York, 1866); Lenoir Chambers, *Stonewall Jackson, the Legend and the Man* (2 vols., New York, 1959).

licans, were eager to put down the facts of history as they saw them.[6] And in our own generation we have seen the beginning of a resurgence of respect and admiration for "the great agitators."

Dwight L. Dumond's new study of the antislavery crusade helps to put the great reform movement in its true perspective but it is only a beginning. Harold Hyman in his biography of Stanton restores to his proper eminence a Radical Republican who had fallen so low in the esteem of historians that they could pay serious heed to the fantastic charge that he had connived in Lincoln's murder. John L. Thomas, Irving Bartlett, Russel B. Nye, John Hope Franklin, Richard Hofstadter, and Oscar Sherwin have all made detailed studies of the abolitionists,[7] and none is apologetic for the "moral causes" underlying what Winston Churchill has called the "noblest and least avoidable of all the great mass conflicts." But for the most part the abolitionists and Radical Republicans have been under remarkably sus-

[6] Henry Wilson, *History of the Antislavery Measures of the Thirty-seventh and Thirty-eighth Congresses, 1861-64* (Boston, 1864), and *History of the Rise and Fall of the Slave Power in America* (3 vols., Boston, 1877); Horace Greeley, *The American Conflict: a History of the Great Rebellion, in the United States of America, 1860-64* (2 vols., Hartford, 1864-66); Alexander McClure, *Abraham Lincoln and Men of War Times* (Philadelphia, 1892); Joshua Giddings, *History of the Rebellion* (New York, 1864); John A. Logan, *The Great Conspiracy, its Origin and History* (New York, 1886); George W. Julian, *Political Recollections, 1840-1872* (Chicago, 1884).

[7] See Dwight L. Dumond, *Antislavery: Crusade for Freedom in America* (Ann Arbor, Mich., 1961); Harold Hyman and B. P. Thomas, *Stanton: The Life and Times of Lincoln's Secretary of War* (New York, 1962); John L. Thomas, *The Liberator, William Lloyd Garrison* (Boston, 1963); Irving Bartlett, *Wendell Phillips, Brahmin Radical* (Boston, 1962); Russel B. Nye, *Fettered Freedom, Civil Liberties and the Slavery Controversy, 1830-1860* (East Lansing, Mich., 1949); John Hope Franklin, *From Slavery to Freedom, a History of American Negroes* (New York, 1948), and *The Emancipation Proclamation* (New York, 1963); Richard Hofstadter, *American Political Tradition* (New York, 1954); Oscar Sherwin, *Prophet of Liberty, the Life and Time of Wendell Phillips* (New York, 1958).

tained attack. A detailed examination of this attack is long overdue.

Even the original fury of the slaveholders against the abolitionists has yet to be adequately explored. If it is true, as Lincoln said, that it is "kindly provided that of all those who come into the world only a small percentage are natural tyrants,"[8] then the American historian must explain better than he has previously why the citizens of a vast area that had once tolerated abolition and colonization societies turned against them in a single generation and made "Death to the abolitionist" a sectional shibboleth. One does not find sufficient explanation simply in the invention of the cotton gin, with all its multiform economic consequences, nor in the favored theory that Southern obstreperousness was a natural reaction to the intemperance of the abolitionist.

As early as 1836 South Carolina's Congressman J. H. Hammond said, "I warn the abolitionists, ignorant and infatuated barbarians as they are, that if chance shall throw any of them into our hands, they may expect a felon's death," [and, as the courageous Southerner, W. J. Cash, pointed out in his *The Mind of the South*, "the overwhelming body of his countrymen cheered him hotly."] Some years later Senator Foote of Mississippi won the sobriquet "Hangman Foote" by saying in the Senate that if abolitionist John P. Hale came to Mississippi he would be hanged to one of the tallest trees in the forest, and that he himself would assist in the operation. Shortly after, Congressman Haskell of Tennessee went on record in the House as proposing that Joshua Giddings should be "hanged as high as Haman." By April 1860, when it was Congressman Roger Pryor threatening to hang Owen Lovejoy "higher than Haman" if he set foot in Virginia, the phrase had become a cliché.[9]

[8] Speech in Peoria, Ill., October 16, 1854, Roy P. Basler, ed. *Collected Works*, II, 264.

[9] W. J. Cash, *The Mind of the South* (New York, 1941), p. 108;

But the threat was no cliché, and certainly it was no jest. These were the nation's lawmakers speaking to other lawmakers, and laws ordering the death penalty for abolitionists peppered the statute books of the South. The state of Georgia officially offered $5,000 for whoever should kidnap Garrison and bring him to Georgia for trial; a Virginia editor offered a reward of $10,000 for the kidnapping and delivery to Richmond of Joshua R. Giddings, or $5,000 for his head. For the head of William H. Seward, mistaken for a burning abolitionist, the offer went up to $50,000.[10] The record is too detailed to be dismissed as a tasteless Southern joke.

After the war moderate Southerners who had originally attacked their own extremists and had opposed secession shifted ground and blamed the abolitionists as being at the root of the prewar trouble. Robert E. Lee publicly fastened the blame in an interview with Britisher Herbert C. Saunders, August 22, 1866. "On the subject of slavery," Saunders wrote, "he assured me that he had always been in favour of the emancipation of the negroes, and that in Virginia the feeling had been strongly inclined in the same direction, till the ill-judged enthusiasms (amounting to rancour) of the abolitionists in the North had turned the Southern tide of feeling in the other direction."[11]

Lee's postwar image swiftly emerged: a gentle, compassionate man who had always favored gradual abolition and who had freed his own slaves, a general who had fought against the Union only because he could not bear the violation of his native state. Actually Lee's own "antislavery" record was cloudier than his devoted admirers

---

George Julian, *Political Recollections* (Chicago, 1884), p. 92, and *Life of Joshua R. Giddings* (Chicago, 1892), pp. 243-44; James F. Rhodes, *History of the United States* (New York, 1906), II, 438.

[10] George W. Julian, *Political Recollections*, p. 173; John F. Hume, *The Abolitionists, 1839-1864* (New York, 1905), p. 13.

[11] Robert E. Lee, *Recollections and Letters of General Robert E. Lee* (New York, 1924), p. 231.

made it out to be. It is true that he had never owned more than half a dozen slaves, several of whom he had freed and sent to Liberia. But for years he had participated actively in all the pleasant aspects of plantation life on the beautiful Arlington estate of his father-in-law, which was home for his wife and children. This estate was willed to Lee's wife in 1857, and Lee was made executor of all Custis' property with express orders to free his 196 slaves within five years and find work for them on his farms. By 1859 none had been emancipated. Lee blamed the delay on legal complications attending the will. Still it happened that when two of the slaves fled toward freedom and were captured in Maryland, he had them brought back and sent to southern Virginia where it was less easy to escape. And he waited until the end of the five-year period before signing the deeds of manumission, December 29, 1862.[12] Certainly during the war, if Lee had had a bad conscience about fighting to preserve the slave system, it had not noticeably impaired his aggressive skill and daring.

When Lee blamed the abolitionists for turning the Southerners against emancipation, he helped raise a lame defense into a respected pattern of thought. Typical of many statements in our own time is that of Robert S. Henry, who in his *Story of the Confederacy* insisted that "Forty years of agitation against slavery, growing more intolerant and impassioned year by year, had effectively killed the movement in the South for gradual emancipation." Avery Craven in his *Coming of the Civil War* wrote that the whole intellectual life of the South was "almost frozen, not so much to justify a questionable labor system as to repel a fanatical attack."[13] Surely the prewar Southern fury against the abolitionist can hardly

[12] Douglas Southall Freeman, *Robert E. Lee, a Biography* (4 vols., New York, 1935), I, 371, 380-87, 390-93, 637.
[13] Robert S. Henry, *The Story of the Confederacy* (New York, 1931), p. 14; Avery Craven, *The Coming of the Civil War*, p. 162.

be explained as the anger of one man against another over a system both wanted to see extinct.

Lincoln said in 1858, "There is vigor enough in slavery to plant itself in a new country even against unfriendly legislation. It takes not only law, but the *enforcement* of law to keep it out."[14] It is the *vigor* in slavery that needs exploring—the psychic as well as economic rewards derived from practicing it. Who has bothered to examine clinically the pathology of men like Representative Lawrence Keitt, who helped Brooks in his assault on Sumner by holding at bay with his pistol the Senators who tried to interfere, and who in July 1860 accused the Republican party of being "stained with treason, hideous with insurrection, and dripping with blood"? Or of fire-eater George Fitzhugh, who reversed the eloquent antislavery statement of Jefferson to read as follows: "Some were born with saddles on their backs, and others booted and spurred to ride them—and the riding does them good."[15]

The slaveholders' assaults on the abolitionists are more easily understood, nevertheless, than the similar attacks by Northerners. The plantation owners, after all, had much to lose, including—as they saw it—two billion dollars worth of property. But it was Northerners who burned abolitionist meeting halls, who mobbed Garrison and Weld, who murdered Elijah Lovejoy. It was Horatio Seymour, distinguished Governor of New York, who met the tragedy of secession with a cynical letter to ex-President Franklin Pierce: "The Union is about gone already. . . . We have deferred cutting throats long enough. . . . I should like to begin with the Abolitionists at once."[16] And it is in the speeches of Northerners like

14 Speech at Jonesboro, Ill., September 15, 1858, Basler, ed. *Collected Works*, III, 130.

15 Keitt is quoted in Allan Nevins, *Emergence of Lincoln* (2 vols., New York, 1950), II, 288; Fitzhugh is quoted in Harvey Wish, *George Fitzhugh, Propagandist of the Old South* (Baton Rouge, La., 1943), p. 97.

16 Quoted in George Fort Milton, *Stephen A. Douglas and the Needless War* (Boston, 1934), p. 506n.

Daniel Webster and Stephen A. Douglas that one hears truly modern overtones, suspicion and hatred of radicalism, cynicism, apathy, and simple dislike of the Negro.

Webster had said in his famous speech of March 7, 1850, "If the infernal fanatics and abolitionists ever get the power in their hands, they will override the Constitution, set the Supreme Court at defiance, change and make Laws to suit themselves. They will lay violent hands on those who differ with them politically in opinion, or dare question their infallibility; bankrupt the country and finally deluge it with blood."[17] Douglas, who has emerged in much revisionist literature as "a realist in an emotional age," a man whose "national" view was superior to Lincoln's sectional view, said frankly of slavery: "I don't care whether it be voted up or down. . . . It is merely a matter of dollars and cents." And again, "When the struggle is between the white man and the negro, I am for the white man; when it is between the negro and the crocodile, I am for the negro."[18]

Lincoln more than any man of his time felt the full pressure of the anti-Negro, anti-abolitionist tradition of the Democrats and Copperheads, which plagued him throughout the war and rose to formidable proportions during the election of 1864. His most patient public and private pleadings failed to persuade the border states to accept gradual emancipation, even with compensation. His Emancipation Proclamation met a mixed reception, a typical border state reaction being that of Representative Wadsworth of Kentucky, who protested in the House, "As to that proclamation, we despise and laugh at it. . . . The soldiers of other States will not execute it. May my curse fall upon their heads if they do!"[19] A year after the Proclamation Lincoln's own cabinet member, Mont-

[17] Allan Nevins, *Ordeal of the Union*, I, 295.
[18] For a discussion of revisionist attitudes toward Douglas see Thomas J. Pressly, *Americans Interpret Their Civil War* (Princeton, 1954), pp. 261-67.
[19] *Congressional Globe*, 37 Cong., 3 sess., January 8, 1863, p. 243.

gomery Blair, publicly accused the "Abolition party" of favoring "amalgamation, equality, and fraternity," and told his Maryland constituents that they would not lose their slaves.[20] The war was almost over—January 31, 1865—before the Republicans could muster enough votes to pass a resolution calling for a Thirteenth Amendment prohibiting slavery, and then it passed only with the aid of Lincoln's quiet backstage pressure. As Thaddeus Stevens commented cryptically, "The greatest measure of the nineteenth century was passed by corruption, aided and abetted by the purest man in America."[21]

The sobering story of the Democratic and Copperhead opposition to Lincoln, and the extraordinary persistence of proslavery sentiment in the North, needs retelling. What we have had instead—as in *Lincoln and the Radicals* by T. Harry Williams—is a minute examination of the differences between Lincoln and the abolitionists and Radicals in his own party. To all the crimes already laid at the feet of the abolitionists a new one was added— the crime of differing with Lincoln. And though the actual differences had much to do with timing and very little to do with principle or compassion, many historians have so magnified them that they have gravely distorted the image of Lincoln himself.

Back in 1862 Edward Pollard, writing his *Southern History of the War*, called Lincoln a "Yankee monster of inhumanity and falsehood." Now historians from every section and representing every shade of opinion try desperately to claim him for their own. But the attempt to turn Lincoln into something close to an anti-abolitionist would have astonished the old Confederates, who realistically—from their point of view—labeled Lincoln an abolitionist despite his public protestations that he was

[20] William E. Smith, *The Francis Preston Blair Family in Politics* (2 vols., New York, 1933), II, 228, 238, 269.

[21] James M. Scovel, "Thaddeus Stevens," *Lippincotts' Magazine*, 6 (April 1898), 550.

not one at all but only antislavery. For them it was enough that he was on public record as "hating" slavery, as hoping for its "ultimate extinction," and resolutely opposing its expansion.

They did not overlook the fact that as early as 1854 he had said that slavery was "hid away in the constitution, just as an afflicted man hides away a wen or cancer, which he dares not cut out at once, lest he bleed to death; with the promise, nevertheless, that the cutting may begin at the end of a given time."[22] Lincoln had been fond of this simile, returning to it often in the debates with Douglas. No one knows if ever he secretly fantasied himself as surgeon. But certainly when the war powers gave him the right to cut, he did not refrain from using the knife, and his timing and skill were of the highest professional quality.

In our time E. Merton Coulter writes that Lincoln "held out tenaciously against issuing a proclamation freeing the slaves," and Hudson Strode holds that Lincoln "could foresee no bright destiny for Negroes in the United States, and, by his own testimony he wanted them out of the country." David Donald in his *Lincoln Reconsidered* asserts, "On all crucial issues Lincoln was closer to George B. McClellan or Horatio Seymour than to many members of his own party." And Donald reduces the whole abolitionist Zeitgeist to a neurotic disturbance by writing cynically, "The freeing of the slaves ended the great crusade that had brought purpose and joy to the abolitionist. For them Abraham Lincoln was not the Great Emancipator; he was the killer of the dream."[23]

Such statements are bolstered by a dexterous selection of early Lincoln statements and by ignoring the steady

[22] Speech at Peoria, Ill., October 16, 1854, Basler, ed. *Collected Works*, II, 274.

[23] E. Merton Coulter, *The Confederate States of America, 1861-1865* (Baton Rouge, La., 1950), p. 264; Hudson Strode, *Jefferson Davis, Confederate President*, II, 310; David Donald, *Lincoln Reconsidered* (New York, 1956), pp. 61, 36.

evolution of Lincoln's attitude toward Negro rights and the massive evidence of his cooperation with men in the radical wing of his party and they with him. The total Lincoln antislavery record, beginning with his earliest attempts as Congressman to get slavery abolished in the District of Columbia, and continuing to the passage of the Thirteenth Amendment, which he described with satisfaction as "the king's cure for all the evils," and "the great event of the nineteenth century,"[24] is as certain a march in the direction of Negro freedom as that of Jefferson Davis and Robert E. Lee was away from it.

The record includes Lincoln's friendship and affection for Radicals like Edwin M. Stanton, Owen Lovejoy, and Charles Sumner, as well as his respect for and sagacious use of the great parliamentary talents of Thaddeus Stevens. In includes Lincoln's approval of Congressional bills providing for abolition of segregation on horse-drawn streetcars in Washington, for the acceptance of Negro witnesses in Federal courts, for the equalizing of penalties for the same crime. It includes his friendship for the famous ex-slave Frederick Douglass, and his easy willingness to break a precedent and accept a Negro as Ambassador from Haiti. It includes his urging of Federal aid for the welfare and schooling of the newly freed slave. In his last public address Lincoln urged *immediate* suffrage for the educated Negro and the Negro soldier.[25] This pointed the way to eventual universal Negro suffrage.

If the reputation of the abolitionists has suffered by their being dexterously separated from Lincoln, it has suffered also by their being warmly embraced in recent times by the American Communists, who heralded them as forerunners of the Second American Revolution. The resulting damage by association has been deadly. The

[24] Speech from the White House, February 1, 1865, Basler, ed. *Collected Works*, VIII, 254; Frank B. Carpenter, *The Inner Life of Abraham Lincoln, Six Months at the White House* (New York, 1868), p. 90.

[25] Basler, ed. *Collected Works*, VIII, 403.

label of the "abolitionist-Marxist stereotype" has been used to condemn so able a writer as W. E. B. DuBois, whose embracing of Marxism actually accounts very little for the distortions in his admittedly impassioned early histories of his own people, histories which were much-needed correctives to numerous white stereotypes.

The neo-Marxists, on the other hand, stimulated by the writing of Charles Beard, did not glorify the abolitionists, but by overemphasizing the economic differences dividing the North and South tended to minimize and obscure the profoundly moral issue of slavery and to support those who insist on the "needlessness" of the Civil War. Many revisionist historians, impressed by the seeming sophistication of this historical posture, accepted it enthusiastically. More than ever they came to dismiss the idealism of the abolitionists and Radicals as—in the words of William B. Hesseltine—"humanitarian gabble."[26]

Perhaps the most subtle attack on the abolitionists is that which exploits the vocabulary though not much of the insight of modern psychiatry. It is commonplace now for historians to assert or imply that abolitionist indignation over slavery was a kind of collective neurosis, and that the agitators were all likely to be somewhat obsessional or paranoid. Hazel C. Wolf, for example, in her book *On Freedom's Altar, the Martyr Complex in the Abolition Movement*, describes Theodore Weld as one who "gloried in the persecution he suffered," and who "lovingly wore the martyr's crown of thorns." Garrison, she says, "knew he wanted a cause; he had a certain facility with words; he had a mania for uniqueness and for attention." All the abolitionists, she adds, were "eagerly bidding for a martyr's crown."[27]

David Donald in his biography *Charles Sumner and the Coming of the Civil War*, wielding a deft scalpel, lays

[26] Wm. B. Hesseltine, *Lincoln and the War Governors* (New York, 1948), p. 285.
[27] (Madison, Wis., 1952), pp. 3, 194.

bare certain signs of impotence and latent homosexuality in his hero with such subtlety that the reader is scarcely aware that he is witnessing a surgical operation. It is proper that Professor Donald should be aware of the immense legacy of Freud; what is disturbing is that in fitfully employing the psychiatrist's tools he shows little of the psychiatrist's compassion. Instead he betrays a pervasive distaste for Sumner and an absence of respect for the nobility of his cause. "This holy blissful martyr thrived upon his torments," Donald writes, and he leads one to believe that Sumner's championing of the unpopular cause of antislavery was only an expression of his neurotic craving for persecution.

It is good to see that Donald, in describing Sumner's three-year search for health after the Brooks beating, disagrees with the conventional Southern view that he was a poltroon and coward and was faking illness out of fear of returning to his seat. "The diagnosis," writes Donald, "is that Sumner was not shamming, but that his ailments were not, neurologically, the result of Brooks' beating . . . modern specialists classify Sumner's illness as 'post-traumatic syndrome,' . . . the Brooks assault produced psychic wounds that lingered long after the physical injuries had disappeared."

What one misses, however, is a comparable clinical look—however brief—at the sick psyche of Preston Brooks. "I gave him about 30 first rate stripes," Donald quotes him as saying. "Toward the last he bellowed like a calf. I wore my cane out completely, but saved the Head which is gold." All Donald tells us by way of explaining Brooks' motivation is that "under his placid exterior, there burned a smoldering hatred of abolitionists, a proud devotion to the South and to South Carolina, an intense loyalty to his family, and a determination to live by the code of a gentleman."[28]

[28] David Donald, *Charles Sumner and the Coming of the Civil War* (New York, 1961), pp. 176, 336, 295, 290.

"I hope," says Donald in his preface, "that no one will accuse me of sympathizing with Negro slavery because I have not interjected a little moral discourse after each of Sumner's orations to the effect that he was on the side of the angels. Surely in the middle of the twentieth century there are some things that do not need to be said." Unfortunately, the student is easily snared by a fine writer. And where moral judgments are implicit in ironic phrases, where hostility determines the selection and omission of quotations, an atmosphere can be created where the student has no consciousness of the extent of the historical distortion. Certainly one gets from the book the author's feeling that Sumner was somehow responsible for the *sin* of the Civil War. That slavery itself was so great a sin that many people could fight against it with a passion that was not neurotic seems with Donald to be inadmissible.

It is likely that the continuing modern attacks on the abolitionists stem in part from anxiety over contemporary racial problems, and especially over the mounting militancy of the Negro himself. The old radicalism, many have said, brought on the holocaust of the Civil War; the new radicalism, many now assert, with its integrationists and Freedom Riders, may well also end in a gigantic blood bath. To these people Martin Luther King has much in common with Garrison and Wendell Phillips, though neither was as self-disciplined. The fact, however, that King is permitted to preach in the South at all is a measure of the improvement in the nation's moral health since 1850. But he might well repeat today what Garrison said more than a century ago when reproached for the heat and severity of his language: "I have need to be all on fire, for I have mountains of ice about me to melt."

PART II: INDIVIDUALS

CHAPTER 4

ORANGE SCOTT:

THE METHODIST EVANGELIST

AS REVOLUTIONARY

BY DONALD G. MATHEWS

ORANGE SCOTT'S credentials as an antislavery captain were a laborer's tools, a minister's Bible, and a Methodist's vocal and inexorable piety. As he lay dying on a hot summer day in 1847, Scott could recall a tumultuous life which began the winter of 1800 in the home of a poverty-stricken Vermont day-laborer. The eldest of eight children, he had followed in his father's uncertain footsteps until conversion at a Methodist meeting made his life more purposeful. And then like other poor and unlettered young men, he found that he possessed gifts of organization and oratory which he offered the Methodist Episcopal Church in 1826 at his ordination as a minister. One of the most promising soldiers in the Methodist attack upon the dispassionate Jericho of New England, Scott became a Presiding Elder over Methodist ministers around Springfield, Massachusetts in 1830, and a delegate to the General Conference of the entire church in 1832. Thus, at a relatively early age, the determined former laborer was on the road which had led less talented and ambitious men to the Episcopacy, power, and relative respectability.[1]

Yet Scott left the path of ecclesiastical advancement to become an abolitionist. Recalling his "conversion" to

[1] Lucius C. Matlack, *The Life of Rev. Orange Scott* (New York, 1851), pp. 5-28, 299.

radical antislavery ideas, he later said that he had been "exceedingly ignorant of the question of slavery up to July 1833." He had apparently been unmoved when in 1828 the New England Conference of which he was a member had unanimously pleaded that "a system so degrading as that of Slave-holding [might] soon be extirpated from [the] nation."[2] Later as a delegate to the General Conference of 1832, he was not openly affected by that body's refusal to receive a mild antislavery petition from free Negroes, or by the discussion over whether or not to elect a slaveholding Bishop. Nevertheless, these experiences, plus the knowledge that the Methodist Book of Discipline anticipated a millennial freeing of the slaves, probably made him receptive to the arguments of the rising antislavery movement. Leaning at first toward the American Colonization Society, he yielded in 1833 to the influence of some of his abolitionist colleagues, subscribed to the *Liberator* of William Lloyd Garrison, and read the editor's *Thoughts on African Colonization*. He also devoured the antislavery tracts of Lydia Maria Child, George Bourne and Amos A. Phelps. Then sometime in 1834, Scott fused Garrison's appeal to conscience, Bourne's appeal to John Wesley, and Phelps' appeal to the ministry into a final decision to become an abolitionist.[3]

Why did he make such a decision? As a Christian, he believed that life was a probation period for a more meaningful existence. As a former laborer, he had known his own special kind of slavery. And as a young revivalist,

[2] *Zion's Herald*, August 13, 1828, p. 2.

[3] *Journals of the General Conference of the Methodist Episcopal Church, 1796-1836* (New York, 1845), I, 413, 415; *The Liberator*, July 28, 1832, p. 118; William Winans, Diary, May 22, 1832, Winans Collection in Millsaps College Library; Lydia Maria Child, *An Appeal in Favor of That Class of Americans Called Africans* (Boston, 1833); George Bourne, *Pictures of Slavery in the United States of America* (Boston, 1834); Amos A. Phelps, *Lectures on Slavery and its Remedy* (Boston, 1834).

it is quite possible that he wished conversion under his preaching to have more far-reaching social consequences than mere forms of personal goodness. Perhaps, too, he wondered why so many people had been converted at so many Methodist revivals while an evil as great as slavery went undenounced. Whatever his reasons, he was swept along by the moral crusade that proposed to effect the spiritual and physical well-being of other men. Freed by background and ethics from stressing the stability of society, he could preach against its structures and its mores. Such freedom was especially characteristic of his position in the Methodist Episcopal Church. Since his ecclesiastical office was more local than national, he did not have to conciliate Southern opinion. Since he was too young to have been a party to the initial compromises that crippled the early Methodist antislavery enterprise, he did not have to defend them. But his dedication to the fight against slavery was necessitated by more than his morally fortuitous place in or out of society. Other men very much like Scott did not become abolitionists; Scott explained his own conversion as having been induced simply by the logic of abolitionist arguments. Why this happened was a mystery he scarcely pondered. Instead of fondling the problems of his motivation, he dedicated himself to the ceaseless, merciless antislavery activity which was consummated in his early death.

Scott derived the intellectual content of his dedication from the ideas of Phelps and Garrison. He repudiated the plan of the American Colonization Society to send free Negroes to Africa as impracticable, unjust, and morally reprehensible. Only abolitionists saw slaveholding for what it was, he said in Phelps's words: ". . . falsehood in theory, tyranny in practice, a violation of God's law, and the parent of all abominations."[4] Although

4 Phelps, *Lectures*, pp. 38-41.

Scott condemned the cruelties inherent in slavery, he understood its essential evil to be the making of man into merchantable property with neither the dignity nor legitimacy of humanity. Such degradation was not only a denial of the principles assumed by Americans in the Declaration of Independence, it was the granting of absolute authority to a master and therein making him a god; this was contrary to the teaching of the Christian religion and essentially blasphemous. Never mind that circumstances might make slavery different from place to place; never mind that many good men held slaves. Since in its best forms slavery denied men their rightful place as men, Scott said, "the principle remains unchanged— it is *evil*, only evil, and that *continually.*—It is too bad to be converted—it is a reprobate—in the hands of a good man or a bad man this, *this principle is the same*. It possesses not one redeeming quality. It is a usurper, a thief, a ROBBER, a MURDERER!!!" Such a social institution must not be reformed, but destroyed. And to those who pleaded that the consequences forbade emancipation, he was short: "I am of the opinion," he said, "that we should ascertain our duty from the Bible, and from the laws of equity and justice."[5]

Scott's oratorical disregard for "consequences" did not mean that he or many of his fellows were thoughtlessly indifferent to the problems of emancipation; they simply did not sanctify those problems. Scott joined the rest of the American antislavery "left" when he proposed the primary solution to slavery to be immediate emancipation of the slaves. By 1832 American antislavery men, like their British brethren, had despaired of "gradual abolition" and were using a new formula. Benjamin Lundy, who had printed many gradualist plans in his *Genius of Universal Emancipation*, by the end of 1832 had begun

[5] *Zion's Herald*, February 24, 1836, p. 30. Scott's ideas as he first worked them out are found in the *Herald* for the first five months of 1835.

to support the "IMMEDIATE ADOPTION of measures that [should] break the fetters of the slave."[6]

Orange Scott agreed. The key to immediatism was its appeal to do something at once about slavery. This appeal was natural to an evangelist who was accustomed to demanding an immediate and willful repentance from sin. Thus, as a preacher, Scott did not have a *plan* for emancipation, for in his world of Jacksonian political oratory and revivalistic Protestantism, he knew that men's minds were not changed by rational appeal or intricate argument. Radical change would come, he thought, when men repented of their sinful support of slavery and decided to destroy it. And then what? As a seasoned revivalist Scott had a *vision* if not a plan—a vision of the immediate emancipation of the slaves, the immediate provision for their education, the immediate passage of laws to guarantee them civil and legal rights so that "at the *earliest possible period, consistent with the best good of the slaves*, they should be FULLY EMANCIPATED." The preaching of this vision would encourage antislavery converts to force their elected representatives in states' legislatures to enact proper laws on behalf of the slaves.[7] Although Scott's vision of a converted Democracy was somewhat vague, it was also simple and essentially easy to understand. He never got involved in the doctrinal debate over the correct formula in which to present immediatist ideas. As a revivalist his first concern was with the moral decision; but he never preached "Repent and be saved!" Rather he pleaded, "Repent and do right!"

As an evangelist, Scott was particularly valuable in his dual role in the antislavery crusade: for he was an agent for antislavery societies as well as a disturber of the

[6] *Genius of Universal Emancipation*, November 1832, p. 1; also December 1832, p. 26.

[7] Phelps, *Lectures*, pp. 177-79, *Zion's Herald*, January 7, 1835, p. 2, March 16, 1836, p. 42; Orange Scott, *An Appeal to the Methodist Episcopal Church* (Boston, 1838), p. 45.

peace in the Methodist Episcopal Church. Although his oratory could be turgid and shapeless, it could also hold an audience for hours, as he suggested, pleaded, and finally demanded repentance and dedication. When he was explaining his position to a hostile audience, Scott was in complete control of himself, perhaps even "dispassionate and conciliatory." But an overheated argument would bring a torrent of words and accusations that would dash against his opponents' sensitivities. Later, he might repent of his "unruly" words, but never of the principles which had prompted them. Self-educated, self-disciplined and ever-restless, Scott was determined to bring order to the moral chaos which suffered the existence of slavery.[8]

Given this determination, it was not surprising that officials of the American Anti-Slavery Society should be pleased when he accepted their commission in August of 1836 as one of the famous "Seventy." Already a frequent speaker at antislavery meetings, a vice-president of the Massachusetts Anti-Slavery Society, and one of the most vigorous of Methodist abolitionists, he henceforward divided his time between trying to convert the Methodist Episcopal Church to abolitionism and building local antislavery societies. A typical mission was that of early 1837 when the executive committee of the national society sent him to Harrisburg, Pennsylvania, to help direct the state antislavery convention there. Scott's ability to organize and arouse action was always an asset, and his words in Harrisburg were as ever full of confidence and spirit. "What have [abolitionists] done?" he asked. "We have aroused a slumbering nation. . . . And have converted eight-hundred thousand goods and chattels into men, in the West Indian Islands! For aboli-

[8] Matlack, *Scott*, pp. 299-305, 60-62; also *Herald of Freedom*, April 27, 1839, pp. 34-35; *Christian Advocate and Journal*, May 29, 1840, p. 162.

tionism in all parts of the world is *one*."[9] And Scott could not only sway the Harrisburg meeting, but also those at Natick, Northfield, Wilbraham, and Andover. When he spoke, his audiences wept with him for the martyred Elijah Lovejoy, applauded the freedmen of the Indies, and gave so much of their money to the "cause" that one of Scott's enemies called him "avaricious."[10]

His "avarice," however, consisted only in his single-mindedness, in his ability to encompass only one "cause" at a time; and it was this quality which made Scott join other abolitionists in their attacks upon William Lloyd Garrison. Impressed with John Humphrey Noyes's "perfectionism," and Henry C. Wright's "nonresistant" theories of no government but God's, Garrison began to support these ideas in *The Liberator*. Dismayed, Scott became one of the editor's most frequent and active critics. "Trust in God and leave all to him?" he asked incredulously. "As well might you trust God to edit and print your paper, without any human agency." Trust in God and no human government? "What is it shields you from northern and southern vengeance now?" Scott demanded. "Not the irresistible power of God as much as the fear of human laws." The way to destroy slavery was not to create chaos by repudiating human laws, Scott insisted, but to reform the existing government—to abolish the laws which upheld racial servitude. To reform government, abolitionists would have to vote for men who would be most likely to work against slavery.[11]

[9] *Zion's Herald*, February 15, 1837, p. 26; *Emancipator*, March 16, 1837, p. 181; Matlack, *Scott*, pp. 119-21. Elizur Wright to Theodore Dwight Weld, August 18, 1836 in Gilbert H. Barnes and Dwight L. Dumond, eds. *Letters of Theodore Dwight Weld, Angeline Grimké Weld and Sarah Grimké, 1822-1844* (New York, 1934), I, 333-34.

[10] W. Booth to Willbur Fisk, April 1838, Fisk Papers, Wesleyan University; *Zion's Watchman*, January 6, 1838, p. 2; Matlack, *Scott*, p. 135.

[11] *The Liberator*, October 26 and November 16, 1838, pp. 171-72, 184.

In November 1838 a Methodist antislavery convention at Lowell, Massachusetts, urged abolitionists to follow Scott's advice. With this and other signs of Methodist disapproval of Garrison's course, Scott anticipated a successful subversion of the editor's influence in the Massachusetts Anti-Slavery Society.[12]

The signs were wrong. Henry B. Stanton, Amos A. Phelps, and Scott were disastrously unsuccessful in their attempts to dislodge Garrison from his powerful position. The harried editor himself was disheartened to find among his enemies the best known antislavery agents in the state, but he struck back vigorously and won his fight at the convention in January of 1839. Stanton hoped to get Scott appointed general agent of the Massachusetts Anti-Slavery Society in order to have an anti-Garrisonian in that important job—but he failed. Stanton had also wanted the society to support a new abolitionist paper— but it would not. He tried to get the convention to require abolitionists to "vote for the slave"—but it refused. As Scott had warned him, most of the delegates were *Liberator* abolitionists and they supported their leader with "clamor" and votes. One of the few good things that Stanton could recall after the disaster was that "a very large corps of Methodists were present, and went right with their whole hearts, almost to a man."[13]

As one of the chief conspirators, Scott threw himself into the succeeding fight against Garrison. He charged that the editor's *"consummate nonsense"* about "no human government" could very easily subvert the abolitionist or-

12 *Zion's Watchman*, December 1, 1838, p. 190; *The Liberator*, March 22, 1838, p. 43.

13 Henry B. Stanton to James G. Birney, January 26, 1839 in Dwight Dumond, ed. *The Letters of James G. Birney* (2 vols., New York, 1938), I, 481-82; William Lloyd Garrison to George N. Benson, January 5, 1839, William Lloyd Garrison Papers, Boston Public Library; Henry B. Stanton to Amos A. Phelps, January 13, 1839, Orange Scott to Phelps, January 15, 1839, in Amos A. Phelps Papers, Boston Public Library; Henry B. Stanton to Elizur Wright, January 26, 1839, Elizur Wright Papers, Library of Congress.

ganization itself. He scolded the editor of the *Herald of Freedom* for not joining the fight to save abolitionism, urged Phelps to be more active in opposing Garrison's "foolery," and joined in forewarning fellow abolitionists of the danger of Garrisonianism if it should prevail at the national convention in May 1839. In order to institutionalize their opposition to both Garrison and slavery, the dissidents formed the Massachusetts Abolition Society which Scott supported vigorously. In his campaign to strengthen the new organization, Scott optimistically pledged "*nine tenths* of the Methodist influence in the state."[14] He stumped local abolition meetings, talking so much about going to the polls for the slave that someone started a rumor that Scott would shortly run for Congress. Once he was heard "screaming at the top of his voice about Slavery's being a creature of law" and therefore capable of being destroyed only by law. And when a meeting at Lowell voted to hear both sides of the question concerning abolitionists' obligation to vote, the canny evangelist spoke first and then, before his opponent could reply, had moved and carried a vote to adjourn. Such tactics made Theodore Dwight Weld deplore Scott's attitude as "the spirit of slave holders undiluted."[15]

The almost frantic energy which Scott displayed in fighting Garrison had been expended futilely. The Massachusetts Abolition Society soon became powerless. The Garrisonians captured the American Anti-Slavery Society in 1840, whereupon Scott followed James G. Birney and the Tappan brothers into the American and Foreign

[14] Orange Scott to James G. Birney, May 12, 1839, Weston Family Papers, Boston Public Library; circular letter sent by Scott and Phelps, April 16, 1839, Scott to Phelps, June 27, 1839, Phelps Papers; *Herald of Freedom*, April 6, April 13, April 27, 1839, pp. 23, 26, 34-35; *The Liberator*, April 5 and April 19, 1839, pp. 54, 64.

[15] Theodore D. Weld to Gerrit Smith, October 23, 1839, in Barnes and Dumond, *Weld-Grimké Letters*, II, 810; *Friend of Man*, October 30, 1839, p. 12; Lucia Weston to Deborah Weston, July 1839 and n.d. [1839], Maria Chapman to Mary Weston, n.d. [1839], Weston Family Papers.

Anti-Slavery Society to join three of his co-religionists on the executive committee.[16] After 1840 he continued his interest in the "new organization" as well as in the Liberty party, but he had by then become primarily involved in his fight within the Methodist Episcopal Church.

Scott had eschewed general reform for a consistent and relatively uncluttered attack upon slavery. He found this task sufficiently absorbing, for as a minister of the Methodist Episcopal Church, he had to fight slavery in the Church as well as in the world—and he required all his strength for that task. As a Methodist minister he was especially sensitive to the discrepancy between the Church's formal statement of opposition to slavery (a relic of the eighteenth century), and its refusal to act upon it. As a revivalist he hoped to preach the Church into repentance. But as a "troublemaker"—perhaps even a revolutionary schismatic—he faced difficulties and disappointments which would have humiliated and defeated less determined men. When he finally was forced to cease his abolitionist activities, he had accomplished less than he had hoped but more than he realized.

Scott's antislavery evangelism had begun the summer of 1834 when he had joined some of his colleagues in the work of converting the New England Conference of Methodist ministers to abolitionism. Adding his own influence to that of the few who had already become abolitionists, Scott cooperated in persuading the New England Conference to refuse to support the American Colonization Society. He then spent one hundred dollars of his own money in order to send *The Liberator* for three months to every man in the conference. Further, he persuaded camp meetings to enjoin the conference newspaper, *Zion's Herald*, to print a discussion of slavery. Fearing that the abolitionists would start a new paper unless given space in the *Herald*, the publishers acceded

16 *Anti-Slavery Reporter*, June 1840, p. 3.

to Scott's demand. Confident of success, the energetic abolitionist had already written part of a series of anti-slavery articles which began to appear in January 1835.[17] These articles were almost immediately accompanied by "An Appeal on the Subject of Slavery Addressed to the Members of the New England and New Hampshire Conferences," published February 4, 1835 by five of Scott's colleagues. While Scott's articles were confined to a condemnation of slavery and only infrequently appealed to the Wesleyan antislavery heritage, the "Appeal" forcefully demanded that Methodists be true to John Wesley and their *Discipline* by urging laws for the immediate destruction of the flagrant "sin" of slavery.[18]

The purpose of Scott's essays and the "Appeal" was achieved at the annual meeting of the New England Conference in June 1835. In May, Scott announced a pre-conference meeting of "true abolitionists" at Lynn, Massachusetts, to discuss the formation of an antislavery society, the election of abolitionist delegates to the General Conference of 1836, and the passing of antislavery resolutions at the annual conference. Scott also thought it would be a good idea to have the meeting hear George Thompson, the English abolitionist lecturer who was having much success among the Methodists of Massachusetts. Although the presiding bishop and his friends were angered by the proceedings, the abolitionists proved the power of their newly formed Wesleyan Anti-Slavery Society by electing six of their colleagues to the seven-man delegation to the General Conference. Scott was to be the unofficial leader of this group which was sub-

[17] *Zion's Herald*, January 7, 1835, p. 2, *et seq.*; Benjamin Kingsbury, Jr. to Willbur Fisk, January 5, 1835, Fisk Papers; Matlack, *Scott*, pp. 38ff.; Scott to Garrison, December 30, 1834, Garrison Papers.

[18] Shipley Willson, Abram D. Merrill, La Roy Sunderland, George Storrs, and Jared Perkins, "An Appeal on the Subject of Slavery Addressed to the Members of the New England and New Hampshire Conferences of the Methodist Episcopal Church . . . ," (Boston, 1835), *passim*.

sequently joined by seven antislavery preachers from the New Hampshire Conference: they would be a small but determined band of prophets.[19]

The opposition to the abolitionists within the Church was formidable. The powerful ecclesiastics were all opposed to abolitionism. After a generation of repeated failures in trying to enforce antislavery rules, institutional Methodism had channelled its concern for Negroes into missions to the slaves and the colonization scheme. One anti-abolitionist explained that Negroes were helped not "by inflammatory harangues, but by deeds of charity."[20] In fact, abolitionist demands for *justice* instead of charity were so alien to nineteenth-century ideas of the proper moral relationship between white and black people that many Americans could not begin to accept abolitionist arguments. Believing that different peoples could live together in equality only if they intermarried, the anti-abolitionists condemned abolitionists as "amalgamationists." Fearful of radical social change they falsely accused the reformers of proposing "unconditional" emancipation. Aghast at the sometimes color-

[19] James Mudge, *History of the New England Conference of the Methodist Episcopal Church, 1796-1910* (Boston, 1910), p. 279; Scott to J. A. Merrill, May 7, 1835, New England Methodist Historical Society Papers, Boston University School of Theology; "Mr. Thompson's Journal" [Printed] and Henry E. Benson to George W. Benson, February 2, 1835, Garrison Papers. In his attempt to represent the English influence upon New England Methodism as more direct and pervading than it actually was, Professor Thomas Harwood intimates that Thompson was primarily rather than incidentally responsible for the organization of the ministers into an antislavery society. It is quite true that the British exerted some pressure upon the Americans as Harwood says, but it was sporadic—almost quadrennial. The Americans used the English Methodist addresses to the General Conferences as propaganda, but three letters and two delegates who brought them are hardly the continual influence which Harwood suggests the English exerted. See Thomas F. Harwood, "British Evangelical Abolitionism and American Churches in the 1830's" *Journal of Southern History*, 28 (August 1962), 287-306, especially 292-96.

[20] *Christian Advocate and Journal*, August 15, 1834, p. 202.

ful and harsh denunciation which the antislavery evangelists perfected, their antagonists condemned them as dangerous incendiaries who incited to riot and invited slave
insurrection. Furthermore, as Christians, Methodist
churchmen could not condone condemnation of "good
and innocent men" who, they believed, had had slavery
entailed upon them through no fault of their own. The
abolitionists were not only alienating themselves from
Southern Christians, their opponents claimed, but also
from the best interests of the slaves. Antislavery pronun-
ciamentos in the North, they argued, inclined masters
who were wary of slave insurrections to curtail what
little freedom the slaves had, and made them suspicious
of any solicitude for the Negroes, including the preaching of the Gospel. Finally, the attacks upon the South
were considered anti-republican and un-American inasmuch as they endangered the Union. President Willbur
Fisk of Wesleyan University explained his unfavorable
reaction to Orange Scott and the "Appeal" of 1835 by
saying: "All the political and moral elements of the
country are in a state of feverish excitement, and it is
but *moral quackery*, at such times, to administer stimulants or apply caustics to the social system. . . . A portion
of the North, particularly, are [sic] getting too much
excited against the South. This state of things requires
assuasives instead of stimulants."[21]

The anti-abolitionist position was deeply entrenched
among the powerful men in the Church. The official
Methodist weekly, the *Christian Advocate and Journal*,
refused to allow a discussion of slavery in its columns.
Nathan Bangs, more powerful than any bishop because
of his various editorial and administrative positions, had
fought the abolitionists ever since Garrison had pub-

[21] *Zion's Herald*, March 11, 1835, p. 37; *Christian Advocate and
Journal*, July 25 and August 15, 1834, pp. 190, 202; September 25,
1835, p. 17; *Maine Wesleyan Journal*, April 30, 1835, pp. 69, 72;
Western Christian Advocate, November 27 and December 4, 1835,
pp. 121, 125.

lished his *Thoughts on African Colonization*. And Bishop
Elijah Hedding joined his colleague, Bishop John Emory,
in admonishing New England abolitionists for their irresponsible and "arbitrary denunciations."[22] Annual conferences as diverse as those in Maine and Missouri responded to Scott's antislavery triumph in New England
with resolutions denouncing abolitionism and reaffirming
Methodists' faith in the American Colonization Society,
in religious instruction of the slaves, and in "states'
rights." Even more extreme was the reaction of the South
Carolina Conference which claimed that the abolitionists
were heretics, denied that the Church had a right to
discuss the "civil" question of slavery, and then added
that the relationship of master and slave was not immoral.[23] With such opposition mustered against him,
Scott arrived in Cincinnati, Ohio, in May 1836 to attend
the quadrennial meeting of the General Conference—
outnumbered, "outgunned," but certainly not outwitted.

The intrepid Massachusetts abolitionist must have
listened with much satisfaction as the fraternal address
of the English Methodist Conference was read to the
conference by one of his chief opponents, Nathan Bangs.
The English urged the conference to lead public opinion
by rejecting "slavery and its social mischiefs, on the
ground of its repugnancy to the laws of Christ."[24] Scott
was certainly not surprised when the conference refused
either to print the British address or to honor its advice.
Nor could he have been surprised when a Marylander
offered two resolutions—one which condemned two con-

22 *Christian Advocate and Journal*, September 25, 1835, p. 17.

23 "Minutes of the South-Carolina Conference of the Methodist
Episcopal Church for the year 1836" (Charleston, 1836), pp. 30f.;
Western Christian Advocate, September 11, October 16, October 23,
December 4, 1835, pp. 97, 99, 103, 126; "Holston Conference Minutes," October 12, 1835, Baltimore Conference Journals, III, 67-68,
in Baltimore Conference Historical Society Papers, Baltimore, Maryland.

24 *Minutes of the Methodist Conference* [English] (London, 1838),
VII (1835), 616.

ference delegates for speaking at a recent abolition meeting in Cincinnati, and another which disclaimed any Methodist interest in discussing slavery. Scott was ready to fight the resolutions, but his first attempt to speak was greeted with an uproar. When he finally won the recognition of the chairman he tried to explain that preachers ought not to be condemned for opposing sin and trying to get the slaves emancipated "into law." Scott was answered by a conference vote which obliterated his proposal to preface the inevitable censure with the traditional Methodist statement of opposition to "the great evil of slavery." This done, the conference then went on to register overwhelming disapproval of the conduct of their two "wayward" colleagues and to disclaim any "right, wish, or intention to interfere in the civil and political relation between master and slave as it exist[ed] in the slaveholding states of this union."[25] These actions might have ended the matter for a time had it not been for the indefatigable Orange Scott.

In order to carry on the fight, he printed an anonymous pamphlet and distributed it to the conference. He first accused the speakers in the debate of failing to take cognizance of his arguments; and then he clearly and forcefully indicted slavery and its defenders.[26] The pamphlet created a storm, especially in the mind of gruff, unbending William Winans. This Mississippi delegate offered a resolution accusing the broadside of "palpably false" and injurious statements which constituted

[25] "Debate on Modern Abolitionism in the General Conference of the Methodist Episcopal Church held in Cincinnati, May 1836," Cincinnati, 1836, pp. 22-27; *Zion's Herald*, May 25, 1836, p. 82; *Journals of the General Conferences, 1796-1836*, I, 474, 477.

[26] [Orange Scott], "An Address to the Members of the General Conference of the M. E. Church (by a member of that body)." Printed in *Zion's Watchman*, June 8, 1836, pp. 87-91, and later in pamphlet form for wider distribution and with Scott's name attached.

an "outrage on the dignity of this body, and meeting unqualified reprehension." When Scott identified himself as the author, Winans called him a "reckless incendiary or *non compos mentis*." The ensuing debate, which turned into a long attack upon abolitionism and Scott, ended in the passage of Winans' resolution by the lopsided vote of 97-19.[27] This all but complete victory of the ecclesiastical defenders of the status quo was summarized in the Bishops' Pastoral Address. The only scriptural way to deal with slavery, Methodists were told, was "to refrain from this agitating subject" and to support the civil and religious institutions "which we so highly and justly value as freemen, as Christians, and as Methodists."[28] Apparently but few of the delegates wondered whether eighty thousand Methodist slaves valued American civil and religious institutions, or had any reason to do so.

The General Conference of 1836 was the event which cast Scott into the symbolic leadership of Methodist abolitionism. Before he went to Cincinnati he had been a locally known abolitionist, but he returned to Massachusetts as the Church's representative antislavery prophet. So many people began to read his "Address" that he reported that it was "producing a *tremendous excitement*"; James G. Birney's account of the General Conference debate which Scott had triggered was doing almost as well. Enthusiastically, Scott and eighty-eight of his fellows sent a message to the English Wesleyans explaining that they, at least, if not the General Conference, were opposed to slavery.[29] In *Zion's Herald* and in La Roy Sunderland's abolitionist paper for Methodists, *Zion's Watchman*, Scott and his activities were given increasing space, and even the hostile *Christian*

27 *General Conference Journals*, I, 486.

28 *Christian Advocate and Journal*, June 17, 1836, p. 171.

29 Scott to William M. Chace, July 5, 1836, Garrison Papers; James G. Birney to Lewis Tappan, August 10, 1836 in Dumond, *Letters of James G. Birney*, I, 349-52; *Herald of Freedom*, July 23, 1836, p. 81.

Advocate and Journal gave Scott special attention by reporting that the New England Conference had declared his reputation "for truth and veracity [stood] fair and unimpeached"—in spite of the censure of his pamphlet at the General Conference.[30] Publicity and personal commendations, however, could hardly crack the solid wall of ecclesiastical opposition to abolitionism.

Following the advice of the General Conference, Church officials tried to muzzle their abolitionist numbers. The New York conference refused to ordain abolitionists, and antislavery activity was officially proscribed in all but the New Hampshire and New England conferences; and even the latter were forbidden to condemn slavery in an official capacity. When the New England conference's committee on slavery reported antislavery resolutions in June 1836, Bishop Elijah Hedding postponed them indefinitely. Nevertheless, *Zion's Watchman* printed the resolutions which declared slavery a sin and therefore fair subject for agitation. Scott made an issue of Hedding's delaying tactics, accusing the bishop of exercising "zeal to put down" the abolitionists, of "hostility," of oppression, and of acting with "partiality." He also accused Hedding of depriving him of his post as Presiding Elder because he was an abolitionist.[31] The resulting controversy ended in Scott's recanting certain parts of his accusations and then suffering Hedding's publication of what the abolitionist believed was personal correspondence. Scott soon began to see the actions of the General Conference, of the New York Conference, and of Bishop Hedding as tyrannical oppression of just and conscientious prophets.

Thus convinced, Scott began to include institutional Methodism in his assaults upon slavery. The action of

[30] *Christian Advocate and Journal*, August 26, 1836, p. 3.
[31] *Zion's Watchman*, August 24 and August 31, December 7, 1836, pp. 133, 139, 193; D. W. Clark, *Life and Times of Rev. Elijah Hedding, D.D.* (New York, 1855), pp. 498-502; *Zion's Watchman*, August 12, 1837, p. 127.

the General Conference of 1836 and Bishop Hedding's crusade against agitators in one sense made Scott's fight easier, for the enemy had now taken on an institutional and personal identity. In fighting the officials of the Methodist Episcopal Church, Scott fought slavery. The goal of his struggle was to convert enough Methodists to abolitionism to be able to override the objections of his antagonists, and turn the power of the Church against slavery. Thus, he temporarily ceased his activities as a Methodist minister on grounds of ill-health, and devoted all of his time to being an agent of the antislavery movement. In the late summer of 1837 he visited six Methodist conferences which exercised pastoral care over more than one hundred thousand people. The majorities of the three New England conferences welcomed him and his frequent companion, the impetuous George Storrs. Although he found that the majority of ministers in western New York were less enthusiastic, he nonetheless spoke to antislavery meetings and attended conferences there—as if to remind the bishops, particularly Hedding, that they could not escape the watchful eyes of the abolitionists.[32] Watching, however, was not enough—nor were mild antislavery resolutions from the Genesee and Oneida conferences, or the continual and slow increase in local Methodist antislavery societies. What Scott still wanted and needed were weapons with which to capture the centers of Methodist power and thereby strike a decisive blow against slavery. He finally found his weapons in the controversy over "Conference Rights," and in the unofficial Methodist antislavery conventions.

As the general antislavery movement found sustenance in the battle over the right of citizens to petition Con-

[32] *Zion's Watchman*, August 26 and September 16, 1837, pp. 134, 147. *Emancipator*, August 24, September 7, September 21, October 26, 1837, pp. 67, 73, 80, 100; *Maine Wesleyan Journal*, July 8, 1837, p. 2; F. W. Conable, *History of the Genesee Conference of the Methodist Episcopal Church* (New York, 1876), pp. 406-10.

gress, so Methodist abolitionism increased through a battle over the right of conferences to speak as they chose. At the New England Conference of 1837 Bishop Beverly Waugh refused to put antislavery resolutions to a vote, and Bishop Hedding followed the same course at the New Hampshire Conference. In reaction, Orange Scott wrote confidently to Elizur Wright: "It is my opinion that the discussion to which the course of our Bishops will give rise, will be of more service to the cause of God and the slave than any conference action could have been at the last session. A full discussion of the powers of bishops will create a public sentiment in the Methodist Church which they will not be able to resist . . ."[33] "Full discussion" was an understatement. Scott and La Roy Sunderland lost no opportunity to denounce the episcopacy for having wielded "unconstitutional" and "usurped" powers: not the bishops they insisted, but the conference majorities should determine what resolutions should be voted upon. In October Scott issued a "call" for a Methodist antislavery convention to meet at Lynn, Massachusetts: "Brethren in the ministry, who believe that Annual Conferences have a right to express an opinion on a moral question, rally to the Convention, and remonstrate against recent attempts to prevent Annual Conferences from bearing their testimony against slavery."[34]

Thus the abolitionists, when denied usual channels of expression and protest, turned to extra-ecclesiastical meetings. At Lynn they took advantage of their freedom by attacking the episcopal administration, the "negro-hating spirit" of both North and South, the "FLAGRANT SIN" of slavery and the "professed Christians" who were its apologists.[35] Pleased with the success of the Lynn Con-

[33] Scott to Elizur Wright, June 23, 1837, Elizur Wright Papers.
[34] *Zion's Watchman*, January 6, 1838, *et seq.*; *Zion's Herald*, October 18, 1837, p. 166.
[35] Orange Scott, *An Appeal to the Methodist Episcopal Church* (Boston, 1838), pp. 138-139.

vention, Scott and his cohorts arranged for another in May 1838. The occasion—if one were needed—was the proslavery resolution of the Georgia conference that "slavery as it exists in the United States, *is not a moral evil.*"[36] Scott was no more horrified than his opponent, Bishop Hedding, but unlike Hedding, Scott did something about it: together with other abolitionists he set out to organize a convention at Utica, New York. As he wrote to one of his colleagues with typical urgency, "Now, dear brother, are you prepared to submit to such things *in silence?* Will you not *remonstrate?* Will you not fly to the rescue?" Over two hundred delegates from thirteen conferences from Maine to Michigan did "fly to the rescue," and at Utica abolitionist addresses and resolutions poured forth—even as they did five months later at still another convention in Lowell, Massachusetts.[37] Orange Scott was skillfully and forcefully converting the official proscription of abolitionists into a prescription for abolitionism.

Although Scott claimed that his activities were for the sake of rescuing the Methodist Episcopal Church for "true Wesleyan Methodism," his ecclesiastical opponents believed him to be a dangerous schismatic and revolutionary. Indeed, his attacks on episcopal power, his refusal to accept the advice of the General Conference, and his extra-ecclesiastical conventions were the very "stuff" of schism. Scott, his opponents recognized, had nothing but revolutionary disdain for that quality of moderation so necessary to the preservation of institutional power. Had not the abolitionist agitator said, "Our statesmen and doctors of divinity can fold their hands and calmly say, 'Keep still. . . .' It is nothing to them that two and

[36] *Southern Christian Advocate*, January 5, 1838, p. 114.

[37] Scott to W. Lindsey, March 29, 1838, New England Methodist Historical Society Papers; Elijah Hedding to Willbur Fisk, April 19, 1838, Fisk Papers; *Friend of Man*, May 9, 1838, p. 182; *Zion's Herald*, February 5, 1838, p. 193.

a half millions of American citizens are groaning in chains! 'They are not their brother's keeper.' Opposition to SIN is a dreadful *thing*; but *sin itself* is a small matter, compared with agitation! What a paradox we are to surrounding nations—and what a stench in the nostrils of the Almighty! I blush for our institutions; I blush for our religion!"[38] When this open contempt for the Church's cautious ethics was institutionalized in unofficial conventions, Scott's opponents not only maligned him personally, but also wrote didactic and anxious articles against schism. Although the bishops now began to allow some discussion of slavery in the conferences, they still refused to sanction abolitionist resolutions. The battle increased in intensity as constant repression and harassment led the antislavery prophets into language reminiscent of Amos' denunciation of the "fat cows of Bashan." And as the battle waxed, so did the strength of abolitionism in Methodist ranks—cheering both Scott and the American Anti-Slavery Society.[39]

The growth of Methodist abolitionism, however, did not mean that the officials in the Church were yielding to it. In fact, La Roy Sunderland in 1840 lamented that "the servile power in the M. E. Church was so extensive that it would never be subdued" except by a "convulsion" and schism.[40] Orange Scott, nevertheless, was willing once more to attempt the seemingly impossible task of converting the highest Methodist judicatory to a proscription of slavery. In 1839 he withdrew from the civil war in Massachusetts abolitionism, re-entered the active ministry, and was again elected delegate to the General Conference. In anticipation of its meeting, Scott began to publish the *American Wesleyan Observer* as a

[38] Scott, *An Appeal*, p. 128.

[39] *The Liberator*, August 24, 1838, p. 135; "Fifth Annual Report of the Executive Committee of the American Anti-Slavery Society . . . ," New York, 1838, p. 52; *Christian Advocate and Journal*, January 26 and February 23, 1838, pp. 90, 105.

[40] *Zion's Watchman*, January 4, 1840, p. 2.

special guide to what the conference ought to do. He enjoined thousands of Methodists to sign antislavery petitions and to pass abolitionist resolutions.[41] His was a great effort at moral suasion. But it did not succeed.

During the General Conference of 1840 Orange Scott acted the role of prophet as best he could—although it may have seemed to him that he was Samson in the temple of Dagon. For several days he introduced antislavery memorials one by one, reading each of them aloud; then when they were all rejected by the committee on slavery, he spoke for almost two hours in their defense. Although rejection of the antislavery petitions made Scott believe that the increase in the number of Methodist abolitionists had had no effect upon the General Conference of the Church, the votes on the issues which could have been interpreted as dividing strictly between "antislavery" and "proslavery" gave the former 35 per cent of the tally, almost a threefold increase over 1836. Abolitionists like Scott could be little satisfied with such "antislavery" feeling, however, for it was primarily a refusal to defend slavery rather than a willingness to condemn it openly. Northern churchmen were also becoming more and more disillusioned with Southern ministers because of the latter's proslavery declarations, but no matter how wary of Southern attitudes, the anti-abolitionists would not surrender to the abolitionists. The conference rejected abolitionist contentions on "conference rights," and refused once again to follow British suggestions to declare the "*principle* of opposition to slavery."[42] Indeed, the delegates actually came close to acceding to slavery by voting to forbid Negro testimony in church trials wherever civil trials

[41] *Journal of the General Conference of the Methodist Episcopal Church* (Baltimore, 1840), pp. 14-40; *Zion's Herald*, November 13 and December 25, 1839, pp. 182, 206.

[42] *Christian Advocate and Journal*, September 30, 1840, p. 26; *Friend of Man*, August 5, 1840, p. 171; *General Conference Journals* (1840), pp. 17-40.

precluded it also. To seal its contempt for abolitionism, the General Conference proclaimed that some of the names on an antislavery petition from New York were "forgeries."[43] Thus the whole meeting could only have been taken by Scott as a complete defeat. His "revolution" had failed, and largely because moral suasion was not enough; as a proponent of the use of political power for abolitionists ends, he should have known that. Perhaps he expected too much ethical purity from a church which valued its national character and its institutional power. In any case, there was much for Scott to mull; and, although he did not know it, his personal ordeal had just begun.

The failure of 1840 greatly depressed him. For the next two years he wrestled with his conscience, reconsidered the forces he had unleashed, and raised with himself the question of whether or not he should leave the Church. He called one more convention, which created the American Wesleyan Anti-Slavery Society in October of 1840; but the society barely survived its first anniversary. The internal troubles of the general antislavery movement, the great political campaign of 1840, the continuing economic depression, and the general dispersion of antislavery ideas all combined to bank the fires of enthusiastic Methodist abolitionism. Although Scott was pleased with the growth of Methodist antislavery societies in the West, he was becoming increasingly concerned over mounting charges in the East that he was a schismatic. The new editor of the *Christian Advocate and Journal*, the witty and capable Thomas E. Bond, Sr., was joined by *Zion's Herald* in an open, continual, and effective warfare against Scott's brand of "extreme" abolitionism which they claimed would lead eventually to schism.[44]

[43] *Ibid.*, June 5, 1840, pp. 165-66; *General Conference Journals* (1840), p. 60.

[44] *Ibid.*, September 23, 1840, *et seq.*; *Zion's Herald*, December 9, 1841, p. 198; *Zion's Watchman*, August 1 and October 31, 1840, pp. 123, 174, May 15 and October 16, 1841, pp. 78, 166.

Bond's concern was genuine; the threat he envisioned, real. Gradually, abolitionists were leaving the Methodist Episcopal Church—in Michigan, Ohio, New York, and New Jersey. And gradually, too, this mounting tide of secession intruded itself upon Scott—in personal letters to him, and in his election as vice-president of a Wesleyan Anti-Slavery Missionary Society.[45] In addition, his old friends in the antislavery movement increasingly taunted him for remaining in the Methodist Episcopal Church which, they said, was no better than a "brothel" —a bulwark of slavery. Garrison charged that denominational antislavery societies served the Church instead of humanity. Where, he asked scornfully in *The Liberator*, is Orange Scott, "who once shook the Methodist hierarchy to its foundation with his antislavery thunder? Morally defunct."[46]

The charge was not true. Forced to rest because of ill-health, Scott pondered the low fortunes of abolitionism within the governing body of the Church and his defeat at the General Conference. Oppressed in body he became depressed in spirit; he desperately wanted peace and silence after so much "sound and fury." But there was conscience—perhaps he should leave the Church in one last protest against slavery. First, however, he tried to atone for the animosity he felt his violence might have wrought. He wrote letters of apology to the bishops, who, he had already admitted in *Zion's Herald*, were not so guilty of usurpation as he had once thought. In June of 1842, in this current mood of reconciliation, he wrote what must have been for him a difficult letter to *Zion's Herald*. In it he compared his impetuosity to that of St. Peter's in Gethsemane and added, "I now regret that the debate on both sides assumed, at so early a period, so hostile a character . . . ; and that I contributed my

---

[45] *Zion's Watchman*, June 12, 1841, p. 94; *Zion's Herald*, October 28, 1840, p. 173; Matlack, *Scott*, pp. 187-91.

[46] *The Liberator*, August 12 and October 21, 1842, pp. 127, 166.

full quota to such a result." He went on to repudiate the usefulness of antislavery conventions and even denominational antislavery societies, suggesting that political action was the best solution to slavery.[47] Then, purged by his confession and pressed by his conscience and the secessions which he himself had occasioned, Orange Scott finally seceded from the Methodist Episcopal Church—its position on slavery and its episcopacy—on November 8, 1842.[48]

His act of secession was an admission of failure. As evangelists Scott and his friends had failed to revolutionize and convert the Church—and for several reasons. There is a basic and frustrating inconsistency in a Christian evangelist's belief that those implicated in sin can willfully extricate themselves from it: for if men are sinners, as Scott believed, their wills are as sinful as any other part of them. Thus, they could not change their lives wholly through self-will; they would have to rely in part on outside influences. It was a commonplace assumption even among revivalists that men could not wholly "save" themselves. They could transcend guilt either by accepting the evangelists' moral authority or by refusing to be implicated in the particular sin under condemnation. The Southern ministers and the officials of the Church could not accept the moral superiority of the antislavery evangelists because the latter defied institutional authority and demanded what Methodist ministers before 1800 had "learned" was impossible to demand—the emancipation of the slaves. Nor could the anti-abolitionists extricate themselves from implication with slavery by an effort of the will. Their past decisions on what was best for the Negro in his relations with the Church, and their ambitions for a peaceful and pros-

[47] *Zion's Herald*, June 15, 1842, p. 96; Matlack, *Scott*, pp. 185, 193, 195-203.
[48] Orange Scott, *The Grounds of Secession from the M.E. Church* (New York, 1848), pp. 6, 14.

perous national church necessitated accepting slavery as an unfortunate but unassailable fact of life. This implication with slavery seemed to Scott to be a degenerate subservience to the "slave power," and he came bitterly to condemn institutional Methodism as he failed to convert it. Instead of staying within the Church to continue the battle, Scott gave up the fight, withdrew from moral ambiguity, repudiated the social complexities of history, and created a community presumably free from guilt. If the leaders of the Methodist Episcopal Church could not act on principle alone, Scott would try to demonstrate that he and his friends could.

The "Scottite" secession was sufficiently extensive to be a primary factor in moving Northern churchmen toward a position more favorable to antislavery sentiment. In May 1843 at Utica, New York, Scott and some of his colleagues led delegates from eight Eastern states and Michigan in organizing the Wesleyan Methodist Church. In reaction, the *Christian Advocate and Journal*, and Northern conferences which had previously been moderate or silent on Negro servitude, became more vocal against slavery in an attempt to keep abolitionists within the Church. The conferences in New England petitioned the General Conference not only to rescind the resolution of 1840 against the acceptance of Negro testimony, but also to refuse to elect any slaveholder to high office in the Church. And the general theme of all official pronouncements in the North became that good Methodists could be good abolitionists and vice versa.[49]

The new stand of the Northerners combined with the

[49] Lucius C. Matlack, *The History of American Slavery and Methodism from 1780 to 1849* (New York, 1849), pp. 322, 328ff., 334, 344, 346; *Christian Advocate and Journal*, March 9 and March 16, 1842, pp. 119, 121; May 31, 1843, p. 166; *Zion's Herald*, January 3, 1844, *et seq.*, July 19 and August 9, 1843, pp. 116, 126; *Pittsburgh Christian Advocate*, August 17, 1843, p. 118, February 14, 1844, p. 15; *Western Christian Advocate*, September 29, 1843, pp. 94-95, January 12, 1844, p. 155; *The Liberator*, August 25, 1843, p. 133.

proslavery apology of the Southern Methodists to split the Methodist Episcopal Church at its General Conference of 1844. The controversy over the acceptability or unacceptability of slavery was signaled by the fact that Bishop James O. Andrew of Georgia had married a slaveholder. Even though Andrew did not own his wife's slaves, New England Methodist abolitionists were incensed at the bishop's "connection" with slavery and demanded that he free her slaves. When the abolitionists later found that he had himself inherited two slaves, they were even more insistent that he purge himself of the "sin" of being a master. Andrew explained to the General Conference that his wife's slaves did not belong to him and that he could not legally or morally emancipate the Negroes whom he had received by legacy. In regard to his own slaves, however, Andrew had clearly broken the tradition that bishops could not be slave-owners; indeed, he had been elected a bishop for the very reason that he was a Southerner who did not own slaves, a fact which made his present position even more difficult. Northern churchmen, fearing further secession in their section unless they removed the taint of slavery from the episcopacy, and more than a little disgusted with Southern defenses of slavery, carried a General Conference vote to relieve Andrew of his office until he was no longer personally "connected" with slavery. Southerners, fearing rejection of Methodism and their missions to the slaves in the South after this "attack" upon that section's morality, announced that they could no longer remain associated with the North. The General Conference then arranged to divide the Methodist Episcopal Church, a split which lasted until 1939.[50]

[50] Orange Scott, *The Methodist E. Church and Slavery* (Boston, 1844); *Western Christian Advocate*, October 11, 1844, p. 101; James Porter, "General Conference of 1844," *Methodist Quarterly Review*, 53 (April 1871), 242; *Journal of the General Conference of the Methodist Episcopal Church* (New York, 1844), pp. 84, 86; *Christian Advocate and Journal*, June 12, 1844, p. 174; July 3, 1844, p. 185.

Orange Scott's view of the separation revealed his growing disillusionment not only with Episcopal Methodism, but also with a nation whose Constitution he believed condoned slavery. The Church had acted not from principle, but from expediency, Scott pointed out. To have been consistent in their conduct toward Andrew, he went on, the conference "should have made a law expressly against slavery." He wondered if Bishop Andrew as a slaveholder had done "a hundredth part as much to sustain [slavery] as Bishop Hedding? Nay, verily!" Scott, however, did not bewail the division, rather he rejoiced in it. "A division of the M. E. Church will hasten the abolition of slavery in our country; it cannot be otherwise," he wrote. "Withdraw all Northern support from the abominable system of man stealing, and the traffic in human souls will soon wind up." Other churches must split also, he insisted. "And blessed be that day when the ungodly national compact [should] be broken up! Slavery never would, never could have flourished in this land . . . but for the connivance and support of the North."[51] Scott's disillusionment with governing institutions—political or ecclesiastical—was completed with his advocating the dissolution of the Union. His despair had been induced by a thwarted faith in moral action, moral influence, and moral principle. Demands for unambiguous moral action are essentially disrespectful of the moral ambiguity of historical institutions. Scott would have no compromise for the sake of institutional integrity if Christian moral principles, as he understood them, were involved. But if he insisted on moral purity, he did in part understand that morality often became besmirched with self-interest. The final consummation of the abolitionists' moral influence, however,

[51] *The True Wesleyan*, June 15 and August 3, 1844, pp. 94, 123. Scott gave Garrison satisfaction he did not intend. See *The Liberator*, August 9, August 30, September 13, September 27, 1844, pp. 126, 138, 146, 153.

he never saw. As one who believed in the immorality of physical violence he was spared the final disillusionment.

In 1847, Orange Scott died—only a few days before his mentor and fellow abolitionist, Amos A. Phelps. Refusing the presidency of the separate Methodist Church he had done so much to create, Scott had thrown himself into developing the new sect's publishing house and its paper, the *True Wesleyan*. His battle with slavery had mellowed him. He warned against stubbornness, un-Christian condemnation, "heated and intemperate controversy," and "worship of sect." Although his brashness had diminished, his energy had not. He had mortgaged his property to help start the Wesleyan Methodist Church upon its way; he wrote and worked with an energy his body no longer could spare—and by March 1846 he had worked himself out. For over a year he fought a losing battle with tuberculosis. As he lay in bed he remembered the valiant years he had spent lecturing against slavery, and regretted that he had done "so little." He had hoped some day to have convinced the wealthy classes of "their duty to the millions enduring poverty and toil." But he had already done too much, and on July 31, 1847, he died. A close friend preached his funeral sermon on the text, "Know ye not that there is a prince and a great man fallen this day in Israel."[52]

Orange Scott's assault on ecclesiastical ethics made him one of the most important men in the antislavery enterprise before 1845. As an evangelical demanding repentance from sin, Scott attempted to enlist institutional Christianity in his cause. Although claiming less than 20 per cent of all Americans as even nominal members, the churches and their clergy exercised a great moral influence in Jacksonian America through their newspapers and their pulpits. By 1844 much of that influence was wielded by the Methodists who were the largest denomination of Protestant Christians in the United States

[52] Matlack, *Scott*, pp. 245-47, 253, 262-65, 283.

with 1,200,000 members and 8,000 ministers. In fact, aside from the Federal government and the political parties, the Methodist Episcopal Church was the largest single national institution. Orange Scott, as the man who came to symbolize Methodist abolitionism, tried to link the nationalism of institutional Methodism to more than geography—to the ideal of a totally free America which the Church had held in its earlier days. His activities led on the one hand to the conversion of thousands of Methodists to antislavery ideas, and on the other, to his own disillusioned secession from the Church. Scott's schism was one of the events which helped to frighten Northern clerics into a position that Southerners could not tolerate. The resulting split of the Church revealed institutionally the yawning moral chasm between the two sections, and prepared thousands of Americans to think even more concretely of the differences between North and South.

Rarely considered more than a member of the supporting cast in most dramas of the antislavery crusade, Orange Scott actually played a vital and significant role as antislavery evangelist, as a disturber of consciences, as a shaker of institutions. To call him a reformer would be to misunderstand his importance; rather, he was a revolutionary. He emphasized justice rather than charity; he valued moral purity more than institutional adjustment; and he opposed a whole social system. He demanded not the reform of slavery, but its abolition, and in doing so, implied the destruction of Southern and even American society as he and his contemporaries knew it. For white Americans in Jacksonian America were quite satisfied to separate the Negro and to enslave him. The implication of the abolitionist preaching was a new kind of society much different from the old—an implication only gradually being realized in the twentieth century.

But Scott was revolutionary not merely by implication.

In his monumental study, *The Age of the Democratic Revolution*, Professor Robert R. Palmer has suggestively described what he understands a revolutionary situation to be. This description, when applied to Orange Scott and his predicament, clearly suggests that he was more than a reformer. Scott had lost confidence in the "justice" and "reasonableness" of the authorities of the Church; and his "obligations" he began to understand as "impositions." The actions of his superiors, especially Bishop Hedding, began to seem arbitrary; the government of his church and his country seemed no longer representative of their moral heritage.[53] Furthermore, institutional power had so opposed the high moral principles to which he tenaciously adhered that Scott had begun to feel alienated from the country's basic contract—the Constitution. In his warfare with power and institutions Scott was willing not only to revolutionize American society by freeing the Negroes, and to revolutionize the Church by seizing power from the bishops, but also to revolutionize American political institutions by dissolving the Union. Orange Scott was the epitome of the "Methodist evangelist as revolutionary."

[53] Robert R. Palmer, *The Age of the Democratic Revolution* (Princeton, 1959), p. 21.

CHAPTER 5

THE PERSISTENCE

OF WENDELL PHILLIPS

BY IRVING H. BARTLETT

"The antislavery agitation is an important, nay, an essential part of the machinery of the state. It is not a disease nor a medicine. No; it is the normal state,—The normal state of the nation" [*Lecture on Public Opinion*].

WHEREVER Wendell Phillips walked on the Harvard campus he carried the aura of Beacon Hill with him. He was as well born as any Winthrop or Saltonstall and had been brought up in an imposing brick mansion on Beacon Hill only a few steps from the State House. The son of Boston's first mayor, a man universally respected for sound conservative principles, young Phillips seemed intent on following in his father's footsteps. He gained a reputation as being "the pet of the aristocracy," and in orations at the college exhibitions went out of his way to attack reformers and defend the standing order. One of his friends later recalled that Phillips would probably have been chosen by his classmates as the man *"least likely* to give the enthusiasm and labor of [his life] to the defense of popular rights."[1]

Fifteen years after he left Harvard Phillips was asked by the secretary of the class of 1831 to fill out a questionnaire. He noted that he was in good health but growing bald. Under occupation he said he had prepared for the law "but grew honest and quitted what required an oath to the Constitution of the United States."

[1] John H. Morison to T. D. Weld, n.d., Clements Library, Ann Arbor, Michigan.

Asked to note any other remarks that might be interesting to his classmates, he wrote: "My main business is to forward the abolition of slavery. I hold that the world is wrong side up and maintain the propriety of turning it upside down. I go for Disunion and have long since abjured that contemptible mockery, the Constitution of the United States."[2]

To understand Phillips' career as an abolitionist and free-lance radical it is first necessary to account for his transformation from gentility to "fanaticism." Certainly it was not a natural development. After graduating from Harvard College Phillips entered the Harvard Law School. His career there and later as a practicing attorney was uneventful. Like most of the other sons of the old Federalists, he was happy to follow Daniel Webster into the Whig party which continued to serve the bulwarked conservatism of Massachusetts. He shared an office at this time with a man who later led a mob against abolitionists, and most of his social contacts were with the old aristocratic families who, if they knew anything about William Lloyd Garrison, naturally "supposed him to be a man who ought to be hung," and were unanimously determined to outlaw anyone, even the saintly William Ellery Channing, for expressing the slightest sympathy with his principles.

Phillips' first personal encounter with the antislavery movement came in October 1835, when he stood on a Boston street corner and watched a jeering mob drag Garrison through the street at the end of a rope. A few weeks later he met Ann Terry Greene, one of Garrison's disciples, and in less than a year, to the consternation of his mother and most of Boston society, married her. A few months later he made his first antislavery speech.

As with most of the early abolitionists, religion played a dominant role in making Phillips an abolitionist. We will never know how successful he might have been in

[2] W. P. MS. Harvard Archives.

law or politics, but his advantages in family background
and education, his intelligence, and his remarkable
oratorical talent suggest that the achievements of a
Webster, Choate, or Sumner were not beyond his reach.
The fact is, however, that between the time he graduated
from college and met his wife, Phillips appears to have
been in a melancholy state of mind largely because he
lacked a sense of vocation. He had been brought up as
a devout Calvinist, and it was a fundamental article in
his belief that a man must make his life count for something. Like all new lawyers he found it slow going to
get a practice started, but even more important he found
no great satisfaction in the profession. He needed to
find a calling. As it turned out he fell in love and found
his calling at the same time. His bride introduced him
to William Lloyd Garrison and other Boston abolitionists, and in the early days of their marriage, when her
health permitted, accompanied him to antislavery meetings. Phillips had undergone religious conversion years
before under the powerful preaching of Lyman Beecher.
As he joined hands with the abolitionists he felt he was
being born a third time. "None know what it is to live,"
he wrote in 1841, "till they redeem life from its seeming
monotony by laying it a sacrifice on the altar of some
great cause."[3]

Phillips never forgot the importance of religion to the
antislavery movement. "Our enterprise is eminently a
religious one," he said, "dependent for success entirely
on the religious sentiment of the people."[4] When Phillips refused to take an oath to support the "proslavery
constitution" of the United States, he thought of himself as following in the tradition of his forbear, the
Reverend George Phillips, who had come to America in
1630 to put the Atlantic Ocean "between himself and a

[3] W. P. *Speeches, Lectures, and Letters* (Second Series, Boston,
1900), p. 223.
[4] *Ibid.*, p. 8.

corrupt church." He did not think of himself as an ordinary lecturer or orator, but as a kind of minister to the public, preaching the gospel of reform. When he was called to fill Theodore Parker's pulpit in the Boston Music Hall in 1860, it was natural for him to begin a sermon by announcing that "Christ preached on the last political and social item of the hour; and no man follows in his footsteps who does not do exactly the same thing."[5] Phillips' sermons before Parker's congregation were the same sermons that he preached in Faneuil Hall before antislavery meetings, and he was convinced that he did his duty to God in both places by flaying the public sinners of the day whether their names were Webster, Everett, Jefferson Davis, or Abraham Lincoln.

The idealism of the American revolutionary tradition also played a decisive role in shaping Phillips' career. When he was a boy, he remembered later, the Boston air still "trembled and burned with Otis and Sam Adams." He had been born practically next door to John Hancock's mansion, within site of Bunker Hill and only a few steps from the site of the Boston massacre. When he was thirteen years old and a student at the Boston Latin School he stood for hours in a crowd on the Common to catch a glimpse of Lafayette upon his visit to the city. Two years later, while poring over his lessons at the school, the sound of tolling bells came through the open windows announcing the deaths of Thomas Jefferson and John Adams.

Phillips never doubted that the revolutionary fathers were on his side. His first antislavery speech was given to support John Quincy Adams in his fight to get the Congress to hear petitions attacking slavery. Phillips argued that the right of petition was a traditional right for free men and that in attacking it the South threatened the freedom of all men. "This is the reason we render to those who ask us why we are contending against

[5] *The Liberator*, May 18, 1860.

southern slavery," he said, *"that it may not result in
northern slavery . . .* it is our own rights which are at
issue."[6]

The speech which made Phillips famous in Boston
was given at a Faneuil Hall meeting to honor the
memory of Elijah Lovejoy who had been killed by a
mob in Alton, Illinois. The meeting was called to pay
tribute to Lovejoy, but the abolitionists almost lost control of it when James Austin, the Attorney General for
Massachusetts, stood up and made a violent speech
attacking Lovejoy for having published an incendiary
antislavery newspaper. Austin likened the mob which destroyed Lovejoy and his press to the patriots responsible
for the Boston Tea Party. Phillips was able to get the
floor after Austin, and overcome the hooting and jeering
of the proslavery faction in the audience with an eloquent
defense of Lovejoy. Again Phillips was defending a traditional American right, freedom of the press, and he
insisted that the spirit of the American revolution supported him.

> Sir, when I heard the gentleman lay down principles
> which place the murderers of Alton side by side
> with Otis and Hancock, with Quincy Adams, I
> thought those pictured lips would have broken into
> voice to rebuke the recreant American,—The slan-
> derer of the dead. . . . In the sentiments he has
> uttered, on soil consecrated by the prayers of Puri-
> tans and the blood of patriots, the earth should
> have yawned and swallowed him up.[7]

In his reliance on religion and the spirit of the Declaration of Independence, Phillips was like most other
abolitionists. As an orator, however, despite the fact that
he was part of a movement full of celebrated speakers, his
uniqueness is unchallenged.[8]

[6] *Speeches, Lectures, and Letters* (Second Series), p. 5.

[7] W. P. *Speeches, Lectures, and Letters* (Boston, 1863), p. 3.

[8] The discussion of Phillips' oratory which follows has been fully

For at least a quarter of a century, from 1850 to 1875, Wendell Phillips was the commanding figure on the American lecture platform. Not only was he a spectacular success on the Lyceum circuit, but during the critical years surrounding the Civil War, his reputation as a critic of public policy was so great that each of his major addresses became a national event widely reported by the Boston and New York press and copied in papers throughout the northern and western states. Chauncey Depew, who lived to be ninety and claimed to have heard all the great speakers including Webster and Clay, declared that Phillips was "the greatest of all American orators." Thomas Wentworth Higginson placed Phillips and Webster together as the two most powerful orators in the post-revolutionary period, while Bronson Alcott said that Phillips' speeches "in range of thought, cleverness of statement, keen satire, brilliant wit, personal anecdote, wholesome moral sentiments, patriotism and Puritan spirit" were "unmatched by any of the great orators of the day." A critical piece in the *New Englander* in 1850 may be considered typical of the way in which a performance by Phillips was reviewed. Taking pains to disassociate himself from the speaker's radical doctrines, the writer went on to say that he was a "more instructive and more interesting speaker" than Clay, Webster, Choate, Adams, or Benton. Nor was Phillips' power entirely lost on the generation which grew up after his death in 1884, for as late as 1927 Senator William E. Borah, one of the few great American orators of this century, confessed to the habit of reading one of Phillips' speeches every three weeks or so to keep the famous radical's "style" fresh in his mind.

What sets Phillips off from the other lecturers within the Garrisonian camp, such colorful individuals as Parker Pillsbury and Stephen and Abby Kelly Foster, is that

---

documented in my essay, "Wendell Phillips and the Eloquence of Abuse," *American Quarterly*, Winter 1959.

Phillips alone was consistently recognized as great even by those who detested his ideas. After hearing him declare in what was perhaps an unconscious parody of Webster's famous words, that he hoped to witness before he died "the convulsion of a sundering Union and a dissolving church," a New York reporter remarked that Phillips' sentiments "however repugnant to general opinion were expressed with a clear and lofty eloquence and extraordinary felicity and beauty of illustration." In Boston, where Phillips was loved and hated the most, a writer for the *Courier* made the same point in plain language. "It is a dish of tripe and onions served on silver," he wrote, "or black-strap presented in a goblet of Bohemian glass . . . Mr. Phillips thinks like a Billingsgate fishwoman, or a low pothouse bully, but he speaks like Cicero."

The sources of Phillips' power on the platform were deceptive. Those seeing him for the first time were invariably surprised to discover that he was not an orator in the grand manner. Shortly before the Civil War an Andover student, hearing that Phillips was to lecture in Boston, made a twenty-two-mile pilgrimage on foot to hear him. At first the trip seemed hardly worthwhile, for Phillips stood on the platform, one hand lightly resting on a table, talked for what seemed about twenty minutes and suddenly sat down. When the astonished young man consulted his watch he found that he had been listening for an hour and a half.

There was, as the Andover student discovered, nothing ponderous about Phillips as a speaker, no bombast, no flights of empty rhetoric. He spoke almost conversationally; his appearance was invariably one of calm poise, and he relied little on the kind of theatrics that led Henry Ward Beecher to auction off a slave girl from the pulpit. "The most prolonged applause could not disturb a muscle in his countenance," one listener remembered, "and a storm of hisses seemed to have as little effect on him." His customary serenity enhanced the effect of those few occasions when Phillips did make some spectacular gesture, as for example, when after mentioning the name of the fugitive slave commissioner George Ticknor Curtis, he would rinse his mouth out with water and spit it on the floor.

Webster with his bull-like body and cavernous, smoldering eyes could overpower an audience with sheer physical magnetism. Phillips did not have this power. He was a man of average height, rather slightly built, with finely drawn features which most easily lent themselves to expressions of scorn and resolution. What everyone did notice about him was his aristocratic bearing. An Englishman visiting Boston saw Phillips and Edmund Quincy walking together down Park Street and remarked that they were the only men he had seen in this country "who looked like Gentlemen." As a matter of fact, Phillips came as close to being a native-born aristocrat as any American could. And his assurance on the platform was undoubtedly related to the fact that he did not have to make a name for himself. He had a way of treating his opponents as if they were socially beneath him as well as morally loathsome. Because of this he was nearly immune to criticism, and absolutely invulnerable to a heckling audience. He would never lose his temper, but would reply to his critics in a tone so witheringly contemptuous that it was like a blast of air from an iceberg. Neither rotten eggs nor brickbats could startle him, and hissing so consistently aroused him to his best effort that his admirers sometimes sat in a back row and hissed merely to make him warm to the subject.

By far the most sensational characteristic of Phillips as a speaker was the contrast between his perfectly controlled, poised, almost dispassionate manner, and the inflammatory language he employed. It was the apparent effortlessness of his delivery that impressed many listeners most. "Staples said the other day that he heard

Phillips speak at the State House," wrote Thoreau in his *Journal*. "By thunder! he never heard a man that could speak like him. His words come so easy. It was just like picking up chips." In an effort to explain how the speaker remained somehow detached from his own eloquence, another observer compared him to "a cold but mysteriously animated statue of marble." Time and time again when Phillips was on tour, talking before new audiences, the reporter would register the audience's surprise. "They had conceived him to be a ferocious ranter and blustering man of words. They found him to be a quiet, dignified and polished gentleman and scholar, calm and logical in his argument."

One of the reasons why abolitionist meetings in the middle and later 1850's began to draw impressively large crowds, as the critics of the abolitionists pointed out, was that for many people an antislavery meeting had all the elements of a theatrical performance. The star performer was usually Wendell Phillips, and his stock in trade, according to the unconverted, was "personal abuse." To the abolitionists themselves he was, as his publisher remarked, the greatest "master of invective" in the nineteenth century. With sublime confidence, almost as if he were reading from a sheaf of statistics or reciting a series of scientific facts, Phillips would take the platform to announce that Daniel Webster was "a great mass of dough," Edward Everett "a whining spaniel," Massachusetts Senator Robert C. Winthrop "a bastard who had stolen the name of Winthrop," and the New England churches an ecclesiastical machine to manufacture hypocrisy "just as really as Lowell manufactures cotton." It was the way Phillips uttered his epithets that fascinated most critics. The shrewd Scottish traveler David Macrae who had been led "from the ferocity of his onslaughts on public men and public measures . . . to form a false conception of his delivery" noted with surprise that vehemence and declamation were replaced by sarcasm, "cold, keen, withering." Macrae was impressed by the relentless manner in which Phillips pursued his opponents. "He follows an enemy like an Indian upon the trail. . . . When he comes to strike, his strokes are like galvanic shocks; there is neither noise nor flash but their force is terrible."

A writer for an English paper who was contrasting Phillips' speeches with "the rounded periods of Mr. Seward" and "the finished artistic rhetoric of the patriotic Mr. Everett" noted one quality which grated on European ears, and that was "the concentrated bitterness, the intense spirit of hatred with which they are frequently suffused." Because Phillips did not like to talk in general terms about issues, because he always took dead aim on personalities and heaped "the concentrated bitterness" of his rhetoric upon the heads of men prominent in public life, and because the people turned out in droves to hear him, Robert C. Winthrop believed that Phillips had "gradually educated our people to relish nothing but the 'eloquence of abuse.' "

A good many later critics have been much harsher than Winthrop in criticizing Phillips. Theodore Roosevelt called him a wild-eyed fanatic and Professor Randall has dismissed his speeches as "a kind of grandiloquent, self-righteous raving."[9] A careful reading of his career shows these estimates to be incorrect. What distinguishes Phillips from the other abolitionists more significantly than anything else is that he was an intellectual, a philosopher of reform as well as a practical agitator. It is impossible to understand him, therefore, without knowing more about his political ideas and his conception of the role of the reformer in America.

Like other abolitionists Phillips believed in the Higher Law and judged every public question from an absolute

[9] Theodore Roosevelt, *Letters*, Elting Morison, ed. (Cambridge, Mass., 1951-54), VII, 785; James G. Randall, *Lincoln The President: Springfield to Gettysburg* (New York, 1945), I, 190.

moral standard. He believed that a man's first duty was to God, and that men should do their duty at whatever cost. He was convinced that anything right in principle had to be right in practice. He accepted Garrison's demand for immediate emancipation without question. Phillips' Calvinism, his belief in Divine Providence, made it possible for him to dismiss whatever doubts he might have had about the practicality of this radical solution. "No matter if the charter of emancipation was written in blood," he said in one of his early speeches, "and anarchy stalk abroad with giant strides—if God commanded, it was right."[10] Phillips' Calvinism reinforced his radicalism. He did not have to worry about the consequences of his agitation. A man could only do his duty and let God do the rest.

As the most eloquent and intellectual of all the radicals, Phillips was called upon to defend the position that abolitionists should not support a constitution or government which supported slavery. Although the refusal of the radical abolitionists to vote or hold office, and their continued agitation to get the North to secede from the union seemed incomprehensible to most people, the position was perfectly consistent with Phillips' principles. Slavery was evil and this evil was supported by a Federal government which protected slave states from insurrection, undertook to return their fugitives and gave them special representation in Congress. Therefore anything voluntarily done in support of this government (i.e. taking an oath to support the Constitution or voting for a candidate who would be required to take such an oath), supported slavery also and was evil.

Despite the fact that his position was condemned in the public mind from the beginning, Phillips, through pamphlets and lectures, did as much as anyone could do to persuade people of its worth. He never once doubted its soundness. When friends like Charles Sumner

10 *The Liberator,* June 21, 1839.

argued that the course he advocated would impede the struggle for emancipation, he replied that "honesty and truth are more important than even freeing slaves." When Sumner asked how he could consistently pay taxes or even remain in the country, he reminded him that a man's choices were always limited by the social and historical situation in which God placed him. A man had to live in the world, but he did not have to collaborate with the devil, which is what Sumner and all other "loyal citizens" were doing. "To live where God sent you and protest against your neighbor—this is certainly different from *joining him* in sinning, which the office holder of this country does."[11]

Phillips' moralism supplied the ballast for his career. His solutions to difficult problems were both "right" and simple. When he continued to badger the government long after Garrison and other abolitionists had retired from the field after the war, it was because he sought "*justice*—absolute, immediate, unmixed justice to the negro."[12] He did not, however, live by shibboleths alone, and his tactics as a reformer were based on a surprisingly sophisticated conception of American politics and society.

Phillips recognized that slavery was a threat to the freedom of all Americans. This conviction developed gradually out of his early experiences. He had the grisly reminiscences of the Grimké sisters to remind him of the evils of slavery in the south—the whippings and mutilations, the ruthless separation of husband and wife, of parent and child. Closer to his personal experience was what slavery had done to supposedly free American citizens. It had jailed Prudence Crandall for opening a school for Negro girls. It had publicly whipped Amos Dresser for daring to distribute antislavery literature. It had tried to gag John Quincy Adams in Congress,

[11] W. P. to Sumner, February 17, 1845, Sumner Papers, Boston Public Library.
[12] *The Liberator*, February 17, 1865.

had mobbed Garrison within the shadow of Faneuil Hall, and had finally killed Lovejoy. The pattern seemed always to be the same; principle was overcome by power. For the first time Phillips sensed the demonic possibilities of a slave power supported by public opinion in America.

> A lawyer, bred in all the technical reliance on the safeguards of Saxon liberty, I was puzzled, rather than astounded, by the fact that, outside of the law and wholly unrecognized in the theory of our institutions, was a mob power—an abnormal element which nobody had counted in, in the analysis of the system, and for whose irregular actions no check, no balance, had been provided. The gun which was aimed at the breast of Lovejoy on the banks of the Mississippi brought me to my feet conscious that I stood in the presence of a power whose motto was victory or death.[13]

Having recognized the importance of public opinion in America Phillips began to examine American institutions more closely. He distinguished a fundamental tension between the American ideal, a society based on the rights of man, and an American political system based on numbers. "The majority rules, and law rests on numbers, not on intellect or virtue," thus "while theoretically holding that no vote of the majority can authorize injustice, we practically consider public opinion the real test of what is true and what is false; and hence, as a result, the fact which Tocqueville has noticed, that practically our institutions protect, not the interest of the whole community but the interests of the majority."[14]

Phillips was acute enough to see that while the tyranny of the majority might occasionally express itself violently, as in the lynching of Lovejoy, a more common and insidious threat to liberty came through the intimidation

[13] *National Anti-Slavery Standard* (New York), May 25, 1867.
[14] *Speeches, Lectures and Letters* (Boston 1863), p. 321.

of citizens holding unpopular ideas. "Entire equality and freedom in political forms" naturally tended to "make the individual subside into the mass, and lose his identity in the general whole." In an aristocratic society like England a man could afford to "despise the judgment" of most people so long as he kept the good opinion of those in his own class. In America there was no refuge. Every citizen "in his ambition, his social life, or his business" depended on the approbation and the votes of those around him. Consequently, Phillips said, "instead of being a mass of individuals, each one fearlessly blurting out his own convictions,—as a nation, compared with other nations, we are a mass of cowards. More than any other people, we are afraid of each other."[15]

Although Phillips knew that in some nations public opinion was shaped by political leaders, he could find nothing to show that this was true in the American experience. Theoretically every American male citizen was supposed to be eligible for office, but in practice, "with a race like ours, fired with the love of material wealth," the best brains were drawn into commerce. As a result politics took up with small men, "men without grasp enough for large business . . . men popular because they have no positive opinions."[16] Even if an occasional man of the first rank (a Charles Sumner for example), did emerge in politics, he would be lost to the reformer because the whole art of politics in America was based on the ability to compromise. "The politician must conceal half his principles to carry forward the other half," Phillips said, "must regard, not rigid principle and strict right, but only such a degree of right as will allow him at the same time to secure *numbers*."[17]

These considerations led Phillips to conclude that the

[15] *Speeches, Lectures and Letters* (Second Series), p. 399.
[16] *Speeches, Lectures and Letters* (Boston, 1863), p. 333.
[17] *The Liberator*, May 16, 1845.

reformer in America had to confront the people directly. "Our aim," he said in his lecture *The Philosophy of Abolitionism*, "is to alter public opinion." Slavery endured and abolitionists were mobbed because a majority of Americans refused to face the moral issues involved. Phillips was too much of a realist to believe that he could suddenly convert the nation, but he did feel that he could force the issue and change the public attitude toward slavery.

Phillips knew that most people in the North disliked slavery, but he also knew that it was to their self-interest to leave it alone. To stir up controversy was dangerous: no one wanted to be known as a troublemaker; mill owners were concerned for their capital; mill hands were concerned for their jobs; the respectable middle class was concerned for its reputation. The easy thing for everyone was to turn away from the problem. The abolitionist's job was to scatter thorns on the easy road by dramatizing the moral issue and insisting that every man who did not throw his whole influence into the scales against slavery was as guilty as the slaveholder. "We will gibbet the name of every apostate so black and high," Phillips warned, "that his children's children shall blush to hear it. Yet we bear no malice—cherish no resentment. We thank God that the love of fame is shared by the ignoble."[18]

What this could mean in practice is perhaps best seen in Phillips' criticism of Henry Gardner, a Boston politician who was the leader of Know-Nothingism in Massachusetts and Governor of the Commonwealth from 1855 to 1858. Gardner usually made a few antislavery sounds during election campaigns, but his great appeal was to nativism, and it was he who had blocked Phillips' attempt to get Judge Edward Loring recalled after the rendition of Anthony Burns. Phillips believed that Gardner dabbled in antislavery politics for personal gain

[18] *Speeches, Lectures and Letters* (Boston, 1863), p. 115.

and frustrated the abolitionists' effort to educate the public. He called the Governor "a consummate hypocrite, a man who if he did not have some dozen and distinct reasons for telling the truth would naturally tell a lie." On another occasion he said, "Our course is a perfect copy of Sisyphus. We always toil up, up, up the hill until we touch the soiled sandals of some Governor Gardner, and then the rock rolls down again. Always some miserable reptile that has struggled into power in the corruption of parties—reptiles who creep where *man* disdains to climb; some slight thing of no consequence till its foul mess blocks our path; and dashes our hopes at the last minute."

The denunciation could hardly have been more savage. Phillips insisted, however, that there was nothing personal in it.

> Do not say I am personal in speaking thus of Governor Gardner. . . . Do not blame me when I speak thus of Henry J. Gardner. What is the duty of the minority . . . what is the duty of a minority in this country? A minority has no right to rebel . . . the majority have said the thing shall be so. It is not to resist, it is to convert. And how shall we convert? If the community is in love with some monster, we must paint him truly. The duty of a minority being to convert, every tool which the human mind knows, it is their right and duty to use; a searching criticism, pitiless sarcasm, bitter invective, rigid analysis of motives, constant recurrence to the admitted facts of a man's career,—these are our rights, if our function is to save the people from delusion.[19]

Phillips was not a fanatic. He used the most violent language dispassionately as a surgeon uses the sharpest steel. He could not actually cut away the diseased tissue with his rhetoric, but he could expose it. Thus when he

[19] *The Liberator*, August 1, 1856, June 15, 1855, August 14, 1857.

called Lincoln a "slave hound" he was reminding his listeners and readers that as a Congressman Lincoln had supported a bill which would have enforced the return of fugitive slaves escaping into the District of Columbia. This was the man who expected to get the antislavery vote. Phillips' intention in attacking Lincoln so savagely was simply to dramatize the rottenness of the American conscience by showing that only a "slave hound" could be elected President. His reply to those who accused him of extravagance and distortion was that "there are far more dead hearts to be quickened, than confused intellects to be cleared up—more dumb dogs to be made to speak than doubting consciences to be enlightened. We have use, then, for something beside argument."[20]

The easiest way to treat nettlesome reformers like the abolitionists is to dismiss them as cranks. Nothing irritated Phillips more than the attempts of his opponents to thrust him outside the mainstream of American life. The antislavery agitation, he insisted, was "an essential part of the machinery of the state . . . not a disease nor a medicine . . . the normal state of the nation."

The preceding statement takes us to the heart of Phillips' philosophy of reform. He recognized that American ideals could ultimately be translated into practice only through politics. At the same time he knew that the American politician's ability to gain and hold power was largely determined by his ability to effect compromises that appealed to numbers rather than to principle. He added to these corruptive tendencies the fact that people in a democracy always tend to have as high an opinion of themselves as possible—always tremble on the edge of national idolatry. The result, Phillips argued, was that "every government is always growing corrupt. Every Secretary of State is by the very necessity of his

[20] *Speeches, Lectures and Letters* (Boston, 1863), p. 107.

position an apostate." A democratic society that trusted to constitutions and political machinery to secure its liberties never would have any. "The people must be waked to a new effort," he said, "just as the church has to be regenerated in each age." In the middle of the nineteenth century the abolitionist was the agency of national regeneration, but even after he had vanished his function in the American system would still remain.

> Eternal vigilance is the price of liberty: power is ever stealing from the many to the few. The manna of popular liberty must be gathered each day, or it is rotten. . . . The hand entrusted with power becomes, either from human depravity or *esprit de corps*, the necessary enemy of the people. Only by continual oversight can the democrat in office be prevented from hardening into a despot: only by unintermitted agitation can a people be kept sufficiently awake to principle not to let liberty be smothered in material prosperity. All clouds, it is said, have sunshine behind them, and all evils have some good result; so slavery, by the necessity of its abolition, has saved the freedom of the white race from being melted in luxury or buried beneath the gold of its own success. Never look, therefore, for an age when the people can be quiet and safe. At such times despotism, like a shrouding mist, steals over the mirror of Freedom.[21]

It should be clear now that Phillips believed the radical abolitionist to be justified as much by his radicalism as by his abolitionism. Phillips preferred the word agitator to radical, and since he himself was frequently accused of demagoguery, he took pains to point out the difference between the demagogue and agitator. A demagogue (he used Robespierre as an example), "rides the storm; he has never really the ability to create one. He

21 *Ibid.*, p. 52.

uses it narrowly, ignorantly, and for selfish ends. If not crushed by the force which, without his will, has flung him into power, he leads it with ridiculous miscalculation against some insurmountable obstacle that scatters it forever. Dying, he leaves no mark on the elements with which he has been mixed." Quoting Sir Robert Peel, Phillips defined agitation as "the marshalling of the conscience of a nation to mould its laws." Daniel O'Connell who, after thirty years of "patient and sagacious labor," succeeded in creating a public opinion and unity of purpose to free Ireland from British tyranny was one of Phillips' models as a successful agitator.[22]

It was because Phillips thought of himself primarily as an agitator and Garrison thought of himself primarily as an abolitionist that the two came to a parting of the ways in 1865. With the war over and slavery prohibited by the passage of the thirteenth amendment, Garrison felt that the "covenant with death" had been annulled. The American nation had become "successor to the abolitionists," and the American Anti-Slavery Society had lost its excuse for being.[23] Phillips did not agree. He argued that the nation needed "the constant, incessant discriminating criticism of the abolitionists as much as ever."[24] The debate grew rancorous and resulted in Garrison's quitting the Society. Phillips was elected President in his place, and for the next five years continued to agitate as fiercely for Negro suffrage as he had for emancipation. Only after the fifteenth amendment was passed did he allow the organization to be dissolved.

Even then Phillips did not relax his efforts. He denounced the decision to remove Federal troops from the South as vehemently as he had the Fugitive Slave Law, and predicted that a " 'solid south'—the slave power

[22] *Speeches, Lectures and Letters* (Second Series), p. 393.

[23] *The Liberator*, November 24, 1865.

[24] *The Liberator*, February 10, 1865.

under a new name" would soon control national politics. Most of the other surviving abolitionists had long since gone over to the Republican party lock, stock, and barrel, but Phillips saw through the moral pretensions of the Republicans as clearly as anyone in the country. They had waved the bloody flag with regularity, but had been unwilling to make the sacrifices and the long-term commitments in reconstruction that were necessary if the moral legacy of the war was not to be squandered away. Accusing the Republicans of "a heartless and merciless calculation" to exploit war memories and Ku Klux Klan atrocities for party purposes, Phillips claimed that no party in history had ever "fallen from such a height to such a depth of disgrace."[25]

The rhetoric was the same but the response was not. The people had grown tired of the war, and newspapers that would have praised him in the sixties now wrote about "Mr. Phillips' Last Frenzy" and called him "the apostle of unforgiving and relentless hate."[26]

Meanwhile, even as he decried the growing popularity of the illusion that the Negro might be safe in the hands of his old master, Phillips turned his attention to the struggle of free labor in the North. "While this delusion of peace without purity persists," he was saying in 1878, "labor claims every ear and every hand."[27] And so, in the declining years of his life, Wendell Phillips, true to his belief that agitation was "an essential part of the machinery of the state," poured his whole influence into the struggle for social justice in an industrial society. His solutions were still simple—passage of an eight-hour law—the unlimited issuance of Greenbacks. His tactics were the same. "The only way to accomplish our object," he said, "is to shame greedy men into humanity. Poison

[25] *Boston Herald*, August 13, 1879.
[26] *Boston Daily Advertiser*, March 29, 1877; New York *Daily Tribune*, April 3, 1877.
[27] *North American Review* (July 1878), p. 115.

their wealth with the tears and curses of widows and orphans. In speaking of them call things by their right names. Let men shrink from them as from slave dealers and pirates."[28] And the response was the same he had received during the hard, bitter years before the war. If anything Phillips was even more of an outsider now than he had been then. His support of unions, the right to strike, shorter hours of work, a graduated income tax, and his derision of laissez-faire ("the bubble and chaff of 'supply and demand' ") offended even the old abolitionists. If Phillips had acted "with ordinary common sense and good temper when slavery was abolished and had gone into politics," Edmund Quincy thought, "he might have been the next Senator . . . but he is 'played out' as we say, and will be merely a popular lecturer and a small demagogue for the rest of his life."[29]

Quincy was a retired reformer. Like most of his contemporaries and most of the American historians who have followed, he could not appreciate Wendell Phillips, a gentleman who understood the difference between agitation and demagoguery, and knew that the radical in America could never retire.

[28] *National Standard* (New York), September 9, 1871.
[29] Edmund Quincy to Richard Webb, November 13, 1870, Quincy-Webb Correspondence, Boston Public Library.

CHAPTER 6

ABOLITION'S DIFFERENT DRUMMER:

FREDERICK DOUGLASS

BY BENJAMIN QUARLES

THE time and place—August 11, 1852, at the Masonic Hall in Pittsburgh. The occasion—the national convention of the Free Soil party, a political group that four years previously had been formed to combat the extension of slavery into the territories. The afternoon meeting had been in progress for more than an hour when a Negro, wearing a white linen coat and dark blue trousers, entered the hall. Before he could find a seat someone shouted his name, and others spontaneously took up the cry. The presiding officer, his voice drowned out, resorted to sign language to welcome the visitor and invite him to speak. Amid cheers, the newcomer proceeded down the aisle.

Facing the audience, he showed no sign of nervousness—he had a talent for talking fluently. For the space of a few moments, however, he said nothing, as if to satisfy those among the two thousand spectators who might wish to size him up as a physical specimen. Broad-shouldered, six feet tall and in the prime of manhood, he could bear scrutiny. His skin was bronze-colored and his mass of black hair was neatly parted on the left. His eyes were deep-set and steady. But at the moment they were less expressive than his well-formed nose that now, as he prepared to say his first words, inhaled deeply, almost critically, as though the air might offer to nonwhites an inferior oxygen, if vigilance were relaxed.

"Gentlemen, I take it that you are in earnest, and therefore I will address you," he began in low but carrying tones that searched the recesses of the auditorium, hinting of a readiness to defy faulty acoustics. But there was no answering challenge to this voice that had tested itself in damp groves, in tents and on ship decks. "I have come here, not so much of a free soiler as others have come," he continued. "I am, of course, for circumscribing and damaging slavery in every way I can. But my motto is extermination—not only in New Mexico, but in New Orleans, not only in California but in South Carolina." The theme was a familiar one with the speaker, but he saw no need of talking about new wrongs as long as the old ones still existed.

He proceeded to criticize the Fugitive Slave Law. Because an alleged runaway might be carried away without trial by jury, "the colored man's rights are less than those of a jackass," since the latter could not be seized and taken away without submitting the matter to twelve men. He had a solution, said the speaker: "The only way to make the Fugitive Slave Law a dead letter is to make half a dozen or more dead kidnappers. The man who takes the office of a bloodhound ought to be treated as a bloodhound." The crowd applauded, many of them knowing that the speaker's strong language resulted in part from his twenty-year experience as a slave.

When the noise died down, the speaker continued along a different line—denunciation was but one of his weapons. The Constitution, he contended, was against slavery inasmuch as "human government is for the protection of rights and not for the destruction of rights." But even if the Founding Fathers had expressly said that one man had the right to possess another man, such a stipulation would lack the binding quality of rationality: "Suppose you and I made a deed to give away two or three acres of blue sky; would the sky fall, and would anybody be able to plough it?" The speaker's sentences had now gained momentum. Those who were listening to him for the first time became aware of a voice that employed every degree of light and shade, a rich baritone giving emotional vitality to every word.

He resumed in a conversational manner—he had all the gifts requisite to an orator—"You are about to have a party, but I want to be independent and not hurried to and fro into the ranks of Whigs and Democrats." Possibly some in the audience may have reflected that it was this desire for independence that had led him to break with his slave past and to strike out on his own.

Now that he was at the point of bringing his remarks to a close, he had a parting bit of advice. "It has been said that we ought to take the position of the greatest number of voters. That is wrong. Numbers should not be looked to so much as right. The man who is right is a majority. If he does not represent what we are, he represents what we ought to be."

The crowd cheered again and again as the speaker concluded in this high strain. He had difficulty making his way down the aisle, past those who wished to shake his hand.[1] The clapping and shouting, however, were not primarily an approval of what the speaker had said. Rather they were a personal tribute to a man who had devoted his talents to the building of a better America.

For to Frederick Douglass this address differed from his others only in externals. All his public appearances grew out of a career that had sought the storms in a period that was itself shaped by stress and passion. By the time he delivered this impromptu speech his career had been inexorably charted, Douglass having become a reformer of the first water.

Douglass acquired prominence in his day because of his qualities of mind and spirit and the fact that he was a

[1] Quotations from this speech are from the New York *Herald*, August 12, 1852.

Negro. These two outstanding causative factors may be examined in turn.

Douglass had become a professional reformer by having come to the attention in August 1841 of the Massachusetts school of abolitionists, headed by William Lloyd Garrison and Wendell Phillips. Persuaded to join the cause as a paid lecturer, Douglass cut loose from his odd-jobs work in New Bedford to become a careerist in reform. To say that Douglass became an abolitionist solely as an alternative to sawing wood, sweeping chimneys, and blowing bellows is to venture beyond the record. Outward circumstance may have been reinforced by inner calling. But whatever the motivation, Douglass had no difficulty in internalizing his role, becoming a typical reformer in outlook and style.

As one who was single-mindedly bent on wiping out institutions he regarded as outworn, Douglass viewed things with an almost theological purity. He was given to absolutes of feeling, making him tend to overstate his case. To him the slave system was "a grand aggregation of human horrors." For the master class he had no charity: "Every slaveholder is the legalized keeper of a house of ill-fame, no matter how high he may stand in Church or State. He may be a Bishop Meade or a Henry Clay—a reputed saint or an open sinner—he is still the legalized head of a den of infamy."[2]

But if Douglass tended to overreact, it was due to the failure of the great majority to react at all. Charged with irritating the American people, Douglass replied that this was what they deserved: "The conscience of the American public needs this irritation. And I would blister it all over, from center to circumference, until it gives signs of a purer and better life than it is now manifesting to the world."[3]

[2] Philip S. Foner, *The Life and Writings of Frederick Douglass* (4 vols., New York, 1950-55), II, 142.

[3] Speech before the American Anti-Slavery Society, May 11, 1847,

Douglass was not a gradualist, prepared to await for abuses to be corrected "in the fulness of time." At one of the reformist gatherings Henry Ward Beecher stated that rather than see slavery abolished as a result of mercenary motives, he would prefer to wait seventy-five years to have the evil struck down by the power of Christian faith. Douglass, who followed Beecher on the program, immediately replied that "if the reverend gentleman had worked on plantations where I have been, he would have met overseers who would have whipped him in five minutes out of his willingness to wait for liberty."[4]

Douglass' whole philosophy of reform was one of no quarter. He had little patience with well-intentioned men like the influential Unitarian pastor, William Ellery Channing, who deplored harsh language, seeking instead to win over the slaveholder by a policy of sweet reasonableness. Douglass, in a West India Emancipation celebration speech in August 1857, pointed out that "those who profess to favor freedom and yet deprecate agitation are men who want rain without thunder and lightning. Power concedes nothing without a demand. It never did and it never will."[5]

Douglass brought more to the reform movement than a "hard line" against the opposition. He had the gift of words. His sentences, although sonorous as befit the style of his day, arrested the attention. One example may suffice. Speaking in Rochester in 1852 on "The Meaning of July Fourth to the Negro," he posed a long rhetorical question concerning the "equal manhood of the Negro race":

Is it not astonishing that, while we are ploughing, planting, and reaping, using all kinds of mechanical

"The Right to Criticize American Institutions," Foner, *Life and Writings*, I, 237.

[4] *Annual Report of the American Anti-Slavery Society for 1853* (New York, 1853), pp. 51, 55.

[5] Foner, *Life and Writings*, II, 437.

tools, erecting houses, constructing bridges, building ships, working in metals of brass, iron, copper, silver and gold; that, while we are reading, writing and ciphering, acting as clerks, merchants and secretaries, having among us lawyers, doctors, ministers, poets, authors, editors, orators and teachers; that, while we are engaged in all manner of enterprises common to other men, digging gold in California, capturing the whale in the Pacific, feeding sheep and cattle on the hill-side, living, moving, acting, thinking, planning, living in families as husbands, wives and children, and, above all, confessing and worshipping the Christian's God, and looking hopefully for life and immortality beyond the grave, we are called upon to prove that we are men![6]

Douglass tinged his eloquence with humor. When Stephen A. Douglas was debating with Abraham Lincoln in 1858, Douglass had this to say of the Illinois Senator: "Once I thought he was about to make the name respectable, but now I despair of him, and must do the best I can for it myself."[7] In mockery Douglass was devastating, as evidenced in an address at Faneuil Hall on a June day in 1849: "I want to say a word about the Colonization Society of which Henry Clay is President. He is President of nothing else."[8] Cheers and applause greeted this quip at Clay's long-held White House ambitions. A clever mimic, Douglass was often called upon to deliver his "slaveholder's sermon"—a white clergyman's address to the bondmen.[9]

A typical example of Douglass' raillery was his account of the plight of Bishop James O. Andrew, whose family holdings in slaves precipitated the shattering

[6] *Ibid.*, p. 191.

[7] New Orleans *Daily Delta*, September 19, 1858.

[8] Foner, *Life and Writings*, I, 390.

[9] An excerpt from this sermon is reproduced in Benjamın Quarles, *Frederick Douglass* (Washington, 1948), p. 363.

sectional split in Methodism at the General Conference in New York in 1844:

> A slaveholding bishop, Bishop Andrew of South Carolina, married a slaveholding wife and became the possessor of fifteen slaves. At this time the Methodist Church in the North was of the opinion that bishops should not hold slaves. They remonstrated with the Conference to induce Bishop Andrew to emancipate his slaves. The Conference did it in this way. A resolution was brought in, when the Bishop was present, to the following effect: "Whereas Bishop Andrew has connected himself with slavery, and has thereby injured his itinerancy as a bishop . . ." It was not, "Whereas Bishop Andrew has connected himself with slavery, and has thereby become guilty, or has done a great wrong," but "has thereby injured his itinerancy as a bishop, we therefore resolve that Bishop Andrew be, and he hereby is,"—what?—"requested to suspend his labors as a bishop until he can get rid of"—what?—slavery?—"his impediment." (Laughter.) This was the name given to slavery. One might have inferred from the preamble that it was to get rid of his wife. (Laughter and loud cheers.)[10]

Douglass' considerable abilities as an abolitionist lecturer were heightened by the fact that he was a Negro. Here was no stammering fugitive from the South; here was no shiftless former slave unable to cope with the responsibilities of freedom. Here was a different breed of Negro, a different brand of abolitionist—a symbolic figure in race relations and in reform.

Douglass' accomplishments were trumpeted by abolitionists as an example of Negro improvability. As

[10] *Report of a Public Meeting Held at Finsbury Chapel, Moorfields, to receive Frederick Douglass, An American Slave on Friday, May 22, 1846* (London, 1846), p. 16.

no other colored man or woman, Douglass was a challenge to the widespread belief that the Negro was innately inferior in character, intelligence, and ability. To those who held that the rightness or wrongness of slavery pivoted on the capacity of the colored man, Douglass was a figure who could not be overlooked.

This image of Douglass as an able Negro had owed much to the publication of his autobiography, *Narrative of the Life of Frederick Douglass*, in 1845. Slave narratives were effective weapons in the abolitionist crusade. "It is often said that the evils of slavery are exaggerated. This is said by the masters," wrote Theodore Parker in 1847, after reading a number of slave narratives.[11] Douglass' book was by far the most effective of the lot, in part because he had written every line.[12] If its prose was simple and unadorned, the Douglass autobiography was forceful and vivid, a tribute to a man who less than seven years previously had been a slave calker in a Baltimore shipyard. Aside from what it said in the text, the *Narrative* spoke volumes for the capacity of the Negro. Indeed, Douglass always recognized that whatever he said or wrote had a meaning beyond the letter. When he launched his own weekly in Rochester in 1848, he appended his initials to his editorials in order to demonstrate that a former slave could write good English.[13]

If others saw him as a Negro before all else, the maturing Douglass never sought to escape such an identification. If some Negroes affected a studied indifference to race problems, he did not. He had no trace of the self-hate that leaves its mark on many members of an oppressed minority. "Whatever character or capacity you ascribe to us, I am not ashamed to be numbered

[11] "Letter to the People of the United States Touching the Matter of Slavery," December 22, 1847, in James K. Hosmer, ed. *The Slave Power*, by Theodore Parker (Boston, American Unitarian Association, n.d.), p. 55.

[12] Benjamin Quarles, ed. *Narrative of the Life of Frederick Douglass* (Cambridge, Mass., 1960), pp. xvi and following.

[13] *Frederick Douglass' Paper* (Rochester, New York), June 26, 1851.

with this race," he said in an address to the American and Foreign Anti-Slavery Society in May 1853.[14] "I shall bring the Negro with me," he once wrote in response to an invitation to lecture. " 'I am black, but comely,' is as true now as it was in the days of Solomon," he wrote in April 1849 in reviewing Wilson Armistead's lengthy book, *A Tribute for the Negro*.[15]

Douglass' sense of identification with his Negro fellows expressed itself in his concern over their plight. In the August 10, 1849 issue of his newspaper, *The North Star*, he proposed that an organization be formed exclusively of Negroes, for the purpose of opposing slavery and improving their own condition. The society would bear the title "The National League," with the motto "The union of the oppressed for the sake of freedom." After more than two months the suggestion had met with almost no response in Negro circles, much to the mortification of its sponsor. "We have among us our little Popes and Bishops," Douglass wrote in an acid editorial on October 26, 1849.[16]

Although Douglass had proposed an all-colored improvement society, he never thought of the Negro as apart from the mainstream of American life. As he put it, it was better to be a part of the whole than the whole of a part. "We are Americans, and as Americans we would speak to Americans," ran a sentence in a statement which the Colored Convention of 1853, meeting in Rochester, addressed to "the People of the United States." This lengthy address, composed in the main by Douglass, was entitled, "The Claims of Our Common Cause," and its insistent theme was the Americanism of the Negro.[17]

To Douglass one of the best ways that the Negro

14 Foner, *Life and Writings*, II, 246.
15 *Ibid.*, I, 380.
16 *The North Star* (Rochester, New York), August 10, October 26, 1849.
17 *Proceedings of the Colored National Convention held in Rochester, July 6th, 7th and 8th*, Rochester, 1853.

could exercise his full rights as an American citizen was to make contacts across the color line. Setting an example himself, he made it a point to defy Jim Crow practices in restaurants and on common carriers. To be "roughed up" for seeking service in places open to the public was no novelty to Douglass. Prominent Negroes who accepted segregation drew his fire. He wrote a bitter editorial chastising Elizabeth Taylor Greenfield (the "Black Swan") for giving a concert at Metropolitan Hall in New York in April 1853, to which whites only were admitted.[18]

Douglass was a protagonist for "integrated" schools. When his nine-year-old daughter was put in a room and taught separately at Seward Seminary in Rochester, his protest could be heard throughout the city. But his indignation did not spring solely from the protective sympathies of a parent. "If this were a private affair, only affecting myself and family, I should possibly allow it to pass without attracting public attention to it; but such is not the case," he wrote to the editor of the *Rochester Courier* on March 30, 1849. "It is a deliberate attempt to downgrade and injure a large class of persons, whose rights and feelings have been the common sport . . . for ages."[19]

Because he mixed with whites as a matter of principle, the Douglass of the abolitionist crusade felt no uneasiness in their presence. Within a few years after his flight from his master, his slavery-days dislike of whites had evaporated. His close association with them as fellow reformers left him permanently shorn of racist thinking. He viewed whites individually, not lumping them together.

By the time he had reached his prime as a man and as a reformer, Douglass had placed himself "upon

---

[18] *Frederick Douglass' Paper*, April 8, 1853.

[19] Foner, *Life and Writings*, I, 373. For a brief account of this episode, see Quarles, *Frederick Douglass*, p. 108.

grounds vastly higher and broader than any founded upon race or color," to use his own language. His own freedom from preconceptions enabled him to view things in the round. To him the abolitionist crusade had become less a separate movement than a national impulse; to him the struggle of the Negro was more of a human struggle than one of race. Paradoxically, it would seem, his belonging to a despised group had given him a deeper, more inclusive sense of human brotherhood. This broad concern led him to take an active role in reforms that were not Negro-centered, among them the woman's rights movement.[20]

In the closing years of the abolitionist crusade, Douglass was one of its chief ornaments. He carried himself with the assurance of one who had risen above obscure birth, color prejudice and all the Pandora's box of human besettings. Of the many assessments made of him by contemporaries, the words of Albion W. Tourgée would not seem wide of the mark: "Three classes of the American people are under special obligations to him: the colored bondman whom he helped to free from the chains which he himself had worn; the free persons of color whom he had helped make citizens; the white people of the United States whom he sought to free from the bondage of caste and relieve from the odium of slavery."[21]

Douglass' chief claim to enduring recollection has been voiced by a present-day poet, Robert E. Hayden, akin to Douglass by color if not by century. When freedom, writes Hayden, is finally won:

[20] At the convention at Geneva Falls, New York in July 1848, which formally inaugurated the women's rights movement in the United States, Douglass was the only male to play a prominent role. "We bid the women engaged in this movement our humble Godspeed," he wrote in an editorial in *The North Star*, July 28, 1848. The August 11, 1848, issue of this weekly carried a complete report of the proceedings of this historic meeting.

[21] *A Memorial of Frederick Douglass from the City of Boston* (Boston, 1896), p. 29.

this man, this Douglass, this former slave,
    this Negro
beaten to his knees, exiled, visioning a world
where none is lonely, none hunted, alien,
this man, superb in love and logic, this man
shall be remembered . . .[22]

[22] Langston Hughes and Arna Bontemps, eds. *The Poetry of the Negro, 1746-1949* (New York, 1949), p. 171.

PART III: THE ABOLITIONISTS
AND THE NEGRO

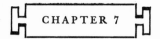
THE EMANCIPATION
OF THE NEGRO ABOLITIONIST

BY LEON F. LITWACK

WHEN William Lloyd Garrison launched his antislavery offensive, Negro abolitionists responded with warm enthusiasm. It "has roused up a Spirit in our Young People," one Negro leader wrote, "that had been slumbering for years."[1] Encouraged by this emergence of antislavery militancy among whites, Negroes helped to sustain *The Liberator*, joined the newly formed abolition societies, and cheered the announced intention of white abolitionists to establish a Negro industrial college. It appeared to be an auspicious beginning of effective interracial cooperation for mutual goals. But the attempted coalition, though not unproductive, was to reveal to the abolitionists—white and black—fundamental differences in assumptions, goals, and emphasis. "Thus, was the cause espoused," Negro leader Martin R. Delany wrote in 1852, "and thus did we expect much. But in all this, we were doomed to disappointment, sad, sad disappointment. Instead of realizing what we had hoped for, we find ourselves occupying the very same position in relation to our Anti-Slavery friends, as we do in relation to the proslavery part of the community—a mere secondary, underling position." The time had come, he insisted, for Negroes to break the chains of this bondage.[2]

[1] James Forten to William Lloyd Garrison, March 21, 1831, Garrison Papers, Boston Public Library.

[2] Martin R. Delany, *The Condition, Elevation, Emigration, and*

The Negro's initial enthusiasm was readily under-standable. Several years of independent Negro agitation had produced few results. And now, in the wake of the Nat Turner insurrection, new racial tensions gripped large sections of the country, for not only the South but the North, too, was forced to consider the possible conse-quences of a disgruntled racial minority in its midst. Both sections embraced the prevailing image of the Negro as an inferior race, incapable of assuming any of the responsibilities of citizenship, but in the North the Negro could at least challenge this assumption and strive to improve his position. Thus Garrison's anti-slavery debut had come at an opportune moment. Sub-jected to incessant harassment and racist propaganda, the Negro found encouragement in the advent of a movement which forcefully challenged the colonization-ists, the doctrine of racial inferiority, and any antislavery which did not include as an objective the elevation of the free Negro—politically, socially, and economically. The publication of *The Liberator*, Garrison declared, had "operated like a trumpet-call" on the Northern Negro community. "They have risen in their hopes and feelings to the perfect stature of men: in this city, every one of them is as tall as a giant."[3]

Notwithstanding some opposition or misgivings, most of the white abolition societies admitted Negroes, and some elevated them to positions on the executive com-mittee. The Negro's most important function, however, was that of an antislavery lecturer, for "eloquent" Negro speakers were able to draw "in most places far larger" audiences than their white counterparts. "The public have itching ears to hear a colored man speak," one abolitionist wrote to Garrison, "and particularly *a slave*.

Destiny of the Colored People of the United States (Philadelphia, 1852), p. 27.

[3] Garrison to Samuel Joseph May, February 14, 1831, Garrison Papers.

Multitudes will flock to hear one of this class speak."[4] Such was the response to Frederick Douglass, for example, that he soon became a leading abolitionist orator. The Negro who committed himself to the abolitionist cause incurred obvious risks. If the average white man expected anything of the Negro, it was that he acquiesce in the racial status quo and act the clownish, childish, carefree, irresponsible Uncle Tom that whites had long presumed him to be. But the Negro abolitionist betrayed the white man's trust and confidence; more than that, he confounded by his very example the white man's rationale for a benevolent guardianship over an inferior and helpless race. Rare, indeed, was the Negro abolitionist who did not have to face a hostile mob at some point in his antislavery career; it was the price he paid for having committed the most unpardonable sin of all— impudence.

In a society racked by racial tensions, misunderstanding and suspicion were almost bound to precipitate divisions between white and black abolitionists. Such questions as Negro membership in abolition societies and race mixing at antislavery functions, for example, provoked considerable debate among white abolitionists.[5] Many feared that a bold defiance of prevailing customs might endanger the eventual success of the antislavery cause. Outside of official gatherings, such intercourse also posed challenges to well-meaning white abolitionists. Sarah Forten, a Philadelphia Negro, recalled a white friend who told her that when walking with a Negro "the darker the night, the better Abolitionist was I."

[4] Theodore Weld to Gerrit Smith, October 23 [1839], in Gilbert H. Barnes and Dwight L. Dumond, eds., *Letters of Theodore Dwight Weld, Angelina Grimké Weld and Sarah Grimké, 1822-1844* (2 vols., New York, 1934), II, 811; John A. Collins to Garrison, January 18, 1842, quoted in Philip S. Foner, *The Life and Writings of Frederick Douglass* (4 vols., New York, 1950-55), I, 46.

[5] See Leon F. Litwack, *North of Slavery: The Negro in the Free States, 1790-1860* (Chicago, 1961), pp. 216-22.

Nevertheless, she was willing to forgive such conduct on the ground that abolitionists were often forced to make "great sacrifices to public sentiment." Still, it was disconcerting. "Many, very many anxious to take up the cross," she lamented, "but how few are strong enough to bear it."[6] Less forgiving was the Rev. Theodore S. Wright, who entreated white abolitionists to "annihilate in their own bosoms the cord of caste. We must be consistent—recognize the colored man in every respect as a man and brother." And this must be applied, he said, to "the church, the stage, the steamboat, the public house, in all places."[7]

Equally annoying to Negroes was the patronizing attitude of some white abolitionists and the application of a double standard which strongly suggested the Negro's inherent inferiority. After exiling himself to England, along with his white wife, Negro abolitionist William G. Allen wrote to Garrison that the English had treated him warmly, in contrast to the "patronizing (and, of course, insulting) spirit, even of hundreds of the American abolitionists," who had always seemed so overly conscious of color differences.[8] More pointedly, however, some Negroes complained that white abolitionists tended to establish different standards by which to judge the respective abilities of the two races. Thus whites expected less of Negro students in the classroom, spoke exultantly of the academic work of Negroes which would have been barely passable if performed by whites, and willingly tolerated Negro ministers and teachers who fell far short of the quali-

[6] Sarah Forten to Angelina Grimké, April 15, 1837, in Barnes and Dumond, eds., *Weld-Grimké Letters*, I, 380.

[7] *Address of the Rev. Theodore S. Wright before the Convention of the New York State Antislavery Society, . . . held at Utica, Sept. 20, 1837*, in Carter G. Woodson, ed., *Negro Orators and Their Orations* (Washington, D.C., 1925), p. 91.

[8] William G. Allen to Garrison, June 20, 1853, in *The Liberator*, July 22, 1853.

fications of whites for the same positions. "Our white friends," commented a Negro newspaper, "are deceived when they imagine they are free from prejudice against color, and yet are content with a lower standard of attainments for colored youth, and inferior exhibitions of talent on the part of colored men. This is, in our view, the worst feature of abolitionism—the one which grieves us most. It is the highest rock of danger; the only one on which we fear a shipwreck of our high and holy cause."[9]

But that was not all. Of what use, asked Negroes, was the right to vote, attend school, and enter the homes of abolitionists if it was still impossible to gain access to any but the most menial employment. The economic condition of the Negro was at best deplorable, and the new waves of immigrants, competing for many positions which Negroes had long monopolized, only made matters worse. Although some white abolitionists had agitated vigorously in the areas of civil rights and educational opportunities, little had been done in the way of economic assistance, except to call upon Negroes to improve themselves. Perhaps this simply reflected the dominant middle-class ideology of self-help which affected abolitionists, like other whites, but Negroes found little encouragement in such a doctrine and appealed to the antislavery movement to meet this true test of its stated determination to elevate the free Negro.

That the Negro should have placed considerable emphasis on the economic question is understandable. To many Negroes, in fact, this was a key point if they were ever to achieve the respect of white society. The abolitionist, then, was called upon to render practical assistance. But when the *Colored American* reviewed the economic plight of the Negro in the wake of the Panic of 1837, it noted that not one local abolitionist had placed a Negro in any conspicuous po-

[9] *The Colored American*, November 4, 1837.

sition in his business establishment; in fact, it could not even find a Negro in the offices of the New York Anti-Slavery Society. The newspaper beseeched abolitionists to correct this grievous situation, and preferably not by passing a resolution at their next convention.[10] In the absence of any measurable progress along these lines, Negro delegates to an abolition convention in 1852 charged that the antislavery movement had failed in its responsibility. Proposals had been made to leading abolitionists to employ Negroes in their commercial establishments but the appeal had been largely in vain. True, one delegate conceded, Negroes had found employment in Arthur Tappan's department store, but, he added, only in a menial capacity. "Wherever the colored man is connected with the houses of these gentlemen, it is as the lowest drudges."[11]

In demanding economic assistance, the Negro denied any desire for preferential treatment; he simply wanted an equal opportunity to compete for respectable employment. And since many white abolitionists were in a position to make this possible, they were asked to give practical implementation to their antislavery professions. After all, one Negro leader argued, the struggle for equal rights cannot be won on "the bare ground of abstract principles"; abolitionists must strive not only to abolish chattel slavery but "that other kind of slavery" which doomed the free Negro to economic dependence and pauperism; indeed, he deplored the preoccupation of abolitionists with such reforms as capital punishment, temperance, and women's rights, while they refused in their own establishments to afford equal economic opportunities to depressed Negroes.[12] But such strictures

10 *Ibid.*, July 28, 1838.
11 *The* [12th] *Annual Report of the American and Foreign Anti-Slavery Society, presented at New York, May 11, 1852* (New York, 1852), pp. 29-30.
12 Charles L. Reason, "The Colored People's 'Industrial College,'"

yielded few concrete results, thus prompting a Negro convention delegate to charge that some of those who professed to be "the strongest abolitionists" have refused to grant Negroes anything but sympathy; they have persistently evaded a more practical application of their principles. True, some "might employ a colored boy as a porter or packer," but most abolitionists "would as soon put a hod-carrier to the clerk's desk as a colored boy, ever so well educated though he be."[13] It was left to Frederick Douglass to issue a more direct challenge to the abolitionists: "What boss anti-slavery mechanic will take a black boy into his wheelwright's shop, his blacksmith's shop, his joiner's shop, his cabinet shop? Here is something *practical*; where are the whites and where are the blacks that will respond to it?"[14] The response was difficult to discern. This "is not the song that anti-slavery sung," wrote the disillusioned Delany, "in the first love of the new faith, proclaimed by its disciples."[15]

Perhaps the Negro had been unrealistic in his expectations. By the late 1830's, at any rate, Negro leaders began to reassess their role in the antislavery movement; increasing factional quarrels among the whites made such a reappraisal all the more necessary. Although some Negro abolitionists, such as Robert Purvis and Charles Remond, remained loyal Garrisonians, a growing restlessness within the Negro abolitionist camp manifested itself in more frequent demands for ideological and political independence; moreover, as Negroes became more articulate themselves, they tended increasingly to voice their own aspirations and to question the white

---

in Julia Griffiths, ed., *Autographs for Freedom* (Second Series, Auburn, Rochester, 1854), pp. 12-15.

[13] *Frederick Douglass' Paper*, May 18, 1855.

[14] *Ibid.*, March 4, 1853.

[15] Delany, *The Condition, Elevation, Emigration, and Destiny of the Colored People*, p. 28.

abolitionist's prerogative to speak for them. "As long as we let them think and act for us," the *Colored American* warned in 1839, "as long as we will bow to their opinions, and acknowledge that their word is counsel, and their will is law; so long they will outwardly treat us as men, while in their hearts they still hold us as slaves."[16]

Under the editorial supervision of Charles B. Ray and Philip A. Bell, the *Colored American* was the most prominent voice of this quest for independent expression. Published in New York, the newspaper first took to task the recently formed American Moral Reform Society, dominated largely by pro-Garrison Philadelphia Negroes, for its criticism of separate Negro conventions and the term "colored people," both of which allegedly implied degradation. To the *Colored American*, such positions not only were preposterous but they ignored the primary problems facing the Negro in a hostile society. "[W]hile these sages are frightened half to death, at the idea of being called colored, their FRIENDS and their FOES, in the convention, in the Assembly and in the Senate; through the pulpit and the press, call them nothing else but NEGROES, NEGROES, THE NEGROES OF PENNSYLVANIA."[17]

But the *Colored American* found even more distasteful the destructive factional warfare among abolitionists, for it threatened to undermine the antislavery effort. "The controversy," the newspaper asserted, "has . . . engrossed all their powers, and been prosecuted with a spirit wholly unworthy the character of the brethren engaged in it. . . . There is nothing to be gained by brother contending with brother."[18] That was heresy enough, in the eyes of some Garrisonians, but what followed must have confirmed their suspicions. Accepting political action as a legitimate antislavery weapon, the

16 *Colored American*, October 5, 1839.
17 *Ibid.*, August 26, September 2, 9, 1837; March 15, 1838.
18 *Ibid.*, October 7, 1837.

Colored American urged qualified Negroes to vote. When the Garrisonians then attacked the newspaper for abandoning the true faith (which deprecated political action), the editors affirmed their right to take an independent position. Notwithstanding the noble motives of most abolitionists, the *Colored American* insisted that they had no right to dictate antislavery doctrine to the Negro. "Sooner than abate one jot or tittle of our right to think, speak and act like men, we will suffer our enterprise to perish, and the *Colored American* will be numbered with the things that were."[19]

When the Garrisonian press claimed that separate Negro conventions perpetuated the idea of segregation, the *Colored American* and its supporters reaffirmed their defense of independent action. The multiplicity of wrongs inflicted on the Negro, Samuel Ward argued, made frequent meetings and independent organization indispensable; his white friends, he thought, would appreciate this need if they had "worn a colored skin from October '17 to June '40, as I have, in this pseudo-republic." Although conceding some valuable service by the white antislavery men, Ward was still dissatisfied, especially with those "abolitionists in *profession*" who had yet to conquer prejudice within themselves. "Too many," he regretted, ". . . best love the colored man at a distance."[20]

If there remained any doubts as to the determination of Negroes to voice their opinions, regardless of prevailing antislavery creeds, Henry Highland Garnet quickly dispelled them in 1843 when he told a national Negro convention that slaves would be justified in using violent means to win their freedom.[21] The convention refused by a single vote to endorse the address; nevertheless, the

[19] *Ibid.*, October 5, 1839.
[20] New York *National Anti-Slavery Standard*, July 2, 1840.
[21] Reprinted in Woodson, ed., *Negro Orators and Their Orations*, pp. 150-57.

issue had been permanently raised and the narrow vote suggested a growing impatience among Negroes with the traditional reliance on moral force to conquer slavery. But the aftermath of this debate was in many ways even more revealing. Condemned by *The Liberator* for his militant appeal to the slaves and for his endorsement of the Liberty Party, Garnet accepted the challenge. "If it has come to this," he replied, "that I must think and act as you do, because you are an abolitionist, or be exterminated by your thunder, then I do not hesitate to say that your abolitionism is abject slavery."[22] Six years later, an Ohio Negro convention ordered the "gratuitous" circulation of Garnet's convention address;[23] and by this time Frederick Douglass, who had opposed Garnet at the convention, was on the verge of breaking with the Garrisonians and adding his considerable force and prestige to the cause of independent Negro expression and agitation.

The Douglass heresy, made public at the American Anti-Slavery Society convention of 1851, struck particular dismay into the Garrisonian camp, for he had been their principal Negro spokesman. The estrangement stemmed from Douglass' revised position on the dissolution of the Union, political action, nonresistance, and the nature of the Constitution. In each case, he broke with prevailing Garrisonian ideology. To seek the dissolution of the Union, he now argued, was to violate his duty as an abolitionist, for it left the slave helpless; to abstain from voting was to ignore "a legitimate and powerful means for abolishing slavery"; and to hold that the Constitution was a proslavery document was to distort both its letter

[22] Henry Highland Garnet to Mrs. Maria W. Chapman, November 17, 1843, in Carter G. Woodson, ed., *The Mind of the Negro as Reflected in Letters Written During the Crisis, 1800-1860* (Washington, D.C., 1926), p. 194.

[23] *Minutes and Address of the State Convention of the Colored Citizens of Ohio, convened at Columbus, January 10th, 11th, 12th, and 13th, 1849* (Oberlin, 1849), p. 18.

and spirit.[24] The Garrisonians, Douglass charged, had abandoned the original purposes of the antislavery movement. "It started to free the slave," he contended. "It ends by leaving the slave to free himself. It started with the purpose to imbue the heart of the nation with sentiments favorable to the abolition of slavery, and ends by seeking to free the North from all responsibility of slavery." To Douglass, this was not practical antislavery; his alleged apostasy, he insisted, was not from "the Anti-Slavery Cause, for all know that I am as faithful to that cause as I ever was," but from "Garrisonism."[25]

Even before these ideological differences, there had been indications that Douglass was growing restive in the Garrisonian camp. When he first began to lecture, his white friends told him to confine his remarks to his experiences as a slave, for that was what the audiences wanted to hear. "Give us the facts," an abolitionist remarked to Douglass, "we will take care of the philosophy."[26] But Douglass soon found it impossible to confine himself in this way; indeed, his rapid intellectual development had already created some concern among his friends. "People won't believe you ever were a slave, Frederick, if you keep on this way," one abolitionist exclaimed, and another added, "Be yourself and tell your story. Better have a little of the plantation speech than not; it is not best that you seem too learned."[27]

When Douglass went to England in 1846 on a lecture tour, a Boston abolitionist, Mrs. Maria W. Chapman, expressed her concern to an English friend that Douglass might not be able to withstand the pressure of the anti-Garrison faction. Hearing of this letter, Douglass wrote Mrs. Chapman that "if you wish to drive me from the

[24] Frederick Douglass, *Life and Times of Frederick Douglass* (Boston, 1892), p. 322; see also Foner, *Life and Writings of Frederick Douglass*, II, 52-53, 149-50, 152-53, 155-57.

[25] Foner, *ibid.*, pp. 350, 425.

[26] Douglass, *Life and Times*, p. 269.

[27] *Ibid.*, pp. 269-70.

Anti-Slavery Society, put me under overseership and the work is done."[28] Three years earlier, Douglass had objected to abolitionist John Collins' injection of utopian socialism into antislavery meetings, for it imposed "an additional burden of unpopularity on our cause"; reprimanded by Mrs. Chapman for his remarks, Douglass later recalled that this "first offense against our antislavery Israel" had been "a strange and distressing revelation to me, and one of which I was not soon relieved."[29]

When the still restive Douglass decided to establish a newspaper in Rochester, despite the contrary advice of his Garrisonian friends, the subsequent break was almost assured, for he now had an independent means of expression. The newspaper project, Douglass contended, was no reflection on the quality of existing antislavery journals; the time had come, however, for Negroes to demonstrate their own capabilities, to produce their own authors, editors, and journals, and to be their "own representatives and advocates, not exclusively, but peculiarly—not distinct from, but in connection with our white friends."[30] But since independence also involved divergence in antislavery creed, it was insufferable to the Garrisonians. Before long, Garrison and Douglass were engaged in a vituperative editorial war, while other abolitionists looked on in dismay. To Douglass, it was ironic that the proved champions of human freedom—the Garrisonians—should presume to suppress dissent within their own movement. Apparently the only true faith was that proclaimed in Boston. "They talk down there," he wrote to Gerrit Smith, "just as if the Anti-

28 Frederick Douglass to Maria W. Chapman, March 29, 1846, in Foner, *Life and Writings of Frederick Douglass*, I, 144.

29 Douglass, *Life and Times*, pp. 282-83. See also Douglass to Chapman, September 10, 1843, in Foner, *Life and Writings of Frederick Douglass*, I, 110-12.

30 *The North Star*, December 3, 1847.

Slavery Cause belonged to them—and as if all Anti-Slavery ideas originated with them and that no man has a right to 'peep or mutter' on the subject, who does not hold letters patent from them."[31] Such subordination was more than an ex-slave could accept.

Whatever the merits of the conflicting abolition doctrines, Douglass' actions, when combined with those of various state and national Negro conventions, dramatized the increasing demand of Negro abolitionists for a greater voice in the tactics, strategy, and creed of the movement. And this reflected not only conflict over doctrine but considerable dissatisfaction with the pace of the equal rights struggle in the North. Some Negroes questioned whether or not racial equality had been relegated to a position of secondary importance in the abolition crusade. "I have seen constitutions of abolition societies," one Negro leader charged, "where nothing was said about the improvement of the man of color! They have overlooked the great sin of prejudice. They have passed by this foul monster, which is at once the parent and offspring of slavery."[32] Pursuing this subject, the *Colored American* charged that the American Anti-Slavery Society had made "secondary and collateral what ought to have been the primary object of all their efforts. In their strong zeal and fiery indignation against slavery in the South, they half overlooked slavery in the North." Indeed, more is known of slavery in the Carolinas "than of the deep and damning thralldom which grinds to the dust, the colored inhabitants of New York."[33] On the eve of the election of 1860, Douglass noted with regret that the equal suffrage movement in New York was almost exclusively in the hands of Negroes, for neither

[31] Douglass to Gerrit Smith, August 18, 1853, in Foner, *Life and Writings of Frederick Douglass*, II, 270.
[32] *Address of the Rev. Theodore S. Wright . . . Sept. 20, 1837*, in Woodson, ed., *Negro Orators and Their Orations*, pp. 90-91.
[33] *Colored American*, May 18, 1839.

abolitionists nor Republicans "seem to care much for it."[34] But these differences in emphasis were perhaps inevitable and never effectively reconciled; the black abolitionist was generally moved by compelling personal need, his white cohort acted more from the abstractions of conscience; for one, the primary problem was the Negro; for the other, the slave. Each sought, in his own way, to enlarge the area of freedom.

During the crucial decade of the 1850's, the Negro abolitionist grew ever more restive and impatient. The Fugitive Slave Act, the resurgence of the American Colonization Society, the unsuccessful attempts to win equal suffrage, and, finally, the Dred Scott decision, impressed many Negroes with the increasing helplessness of their position in the face of the white man's apparent determination to maintain racial supremacy. Despite two decades of militant antislavery, the Negro's position seemed little improved. Moreover, the emergence of the Republican party made the very term "antislavery" difficult to define with any precision. If the Republican party was "antislavery," why did it refuse to move against racial oppression in the free states? and why in some areas did it proclaim principles of white supremacy? If the Kansas free staters were, indeed, "antislavery," how does one account for their determined efforts to keep all Negroes out of the territory? The answer was obvious: it was possible to be both "antislavery" and anti-Negro, to proclaim both free soil and white supremacy. "Opposing slavery and hating its victims," Douglass observed, "has come to be a very common form of abolitionism."[35] Disillusioned with Republican pronouncements, an Illinois Negro leader was moved to declare that he cared "nothing about that antislavery which wants to make the Territories free, while it is unwilling to extend to me, as a man, in the free

[34] *Douglass' Monthly*, November 1860.
[35] *Frederick Douglass' Paper*, April 5, 1856.

States, all the rights of a man."[36] Of course, many white abolitionists had come to an identical conclusion about the "cowardly and contemptible" antislavery of the Republican party. When Stephen S. Foster accordingly called for a convention to reorganize the abolitionist movement, Douglass enthusiastically endorsed the proposal. Reviewing the history of the antislavery struggle, the Negro leader contrasted the heroic beginnings of militant abolitionism with the "Sentimental Abolitionism" of the Republican party, the "fratricidal conduct" of the American Anti-Slavery Society, and the political impotency of the Liberty party. If the "noble objects" of Foster's convention were put into effect, abolitionists— white and black—might once again unite into "one solid abolition organization" which would agitate for the exercise of Federal and State power to abolish the institution of slavery. Thus might the confusion between Republican antislavery and true abolitionism be ended.[37]

But in the absence of any such unified movement, the Negro abolitionist continued to advance an increasingly independent position. Tired of exhortations to be patient and await that "impartial and just God" who would inevitably rid the nation of slavery, Negroes began to talk of organized insubordination, slave insurrections, the use of physical force to resist the newly passed Fugitive Slave Act, the organization of state leagues to combat repressive legislation, and, in view of the Dred Scott decision, some even argued that Negroes no longer had any obligation to the United States and should welcome the overthrow of the government if necessary to exterminate slavery.[38] The vindication of the Negro's

[36] *The Liberator*, July 13, 1860.
[37] *Douglass' Monthly*, October 1860.
[38] See, for example, the speeches of Dr. John S. Rock and Robert Purvis, as reported in *The Liberator*, May 22, 1857; March 16, May 18, 1860, and H. Ford Douglass, in Herbert Aptheker, ed., *A Documentary History of the Negro People in the United States* (New York, 1951), pp. 366-68; *Proceedings of a Convention of the Colored*

rights now seemed to demand a position more advanced than that of moral suasion. "Every slavehunter who meets a bloody death in his infernal business," Douglass wrote, "is an argument in favor of the manhood of our race."[39] Had not John Brown demonstrated, a Boston Negro leader asserted, that physical force might prove more effective than the "gradual diffusion of anti-slavery gospel." Although he hoped that slavery might be abolished peaceably, "if, as appears to be the case, there is no use in crying peace, then let us not shrink from the responsibility. My motto has always been, 'Better die freemen than live to be slaves.' "[40]

The espousal of increasingly radical measures mirrored the Negro's deepening sense of alienation from American society. The antislavery crusade had not altered the image of the Negro in the eyes of white America, nor measurably improved his position. "We are slaves in the midst of freedom," Delany wrote, "waiting patiently, and unconcernedly—indifferently, and stupidly, for masters to come and lay claim to us, trusting to their generosity, whether or not they will own us and carry us into endless bondage. . . . I must admit, that I have no hopes in this country—no confidence in the American people."[41] The movement which Delany advocated in the 1850's, that of emigration, began to attract more Negroes; it enunciated a vigorous race nationalism, rejected the democratic pretensions of white Americans, questioned the motives and effectiveness of white abolitionists, and urged the establishment of an independent Negro state.

Men of Ohio, held in the City of Cincinnati, on the 23d, 24th, 25th and 26th Days of November, 1858 (Cincinnati, 1858), pp. 6-7; *Proceedings of the Second Annual Convention of the Colored Citizens of the State of California* (San Francisco, 1856), pp. 14, 19.

[39] *Frederick Douglass' Paper*, June 2, 1854.

[40] *The Liberator*, March 16, 1860.

[41] Delany, *The Condition, Elevation, Emigration, and Destiny of the Colored People*, p. 155; Delany to Garrison, May 14, 1852, in Woodson, ed., *Mind of the Negro*, p. 293.

To remain any longer in the United States was to remain "the dupes of, and deluded by the whites, even our most professed anti-slavery friends." The Negro must find his own identity, apart from that of the whites. "The truth is," an emigration convention declared, "we are not identical with the Anglo-Saxon or any other race of the Caucasian or pure white type of the human family, and the sooner we know and acknowledge this truth, the better for ourselves and posterity."[42] Although most Negroes rejected emigration, they did so uneasily, for the logic of the argument seemed difficult to refute.

The emigrationists had challenged the assumption of most white and Negro abolitionists that racial equality was a realizable goal in the United States and that some day Negroes would attain the level of the white man's civilization. But some Negroes chose to question that level. Were white standards of success worthy models for the Negro? Did success in war and material gain, for example, truly constitute "the great ends of human existence"? Was there any other standard of excellence than that "which revolves around the almighty dollar"? In raising these questions, *The Anglo-African Magazine* regretted the fact that most Negroes wanted only to reach the level of the white man; the apparent ideal is "comfortable subsistance; with many, a comfortable room and bedroom, on the same floor, in a front building; with many, in addition, a handsome carpet, a few mahogany chairs, a sofa, and a piano." Most Negro men, it found, would be well satisfied with a "Morphy cap, one well-fitting suit of clothes, patent-leather boots of the latest fashion, an ingot or two of gold in the form of a chain hanging over their breast, a long nine and a sherry cobbler at the St. Charles." And the ideal for Negro women "reaches no higher than the polka and redowa, and agreeable

[42] *Proceedings of the National Emigration Convention of Colored People; held at Cleveland, Ohio, . . . the 24th, 25th, and 26th of August, 1854* (Pittsburgh, 1854), pp. 5, 40.

flirting at a picnic." Such goals, the magazine argued, were unoriginal, "imitative and artificial." The Negro must seek a higher goal; despite his present degradation, he must "look up, above, and beyond the whites, and determine to whip, to beat, to excel them. . . . Once bent upon beating this Yankee Nation, who are beating all creation, and there will come upon us an inspiration, a power, hitherto unknown—hitherto unfelt by any other men, or race of men." The nature of this higher ideal was not indicated, except to suggest that it would not be money; economic changes, the magazine concluded, were already anticipating a day when "wealth will cease to be God of the American heart" and give way to some "nobler idolatry."[43]

On the eve of the Civil War, most Negroes aspired no higher than the goal of incorporation into white American society. Nevertheless, a strong undercurrent of race pride and consciousness, made explicit in the emigration movement, was clearly present, and white reformers would henceforth have to contend with its implications. Although the "wealth, the intellect, the Legislation (State and Federal), the pulpit, and the science of America" still tended to dismiss the Negro "as something less than a man," one Negro journal prophesied in 1859 that such arguments would become increasingly insupportable and that "this great black sluggard" may yet "shake the pillars of the commonweal."[44] In the meantime, the Negro had begun to produce his own spokesmen and media of expression; he had achieved increased recognition within the antislavery movement, and though he continued to express his appreciation of the efforts and sacrifices of white abolitionists, he made it clear that they were no longer to dominate the cause or confine its limits. The entire question of racial equality was at is-

[43] "A Word to Our People," *The Anglo-African Magazine*, I (1859), pp. 293-98.
[44] "Apology," *ibid.*, p. 1.

sue, not merely the elimination of chattel slavery. "The time is come," a Negro conference announced in 1854, "when our people must assume the rank of a first-rate power in the battle against caste and Slavery; it is emphatically our battle; no one else can fight it for us, and with God's help we must fight it ourselves.—Our relations to the Anti-Slavery movement must be and are changed. Instead of depending upon it we must lead it."[45]

[45] *Frederick Douglass' Paper*, May 18, 1855.

CHAPTER 8

A BRIEF FOR EQUALITY:
THE ABOLITIONIST REPLY TO THE
RACIST MYTH, 1860-1865

BY JAMES M. MC PHERSON

ONE of the most formidable obstacles to the abolition of slavery and the extension of equal rights to free Negroes was the widespread popular and scientific belief, North as well as South, in the innate inferiority of the Negro race. Most white Americans believed that Negroes were by nature shiftless, slovenly, childlike, dull-witted, savage, and thus incapable of assimilation as equals into white society. Since the beginning of the antislavery movement, abolitionists had been confronted by arguments that Negroes belonged to a servile and indolent race; that they would work only under compulsion; that they could not take care of themselves in freedom and would revert to barbarism; and that emancipation would bring economic and social ruin to the South and to the nation.[1]

For thirty years many abolitionists worked tirelessly but without much success to combat these beliefs. When

---

[1] The following studies treat this subject in considerable detail: William S. Jenkins, *Pro-Slavery Thought in the Old South* (Chapel Hill, 1935), pp. 242-84; Guion G. Johnson, "A History of Racial Ideologies in the United States with Reference to the Negro," MS. in the Schomburg Collection of the New York Public Library; William R. Stanton, *The Leopard's Spots: Scientific Attitudes Toward Race in America, 1815-59* (Chicago, 1960). For a good example of the many pamphlets and books arguing the innate inferiority of the Negro, see J. H. Van Evrie, *Negroes and Negro "Slavery"; The First an Inferior Race—the Latter its Normal Condition* (New York, 1853).

Civil War came in 1861 and emancipation became an imminent possibility, the debate about the Negro's racial character was sharpened by a new urgency and a heightened relevance. Abolitionist attempts to make the war a crusade for emancipation and equal rights were handicapped by the prevailing belief in the Negro's genetic inferiority. During the war, abolitionists redoubled their efforts to show that slavery and a hostile environment, not innate inferiority, had caused the degradation of the American Negro. They declared that if this environment was transformed by the abolition of slavery and of racial discrimination, the Negro would prove himself a constructive, capable, and creative member of society.

I

Abolitionists were well aware that the common belief in the Negro's racial inferiority constituted one of the main justifications for slavery. In the final analysis, wrote Sydney Howard Gay[2] in 1860, slavery was based "upon the assumed fact that the negroes are an inferior race, over whom the whites possess not merely an artificial superiority dependent upon the existing circumstances of their mutual position, but a natural superiority, which exists and ever must exist." "In truth," said Frederick Douglass, "this question is at the bottom of the whole [slavery] controversy." Until the doctrine of the diversity and inequality of races was discredited, abolitionists reasoned, the theory and practice of slavery would remain strongly entrenched in America. "We cannot expect," said Gilbert Haven, the militant, red-headed Methodist clergyman, "the complete removal of this curse from our land until we stand boldly and heartily

[2] Gay was a veteran Garrisonian abolitionist. He had edited the New York *National Anti-Slavery Standard*, organ of the American Anti-Slavery Society, from 1843 to 1857. In the latter year he joined the editorial staff of the New York *Tribune*. In 1862 Gay became managing editor of the *Tribune*, a position of great influence.

upon the divine foundation—the perfect unity of the human race."[3]

The abolitionist attack on the concept of racial inequality centered on two fronts: (1) an attempt to demonstrate, from the Bible, from science, from history, and from observed facts, the essential equality of the races; and (2) an attempt to show that the unfavorable environmental conditions of slavery and segregation, rather than natural inferiority, had caused the vices and disabilities of the American Negro.

The ante-bellum generation had been fond of quoting the Bible as a weapon in the slavery controversy, and abolitionists could point to several passages of scripture which "proved" the unity of the human race. The book of Genesis told the story of the creation of *man* (not men) in God's own image. In his famous sermon on Mars Hill, St. Paul told the people of Athens that God "hath made of one blood all nations of men for to dwell on the face of the earth." Gilbert Haven contended that the Bible sanctioned the complete equality and fraternity of the races. Solomon treated the Queen of Sheba, an Ethiopian, "with the utmost respect and cordiality"; Moses married an Ethiopian; a Negro was called by God to be one of the prophets and teachers of the Church at Antioch. "More than this," declared Haven, "the Bible constantly proclaims the absolute oneness of the race of man, in Adam, Noah, and Christ."[4]

By 1860, however, the Bible argument was pretty well played out. Thirty years of controversy had only shown that the Bible could be quoted effectively on both sides of the slavery issue. Science, especially ethnology and anthropology, commanded a large and growing influence in the mid-nineteenth century. Ethnology in the

[3] New York *Tribune*, December 1, 1860; Philip S. Foner, *The Life and Writings of Frederick Douglass* (4 vols., New York, 1950-55), II, 294; Gilbert Haven, *National Sermons, Speeches, and Letters on Slavery and Its War* (Boston, 1869), p. 150.

[4] *Ibid.*, p. 137.

hands of Josiah Nott, Louis Agassiz, Samuel G. Morton, and George Gliddon (a group which came to be known as the "American School" of Anthropology), who taught that the various races of mankind constituted separate and distinct species with the Negro at the bottom of the scale, had become a major weapon in the defense of slavery.[5] Abolitionists realized that to combat these teachings they must themselves use the weapons of ethnology. Few abolitionists had any formal anthropological training, but as a group they were well educated and highly literate; and given the rather crude state of nineteenth century ethnological knowledge, the industrious layman could become almost as well informed as the professional scientist.

Several abolitionists made intensive studies of the question of race. To refute the American School of Anthropology, abolitionists quoted prominent European naturalists who argued for the unity of origin and equality of races. In 1861, for example, the *Anti-Slavery Standard* published a review of *L'Unité de l'Espèce Humaine*, by M. de Quatrefarges, Professor of Natural History and Ethnology at the Museum of Natural History in Paris. Using the classifications of Linnaeus and Lamarck, M. de Quatrefarges defined mankind as a single species; racial differences were the result of variety within the species developed by conditions of environment and transmitted by heredity. M. de Quatrefarges used his vast knowledge to deny the existence of any fundamental and immutable differences in the mental capacities of various races.[6]

Abolitionists cited several other prominent European scientists who maintained the unity and equality of races: Dr. R. G. Latham, the British ethnologist; Dumont d'Urville, the great French geographer and navi-

[5] For a discussion of the American School of Anthropology, see Stanton, *Leopard's Spots.*

[6] *National Anti-Slavery Standard*, November 9, 1861.

gator; George Louis Leclerc Buffon, the brilliant nat-
uralist; and finally, the renowned Alexander von Humboldt, who wrote: "Whilst we maintain the unity of
the human species, we at the same time repel the depressing assumption of superior and inferior races of
men." Through Humboldt, said Charles Sumner, "Science is enlisted for the Equal Rights of All."[7]

Sumner may have overstated the case, since American
science, at least, spoke overwhelmingly for inequality.
But the ethnologists of the world spoke with a discordant
and divided voice on the subject of race in 1860. Abolitionists argued forcefully (and accurately) that science
had failed to *prove* the innate inferiority of the Negro.
"You may read Prichard, and Pinkerton, and Morton,
and Pickering, and Latham, and all the rest—the whole
library of Ethnology," said Theodore Tilton in 1863,
"and in the confusion of knowledge you will find one
thing clear—and that is, science has not yet proved, in
advance, that the negro race is not to be a high-cultured,
dominant race—rulers of their own continent, and perhaps dictators to the world."[8]

The endless refinements of the scientific racial arguments probably passed over the heads of the general
public. The average man was more interested in concrete examples; and the advocates of Negro inferiority
thought they had one incontrovertible example to show
him: the supposed barbarous and uncivilized condition
of Africa. What contribution to civilization and progress
had Africa ever made, asked proslavery writers derisively?

This was a potentially damaging argument, and abo-

[7] Charles Sumner, *Works of Charles Sumner* (15 vols., Boston,
1870-73), XIII, 155-57.

[8] Theodore Tilton, *The Negro* (New York, 1863), p. 5. This was a
speech delivered by Tilton at the annual convention of the American Anti-Slavery Society in 1863. Several thousand copies were published by the Society. Tilton was a young and eloquent abolitionist
who in 1863 became editor of the *Independent*, largest religious-
political weekly in the world.

litionists advanced boldly to meet it. Negro abolitionists were in the forefront of the struggle to vindicate Africa. The central theme of their argument was that the ancient Egyptians, fountainhead of Western civilization, were a Negroid or partially Negroid race. "The ancient Egyptians were not white people," declared Frederick Douglass, "but were, undoubtedly, just about as dark in complexion as many in this country who are considered Negroes." Their hair "was far from being of that graceful lankness which adorns the fair Anglo-Saxon head." "I claim that the blacks are the legitimate descendants of the Egyptians," said William Wells Brown, a prominent Negro abolitionist, lecturer, and author, in 1862. While the ancestors of the proud Anglo-Saxons were roaming the forests of Northern Europe as savages, declared Brown, Africa had created the foundations of Western civilization and passed on this precious heritage to the Jews, Greeks, Romans, and ultimately to Western Europe. In reply to a derisive reference to Negroes by William L. Yancey of Alabama, Brown told a group of Boston abolitionists in 1860: "When Mr. Yancey's ancestors were bending their backs to the yoke of William the Conqueror, the ancestors of his slaves were revelling in the halls of science and learning. If the Hon. Senator from Alabama wants antecedents, he shall have them; and upon such, I claim a superiority for the negro. (Loud applause.)"[9]

But the glories of ancient Ethiopia were not sufficient to convince many skeptics of the inherent equality of Negroes. Modern Africa stood in the way. Most nineteenth century Americans considered Africa a backward, barbaric continent, devoid of any trace of civilization or culture. Most world travelers who visited the dark

---

[9] Foner, *Life and Writings*, II, 296; Brown's statements published by *The Liberator*, June 6, 1862, and October 26, 1860. These concepts of Afro-American equality were most vigorously stated by William Wells Brown in a book entitled *The Black Man, His Antecedents, His Genius, and His Achievements*, published in 1863.

continent concurred with Bayard Taylor's opinion that the Negro was "the lowest type of humanity on the face of the earth." Not being world travelers themselves, abolitionists perforce obtained much of their information about Africa from such unflattering sources. Consequently they admitted that contemporary Africa stood low in the scale of civilization, but they advanced a cyclical theory of history, by which nations rose and fell, and would rise again, to explain Africa's temporary eclipse. At one time Africa was the center of learning and culture, said Gerrit Smith, but in the course of events she declined in importance. Africa's "inherent, inborn faculties," however, "are neither multiplied nor diminished because developed in one age, and undeveloped in another. . . . Changes of circumstances, along with other causes, alternately lift up and depress a people." "Do you call the negro race inferior?" asked Theodore Tilton in 1863.

> No man can yet pronounce that judgment safely. How will you compare races, to give each its due rank? . . . You must compare them in their fulfillments, not in their beginnings. . . . How will you estimate the rank of the Roman people? By its beginnings? By its decline? By neither. You rank it at the height of its civilization. . . . The Germans, today, give philosophy to Europe—but you can count the years backward when the Germans, now philosophers, were barbarians. . . . No man can now predict the destiny of the negro race. That race is yet so undeveloped—that destiny is yet so unfulfilled—that no man can say, and no wise man pretends to say, what the negro race shall finally become.[10]

[10] Gerrit Smith to Montgomery Blair, April 2, 1862, public letter published in *The Liberator*, April 18; Tilton, *The Negro*, pp. 4-5.

Some abolitionists, moreover, did not entirely accept the dark portrait of modern Africa drawn by most travelers. Several months after the outbreak of the Civil War a remarkable little book, written anonymously and entitled *Record of an Obscure Man*, was published in Boston. It purported to be the memoir of a man who had visited a friend in the South in 1842 and had talked with him about the capabilities of the Negro race. In reality it was a fictional essay by Mrs. Mary Putnam, elder sister of James Russell Lowell. Mrs. Putnam asserted that most travelers who visited Africa penetrated no farther than the coastal areas, whose inhabitants had been subjected to debasing contact with rapacious slave traders, "to which their degradation is to be attributed, rather than to inherent depravity or stupidity." Travelers who had ventured into the interior of Africa had found people of finer appearance, gentler manners, greater industry and honesty. "When Central Africa has been fully laid open to the world," she argued, "we shall be called upon to revise many of our opinions."[11]

Displaying great learning, Mrs. Putnam quoted from world-famous explorers who had ventured into Central Africa: Hugh Clapperton, Mungo Park, and Dixon Denham. "Read what Denham says of the inhabitants of the interior," she urged; "of their industry, their skill in weaving and dyeing, of their love of music and poetry." Denham described the natives as "hospitable, kind-hearted, honest, and liberal." Anticipating the findings of modern scholars by nearly three generations, Mrs. Putnam decried the notion that Negroes had been civilized and uplifted by slavery and Christianity. Slavery, she said, had only suppressed their native virtues and intelligence.[12]

[11] [Mary Putnam], *Record of an Obscure Man* (Boston, 1861), pp. 91-92.
[12] *Ibid.*, pp. 92-96.

In one of the best expressions of "cultural relativism" to come out of the nineteenth century, Mrs. Putnam warned against accepting at face value the somber descriptions of Africa by certain Westerners. "All men are prone to judge the manners of other countries by the standard of their own," she wrote, "and the civilized world views from its own stand-point that which it calls savage. We find the Africans barbarians, wherever customs differ from ours; but they are on the road to civilization, when their nonsense suits our nonsense."[13]

Abolitionists warmly praised Mary Putnam's little book. "Such a studied tribute to the negro, in this way, we have never had the fortune to see," said Garrison in his review of *Record of an Obscure Man*. "The African is contemplated as a man apart from his accidents, and heavy must be the load of prejudice against color that is not lightened by the spirit and the truthfulness with which his claims are urged." The *Anglo-African*, a Negro newspaper in New York City, declared that Mrs. Putnam had provided "the best, the fullest and most satisfactory record" of the Negro "it has been our fortune to meet with. . . . She recognizes in the negro an original, inherent germ force of his own, solemn, grand, endowed with energy and vitality enough to develop civil, social, and intellectual greatness out of his own resources."[14] Abolitionists adopted many of Mrs. Putnam's arguments in their crusade for emancipation and equal rights.

II

Some abolitionists, although they argued vigorously for the essential *equality* of the Negro race, nevertheless believed in inherent racial *differences*. James Freeman Clarke had declared that "it is a mistake to speak of the

[13] *Ibid.*, p. 123.
[14] *The Liberator*, November 29, 1861; *Anglo-African*, February 15, 1862.

African as an inferior race to the Caucasian. It is doubtless different from this, just as this is also different from the Malay, the Indian, the Mongolian. There are many varieties in the human family."[15] By today's ethnological standards this was an accurate statement, but Clarke and several other abolitionists parlayed it into a more questionable thesis: that the Negro was inferior to the Caucasian in certain aspects of the hard-headed, practical business and professional world, but superior in the realm of religion and the arts. In 1862, for example, Moncure Conway, the son of a Virginia slaveholder and an abolitionist exile from his own state, penned an article for the Boston *Commonwealth*. Negroes were a graceful people, he said, full of exuberance and picturesque charm. It was the Negro who gave to the South its warmth and radiance. The colored people had fertile, poetic imaginations. They had contributed much to Southern culture, and would contribute more in freedom. "In our practical, anxious, unimaginative country, we need an infusion of this fervid African element, so child-like, exuberant, and hopeful," wrote Conway. "We ought to prize it, as we do rare woods and glowing gems imported from the gorgeous tropics." One year later, writing for an English audience, Conway stated that Negroes

> seem to me to be weaker in the direction of the understanding, strictly speaking, but to have strength and elegance of imagination and expression. Negro sermons, fables, and descriptions are in the highest degree pictorial, abounding in mystic interpretations which would delight a German transcendentalist. My belief is, that there is a vast

[15] James Freeman Clarke, *Slavery in the United States: A Sermon Delivered on Thanksgiving Day, 1842* (Boston, 1843), p. 24. See also James Freeman Clarke, "Condition of the Free Colored People of the United States," *The Christian Examiner*, LXVI, Fifth Series, IV (1859), 246-65; and Clarke to Senator Henry Wilson, April 17, 1860, Clarke Papers, Houghton Library, Harvard University.

deal of high art yet to come out of that people in America. Their songs and hymns are the only original melodies we have.[16]

In his widely publicized speech on *The Negro*, Theodore Tilton proclaimed the Negro "the most religious man among men. Is not the religious nature the highest part of human nature? Strike out the negro then, and you destroy the highest development of the highest part of human nature." It was a mistake, thought Tilton,

> to rank men only by a superiority of intellectual faculties. God has given to man a higher dignity than the reason. It is the moral nature. . . . In all those intellectual activities which take their strange quickening from the moral faculties—processes which we call instincts, or intuitions—the negro is superior to the white man—equal to the white woman. The negro race is the feminine race of the world. . . .
>
> We have need of the negro for his . . . aesthetic faculties. . . . We have need of the negro for his Music. . . . But let us stop questioning whether the negro is a man. In many respects he is a superior man. In a few respects, he is the greatest of men. I think he is certainly greater than those men who clamor against giving him a chance in the world, as if they feared something from the competition.[17]

Among American natural scientists of the mid-nineteenth century, Louis Agassiz was foremost in prestige and authority. His adherence to the "American School" of Anthropology gave it an influence it could not otherwise have commanded. As a Harvard Professor Agassiz had many acquaintances in Boston's intellectual circles; several of these acquaintances were abolitionists, and

[16] Boston *Commonwealth*, October 18, 1862; Moncure D. Conway, *Testimonies Concerning Slavery* (1865, London, 2d edn.), p. 71.

[17] Tilton, *The Negro*, pp. 11-13.

Agassiz's racial ideas could not help but have some effect on their thinking. Samuel Gridley Howe was one
such friend. In 1863-64 Howe served as a member of
the American Freedmen's Inquiry Commission (a body
created by the Lincoln Administration to investigate
the condition and needs of the freed slaves). In connection with his research for this Commission, Howe asked
Agassiz for his views on the effect of race on the problems of emancipation and reconstruction. Agassiz replied that he welcomed the prospect of emancipation,
but warned against granting equal political and social
rights to freedmen. He reviewed the history of the Negro
and concluded that colored people were "indolent, play-
ful, sensual, imitative, subservient, good-natured, versa-
tile, unsteady in their purpose, devoted and affection-
ate." The Negro had never shown himself qualified for
self-government. "I cannot," concluded Agassiz, "think
it just or safe to grant at once to the negro all the privileges which we ourselves have acquired by long struggles. . . . Let us beware of granting too much to the
negro race in the beginning, lest it become necessary
hereafter to deprive them of some of the privileges which
they may use to their own and our detriment."[18]

Howe was torn between his respect for Agassiz's learning and his own equalitarian principles. "I would not
only advocate entire freedom, equal rights and privileges," he told Agassiz, but "open competition for social
distinction." Howe was nevertheless influenced by some
of Agassiz's notions regarding the mental inferiority of
Negroes. In a book on Canadian Negroes published in
1864, Howe lamented that the younger generation, who
had never known slavery and who enjoyed equal civil
and political rights in Canada, had failed to produce
as many outstanding individuals, in proportion to their

[18] Howe to Agassiz, August 3, 1863, Agassiz to Howe, August 9,
10, 1863, in Elizabeth C. Agassiz, *Louis Agassiz: His Life and Correspondence* (2 vols., Boston, 1885), II, 591-608.

numbers, as the white community. Howe took into account the prejudice, discrimination, and lack of opportunity which might have accounted for this failure, but concluded that even with these disabilities the Negro community should have produced more superior men. Teachers to whom he talked testified that Negroes learned just as fast as whites in the lower grades, but fell behind at the higher levels "when they come to studies which tax the higher mental powers, or the reasoning and combining faculties." Colored people, thought Howe, were "quick of perception; very imitative; and they rapidly become intelligent. But they are rather knowing, than thinking people. They occupy useful stations in life; but such as require quick perceptions, rather than strong sense."[19]

To the modern reader familiar with the view of contemporary anthropology that there is no proof of significant differences in the mental capacities of various races, the opinions of Howe and other abolitionists who thought like him appear to border on racism. Even the belief of Tilton, Conway, and others in the inherent superiority of the Negro in the "feminine" virtues— religion and the arts—implies an assumption of Negro *inferiority* in the "masculine" virtues of reason and enterprise. Thus a case of modified racism could be made out against certain of the abolitionists, but only by ignoring the fact that in the contemporary spectrum of opinion on race, even these abolitionists were far in the liberal vanguard. The extraordinary thing about the abolitionists as a group was not that some of them believed in racial differences, but that in a nation where popular belief *and* scientific learning overwhelmingly proclaimed the Negro's absolute inferiority, there were other aboli-

[19] Howe to Agassiz, August 18, 1863, *ibid.*, p. 614; Samuel G. Howe, *The Refugees from Slavery in Canada West* (Boston, 1864), pp. 81-82.

tionists who dared to declare their faith in the essential equality of all men, regardless of race.

III

Most abolitionists agreed that the adverse environmental effects of slavery and discrimination, rather than innate deficiencies, were responsible for the practical inferiority of the Negro in American society. "What stone has been left unturned to degrade us?" asked James McCune Smith, a leading Negro abolitionist of New York City, in 1860. "What hand has refused to fan the flame of popular prejudice against us? What American artist has not caricatured us? . . . What press has not ridiculed and condemned us? . . . No other nation on the globe could have made more progress in the midst of such a universal and stringent disparagement. It would humble the proudest, crush the energies of the strongest, and retard the progress of the swiftest." Theodore Tilton agreed that discrimination was responsible for the Negro's disabilities. "We put a stigma upon the black man's color, and then plead that prejudice against the commonest fair dealing," he stated. "We shut him out of schools, and then bitterly inveigh against the ignorance of his kind. We shut up all learned professions from his reach, and withhold the motives for ordinary enterprise, and then declare that he is an inferior being, fitted only for menial services."[20]

Prejudice and discrimination against the free Negro were debilitating enough, but the effects of slavery were worse still. "Take any race you please, French, English, Irish, or Scotch," said Frederick Douglass; "subject them to slavery for ages—regard and treat them every where, every way, as property. . . . Let them be loaded with chains, scarred with the whip, branded with hot irons,

[20] Smith's statement printed in *The Liberator*, November 2, 1860; Tilton's statement published in *Independent*, May 29, 1862.

sold in the market, kept in ignorance, . . . and I venture to say that the same doubt would spring up concerning either of them, which now confronts the negro." It was little wonder that "the colored people in America appear stupid, helpless and degraded. The wonder is that they evince so much spirit and manhood as they do." Tilton conceded that "slavery has reduced the blacks to the lowest point of ignorance and humiliation of which humanity . . . is capable." The peculiar institution had produced some singular effects on the Negro, making him childlike and dependent, lacking in initiative and self-respect. "Man is, to a certain extent, the creature of circumstances," argued Tilton, "and two centuries of slavery must needs have molded the character of the slave. . . . The faults of the slave . . . come of training, rather than of natural endowment."[21]

In the New York *Tribune* of February 5, 1863, Sydney Gay presented a cogent and eloquent summary of the environmentalist argument. "We have never supposed that the liberation of so many human beings, heretofore irresponsible, would be without some embarrassments," he wrote in reply to proslavery arguments that slaves were not fit for freedom. "It is Freedom that fits men for Freedom. . . . The crime of slavery has been that it has found the incapacity of its victims an argument for the continuation of its emasculating influences, and has continually pointed to the ruin it has wrought as an apology for postponing reparation." Nobody in his right senses, continued Gay,

> has expected to find the Freedman . . . a model of possible excellence, a miracle of virtue, a wonder of wit, a paragon of prudence, and a marvel of industry. In him who was yesterday a Slave, we should expect to find the vices of the Slave—the traces of

[21] Speech by Douglass at Cooper Union, February 12, 1862, published in New York *Tribune*, February 13; article by Tilton in *Independent*, August 20, 1863.

that falsehood which heretofore had been his sole
protection against cruelty—of that thievishness
which may have saved him from the pangs of hunger, or guarded him from the inclemency of the
elements—of that insubordination of the animal passions which his superiors in society have encouraged
for their own profit and by their own example. . . .
Emancipation will not remove the scars which Slavery has inflicted. There is many a brow from which
the brand can never be erased. So much the sooner
should we, with all the courage of a genuine repentance, dock this entail of human misery, and at least
turn the faces of future generations toward kindlier
opportunities and less discouraging vicissitudes![22]

The effects of slavery and racial discrimination on the
Negro's character, according to abolitionists, were felt
primarily in three areas: intelligence, industry, and
morals. The Negro's defects of intelligence, remarked
Frederick Douglass, could be found among the peasants,
laborers, and lower classes of all races. "A man is worked
upon by what *he* works on. He may carve out his circumstances, but his circumstances will carve him out as
well." Douglass recalled his trip to Ireland in the 1840's,
where he found the population of the poorer districts
much like plantation slaves in every respect save color.
"The open, uneducated mouth—the long, gaunt arm—
the badly formed foot and ankles—the shuffling gait—
the retreating forehead and vacant expression—and,
their petty quarrels and fights—all reminded me of the
plantation, and my own cruelly abused people."[23]

Moncure Conway, born and raised on a Virginia plantation, recounted the story of a companion of his youth,

[22] New York *Tribune*, February 5, 1863. See also J. M. McKim to
Gay, January 28, 1863, Gay Papers, Columbia University Library.
[23] Foner, *Life and Writings*, II, 304-5. This is taken from a
speech first delivered by Douglass in 1854, and repeated several
times during the Civil War years.

a slave boy who was popular with the white boys of the neighborhood and excelled in telling stories, playing games, etc. The boy had great native intelligence. He accompanied young Moncure to school every day, but of course was not allowed in the schoolroom. He wanted to know what happened in there, and when he found out, he too wanted to learn to read. He could not understand why he was denied this privilege, and grew bewildered, then saddened, and finally rebellious, forcing Moncure's father to sell him South. Conway never forgot the boy. "I have dwelt upon this case," he wrote in his *Testimonies Concerning Slavery*, "because it is that which represents, in my own experience, one of the most tragical forms in which Slavery outrages human nature." On the basis of his experience Conway also denied the theory that because of some natural disability, Negroes learned quickly until the age of ten or twelve, and then fell behind. "It has been my lot to have much to do with the poor whites of the South, and I have observed precisely the same arrest of development, both physical and mental, in those poor whites. . . . They learn well at first, even with a kind of voracity; but, at about the same age with the Negro child, they become dull." This was the result, not of inherent inferiority, but of the sudden realization at age ten or twelve of the cramped circumstances, limited opportunities, and unhappy future that faced the downtrodden of both races.[24]

The lazy, shiftless Negro who would work only under compulsion was a byword among those who defended slavery and ridiculed the idea of emancipation. Of course slaves were lazy, wrote Lydia Maria Child in her study of emancipation in the West Indies. Slavery "takes away the motive power from the laborers, who naturally desire to shirk as much as possible of the work, which brings them no pay. . . . It makes them indifferent to the destruction of property on estates, in whose pros-

[24] Conway, *Testimonies Concerning Slavery*, pp. 4-7, 65-66.

perity they have no interest. . . . It kills their ingenuity and enterprise." She cited the testimony of planters and missionaries in the West Indies, who said that emancipation had "almost wholly put an end to sulking, or pretending to be sick. . . . Planters treat their laborers more like fellow-men, and that leads them to be respectful in their turn. They have now a growing regard for character; a feeling unknown to them in the days of slavery."[25]

The alleged immorality, dishonesty, and untruthfulness of the Negro were cited by proslavery writers as additional proofs of his inferiority. Of course the slave was immoral, replied abolitionists. Under slavery promiscuity was encouraged, marriage had no legal validity, and the father had no personal responsibility for his children, who belonged, not to their parents, but to their master. "Being regarded as animals, and treated like live-stock, [slaves] unavoidably lived like animals," wrote Mrs. Child. "Modesty and self-respect were impossible to their brutalized condition." In the West Indies, she contended, there was much less immorality a generation after emancipation than there had been under slavery.[26]

"To tell us that Slavery fosters in the enslaved habits of deception, is not to communicate to us any startling novelty," wrote Sydney Gay in 1862. Gay and Conway admitted that Negroes were prone to petty thievery, "but it should be remembered that the rights of property involve some very refined problems," said Conway. "If the Negro is inclined to sympathise with the views of Rousseau on such questions more than the English schools would approve, it must be admitted that the systematic disregard of his own right to his earnings is

[25] Lydia M. Child, *The Right Way the Safe Way* (2d edn., New York, 1862), pp. 5-6, 15-16.
[26] *Ibid.*, p. 6. See also Charles K. Whipple, *The Family Relation, as Affected by Slavery* (Cincinnati, 1858); and [William C. Gannett], "The Freedmen at Port Royal," *North American Review*, CI (July 1865), 11-13.

scarcely the best method of giving him better views. I have never heard yet of a slave who had managed to filch back so much as had been filched from him."[27]

IV

"The difference between the Black and White," thought Sydney Gay, "is no other than the difference between the White and the White—differences occasioned by the accidents of location, and susceptible of removal by the opportunities of culture." Abolitionists realized, however, that these differences would not be wiped out in a year or two. "Men going from slavery to freedom cannot change their habits as they change their garments," wrote Samuel Gridley Howe. "The effects of Slavery will last more than one generation or even two," predicted Wendell Phillips. "It were a very slight evil if they could be done away sooner." The Negro was potentially the equal of the white man, but he had a long, hard road to travel before he reached that potentiality.[28]

During the Civil War and Reconstruction, abolitionists had an opportunity to test their theories of racial equality against the actual experiences of the freedmen. Hundreds of abolitionists went to the South in the 1860's and 1870's as teachers and missionaries of the Northern freedmen's aid societies, which were formed during the war to bring education and economic assistance to the emancipated slaves. A few abolitionists were disillusioned by the immensity of the task, and soon returned to their homes. Others, for the sake of propaganda or self-justification, extravagantly praised the virtues and nobility of the freedmen. But most abolitionists who went South to help the freedmen entered the work with their eyes

[27] New York *Tribune*, January 13, 1862; Conway, *Testimonies Concerning Slavery*, p. 70.

[28] New York *Tribune*, September 17, 1863; Howe, *Refugees in Canada West*, p. 86; speech by Wendell Phillips in Boston Music Hall, December 16, 1860, in New York *Tribune*, December 18.

open, reinforced by their belief in the essential innate equality of the Negro race and the corrosive effects of slavery on the Negro's character.[29]

Several abolitionists kept diaries, wrote letters, and published articles and books describing and reflecting upon their experiences with the freedmen. These writings expressed various shadings in points of view, of course, but most abolitionists would have agreed with the sober and thoughtful analysis of William Channing Gannett, who went to the South Carolina Sea Islands as a teacher of the freedmen in 1862. "I feel no doubt," Gannett wrote from the Sea Islands in 1863, "that under conditions of peace, three years would find these people, with but very few exceptions, a self-respecting, self-supporting population."[30] In 1865 Gannett presented a cautiously optimistic view of the future. But the road to freedom would not be smooth. "Not only do their old habits cling to the freedmen as they rise, but their ignorance will betray them into new and perilous mistakes. We look for slow progress and much disappointment. . . . For a time discouragement and failure await the eager restorer." The final outcome of this experiment of freedom, however, could not be in doubt. "Judging from the activity already shown, the improvement already made, we feel certain that this 'institution' of freedom will at once be far more than self-supporting, and that, with the paralysis of slavery fairly thrown off, the negro will eventually contribute to the strength and honor of the country in relations far more

[29] See Willie Lee Rose, *Rehearsal for Reconstruction: The Port Royal Experiment* (Indianapolis, 1964); and James M. McPherson, *The Struggle for Equality: Abolitionists and the Negro in the Civil War and Reconstruction* (Princeton, 1964), Chaps. VII and XVII.

[30] Elizabeth W. Pearson, ed., *Letters from Port Royal, Written at the Time of the Civil War* (Boston, 1906), p. 178. See also William H. Pease, "Three Years Among the Freedmen: William C. Gannett and the Port Royal Experiment," *Journal of Negro History*, XLII (April 1957), 98-117.

important than that of simply furnishing its cotton, sugar, and rice."[31]

In spite of countless discouragements, most abolitionists, like Gannett, who worked directly with the freedmen maintained their faith in the innate equality of the Negro race. The abolitionists' argument for racial equality and their analysis of the effects of environment on the Negro's personality were perhaps their most sophisticated and significant contributions to the discussion of the racial problem in the United States. But in the final analysis they emphasized that the question was not one of race, but of human rights. "I think races are of secondary importance," said Wendell Phillips in 1863. "I despise an empire resting its claims on the blood of a single race. My pride in the future is in the banner that welcomes every race and every blood, and under whose shelter all races stand up equal." "Looked at through centuries," proclaimed Theodore Tilton, "the question of races sinks into insignificance. The only generalization that will stand is, not that there are five races of men, or seven, or twelve, but only one—the universal human race in which all men are brothers, and God is father over all!"[32]

V

The abolitionist movement was essentially a direct response to the existence of slavery in America. But many strains of Western thought converged and focused in the nineteenth century to produce the particular emotional and intellectual intensity of the antislavery movement in the United States. The rational liberalism of the Enlightenment was synthesized with the romantic mysticism of Transcendentalism; Evangelical Protestantism absorbed elements of both systems and added to them a crusading, unquenchable fervor. In America, all three

[31] Gannett, "The Freedmen at Port Royal," op.cit., p. 28.
[32] The Liberator, May 29, 1863; Tilton, The Negro, p. 8.

intellectual traditions—the Enlightenment, Transcendentalism, and Evangelical Protestantism—were basically equalitarian. The Enlightenment produced the Declaration of Independence; Transcendentalism emphasized the innate goodness and ultimate perfectibility of man; Evangelical Protestantism taught that injustice was a sin, and that every Christian had a duty to cleanse society of its sins.

This equalitarianism was at the heart of the abolitionist movement. Slavery and the denial of equal rights were violations of the Declaration of Independence, of Christianity, and of human dignity. Abolitionists insisted that the Negro was a human being, and that he was entitled to all the rights enjoyed by other men in America. Slavery and inequality could be justified only by denying the equal manhood of the Negro, and the supporters of slavery were finally forced to take this position. They maintained that the Negro was a separate and inferior species of human being; in the scale of creation he was higher than the ape, but lower than the Caucasian. The dispute about the Negro's biological capacities was at the core of the slavery controversy. Abolitionists were driven by the whole ideology and logic of their movement to defend the Negro's equality. Although slavery was finally abolished, the abolitionists' racial equalitarianism was ahead of its time. Not until the twentieth century was the validity of the abolitionist argument confirmed. The history of our own time has demonstrated that the abolitionists had perhaps a deeper understanding of the racial problem than any other men of their time—and many of ours.

CHAPTER 9

"ICONOCLASM HAS HAD ITS DAY":

ABOLITIONISTS AND

FREEDMEN IN SOUTH CAROLINA

BY WILLIE LEE ROSE

WILLIAM LLOYD GARRISON was much troubled by the action of his old friend James Miller McKim. In January of 1862, McKim had suddenly asked to be released from his duties as Corresponding Secretary of the Pennsylvania Anti-Slavery Society, an organization which he had served with credit for many years. Less than ten months following the outbreak of the Civil War, and with emancipation as yet no more acknowledged as a war aim than it had been the day Fort Sumter was fired upon, one of the country's most useful and outspoken abolitionists was saying that abolition work as it had been conducted for the past thirty years was no longer necessary, and that if the organized antislavery movement could not adjust to the new needs of the day, it ought to disband. In May, at the annual meeting of the American Anti-Slavery Society, Garrison, as President, rose to the occasion. He asked McKim to explain himself.[1]

There could be no reasonable doubt of the Pennsylvania abolitionist's sincere dedication to the cause of the slave. In his youth, while still a theological student, McKim had happened one day into a barber shop in Carlisle, Pennsylvania, where he picked up a copy of a new journal called *The Liberator*; in that moment he dis-

[1] *The Liberator*, May 9 and 16, 1862.

covered the purpose of his life. In the service of the antislavery movement he had occupied, according to William Still, a companion-in-arms who knew him well, "a position of influence, labor and usefulness, scarcely second to Garrison." In 1833, as representative of the otherwise all-Negro organization of abolitionists in Carlisle, the young Presbyterian minister went to Philadelphia to attend the signal meeting which launched the American Anti-Slavery Society. At the age of twenty-three, McKim had been the youngest delegate present. In a short time he had given up his ministry, as many another convinced abolitionist had done, to devote himself entirely to abolition work, serving first as one of Theodore Dwight Weld's famous band of antislavery apostles, later as a fearless member of the Pennsylvania Vigilance Committee, then as editor of the *Pennsylvania Freeman*, and continuously as a hard-working officer of the Pennsylvania Anti-Slavery Society. There were no important abolitionists of the day who were not McKim's friends, and the runaway slave crossing Pennsylvania would probably have heard of him as a man who would run risks in his behalf. McKim had been one of the select party who went to Harpers Ferry to escort John Brown's body back to his home in the North.[2] There was small wonder that Garrison would want to know what moved McKim to sever his connection with a movement he had served so loyally for nearly thirty years.

McKim had made it clear at the time of his resignation that he was not abandoning the slave. It appeared certain to him, however, that despite inaction on the part of the government, emancipation was already as-

[2] William Still, *The Underground Rail Road* (Philadelphia, 1872), pp. 665-67; *Proceedings of the American Anti-Slavery Society at its Third Decade, Held in the City of Philadelphia, Dec. 3d and 4th, 1863* (New York, 1864), pp. 82-83; Ira V. Brown, "Miller McKim and Pennsylvania Abolitionism," in *Pennsylvania History*, XXX (January 1863), 56-72.

sured as an important result of the war. In a letter to the editor of the *Anti-Slavery Standard* he outlined his new position. "Iconoclasm has had its day," he wrote. More was now needed than "the old anti-slavery routine," of sending lecturers about, as abolitionists were fond of phrasing it, to educate the public mind and conscience. New methods were required. "For the battering-ram we must substitute the hod and trowel; taking care, however, not to 'daub with untempered mortar.' We have passed through the *pulling-down* stage of our movement; the *building-up*—the constructive part—remains to be accomplished." In direct reply to Garrison's question, McKim explained that he now wished to devote his primary efforts to the slaves whom the progress of the war was releasing in ever growing numbers.[3] His action introduced into the councils of the abolition movement a question which was to prove its divisive effect in the course of the succeeding decade. Even after emancipation there was a legitimate point of difference among friends of the freedmen as to whether pressure could be more effectively applied to remove injustices from law or to assist the Negro in grasping his own boot-straps, by providing him with an education. In the early years of the war the question was especially ticklish, because escaping Negroes were not yet free men.

From the very beginning of hostilities the refugee slave had made his appearance, sometimes alone, sometimes in small groups, but ever informed by an instinct that he would not be remanded to his master. There were times when the fugitive's faith proved to be ill-founded, but no matter what was done about him, he always presented a problem to the Federal authorities, who could not call him "free," but did not want to call him a slave. The question first arose in critical proportions, however, in the fall of 1861, on the Sea Islands of

[3] McKim to Oliver Johnson, January 22, 1862, in New York *Anti-Slavery Standard*, May 3, 1862; *The Liberator*, May 16, 1862.

South Carolina, where the fugitives were not black slaves at all, but rather their white masters. In order to strengthen the blockade of the Southern coast, Federal authorities had determined upon seizing a deep-water port on the South Atlantic, a safe harbor where the blockade ships could ride out storms and be supplied. On November 7, the United States forces seized Port Royal Sound for these purposes, a waterway which forked deeply into the fertile cotton and rice country between Charleston and Savannah. Rich in history from the sixteenth century, this semitropical region was the source of the finest cotton in the world, the home of as old and entrenched an aristocracy as the country possessed, and a land where Negro slaves comprised nearly 83 percent of the entire population.[4]

The Sea Island region had been, before the Civil War, a remote, provincial district of live-oaks and Spanish moss, where life was as slow and orderly as the tides which rose and fell in the quiet back-waters, while Beaufort, the only town on the islands, was notable not at all for its commerce, but for the aristocratic cotton lords and "rice birds" who gathered there in summer. In the overthrow of the old order which resulted from the Federal occupation of the islands, there was ample demonstration of the disorderliness of the historical process; for the United States government was abruptly confronted with a battery of Reconstruction problems before the Civil War had well begun. The white inhabitants fled almost to a man, but Negro slaves, to the number of approximately ten thousand, had stubbornly refused to join their masters' hasty retreat to the interior. They remained instead to greet the invaders and enjoy their sudden liberty, which if not official, was at the least a remission of bondage.

[4] For a fuller treatment of the origins of the Port Royal movement than is given in the paragraphs below see Willie Lee Rose, *Rehearsal for Reconstruction; The Port Royal Experiment* (Indianapolis and New York, 1964), pp. 3-31.

In the first few months, however, the new condition was, to outward appearances, a mixed blessing: the Negroes were stranded in the fall before the issue of winter clothing, with their plantation provisions subject to ruthless seizure by the Federal armies, without doctors or ministers, and generally speaking, without experience or power to care for themselves. Many slaves flocked toward the army camps looking for help and work, but they were abused by the unsympathetic soldiers as often as they were assisted. In any event, the wants of ten thousand semifree people far exceeded the resources available to military officials, and there was a compelling need as well for a means of social control and civil organization to replace the old order which had been so suddenly swept away. The situation which became desperate in the course of the winter would surely become worse by another year if the Negroes were not organized and set to work on a new cotton crop.

It was a lucky circumstance for the Sea Islanders that their masters in their flight had also abandoned several million dollars worth of long-staple cotton. Because the confiscation of this cotton fell to the Treasury Department, it was Salmon P. Chase, the most radical member of Lincoln's original Cabinet, who had the first opportunity to direct and organize the means to assist the late slaves. The Secretary was interested and sympathetic. As a result of the investigations of Edward L. Pierce, a young abolitionist and personal friend whom Chase sent to the islands on an official visit, the Treasury Department lent sanction and support to the organization of several privately supported benevolent societies in Boston, New York, and Philadelphia. Their purpose was to send ministers, teachers, and labor superintendents to the islands.[5] The collective efforts of these freedmen's

[5] For Pierce's reports see, Edward L. Pierce to Salmon P. Chase, February 3, 1862, and same to same, June 2, 1862, in Frank Moore, ed., *The Rebellion Record* (New York, 1866), Supplement to Vol. I, pp. 302-23.

aid societies (although the word "freedmen" was studiously avoided at first) came to be known in the North in the second year of the war as "the Port Royal Experiment." From this first large-scale endeavor, launched in the spring of 1862, grew all the freedmen's aid activities which developed during the war and Reconstruction periods.

This was the work which had eclipsed the "old methods" of the antislavery crusade in the affections of Miller McKim, the challenge to what he called the "building-up" phase of the abolition movement. The failure of many of his fellows to succumb to its appeal, however, was not astonishing; for in the beginning the backers of the Port Royal Experiment were inclined to state their aims very modestly, revealing only part of the ultimate purpose of their movement. While they eagerly pressed before the public the goals of feeding the hungry, caring for the sick, supplying clothes, sending ministers, teachers, and doctors, they were hesitant to reveal the full scope of their intentions. The leaders of the Boston Educational Commission pointed out quite simply that if the Negroes were worse off as a result of the Northern invasion, Northern citizens would stand convicted of "that spurious philanthropy" which Southerners had so often charged upon them. Men of good will might hope to do more for the Negroes than their masters had ever done, but they ought to begin, at the least, by doing for the Negroes those essential things which "their masters did not and could not omit to do."[6] Such reticence resulted undoubtedly from considerations of policy, from an attempt to establish the broadest possible basis of support, but many an old-time abolitionist had learned to distrust "policy" as a mask for hedging on emancipation. Too often "policy" had turned out to be another name for "expediency."

[6] *Address to the Public by the Committee of Correspondence of the Educational Commission* (Boston, n.d., but c. March 1862).

It is a practical certainty that simple relief measures could never have shaken the loyalty of a man like Miller McKim to the "old methods" of the antislavery crusade. The real aims of the Port Royal movement were quickly understood by the trusty abolitionists who participated in its organization, and by those who joined it soon thereafter, to be nothing short of creating on the Sea Islands a model for the regeneration of Southern Society, a model which would include the education and rehabilitation of the slave, and a conclusive demonstration of his capacity for freedom. Without tried and true abolitionists in the movement, reasoned McKim, "untempered mortar" might be applied, and the pattern of reconstruction which developed on the islands might not embody true antislavery principles. McKim regarded Port Royal as offering the most promising field now open to abolitionists.

In shaping his plans Edward Pierce had had the benefit of previous experience with refugee Negroes during his tour of duty as a soldier at Fortress Monroe, Virginia, in the first year of the war. He had already seen enough to feel sure that the Negroes would be dependable allies for the Northern war effort, and that they would be especially eager to learn to read. Even before his departure for the Sea Islands on his commission from Secretary Chase he had conceived a broad approach to his Port Royal assignment. On a cold January morning before his departure, he walked over Beacon Hill with the Reverend Mr. Jacob M. Manning, opening to him "his far-reaching plans" and requesting assistance of the Boston minister in securing teachers and funds for their support.[7]

[7] Jacob M. Manning to Edward A. Atkinson, October 18, 1862, Atkinson MSS, Massachusetts Historical Society; [Edward L. Pierce], "The Contrabands at Fortress Monroe," *Atlantic Monthly*, VII (November 1861), 626-40.

The scope of these plans is roughly indicated in the first report which resulted from Pierce's Sea Island visit. He recommended to Secretary Chase that the government avoid the simple but expedient course of leasing the island acres to private parties, but should itself undertake the culture of cotton, providing able and disinterested supervisors for the Negro laborers, and paying wages to the workers from the start. Pierce's plan included provision for teachers for the children, and missionaries to advise adults in their new responsibilities: to inculcate "practical virtues," "faithful labor," and "clean and healthful habits." But this was to be only the beginning. "The plan proposed is, of course," wrote Pierce, "not presented as an ultimate result: far from it. It contemplates a paternal discipline [only] for the time being . . . with the prospect of better things in the future." As soon as the Negroes should "show themselves fitted for all the privileges of citizens," they were to be "dismissed from the system and allowed to follow any employment they please, and where they please." Most particularly, they should be given liberty and encouragement, advised Pierce, to become landowners in their own right.[8] Although Pierce did not state it, the assumption was implicit that land would be made available to the Negroes (whose subsequent freedom was also assumed) through the confiscation and sale of the estates of their late masters, the fugitive Sea Island planters. While he raised no hope for a large immediate Federal revenue from the islands, Pierce thought the government would cover the expenses incurred in the undertaking, and would accomplish a goal of incalculable importance to the war effort, through "the inauguration [on the islands] of a beneficent system which will settle a great social question, insure the sympathies of foreign nations, now

[8] Pierce to Chase, February 3, 1862, in Moore, ed., *Rebellion Record*, Supplement to Vol. I, pp. 310-12.

wielded against us, and advance the civilization of the age."[9]

Settling that "great social question" once and for all was undoubtedly the most appealing aspect of the work for abolitionists like McKim, for it was one which they had been obliged to confront at every turn during the thirty-year history of their movement, a question leveled at them almost as often by citizens who were otherwise favorably disposed to emancipation as by outright enemies. That question usually assumed one of several provoking forms: Would the Negroes if emancipated work voluntarily for a living? Or would they constitute a dependent element in a free society, living forever upon the charity of the white North? Would they fail, without slavery as a means of social control, in the great competition of life? Would they, as some suggested, become *extinct*? With good antislavery leadership the Negroes at Port Royal might silence such questions forever and give an inestimable boost to the progress of public opinion on the emancipation question. The government would welcome the information which would surely result from such an undertaking, for the problem of a new status for the slave would become greater with each passing month. A radical observer of the Washington scene was enthusiastic about the possibilities. "The active and acting abolitionists ought to concentrate all their efforts" at Port Royal, wrote Adam Gurowski. "The success of a productive· colony there would serve as a womb for the emancipation at large."[10]

Organized abolition was by no means of one opinion on the question. Garrison remained unconvinced. His reservations about the new "experiment" were undoubtedly shared by many of his fellows who saw in it a threat to the Anti-Slavery Society and its work. In the May

[9] *Ibid.*, p. 311.

[10] Adam Gurowski, *Diary from March 4, 1861 to November 12, 1862* (Boston, 1862), p. 147.

meeting when the matter first came before the Society, Wendell Phillips voiced the views of those who acknowledged no problem: "I ask nothing more for the negro than I ask for the Irishman or German who comes to our shores. I thank the benevolent men who are laboring at Port Royal—all right!—but the blacks do not need them. They are not objects of charity. They only ask this nation—'Take your yoke off our necks.' " Phillips assured his fellow abolitionists that the newly released bondsman needed no assistance whatever, only a modicum of justice, and not an ounce of mercy. "They ask their hands—nothing more; they will accomplish books, and education, and work." In debate Phillips frequently overstated his case for calculated effect, and there is some reason to believe that he was more aware of the requirements of the situation on the islands than he was ready to admit. But his unwillingness to identify organized antislavery with the freedmen's aid movement remained remarkably constant over the years.[11] There were other abolitionists who steered clear of the Port Royal work, as they were frank to say, from a dread of damaging publicity. "I feel sure," warned one unidentified albeit "tried and trusty" friend of the slave, "that, while you will benefit individuals, you will, in the broad careless views which the world will take, exhibit a most disastrous failure, and furnish a very good argument against any method of emancipation."[12]

McKim did not take this despairing view. Although he did not sever his connection with the Anti-Slavery

[11] Speech of Wendell Phillips at the annual meeting of the American Anti-Slavery Society, May 6, 1862, in *The Liberator*, May 16, 1862. Phillips had exerted his influence with Charles Sumner as early as December to gain a hearing for a friend who requested government aid to schools for the Sea Islanders. Phillips to Sumner, December 20, 1861, Sumner MSS, Houghton Library, Harvard University.

[12] An unidentified abolitionist, quoted in the *Annual Report of the New York National Freedmen's Aid Society* (New York, 1866), p. 10.

Society, his heart really belonged to the freedmen's aid movement. Within a few weeks following the May meeting of the Society, he was in South Carolina surveying what was already being done there and making notes as to how the work could be used to promote abolition. Those of his fellows who did not follow him into the new work were probably most influenced by the action of Garrison, and their leader's frank reminder that emancipation was not yet accomplished. The work of education was not the same thing. "It is a *popular* work," Garrison declared, "as compared with ours, and we may safely leave it to the support of the community at large, giving it all the incidental help in our power, but not making it our special work."[13]

The question will not down whether Garrison rejected the new movement simply because it *was* popular. Much has been written recently portraying the abolitionist as an intellectual reformer who set himself in resolute opposition to all organized social institutions. In his important book, *Slavery: A Problem in American Institutional and Intellectual Life*, Stanley Elkins describes the anti-institutionalism of the New England abolitionists who marched behind Garrison's banner. The more strident of these Garrisonians richly earned their unpopularity by denouncing the most cherished institutions of their fellow Americans, the churches and the United States Constitution, both sullied by compromises with slavery. This anti-institutional abolitionist was apt, according to Elkins' analysis, to content himself with denunciation; he considered no means of using church or state to improve the lot of the slave while he was working toward the ultimate goal of the extinction of slavery. Taking a moral and emotional stand, this same abolitionist called for root-and-branch measures, "a total solution. Destroy the evil, he cries; root it up,

---

[13] *The Liberator*, May 10, 1862; *An Address Delivered by J. Miller McKim in Sansom Hall, July 9, 1862* (Philadelphia, 1862), p. 4.

wipe it out."[14] For such a reformer the light of the moral issue was so blinding that the social problem was scarcely discernible.

The presence of such attitudes in the ranks of abolitionists, goes a long way to explain the suspicion which certain of the veterans expressed toward the freedmen's aid movement, particularly in its initial phase. Why, they might well ask, should they labor to prepare the slave, in the words of Edward Pierce, "for all the privileges of [American] citizens?"[15] Implicit in the assumption of such a task was the acknowledgement that the slave *required* assistance, the admission that striking off the fetters did not in itself make of a slave a truly free man, and the recognition that there might still be a social problem remaining after the nation's conscience had purged its guilt and thrown off its peculiarly abominable institution.[16]

McKim's "battering-ram" and "hod and trowel" symbolically represent a recurring division among American reformers, and anti-institutionalism is a persistent streak in the intellectual's attitude toward entrenched social evil. In a penetrating article on the contemporary struggle for civil rights for American Negroes, Benjamin De-Mott observes that many of the best friends of the movement are less than enthusiastic about the "Domestic Peace Corps" and similar organizations at work among the culturally deprived young people of Harlem. Mr. DeMott assigns this coolness to the endemic impatience

[14] Stanley M. Elkins, *Slavery, A Problem in American Institutional and Intellectual Life* (Chicago, 1959), pp. 161, 163-64, 175-76. Other writers have applied the concepts of guilt and aggression to individual abolitionists, but Elkins has made the more general application of these ideas to the antislavery movement.

[15] Report of Edward L. Pierce to Salmon P. Chase, Secretary of the Treasury, February 3, 1862, in Moore, ed., *Rebellion Record*, Supplement to Vol. I, p. 311.

[16] For an interesting contemporary application of Elkins' analysis, see Benjamin DeMott, "Project for Another Country," in *American Scholar*, Vol. 32, no. 3 (Summer 1962), pp. 455-57.

and suspicion of liberals with any means of attack upon second-class citizenship which suggests, even by implication, present needs or shortcomings of colored citizens. Social work, operating through the cooperation and support of the churches, civic groups, and the government, pales in comparison with the militant call for right and justice, the regeneration of the heart. Men still feel they must make a choice between movements which should be twin efforts. Even now it comes more naturally to most liberals to ascribe the total problem to "white man's viciousness, the assigned cause of the crippling frame of injustice in which the American Negro lives." Harder by far to face is the concomitant struggle to erase the effects of that frame of injustice. Mr. DeMott takes his departure from Elkins' description of the abolitionist, and sees in the present-day prophets of the apocalypse, those who warn us, in the words of James Baldwin, that it will be ". . . no more water, the fire next time," the spiritual descendants of William Lloyd Garrison and his followers of over a hundred years ago.

Those who have identified and helped to explain the anti-institutional bent in American reform movements have served scholarship well and have brought insight to bear upon important personalities who have been alternately blamed and praised, but little understood. On the other hand, it should be recognized that the abolitionists were often much divided among themselves as to their wisest strategy on questions involving the churches and the government. Numbers of abolitionists always subscribed to church-related emancipation activities, and the coming of civil war stimulated among nearly all of them a willingness to abandon previous hostile attitudes in favor of cooperation in the war effort, hoping thereby to influence public policy on the slavery issue.

While there were those who continued to prefer the "battering-ram" to the "hod and trowel," there were also those who, like McKim, undertook constructive work within an institutional framework. There is some danger that the builders may be overlooked because the iconoclasts had such shocking things to say, and said them so loudly. There is some danger that when the anti-institutional studies are incorporated into the general literature of the period that they may be made to cover too much ground, perhaps more ground than the authors intended.

This would occur not only as a result of a continuing overemphasis on the more strident reformers, but also from a tendency of recent scholarship to define the abolition movement narrowly, either by excluding adherents after the 1830's, as David Donald has done in his essay "Toward a Reconsideration of Abolitionists," or concentrating, as Stanley Elkins has done, on the New England branch of the movement, with its close intellectual ties to Transcendentalism.[17] Although any reasonable and clearly stated definition may be used for purposes of study, it would appear that if one is primarily concerned with the effects of the antislavery movement on the Civil War, and its outcome for American Negroes, then there is much to be said for including in the ranks of the abolitionists all those who were, before the beginning of the Civil War, uncompromising adherents of immediate and unconditional emancipation. Otherwise one is left without a name for individuals who became hearty exponents of emancipation after 1840, as a consequence of what they deemed aggressive acts of the Slave Power, or as a result of the Fugitive Slave Law and the struggle for Free Soil in Kansas, or simply because they were born too late to have had any political convictions whatever in the 1830's. Among these

[17] See Elkins, *Slavery*, pp. 164-75, for an analysis which focuses on the New England Transcendentalists; David Donald, in "Toward a Reconsideration of Abolitionists," in *Lincoln Reconsidered* (Vintage Paperback edn., New York, 1956), pp. 19-36, limits his study to those who became abolitionist before 1840.

younger recruits to the freedmen's aid movement the anti-institutional attitudes of the veterans of the battles of the 1830's are hardly discernible.[18] The antislavery movement had become a much broader stream by 1860 than could be contained in the old channel cut by those earliest pioneers in the cause of the slave.

Just how broad this stream was may be seen in the varied responses of antislavery adherents to the opportunities which opened so early at Port Royal. The wartime movement to aid escaping slaves in their adjustment to the free life had, in addition to the simple ones of relief and education, and the greater one of providing a model for Southern reconstruction, two other objectives: to use the successes of ex-slaves to promote emancipation support, and to use the information gained in such a social experiment to guide the government in further steps. This work originated on the Sea Islands, was carried on most intensively there, and can be understood and studied only as a logical projection of the antislavery movement.

While it is clear that the officers and leading supporters of the freedmen's movement were strongly antislavery, it cannot be contended on the other hand that the movement was exclusively abolitionist in backing, especially if the term is to be construed narrowly. Henry Lee Swint analyzed a group of 135 supporters of freedmen's work, and determined that 66 of the number had been outstanding enough in the abolition movement to merit a comment to that effect in the biographical dictionaries. This does not inform us about the others, but

[18] The social experiment at Port Royal was based from the beginning on a cooperation between private organizations and the government, and the freedmen's organizations were much assisted by the churches of the North. Once at work among the freed Negroes the Northern teacher frequently discovered that much could be gained by making the new concepts of freedom and responsibility relevant to the established religious life of the late slaves.

it is plain that the lists of the standing committees of the freedmen's aid societies included the names of those same distinguished jurists, ministers, and philanthropic men of affairs who supported many another good cause of the day.[19] How many of these men, and others less well known than they, had been before the war sympathetic to the antislavery movement is difficult to determine, for solid information on the less vocal early emancipationists is hard to come by. It is doubtful that many individuals who had no prior commitment to the antislavery movement would have identified themselves with freedmen's work so early as 1862. Yet the presence of certain individuals on these freedmen's commissions was enough to set Wendell Phillips' teeth on edge, and confirm his worst fears. Stephen Colwell, for example, of the Philadelphia organization, had written much in behalf of emancipation, but he usually emphasized the economic necessity of the measure, and he had been at one time an advocate of colonization. There were undoubtedly others who would not have received a clean bill of health from a Garrison or a Phillips.

When this is admitted, however, the fact remains that the pioneering work for freedmen's education was primarily supported by abolitionists, and the numbers of abolitionists involved increased as the war progressed. Even if one adopts the most stringent of definitions as to who was an abolitionist, dismissing adherents to the cause after 1840, there was a healthy leavening, even from the beginning, of what one of McKim's corre-

19 Henry Lee Swint, *The Northern Teacher in the South* (Nashville, 1941), p. 27; for lists of the original officers, consult *Circular of the Port Royal Relief Committee*, March 17, 1862 (Philadelphia, 1862); *First Annual Report of the Educational Commission for Freedmen, May, 1863* (Boston, 1863), p. 4; *A History of the American Missionary Association; Its Churches and Educational Institutions among the Freedmen, Indians and Chinese* (New York, 1874), p. 13; *The National Freedman*, Vol. I, no. i (February 1, 1865), p. 40.

spondents was pleased to call "the true West Point" of the war, "the graduates of the Antislavery school."[20]

Among the first to recognize the new opportunities and responsibilities was Lewis Tappan, of New York, who had sent a missionary to the "contrabands" at Fortress Monroe, Virginia, even before the larger field opened at Port Royal. Cooperating closely with Tappan in organizing the earliest work of the American Missionary Association on the Sea Islands were two redoubtable veterans, Simeon Jocelyn and George Whipple. These same men helped launch the nonsectarian New York National Freedmen's Aid Society. In Boston the Educational Commission had the support of a number of distinguished abolitionists of purest 1830's vintage, including, among others, George B. Emerson and Henry Ingersoll Bowditch. Numbered among the enthusiastic supporters of the new work were John Greenleaf Whittier, Maria Weston Chapman, David Lee Child and his wife, Lydia Maria. Mrs. Chapman clearly regarded the freedmen's work as an extension of abolition. "From the high historic point of view, was ever progress so swift?—But thirty years from the start, and you are organizing the leading slave state in Freedom." In Philadelphia the Unitarian minister William H. Furness and his son Horace, were active. Francis George Shaw and William Cullen Bryant were outstanding officers in the New York association. Many others joined the movement before the war was over.[21] When one reads the hearty letters from notable abolitionists to the or-

[20] William Morris Davis to J. Miller McKim, November 30, 1862, James Miller McKim Papers in the Antislavery Collection at Cornell University.

[21] See *supra*, n. 19, manuscript history of the American Missionary Association in the Educational Division of the archives of the Bureau of Refugees, Freedmen and Abandoned Lands, United States Archives; Lydia M. Child to William Endicott, March 2, 1862, and Edward Atkinson to Edward Philbrick, April 23, 1862, and Maria Weston Chapman to Edward Atkinson (n.d., but c. March, 1862), all in the Edward Atkinson MSS, Massachusetts Historical Society.

ganizers of the work, it is difficult to escape the notion that these individuals would have been more prominently placed in the associations if the directors of the freedmen's movement had not been behaving like sensible fellow-travelers, keeping the most conspicuous of the abolitionists out of the limelight. The full strength of abolitionist influence upon the enterprise, however, is not revealed in the lists of officers. There were also those who took to the field.

A sardonic reporter from the New York *Herald* gave the following highly colored account of the arrival at Port Royal in early March of the first teachers and superintendents. There had been rumors, he reported sagely, of a missionary invasion of the islands. All doubts of these rumors vanished with the appearance at the landing in Beaufort of a number of "light-haired, long-whiskered, spectacled individuals, with umbrellas in one hand and a mysteriously covered package, suggestive of tracts, in the other, followed by several ladies, prim and antiquated, and of a general Bostonian style. . . ." These were just such ladies, observed the reporter, as one might meet at "William Lloyd Garrison's soirees or at Wendell Phillips' sermons." The *Times* reporter, who was also delighted to have fresh copy, declared authoritatively that these newcomers were "mostly Abolitionists, of the most violent kind. . . ."[22] Wendell Phillips and other veteran agitators who took no part in the movement must have experienced a sour amusement to note how swiftly these allegations were refuted by certain prominent officers of the aid societies.[23]

The reporters were obviously at more pains to be amusing than accurate, but they had still come nearer to the truth than those who disclaimed, by implication,

[22] New York *Herald*, March 22, 1862; New York *Times*, March 21, 1862.
[23] Judge J. W. Edmonds, President of the New York National Freedmen's Relief Association, in New York *Times*, March 24, 1862.

any connection with abolitionism. Nor were they far from the mark in supposing that certain of the "evangels" newly arrived had been involved in practically every good cause going, Sabbatarianism perhaps, temperance, tract distribution, and the Magdalen movement, as well as abolition. Such a network of good works was characteristic of the evangelical abolitionists. One bemused observer of the embarkation of the party in New York likened the group to "the adjournment of a John Brown meeting," or "the fag-end of a broken-down" phalanx. An uneasy young volunteer from Boston looked around at his fellows, and concluded that he had joined "a rather motley-looking set." He began to wonder how successful some of them would be at raising cotton.[24] These observations were not without some foundation, but it was still a mistake for the reporters to convey the impression that the majority of the party which Pierce brought to the islands were evangelicals looking for new fields to conquer, or for that matter to conclude that more than a few had been recruited from the lunatic fringe. The most extreme of the pacifist groups had been eliminated as a result of their unwillingness to sign the oath of allegiance (as well as by Pierce's judgment that a military post was a bad place for them to be). Otherwise there were representatives among the missionaries of all the major divisions in the abolition movement, some from the East, some from the West, some who regarded themselves as being Garrisonian and others who had continued to work within the churches to accomplish their ends.

The youth of most of the party precluded an early espousal of abolition, but many, probably the majority, of the young people came from abolition families. Edward Philbrick and Charles Follen, whose father had lost

[24] Sarah Forbes Hughes, ed. *Letters and Recollections of John Murray Forbes* (Boston and New York, 1899), I, 295-96; Elizabeth Ware Pearson, ed. *Letters from Port Royal* (Boston, 1906), p. 2.

his professorship at Harvard for his antislavery views, were both sons of Boston abolitionists. Samuel Phillips was a nephew of Wendell Phillips. Such connections multiplied shortly, for antislavery families began to gather on the islands. Men wrote home for their wives and sisters to come and teach, marriages took place, and homes began to be established by the Northerners in the deserted plantation houses of the old regime. When Lydia M. Child asked the Boston Commission to register her as a member and accept her contribution, she ventured a little advice as well. No one should be sent South, she urged, who had ever been "suspected of a pro-slavery bias," for such "habits of thought" would prevent them from gaining the confidence of the Negroes.[25] Mrs. Child ought not to have worried, for, with very few exceptions, the missionaries would have suited her requirements on the point.

James Miller McKim himself had most to do with the selection of the individuals sent South from Philadelphia, and his applicants were carefully screened. When it was determined that a nonprofit store should be opened for the Sea Islanders, McKim looked for more than probity in the man he would send as the manager. John Hunn, McKim reported at last, was "the right sort of person." This Delaware farmer had earned his laurels in the service of fugitive slaves and had paid heavy fines in Roger Taney's court as a result. Hunn was "an abolitionist of the out and out Quaker stamp, and withal a liberal minded and genial hearted man."[26] McKim offered these assurances to Laura M. Towne, who was representing the Philadelphia organization on the

[25] L. M. Child to Edward Atkinson, March 2, 1862, and M. W. Chapman to Edward Atkinson (n.d., but c. March 1862), Atkinson MSS; Rose, *Rehearsal for Reconstruction*, pp. 43-45, 48-54.

[26] J. M. McKim to Laura Towne, October 2, 1862, Towne MSS, Penn Community Center, St. Helena Island, South Carolina. These manuscripts will be removed shortly to the Southern Historical Collection, Chapel Hill, N.C.

islands, because he knew her to be a woman who could tolerate no milk-and-water abolitionism. As an early arrival among the missionaries, Miss Towne had been exposed to the cautious phase of the Port Royal Experiment, and had not liked it. She complained that the original leaders of the movement had been too much concerned about not arousing the ire of the military officers, whose prejudices were all too evident. These leaders had been silent, she charged, about "the benevolence of their plans, or the justice of them, and merely insist upon the immediate expediency. . . ." The lady saw that in all truth the missionaries were gaining nothing, for the army recognized their purposes anyway. "We have the odium of out-and-out abolitionists, why not take the credit? Why not be so confident and freely daring as to secure respect?" She wished all her fellows would "say out loud quietly, respectfully, firmly, 'We have come to do anti-slavery work, and we think it noble work and we mean to do it earnestly.' "[27]

No matter whether they came from the Garrisonian wing of the abolition movement, or from the Western and evangelical wing, the missionaries regarded themselves as "evangels of civilization," Northern style. They revealed their connections with the antislavery crusade not only in the surveillance they kept each over the purity of others' convictions, in the traces in their motivation of a sense of social sin and expiation, but in their internal conflicts as well. The perspicacious reporter for the *Herald* again piped sarcastically about the "jealousies, reproaches and recriminations" abounding among the evangels, trials which had beset Dickens' famous do-gooders, and made the lives of the "Chadbands, Stiggenses, Mrs. Jellyby's and Mrs. Pardiggles a burthen to them."[28] Again he overshot the mark, but he had seen

[27] Diary entry of April 17, 1862 in Rupert Sargent Holland, ed. *Letters and Diary of Laura M. Towne* (Cambridge, 1912), pp. 8-9.
[28] New York *Herald*, March 22, 1862.

something nevertheless. The long-standing hostility between the evangelical abolitionists of New York City, with their Western following, and the American Anti-Slavery Society was now reflected in the not always polite feuding which sprang up between the New York delegation on one hand and the Boston-Philadelphia missionaries on the other. The latter were generally inclined to distrust the frequent and fervent religious expressions of the former, and the evangelists were distrustful of the cool and practical young New England labor superintendents who were so absorbed in proving the free labor thesis. Unfortunately, the role of supervisors of labor planted the superintendents in a situation which was dangerously suggestive of that of the fugitive planters. Those missionaries who were most serious about demonstrating to a dubious Northern public the superior economics of wage labor were occasionally severe in their management to a degree which deserved criticism. The evangelicals accused some of these men of being "not genuinely" antislavery, an opinion sometimes bolstered by others whose abolitionism was not of religious foundations. On the other hand those evangelicals who went directly into the supervision of labor frequently found themselves ill-suited to raising cotton. "I don't believe in putting Reverends in places where prompt business men are required," complained Edward Philbrick, a successful superintendent of Boston origins, "Some of them don't get through morning prayers and get about their business until nearly noon, and then depend entirely upon their black drivers for their information in regard to plantation matters."[29]

In the early months of the Sea Island enterprise, before the Preliminary Emancipation Proclamation, those

[29] Mrs. A. Mansfield French, *Slavery in South Carolina and the Ex-Slaves; or The Port Royal Mission* (New York, 1862), pp. 222-23; Edward Philbrick to [?], December 26, 1862, in Pearson, ed. *Letters from Port Royal*, p. 124; Rose, *Rehearsal for Reconstruction*, pp. 219-22.

who went to work at the "building-up" stage of the abolition movement were obliged to do so in the knowledge
that the house of bondage was not quite torn down.
As a result, much of the publicity they gave to their efforts centered around the condition of the late slave
population: the willingness of the Negroes to work
without coercion, their extreme eagerness to learn to
read and write, their sympathy with the Union war effort, and their desire to improve their own standard of
living. When McKim returned from his extended visit
to the islands in June, he addressed a large meeting in
Philadelphia, emphasizing all these points, but laying
particular stress on the practical economic benefits which
would ultimately accrue to Northern manufacturing as
a result of emancipation. The discovery that the ten
thousand Sea Island Negroes were anxious to buy with
their wages such creature comforts as "pots, kettles, pans,
brushes, brooms, knives, forks, spoons, soap, candles,
combs, Yankee clocks," caused McKim to call special
attention to *the enlarged market for Northern manufactures that will be created by an enlarged area of freedom.*" The ten thousand Sea Islanders might not alone
influence Northern business interests to an astonishing
degree, but the release of four million Southern slaves
provided "an overwhelming economical argument" in
favor of "pushing this Port Royal experiment to its logical conclusion."[30] Such arguments for emancipation were
by no means regarded as cynical, and were freely urged
by missionaries who might have preferred to see emancipation come about as a result of higher motives than
profit.

The economic arguments presented few complications,
but in several important areas of their early publicity
the evangels were troubled in these first months by a
variant of the problem which had deterred many of

[30] James Miller McKim, *An Address Delivered at Sansom Hall,
July 9th, 1862* (Philadelphia, 1862), pp. 21-22.

their antislavery friends from joining them at the outset. How could they maintain on the one side that slavery was an utterly destructive institution, and on the
other that its victims were ready to adjust to full freedom in one short step?

Nobody involved in the work at Port Royal advocated
gradualism, but the confusion in the missionary accounts
shows that they suffered disadvantages in informing the
public about the condition in which they found the
Negroes. For the first time men and women of their
conviction were getting a good close look, unsupervised,
at the peculiar institution. Rare was the man who had
a kind word to say publicly for the slave housing, which
was in general very poor indeed, for the physical condition of the Negroes, which was not good, for the
food they were accustomed to eat, which was, except
when implemented by their own efforts, inadequate. No
missionary approved the primitive way work was done
in a land where men were cheaper than machines. Gen-
eralizations about family relations, however, and qualities of character such as independence, truthfulness, re-
liability, were considerably more confused. When a missionary wished to emphasize smartly the debilitating
effects of living forever without freedom or responsibility, he might go very far toward presenting a hopeless
picture.[31] It was well enough to stress the fact that the
slaves of the islands had suffered a harsher regime than
almost any other slaves had known, and that their isolation had kept them in exceptionally deep ignorance and
superstition. The missionaries needed, however, some

[31] In the interest of emphasizing the economic advantages of
emancipation to the North, one missionary came close to portraying
the future freedman as a showy spendthrift: "The Colored, in freedom, will not hoard, but spend money. They will dress, and ride,
in good style. The table and house, will be secondary, usually.
Imagine the brisk trade. . . ." Mrs. A. M. French, *Slavery in South
Carolina and the Ex-Slaves; or The Port Royal Mission* (New York,
1862), p. 308.

further argument for freedom in order to resolve the conflict inherent in maintaining the devastating effects of bondage while urging the readiness of its victims to carry on as free men.

The way around the dilemma appeared from a quarter to which Garrisonian abolitionists were infrequently accustomed to look. The "evangels" came to rely upon the prompt and saving effects of the free institutions of the North to raise the slave to real freedom. One young teacher recalled with approval John Adams' maxim that "civil society must be built up on the four corner-stones of the church, the school-house, the militia, and the town-meeting," and declared that any plan for "the great work of the admission of four million negroes to our civil society, and the establishment of their social rights" which did not take these institutions into account would fail.[32] To build a new New England in the South seemed well worth the striving. To gain these ends the missionaries were willing to compromise. They accepted every available assistance from the United States government, which was showing some healthy signs of repentance, but was as yet unshriven from complicity in the "vast national sin," as abolitionists liked to phrase it. The evangels even placed that far from antislavery institution, the army, in the service of the good cause. While still maintaining a stiff criticism of proslavery officers, and the callous impressment of Negro soldiers, the evangels became good recruiters, persuading the colored Islanders that enlistment would be very likely to assure them of their personal liberty, and in the long run help their whole race.[33]

The most exalted role of all, however, was reserved for "the earliest and dearest institution of New England,

[32] [William Channing Gannett and Edward Everett Hale], "The Education of the Freedmen," *North American Review*, 101 (October 1865), 528.

[33] Speech of James A. Strong, in Beaufort, S.C. *Free South*, January 23, 1864; Rose, *Rehearsal for Reconstruction*, pp. 148, 187-88.

the free school. . . ." This was to be the agency which would redeem first the Negro and then the poor whites of the South. The eagerness of colored children to learn, and the hunger of the adults who were "fighting with their letters" so as not to be "made ashamed" by their children, pulled the heartstrings of the Yankee school-marm as no other aspect of her work could do.[84] The teachers never missed an opportunity to affirm the equal learning ability of Negro children, and by the time the war was over there were schools on the islands which visitors compared favorably with good Northern schools. Long after other aspects of the freedmen's work lost public appeal, that of education remained attractive to many Northerners. Long after the nonsectarian freedmen's aid organizations had withered away, the interest in freedmen's education which was safely institutionalized in the churches and the American Missionary Association bore fruit in Negro colleges, making an important contribution to the steady increase in able leadership for Southern Negroes.

By all the reasonable standards which might have been applied, the Port Royal Experiment accomplished its purposes. The leaders did exert much influence upon Federal policy, an example was set for the broader Reconstruction, and the freedmen demonstrated beyond question their willing and able response to freedom. Within three years, reported a proud supporter of the movement, the "imbruted slaves" of the islands were living "as orderly communities of freemen. Under a system of elementary instruction improvised for their benefit, blank ignorance has given place to comparative intelligence, chattel slaves have become landed proprietors, black men tilling the soil on their own account. . . ."[85] These things could not have been accom-

[84] From the Annual Report of the Teachers' Committee, in *Freedmen's Record*, April 1865, p. 56.

[85] *Freedmen's Record*, I (May 1865), 81.

plished so swiftly, however, without the assistance of the antislavery men and women who devoted themselves to the "building-up" phase of their movement. It was not their fault that the true lessons of the Experiment were not well understood or followed by the government or by the people of the North.

William Lloyd Garrison had said the movement was "popular." Unfortunately for the Negro and for the nation, the freedmen's movement never became so popular as to justify the Liberator's faintly belittling praise. Had it not been for abolitionists like McKim and strong antislavery men who picked up "the hod and trowel," it is doubtful if "the support of the community at large" would have proved reliable. Real interest in the work of education flared spectacularly for a few short years following the war, but with the exception of church-supported endeavors, it vanished as abruptly as the most brilliant fireworks display will do. Within a decade of the end of the war secular interest was nearly extinct. In early 1862 when the question of freedmen's work had first come up, Garrison had no way of knowing that by 1865 he too would bid farewell to organized abolition, retiring from the Presidency of the American Anti-Slavery Society, on the grounds that "to-day it is popular to be President of the American Anti-Slavery Society."[36] He took up freedmen's aid work!

The tough old veteran recognized that even though the last rotten egg had been thrown at an abolitionist in the North, there was still much antislavery work to be done in the little country hamlets of the South. He undoubtedly knew that many a Yankee "nigger-teacher" enjoyed a local popularity among the whites which was roughly equal to his own back in Boston, in the days when he had denounced the United States Constitution as a compact with hell. Although he became an impor-

[36] John L. Thomas, *The Liberator; William Lloyd Garrison* (Boston, 1963), p. 435.

tant force in the freedmen's movement in the years immediately following the war, Garrison had already missed a chance to lend his name to one of the most interesting social experiments ever undertaken in the country.

No one can say that he was wrong. He had held the "battering-ram" until slavery was overthrown, and then turned promptly to the new work. Entrenched social wrong will always require the services of iconoclasts as well as builders. But posterity may regret that for the American reformer of a hundred years ago the cause of the freedman never equalled the cause of the slave, that the work of "building-up" never commanded an enduring loyalty.

PART IV: SIDE PERSPECTIVES

CHAPTER 10

THE ABOLITIONIST CRITIQUE
OF THE UNITED STATES CONSTITUTION

BY STAUGHTON LYND

"THE Constitution of the United States.—What is it? Who made it? For whom and for what was it made?" So Frederick Douglass wrote in his paper *The North Star* in 1849.[1]

It was natural for abolitionists to ask these questions. Their efforts to uproot the peculiar institution were continually frustrated by clauses of the United States Constitution: by Article I, Section 2, which gave the South disproportionate strength in the House of Representatives by adding three-fifths of the slaves to the number of white persons in apportioning Congressmen to the several states; by Article I, Section 8, which gave Congress the power to suppress insurrections; by Article I, Section 9, which postponed prohibition of the slave trade until twenty years after the Constitution's adoption; by Article IV, Section 2, which provided for the return of fugitive slaves. Little wonder, then, that John Stuart Mill could say that "abolitionists, in America, mean those who do not keep within the Constitution."[2]

Like the Progressives in a subsequent generation, abolitionists sought to undermine the Constitution's authority. When in 1840 James Madison's notes on the proceedings of the Constitutional Convention were pub-

[1] "The Constitution and Slavery," *The North Star*, March 16, 1849, *The Life and Writings of Frederick Douglass*, ed. Philip Foner (New York, 1950), I, 362.

[2] John Stuart Mill, *Dissertations and Discussions: Political, Philosophical, and Historical* (New York, 1882), I, 11.

lished, abolitionists seized on them to show in detail what they had long suspected: that the revered Constitution was a sordid sectional compromise, in Garrison's words "a covenant with death and an agreement with hell."

On this as on all other policy questions there were a variety of abolitionist views, not a single party line. Abolitionists who believed in political action were naturally reluctant to condemn the Constitution root and branch. Political abolitionists tended to stress the document's preamble, with its promise to "establish Justice . . . promote the general Welfare, and secure the Blessings of Liberty to ourselves and our Posterity," and to explain away the enabling clauses previously cited. Richard Hildreth, for example, argued that the fugitive slave clause was intended to refer only to apprentices and indentured servants; and on the eve of the Civil War Douglass asserted that the three-fifths clause "leans to freedom."[3]

It was the Garrisonian wing of the movement, therefore, which produced the most rigorous critique of the United States Constitution. These men saw the Constitution as a patchwork of incompatible parts. It was, said Wendell Phillips, "a wall hastily built, in hard times, of round boulders"; it was an artificial, not a natural growth; it was "a 'hodge-podge,' . . . a general mess, a bowl of punch, of all the institutions of the nation."[4] Douglass, while still a Garrisonian, contended that no man could consistently take an oath to uphold the Constitution, for the Constitution was contradictory. "Lib-

[3] Richard Hildreth, *Despotism in America: An Inquiry into the Nature, Results, and Legal Basis of the Slave-Holding System in the United States* (Boston, 1854), pp. 235-39; Douglass, "The Constitution of the United States: Is It Pro-Slavery or Anti-Slavery?", March 26, 1860, *Life and Writings*, II 472.

[4] Wendell Phillips, "Disunion," January 20, 1861; "Progress," February 17, 1861; "The State of the Country," January 21 and May 11, 1863 (*Speeches, Lectures, and Letters,* First Series, Boston, 1902, pp. 351, 375, 537).

erty and Slavery—opposite as Heaven and Hell—are both
in the Constitution; and the oath to support the latter,"
Douglass wrote,

> is an oath to perform that which God has made im-
> possible. The man that swears to support it vows
> allegiance to two masters—so opposite, that fidelity
> to the one is, necessarily, treachery to the other. If
> we adopt the preamble, with Liberty and Justice,
> we must repudiate the enacting clauses, with Kid-
> napping and Slaveholding. . . .

Garrison and Calhoun, Douglass continued, both saw
the real nature of the Constitution. "Garrison sees in
the Constitution precisely what John C. Calhoun sees
there—a compromise with Slavery—a bargain between
the North and the South; the former to free his soul
from the guilt of slaveholding, repudiates the bond; and
the latter, seeing the weakness of mere parchment guarantees, seeks a dissociation of the Union as his only
means of safety."[5]

The analysis of the Constitution by abolitionist pub-
licists was given more scholarly form in such works as
Richard Hildreth's *History of the United States of America* (Vol. III, 1849), George Ticknor Curtis' *History of the
. . . Constitution of the United States* (Vol. II, 1858),
Horace Greeley's *The American Conflict* (1865), and
Henry Wilson's *Rise and Fall of the Slave Power in
America* (1872). Like Beard, the abolitionist historians
believed that the American Revolution was betrayed by
what Horace Greeley called a "counterrevolution."[6] But
they saw the Revolution betrayed by its compromise with
slavery rather than by its compromise with capitalism.
These scholars established the tradition according to
which the Constitutional Convention experienced two

[5] *The North Star*, April 5, 1850, *Life and Writings*, II, 118.
[6] Horace Greeley, *The American Conflict: A History of the Great
Rebellion* . . . (Hartford, 1865), I, 53.

great crises: one in late June and early July concerning
the basis of representation in Congress; the other, in mid-
August, arising from the questions of slave importation
and the power of the Federal government over commerce.
In this canon the settlement of the two great crises was
accomplished by two (or, if one counted separately the
agreement about representation in the House and the
agreement about representation in the Senate, three)
great compromises. The first compromise, of course, was
that which gave the states equal representation in the
Senate and apportioned representation in the House on
the basis of a "Federal ratio" adding three-fifths of the
slaves to the white population; the second compromise
permitted the importation of slaves until 1808 while
making it possible for Congress to pass laws regulating
commerce by a simple majority. This way of looking at
the Constitutional Convention was concisely summarized by James Schouler in his *History of the United
States of America under the Constitution*, which appeared
during the last two decades of the nineteenth century.[7]

In 1903, in a paper delivered before the American Historical Association, Max Farrand undertook to correct
this traditional account. "It can not be too strongly emphasized," Farrand argued, "that in 1787 the slavery
question was not the important question, we might say
it was not the moral question that it was in 1850." Stressing the fact that Madison's notes on the Convention had
been published in 1840 in the midst of controversy over
slavery, Farrand remarked that "it is not surprising that
the historical writers of that time, in treating of the formation of the Constitution, should overemphasize the slav-

[7] For early enumeration of the compromises, see Richard Hildreth, *The History of the United States of America* (New York,
1849), III, 520; George Ticknor Curtis, "The Constitution of the
United States and its History," *Narrative and Critical History of
America*, ed. Justin Winsor (Boston and New York, 1888), VII,
238-39, 243-44; James Schouler, *History of the United States of
America, under the Constitution* I (New York, 1894), 45-46.

ery questions in the Convention." In this paper, and more fully ten years later in his *Framing of the Constitution of the United States,* Farrand attacked the view that the important compromises at the Convention were compromises over slavery. The three-fifths ratio, he said, had been devised in 1783 and accepted by eleven states before the Convention met: thus it was not really a Convention compromise. The bargain over slave importation and commercial laws was a compromise of the Convention, but less important than a number of others, such as those concerning the admission of new states and the mode of electing the President.[8]

Farrand's revision of the abolitionist critique found a ready response in an America which was accepting the new Jim Crow laws and beginning to rewrite the history of Reconstruction. Frederick Jackson Turner anticipated Farrand when, in the 1890's, he insisted that the frontier rather than slavery was the major theme of the American experience.[9] Beard, iconoclast though he was, gave slavery and slaveholders a most shadowy role in his analysis of the Constitution: he was uncertain whether slaves were "personalty" or "realty"; he nowhere commits himself as to whether Southern slaveholders, as a group, were for or against the Constitution; he ignores almost entirely the profound sectional antagonisms evident in the

[8] Max Farrand, "Compromises of the Constitution," *Annual Report of the American Historical Association for the Year 1903* (Washington, 1904), I, 73-84.

[9] In an early essay entitled "Problems in American History" (1892), Turner asserted: "The struggle over slavery is a most important incident in our history, but it will be seen, as the meaning of events unfolds, that the real lines of American development, the forces dominating our character, are to be studied in the history of Western expansion"; elsewhere in the essay he called Westward expansion "the fundamental dominating fact in United States history" (*The Early Writings of Frederick Jackson Turner*, eds. Everett E. Edwards and Fulmer Mood, Madison, Wis., 1938, pp. 71-72). Essentially the same argument was repeated a year later in Turner's famous address on "The Significance of the Frontier in American History."

debates of the Convention and of the state ratifying conventions. Thus Beard in his 1913 classic built on Farrand's analysis.[10] In 1923, Robert Livingston Schuyler repeated the gist of Farrand's conclusions in his *Constitution of the United States*.[11] In 1935, Andrew C. McLaughlin concurred, writing: "In later years the Constitution was spoken of as if it were a compact or agreement between the slave states and the free. Nothing can be more false to the fact."[12] As emphasis on slavery had dominated treatment of the Constitution from 1840 to 1900, so a neglect of slavery's role prevailed from the turn of the century to World War II.

More recently, a return toward the abolitionist critique has been evident. Even before the war Charles Warren had suggested, as a consideration "which historians have failed to emphasize," that sectional hostility explains much of the Antifederalist resistance to the Constitution.[13] And the anti-Beardian historians of the 1950's, while insisting that the Constitution was more democratic than Beard supposed, have also (rather inconsistently) brought the question of slavery back into the foreground of debate. One summary of the new revisionism states that "the really fundamental conflict in American society at the time [was] the division between slave and free states, between North and South."[14] The floor would thus seem to be open for a detailed reconsideration of the abolitionist contention that, in the words of Gouverneur Morris at the Convention, "Domestic slavery is

[10] For a detailed discussion of the treatment of slavery by both Turner and Beard, see my "Turner, Beard and Slavery," *Journal of Negro History* (October 1963).

[11] Robert Livingston Schuyler, *The Constitution of the United States* (New York, 1923), p. 100.

[12] Andrew C. McLaughlin, *A Constitutional History of the United States* (New York, 1935), p. 190.

[13] Charles Warren, *The Making of the Constitution* (Boston, 1928), pp. 23-30, 755-58.

[14] Robert E. Brown, *Reinterpretation of the Formation of the American Constitution* (Boston, 1963), p. 48.

the most prominent feature in the aristocratic countenance of the . . . Constitution."[15]

I

According to the abolitionist critique, slavery helped
to shape the Constitution because slavery was the basis
of conflict between North and South, and compromising
that conflict was the main work of the Constitutional
Convention.[16]

Both in the nineteenth and twentieth centuries, one
line of argument against the significance of slavery in the
genesis of the Constitution has stressed the fact that the
words "slave" and "slavery" do not appear in the Constitution, and contended that, to quote Farrand, "there
was comparatively little said on the subject [of slavery]
in the convention."[17] This might be called the argument
from silence.

But we *know* why the Founders did not use the words
"slave" and "slavery" in the Constitution. Paterson of
New Jersey stated in the Convention that when, in 1783,
the Continental Congress changed its eighth Article of
Confederation so that slaves would henceforth be included in apportioning taxation among the States, the
Congress "had been ashamed to use the term 'Slaves' and
had substituted a description." Iredell, in the Virginia
ratifying convention, said similarly that the fugitive slave
clause of the proposed Constitution did not use the word
"slave" because of the "particular scruples" of the "northern delegates"; and in 1798 Dayton of New Jersey, who

[15] *The Records of the Federal Convention of 1787*, ed. Max Farrand (New Haven, London, 1911), II, 222.

[16] My emphasis on sectional conflict in the Revolutionary period
follows Professor Alden's *The First South* (Baton Rouge, 1961).
The corollary contention that slavery was not dying in 1787 is
strongly supported by Robert McColley's *Slavery and Jeffersonian
Virginia* (Urbana, 1964), which came to my attention after this
essay was in proof.

[17] Max Farrand, *The Framing of the Constitution of the United
States* (New Haven, 1913), p. 110.

had been a member of the Convention, told the House of Representatives that the purpose was to avoid any "stain" on the new government.[18] If for Northern delegates the motive was shame, for Southern members of the Convention it was prudence. Madison wrote to Lafayette in 1830, referring to emancipation: "I scarcely express myself too strongly in saying, that any allusion in the Convention to the subject you have so much at heart would have been a spark to a mass of gunpowder."[19] Madison's metaphor hardly suggests that the subject of slavery was of secondary importance to the Convention.

Farrand's own magnificent edition of the Convention records amply refutes his contention that the subject of slavery was little discussed. The South Carolinians in particular were often on their feet demanding security for what one of them called "this species of property."[20] And yet the role of slavery in the Convention went much further than this. For we have it on Madison's authority that it was "pretty well understood" that the "institution of slavery and its consequences formed the line of discrimination" between the contending groups of States in the Convention.[21] Slavery, that is to say, was recognized as the basis of sectionalism; and it is not a difficult task to show that sectional conflict between North and South was the major tension in the Convention.

According to Franklin, debate in the Convention proceeded peaceably ("with great coolness and temper") until on June 11, the rule of suffrage in the national

[18] *Records of the Convention*, I, 561 (Paterson), III, 376-77 (Dayton); *The Debates in the Several State Conventions, on the Adoption of the Federal Constitution*, ed. Jonathan Elliot (Washington, 1836), IV, 182 (Iredell).

[19] James Madison to General LaFayette, February 1, 1830, *Letters and Other Writings of James Madison* (Philadelphia, 1865), IV, 60.

[20] *Records of the Convention*, III, 254. See also *ibid.*, II, 95, 364, 371: III, 135.

[21] *Ibid.*, II, 10.

legislature was discussed.[22] Farrand would have us believe
that the three-fifths ratio which resulted was not a compromise in the Convention, that it had been recommended by Congress in 1783, adopted by eleven states before
the Convention met, and was part of the original New
Jersey Plan.[23] Farrand's statement is misleading, however, for all the above remarks refer to counting three-
fifths of the slaves *in apportioning taxation*. What was
at issue in Convention was the *extension of this ratio to
representation*: what George Ticknor Curtis called "the
naked question whether the slaves should be included
as persons, and in the proportion of three fifths, in the
census for the future apportionment of representatives
among the States."[24] The two applications were very different. As Luther Martin told the Maryland legislature,
taxing slaves discouraged slavery, while giving them political representation encouraged it.[25] Thus tempers rose
in the Convention from the moment that Rutledge and
Butler of South Carolina asserted that representation in
the House should be according to quotas of contribution;
years later Rufus King observed that the three-fifths
clause "was, at the time, believed to be a great" conces-
sion, "and has proved to have been the greatest which
was made to secure the adoption of the constitution."[26]

On June 25 there occurred the first perfectly sectional

[22] *Ibid.*, I, 197. The question had been postponed on May 30 and
again on June 9.

[23] Farrand, *Framing of the Constitution*, pp. 107-8. For the New
Jersey Plan, see *Records of the Convention*, I, 242-45.

[24] *History of the . . . Constitution of the United States* (New
York, 1858), II, 153.

[25] *Records of the Convention*, III, 197.

[26] Speech in the Senate, March 1819, *ibid.*, III, 428-30. While
Farrand presents the compromise regarding representation in the
Senate as more important than the adoption of the three-fifths rule
for elections to the House, a South Carolina delegate said that "the
rule of Representation in the 1st. branch was the true condition of
that in the 2d. branch" (*ibid.*, II, 263).

vote of the Convention, the five States from Maryland to Georgia voting to postpone consideration of the election of the Senate until the three-fifths clause regarding elections for the House had been settled. On June 29, Madison made the first of many statements as to the sectional nature of the issue:

> If there was real danger, I would give the smaller states the defensive weapons.—But there is none from that quarter. The great danger to our general government *is the great southern and northern interests of the continent, being opposed to each other. Look to the votes in congress, and most of them stand divided by the geography of the country, not according to the size of the states.* (Italics in original).[27]

The next day Madison reiterated that "the States were divided into different interests not by their difference of size, but by other circumstances; the most material of which resulted partly from climate, but principally from their having or not having slaves."[28] Farrand comments on these observations that "Madison was one of the very few men who seemed to appreciate the real division of interests in the country."[29] Yet Madison's emphasis on sectional conflict at the Convention was echoed by Pinckney on July 2, by King on July 10, by Mason on July 11, and, with reluctance, by Gouverneur Morris on July 13; and when on July 14 Madison once more asserted that slavery, not size, formed the line of discrimination between the States, as previously remarked, he said that this was "pretty well understood" by the Convention.[30] Slavery was thus the basis of the great Convention crisis,

[27] *Ibid.*, I, 476.

[28] *Ibid.*, I, 486.

[29] *Framing of the Constitution*, p. 110. This statement is a little difficult to reconcile with Farrand's general position that slavery was not an important issue in 1787.

[30] *Records of the Convention*, I, 510, 566, 578, 586, 604.

when, as Gouverneur Morris later said, the fate of America was suspended by a hair.

But this crisis, and the crisis which followed over the import of slaves,[31] cannot be understood from the records of the Convention alone. The great Convention compromises involving slavery were attempts to reconcile disputes which had been boiling up for years in the Continental Congress.

II

Sectional conflict, like the ghost in *Hamlet*, was there from the beginning. When in September 1774 at the first Continental Congress Patrick Henry made his famous declaration "I am not a Virginian, but an American," the point he was making was that Virginia would not insist on counting slaves in apportioning representation; Henry's next sentence was: "Slaves are to be thrown out of the Question, and if the freemen can be represented according to their Numbers I am satisfyed."[32] The next speaker, Lynch of South Carolina, protested, and the question was left unsettled. Thus early did South Carolinian intransigence overbear Virginian liberalism.

Again in July 1776, the month of the Declaration of Independence, the problem of slave representation was brought before Congress in the debate over the proposed Articles of Confederation. The Dickinson draft of the Articles produced three controversies, strikingly similar to the three great compromises of the subsequent Constitutional Convention: "The equal representation of all the states in Congress aroused the antagonism of the larger states. The apportionment of common expenses accord-

[31] As to the magnitude of the crisis over slave importation, George Bancroft concluded that had it not been compromised Georgia, South Carolina, North Carolina and Virginia would have formed a Southern confederacy (*History of the Formation of the Constitution of the United States of America*, New York, 1882, II, 157).

[32] *Diary and Autobiography of John Adams*, ed. Lyman H. Butterfield (Cambridge, Mass., 1961), II, 125.

ing to total population aroused the bitter opposition of the states with large slave populations. The grant to Congress of broad powers over Western lands and boundaries was resisted stubbornly by the states whose charters gave them large claims to the West."[33] In its ten-year existence the Continental Congress succeeded in solving only the last of these controversies, the question of Western lands, and accordingly emphasis has tended to fall on it in histories of the Confederation. But the other two problems were just as hotly debated, in much the same language as in 1787; and on these questions, as Channing observes, there was a "different alignment in Congress" than on the matter of Western lands: a sectional alignment.[34]

The eleventh Article of the Dickinson draft stated that money contributions from the States should be "in Proportion to the Number of Inhabitants of every Age, Sex and Quality, except Indians not paying Taxes." On July 30, 1776, Samuel Chase of Maryland (later a prominent Antifederalist) moved the insertion of the word "white," arguing that "if Negroes are taken into the Computation of Numbers to ascertain Wealth, they ought to be in settling the Representation"; Gouverneur Morris would use this same formula in July 1787 to resolve the deadlock over representation in the House.[35] In the debate which followed the changes were rung upon several themes of the Constitutional Convention. Wilson of Pennsylvania said that to exempt slaves from taxation would encourage slaveholding; in response to the observation that if slaves were counted, Northern sheep should also be counted, Benjamin Frank-

[33] Merrill Jensen, *The Articles of Confederation: An Interpretation of the Social-Constitutional History of the American Revolution, 1774-1781*, paperback edition (Madison, 1959), pp. 138-39.

[34] Edward Channing, *A History of the United States* (New York, 1920), III, 451.

[35] Adams, *Diary and Autobiography*, II, 245.

lin remarked that "sheep will never make any Insurrections"; Rutledge of South Carolina anticipated the August 1787 debate on navigation laws by warning that "the Eastern Colonies will become the Carriers for the Southern. They will obtain Wealth for which they will not be taxed"; and his colleague Lynch again threw down a South Carolina ultimatum: "If it is debated, whether their Slaves are their Property, there is an end of the Confederation."[36]

The war had scarcely ended when the sectional debate resumed. We tend to think of Thomas Jefferson as a national statesman, and of the controversy over whether new states would be slave or free as something subsequent to 1820. How striking, then, to find Jefferson writing from Congress to Governor Benjamin Harrison of Virginia in November 1783 about the Northwest Territory: "If a state be first laid off on the [Great] lakes it will add a vote to the Northern scale, if on the Ohio it will add one to the Southern."[37] This concern would never be out of the minds of Southern politicians until the Civil War. Jefferson did, of course, attempt to exclude slavery from the Territories. But on the ninth anniversary of Lexington and Concord, Congress, on motion of Spaight of

[36] *Ibid.*, II, 246. As early as 1776 one South Carolina delegate voiced fear that Congress would become too powerful, as early as 1778 another demanded that important business be approved by eleven states (Edward Rutledge and William Henry Drayton, quoted in John R. Alden, *The South in the Revolution, 1763-1789*, Baton Rouge, La., 1957, pp. 216, 219). We know from Jefferson's notes on the debates of July-August 1776 that Chase's motion, described in the text, was defeated 7-5 on August 1, 1776 by a strictly sectional vote (*The Papers of Thomas Jefferson*, ed. Julian P. Boyd, Princeton, I, 1950, 323).

[37] Thomas Jefferson to the Governor of Virginia (Benjamin Harrison), November 11, 1783, *Letters of Members of the Continental Congress*, ed. Edmund C. Burnett (Washington, D.C., 1934), VII, 374. Nearly a century ago Hermann von Holst remarked on "The erroneous view . . . that the mischievous political division of the country by a geographical line dates back only to the Missouri compromise" (*The Constitutional and Political History of the United States*, Chicago, 1877, I, 86-87), but that view still prevails today.

North Carolina, seconded by Read of South Carolina, struck this provision from Jefferson's draft proposals.[38]

A principal issue between North and South in these first years of the Critical Period was financial. Southern resistance to Northern financial manipulations did not wait until the 1790's: it began, if one must choose a date, when Delaware, Maryland, Virginia, and both the Carolinas voted against the devaluation plan of March 18, 1780, with every Northern state except divided New Hampshire voting Aye.[39] After the war the issue became still more intense. The Revolutionary campaigns in the South took place largely in the last three years of the war "when neither Congress nor the states," in the words of E. James Ferguson, "had effective money and the troops were supported by impressment." The result was that of the three major categories of public debt—Quartermaster and Commissary certificates issued to civilians; loan certificates; and final settlement certificates issued to the Continental army—the South held only 16 per cent.[40] The public debt of the South was a state debt, while the various kinds of Federal debt were held by Northerners: as Spaight of North Carolina put it, "the Eastern [i.e., Northern] States . . . have got Continental Securities for all monies loaned, services done or articles impressed, while to the southward, it has been made a State debt."[41] Hence when Congress sought to tax all the states to repay the Federal debt, the South protested; and when Congress further provided that Northern states could meet their Congressional requisitions with securities, so that only the South need pay coin, the South was

[38] Bancroft makes the point about the date in his *Formation of the Constitution*, I, 157.

[39] *Journals of the Continental Congress, 1774-1789* (Washington, 1904-1937), ed. Gaillard Hunt *et al.*, XVI, 267.

[40] E. James Ferguson, *The Power of the Purse: A History of American Public Finance, 1776-1790* (Chapel Hill, 1961), pp. 181-83.

[41] Richard Dobbs Spaight to the Governor of North Carolina (Alexander Martin), April 30, 1784, *Letters of Continental Congress*, VII, 509.

furious. Madison told Edmund Randolph in 1783 that unless the public accounts were speedily adjusted and discharged "a dissolution of the Union will be inevitable." "The pious New-Englanders," Read of South Carolina wrote in April 1785, "think tis time to carry their long projected Scheme into Execution and make the southern states bear the burthen of furnishing all the actual money."[42]

Sectional considerations underlay many an action of the early 1780's where they might not, at first glance, seem evident. Jefferson's appointment as United States representative in France is an example. Jefferson had been appointed to the commission to negotiate a peace, as had Laurens of South Carolina; but Jefferson did not go and Laurens was captured by the British en route to Europe, so that three Northerners—John Jay, John Adams, and Benjamin Franklin—carried the burden of the peace talks. The treaty completed, the same three men stayed on in Europe to represent American interests there, and it was this that aroused Southern concern. James Monroe expressed it in March 1784, writing to Governor Harrison. Monroe pointed out that Virginia owed British merchants £2,800,000 in debts, which according to the peace treaty must now be paid. "It is important to the southern States to whom the negotiation of these treaties are committed; for except the fishery and the fur-trade (the latter of w'h Mr. Jeff'n thinks . . . may be turn'd down the Potow'k); the southern States, are as

[42] James Madison to Edmund Randolph, February 25, 1783, *Papers of Madison* (Washington, 1840), I, 512; Jacob Read to Charles Thomson, April 26, 1785, *Letters of Continental Congress*, VIII, 105. See also: Ephraim Paine to Robert R. Livingston, May 24, 1784, *ibid.*, VII, 534-35; John Francis Mercer to the Executive Council of Virginia, April 10, 1784, *ibid.*, VII, 491; William Grayson to James Madison, September 16, 1785, *ibid.*, VIII, 217; James McHenry to John Hall [September 28? 1785], *ibid.*, VIII, 223; Richard Henry Lee to James Monroe, October 17, 1785, *ibid.*, VIII, 238-39; Nathan Dane to Jacob Wales, January 31, 1786, *ibid.*, VIII, 296-97.

States, almost alone interested in it."[43] In May, with Jefferson's appointment achieved, the Virginia delegates in Congress wrote the governor: "It was an object with us, in order to render the Commission as agreable as possible to the Southern States to have Mr. Jefferson placed in the room of Mr. Jay." The previous arrangement, the Virginians went on, involved "obvious inequality in the Representation of these States in Europe"; had it continued, it would have presented "an insurmountable obstacle" to giving the commission such great powers.[44]

Here in microcosm was the problem of the South until its victory at the 1787 Convention: recognizing the need for stronger Federal powers, it feared to create them until it was assured that the South could control their use.

III

Even as early as the 1780's the South felt itself to be a conscious minority. This was evident, for example, in the comment of Virginia delegates as to the location of the national capital. "The votes in Congress as they stand at present," wrote the delegates from the Old Dominion, "are unfavorable to a Southern situation and untill the admission of Western States into the Union, we apprehend it will be found impracticable to retain that Body [Congress], any length of time, Southward of the middle States."[45] In the fall of 1786, when the clash over shutting the Mississippi to American commerce was at its height, Timothy Bloodworth of North Carolina remarked that "it is wel known that the ballance of Power is now in the Eastern States, and they appear de-

[43] James Monroe to the Governor of Virginia (Benjamin Harrison), March 26, 1784, *ibid.*, VII, 478.

[44] The Virginia Delegates to the Governor of Virginia (Benjamin Harrison), May 13, 1784, *ibid.*, VII, 525.

[45] The Virginia Delegates to the Governor of Virginia (Benjamin Harrison), May 13, 1784, *ibid.*, VII, 524.

termined to keep it in that Direction."[46] This was why
such Southerners as Richard Henry Lee, later the nation's
leading Antifederalist pamphleteer, were already opposing stronger Federal powers in 1785. "It seems to me
clear, beyond doubt," Lee wrote to Madison, "that the
giving Congress a power to Legislate over the Trade of
the Union would be dangerous in the extreme to the 5
Southern or Staple States, whose want of ships and sea-
men would expose their freightage and their produce to
a most pernicious and destructive Monopoly."[47] This
was a strong argument, which would be heard throughout the South till 1861; it was this fear which in all prob-
ability caused George Mason and Edmund Randolph of
Virginia to refuse to sign the Constitution in 1787.[48]
Recognizing the force of Lee's argument, Madison wrote
to Jefferson in the summer and fall of 1785 that commercial distress was causing a call for stronger powers in
Congress throughout the North, but that the South was
divided. Lee was "an inflexible adversary, Grayson [Wil-
liam Grayson, another Virginia Antifederalist in 1788]
unfriendly." Animosity against Great Britain would push
the South toward commercial regulation, but the high
price of tobacco would work against it. "S. Carolina I
am told is deliberating on the distresses of her commerce
and will probably concur in some general plan; with a
proviso, no doubt against any restraint from importing
slaves, of which they have received from Africa since the
peace about twelve thousand." Madison concluded by
telling his comrade in France that he trembled to think

[46] Timothy Bloodworth to the Governor of North Carolina (Richard Caswell), September 29, 1786, *ibid.*, VIII, 474.

[47] Richard Henry Lee to James Madison, August 11, 1785, *ibid.*,
VIII, 181.

[48] See Edmund Randolph to the Speaker of the Virginia House of
Delegates, October 10, 1787; George Mason's "Account of certain
Proceedings in Convention"; and on Mason's motives, James Madison
to Thomas Jefferson, October 24, 1787 and The Landholder [Oliver
Ellsworth], VI (*Records of the Convention*, III, 127, 367, 136, 164-65).

what would happen should the South not join the other states in strengthening Congress.[49]

Others beside Madison trembled at this thought: the possibility of disunion was openly and seriously discussed in the 1780's, particularly by those who knew of the fiercely sectional debates in Congress.[50] And if disunion was only the speculation of a few in 1785, the great controversy over the Mississippi in 1786 shook many more from their complacence.

The Mississippi question of the 1780's was a part of the larger question of the destiny of the West which, ultimately, would be the immediate cause of the Civil War. Farrand is less than accurate in his attempt to disengage the question of the admission of new states at the Constitutional Convention from sectional strife. For if there is a single key to the politics of Congress and the Convention in the Critical Period, it is that the South expected the West to be slave rather than free and to tilt the balance of power southward, while in Bancroft's words "an ineradicable dread of the coming power of the Southwest lurked in New England, especially in Massachusetts."[51] That group in Congress recognized as "the Southern Interest" (1786), "the Southern party" (1787) or "the Southern Delegation" (1788)[52] fought throughout

[49] James Madison to Thomas Jefferson, August 20 and October 3, 1785, *The Writings of James Madison*, ed. Gaillard Hunt (New York, 1901), II, 160-65, 178-83.

[50] See Richard Dobbs Spaight to the Governor of North Carolina (Alexander Martin), October 16, 1784; Rufus King to John Adams, November 2, 1785; Nathan Dane to Edward Pullen, January 8, 1786; Theodore Sedgwick to Caleb Strong, August 6, 1786; Timothy Bloodworth to the Governor of North Carolina (Richard Caswell), September 4, 1786 (*Letters of Continental Congress*, VII, 602-3; VIII, 247, 282, 415-16, 462). See also James Monroe to the Governor of Virginia (Patrick Henry), August 12, 1786 and to James Madison, September 3, 1786 (*ibid.*, VIII, 424-25, 461-62).

[51] *Formation of the Constitution*, II, 80.

[52] James Manning to Nathan Miller, May 19, 1786, *Letters of Continental Congress*, VIII, 364; Otto to Vergennes, February 10, 1787, quoted in Bancroft, *Formation of the Constitution*, II, 410;

the 1780's to forestall the admission of Vermont until at least one Southern state could be added simultaneously, to hasten the development of the West, and to remove all obstacles to its speedy organization into the largest possible number of new states.[53] It was here that the Mississippi question entered. What was feared if America permitted Spain to close New Orleans to American commerce was not only a separation of the Western states, but a slackening of the southwestward migration which Southerners counted on to assure their long-run predominance in the Union.

"The southern states," wrote the French minister to his superior in Europe,

> are not in earnest when they assert that without the navigation of the Mississippi the inhabitants of the interior will seek an outlet by way of the lakes, and will throw themselves into the arms of England. . . . The true motive of this vigorous opposition is to be found in the great preponderance of the northern states, eager to incline the balance toward their side; the southern neglect no opportunity of increasing the population and importance of the western ter-

James Madison to Edmund Randolph, August 11, 1788, *Letters of Continental Congress*, VIII, 778.

[53] As early as May 1, 1782, Madison wrote in his "Observations Relating to the Influence of Vermont, and the Territorial Claims, on the Politics of Congress," that the Vermont question excited in the Southern states "an habitual jealousy of a predominance of Eastern interest." (*Papers of Madison*, I, 123). On June 8, 1784, Hugh Williamson of North Carolina wrote James Duane that if Vermont were to be independent he wanted to see "at least two Southern states formed at the same time" (*ibid.*, VII, 547); and at the very moment when the Constitution was being ratified by state conventions, the expiring Congress squabbled bitterly over pairing the admissions of Vermont and Kentucky (*ibid.*, VIII, 708, 714, 724, 733, 741, 757). See the Virginia Delegates to the Governor of Virginia (Edmund Randolph), November 3, 1787, for comment on the South's desire to admit the Western states rapidly (*ibid.*, VIII, 672-73).

ritory, and of drawing thither by degrees the inhabitants of New England. . . . These new territories will
gradually form themselves into separate governments; they will have their representatives in congress, and will augment greatly the mass of the southern states.[54]

Otto is abundantly confirmed by the debates of the Virginia ratifying convention,[55] and still more by Monroe's
correspondence of late 1786. On August 12, 1786, Monroe wrote from Congress to Patrick Henry:

P.S. The object in the occlusion of the Mississippi
on the part of these people so far as it is extended
to the interest of their States (for those of a private
kind gave birth to it): is to break up so far as this
will do it, the settlements on the western waters, prevent any in future, and thereby keep the States
Southward as they now are—or if settlements will
take place, that they shall be on such principles as
to make it the interest of the people to separate
from the Confederacy, so as effectually to exclude
any new State from it. To throw the weight of population eastward and keep it there. . . .

Like many another Southerner in the next seventy-five
years, Monroe ended by saying that, if it came to separation, it was essential that Pennsylvania join the South.[56]
So forceful was the effect of his letter on Henry, Madison
wrote Washington in December, that Henry, who had
hitherto advocated a stronger Union, began to draw back.

[54] Otto to Vergennes, September 10, 1786, quoted in Bancroft,
Formation of the Constitution, II, 392.

[55] *Debates in the State Conventions*, III, especially the debates of
June 13-14, during which for example Grayson stated: "This contest of the Mississippi involves this great national contest: That is,
whether one part of the continent shall govern the other" (*ibid.*,
III, 343).

[56] James Monroe to the Governor of Virginia (Patrick Henry),
August 12, 1786, *Letters of Continental Congress*, VIII, 424-25.

By 1788 he, like Lee, Grayson, and Monroe, would be an Antifederalist.

The upshot of the Mississippi squabble was that the long efforts to vest Congress with power over commerce were threatened with failure at the very brink of success. As delegates made their way to the Annapolis Convention in the fall of 1786, Bloodworth of North Carolina wrote that because of the Mississippi controversy "all other Business seems out of View at present." "Should the measure proposed be pursued," Grayson told the Congress, "the Southern States would never grant those powers which were acknowledged to be essential to the existence of the Union."[57] When Foreign Secretary Jay attempted to have instructions, authorizing him to give up American insistence on using the river, adopted by a simple Congressional majority of seven states, it stirred in many Southern breasts the fear of being outvoted. Even before the Mississippi question came before Congress Southerners like Monroe had insisted that, if Congress were to regulate commerce, commercial laws should require the assent of nine or even eleven states.[58] Jay's attempt (as Southerners saw it) to use a simple majority to push through a measure fundamentally injurious to the South greatly intensified this apprehension. When the Constitutional Convention met, the so-called Pinckney Plan suggested a two-thirds Congressional majority for commercial laws, and both the Virginia ratifying convention (which voted to ratify by a small majority) and the North Carolina convention (which rejected ratification) recommended the same amendment.[59]

[57] Timothy Bloodworth to the Governor of North Carolina (Richard Caswell), September 4, 1786, ibid., VIII, 462; Charles Thomson, Minutes of Proceedings, August 18, 1786, ibid., VIII, 438-40.

[58] See James Monroe to James Madison, July 26, 1785, ibid., VIII, 172.

[59] For the Pinckney Plan, see Records of the Convention, III, 604-9; for the amendments proposed in the Virginia and North Carolina ratifying conventions, Debates in the State Conventions, III, 595 and IV, 241.

In the midst of the Mississippi controversy, men hopeful for stronger government saw little prospect of success. Madison wrote Jefferson in August 1786 that he almost despaired of strengthening Congress through the Annapolis Convention or any other[60]; in September, Otto wrote to Vergennes: "It is to be feared that this discussion will cause a great coolness between the two parties, and may be the germ of a future separation of the southern states."[61]

IV

Why then did the South consent to the Constitutional Convention? If the South felt itself on the defensive in the 1780's, and particularly so in the summer and fall of 1786, why did its delegates agree to strengthen Federal powers in 1787? If a two-thirds majority for commercial laws seemed essential to Southerners in August of one year, why did they surrender it in August of the next? Were Madison and Washington, as they steadfastly worked to strengthen the national government, traitors to the interests of their section, or was there some view of the future which nationalist Southerners then entertained which enabled them to be good Southerners and good Federalists at the same time?

It is Madison, once more, who provides the clue. He saw that if the South were to agree in strengthening Congress, the plan which gave each state one vote would have to be changed in favor of the South. And in letters to Jefferson, to Randolph, and to Washington in the spring of 1787 he foretold in a sentence the essential plot of the Convention drama. The basis of representation would be changed to allow representation by numbers as well as by states, because a change was "recommended to the Eastern States by the actual superiority of their

[60] James Madison to Thomas Jefferson, August 12, 1786, *Writings of Madison*, II, 262.

[61] Otto to Vergennes, September 10, 1786, quoted in Bancroft, *Formation of the Constitution*, II, 391.

populousness, and to the Southern by their expected superiority."[62]

So it fell out. Over and over again members of the Convention stated, as of something on which all agreed, that "as soon as the Southern & Western population should predominate, which must happen in a few years,"[63] the South would be compensated for any advantages wrung from it by the North in the meantime. When Northerners insisted on equality of votes in the Senate, it was partly because they feared what would happen when the South gained its inevitable (as they supposed) majority. "He must be short sighted indeed," declared King on July 12,

> who does not foresee that whenever the Southern States shall be more numerous than the Northern, they can & will hold a language that will awe them [the Northern States] into justice. If they threaten to separate now in case injury shall be done them, will their threats be less urgent or effectual, when force shall back their demands?[64]

Gouverneur Morris echoed this gloomy prophecy the next day. "The consequence of such a transfer of power from the maritime to the interior & landed interest," Madison quoted him,

> will he foresees be such an oppression of commerce, that he shall be obliged to vote for ye. vicious principle of equality in the 2d. branch in order to provide some defence for the N. States agst. it.

[62] James Madison to Thomas Jefferson, March 19[18], 1787, *Writings of Madison*, II, 327; also same to Edmund Randolph, April 8, 1787 and to George Washington, April 16, 1787 (*ibid.*, pp. 11, 340, 345).

[63] These were the words of George Mason on July 11 (*Records of the Convention*, I, 586); see also, e.g., Madison that same day (*ibid.*, I, 585-86).

[64] *Ibid.*, I, 595-96.

"It has been said," Morris added, "that N.C. [,] S.C. and Georgia only will in a little time have a majority of the people in America. They must in that case include the great interior Country, and every thing was to be apprehended from their getting the power into their hands."[65]

This false expectation explains why Georgia and the Carolinas who (as Gunning Bedford noted) should by present population have been "small" states, considered themselves "large" states at the Convention.[66] This expectation clarifies, it seems to me, why the South gave way in its demand that commercial laws require a two-thirds majority; for would not time and the flow of migration soon provide such a majority without written stipulation? At the crucial Virginia ratifying convention no one questioned that the South would soon be the most populous section of the country. The difference lay between those who thought this inevitable event made it safe to strengthen the Federal government now, and those, like Henry and Mason, who counseled waiting until the Southern Congressional majority made absolutely safe a transfer of power.[67]

The irony, of course, was that the expectation was completely erroneous. The expected Southern majority in the House never materialized, and the Senate, not the House, became the bulwark of the South. In 1790, the population of the South had been growing more rapidly than the North's population for several decades, and was within 200,000 of the population north of the Potomac. True to the general expectation in 1787, the Southwest filled up more rapidly than the area north of the Ohio River. In 1820, Ohio, Indiana, Illinois, and Michigan contained a population of almost 800,000, but Missouri,

[65] *Ibid.*, I, 604-5.

[66] *Ibid.*, I, 491, 500.

[67] For the position of Henry and Mason, see *Debates in the State Conventions*, III, e.g., pp. 83, 260-61. For the Federalist position, based on the same assumption of a future Southern majority, see, e.g., George Nicholas, *ibid.*, III, 121-22.

Kentucky, Tennessee, Alabama, Mississippi, Louisiana, and Arkansas held over 1,300,000 persons. Nevertheless, in the original thirteen states the Northern population pulled so far ahead of the Southern that in 1820 the white population of Northern states and territories was almost twice that of Southern states and territories. Thus the South never obtained the Congressional majority which statesmen of both sections had anticipated at the time of the Constitutional Convention.

When the dream of a Southern majority in Congress and the nation collapsed, there fell together with it the vision of a Southern commercial empire, drawing the produce of the West down the Potomac and the James to "a Philadelphia or a Baltimore" on the Virginia coast.[68] It was not, as it so often seems, an accident that the Convention of 1787 grew from the Annapolis Convention, or that Virginians were the prime movers in calling both. Throughout the 1780's Madison, Jefferson, Monroe, and to an almost fanatical degree, Washington, were intent on strengthening the commercial ties between Virginia and the West. As early as 1784, Jefferson suggested to Madison cooperation with Maryland in opening communication to the West, and during that year and the next both Washington and Monroe toured the Western country with their grand plan in mind.[69] Jefferson and Monroe pushed a Potomac location for the national capital partly with the hope that it would "cement us to our Western friends when they shall be formed into separate states" and help Virginia to beat out Pennsylvania and New York in the race for Western trade.[70] Virginia had given up its claims to Western land,

---

[68] James Madison to James Monroe, June 21, 1785, *Writings of Madison*, II, 148.

[69] See Bancroft, *Formation of the Constitution*, I, 151-52, and Book 2, Chapter 3. Bancroft seems to me to have a better grasp of this phenomenon, as well as of the false Southern expectations about population growth (*ibid.*, II, 87), than any subsequent student.

[70] Thomas Jefferson to George Rogers Clark, December 4, 1783,

but its leaders hoped for a commercial dominion just as satisfactory: as Jefferson put it, "almost a monopoly of the Western and Indian trade."[71] "But smooth the road once," wrote the enraptured Washington, "and make easy the way for them, and then see what an influx of articles will be poured upon us; how amazingly our exports will be increased by them, and how amply we shall be compensated for any trouble and expense we may encounter to effect it."[72] The West, then, would not only give the South political predominance but also, as Madison wrote Jefferson, "double the value of half the land within the Commonwealth . . . extend its commerce, link with its interests those of the Western States, and lessen the immigration of its Citizens."[73] This was the castle-in-the-air which Virginians pictured as they worked to bring about the Constitutional Convention, this was the plan for economic development so abruptly and traumatically shattered by Secretary of the Treasury Alexander Hamilton.

In the Spring and Summer of 1788, however, as the South with the North moved to ratify the Constitution,[74] few foresaw the clouds on the horizon. The Constitu-

---

Letters of Continental Congress, VII, 378; also James Monroe to the Governor of Virginia (Benjamin Harrison), June 11, 1784, *ibid.*, VII, 550.

[71] Thomas Jefferson to James Madison, February 20, 1784, *Papers of Jefferson*, VI (Princeton, 1952), 548.

[72] George Washington to the Governor of Virginia (Benjamin Harrison), October 10, 1784, *The Writings of George Washington*, ed. John C. Fitzpatrick, XXVII (Washington, D.C., 1938), 476.

[73] James Madison to Thomas Jefferson, January 9, 1785, *Writings of Madison*, II, 102ff.

[74] The legend was later perpetrated that Southern slaveholders opposed the Constitution. An early instance occurs in *The Works of Fisher Ames*, ed. Seth Ames (Boston, 1854), I, 103. Charles Beard seems to have picked up the idea from Richard Hildreth: see *The Economic Origins of Jeffersonian Democracy* (New York, 1916), p. 399n. For the facts, consult Jackson T. Main, *The Antifederalists: Critics of the Constitution, 1781-1788* (Chapel Hill, 1961), pp. 215-20, 223-33, 242-48.

tional Convention, with a Southern majority (in Bancroft's words) "from its organization to its dissolution,"[75]
seemed to have wrought well for the South. Madison
alone, from his vantage-point in Congress, fretted about
that body's continued preoccupation with sectional issues. After wrangling all Spring about the admission of
Kentucky, Congress turned to that old favorite, the location of the capital. "It is truly mortifying," Madison
wrote to Washington, to see such "a display of locality,"
of "local and state considerations," at the very "outset of
the new Government." The behavior of Congress would
give "countenance to some of the most popular arguments which have been inculcated by the southern antifederalists," and "be regarded as at once a proof of the
preponderancy of the Eastern strength." "I foresee contentions," he wrote the next Spring, "first between federal and anti-federal parties, and then between northern
and southern parties."[76] Before long he would be leading
the opposition.

V

Even this sampling of the printed sources suggests that
sectional conflict based (to quote Madison once more)
on "the institution of slavery and its consequences" was
a potent force in the shaping of the Constitution. The
conclusion seems inescapable that any interpretation of
the Convention which stresses realty and personalty,
large states and small states, or monarchy and democracy, but leaves slavery out, is an inadequate interpretation.

[75] Bancroft, *Formation of the Constitution*, II, 75. The South
had a majority in the Convention because Rhode Island did not
send a delegation, the New Hampshire delegation came late, and
the New York delegation left early.

[76] James Madison to George Washington, August 24, 1788 and
September 14, 1788, *Letters of Continental Congress*, VIII, 786, 796;
letter by Madison (otherwise unidentified), March 6, 1789, quoted
in Bancroft, *Formation of the Constitution*, II, 358.

Scholarly effort to bring slavery back into the story of the Revolutionary and Early National periods might do worse than begin with those much-maligned exponents of the abolitionist critique, Horace Greeley and Henry Wilson. They, like Beard, believed that a counterrevolution took place, but they saw as its victim the slave rather than the white artisan or farmer. Moreover, they viewed the counterrevolution not as a sudden *coup d'état* in the years 1787-88, but as a long-drawn-out process which drew strength from the fatal concessions (as Wilson called them) of the Convention, but required such events as the cotton gin and the Louisiana Purchase for its completion.

Crude though they may be, these early abolitionist historians have the power to show us familiar events in a new light. They knew that Adams would have been President in 1800 had the three-fifths clause not existed,[77] and they understood why the Hartford Convention made the abrogation of that clause the first plank of its platform. They viewed the accession of Jefferson as a triumph for slavery; in their accounts the Louisiana Purchase figures not as a diplomatic triumph or an instance of loose Constitutional construction, but as an event by which slavery acquired "a vast extension of its power and influence."[78] They were fully aware of the part which Southern fear of a San Domingo in Cuba played in the genesis of the Monroe Doctrine, and in the American reaction to the Panama Congress.[79] No doubt all these insights are half-truths, but they are half-truths which have been neglected in this century and deserve to be reincorporated into the mainstream of scholarly interpretation.

[77] Channing remarks on this in his *History of the United States* (New York, 1916), III, 511n.

[78] Greeley, *American Conflict*, p. 57.

[79] See especially Henry Wilson, *History of the Rise and Fall of the Slave Power in America* (Boston, 1872), I, 115-17.

If it be granted that sectional conflict based on slavery was real and intense long before 1820, our final evaluation of the abolitionist critique of the United States Constitution will still depend on how we answer the question, *Could* slavery have been abolished at the time of the Revolution?

It came very close. During the Revolutionary War the importation of slaves ceased. In 1779 the Continental Congress agreed unanimously to arm 3,000 slaves in South Carolina and Georgia, with freedom as a reward. In 1784 Congress failed by one vote to prohibit slavery in the Western territories.[80] These facts support Von Holst in his remark that but "one more impulse" was needed.[81] Jeffrey Brackett, writing in 1889, suggested the sense of lost possibilities that was felt when the South Carolina and Georgia legislatures refused to adopt the plan to enlist slaves of the Deep South against the British:

> It was on hearing of the failure of this plan that Washington wrote, that the spirit of freedom which had so strongly marked the beginning of the war, had subsided. It is private not public interest, he added, which influences the generality of mankind.[82]

Why was the final impulse not forthcoming? Many abolitionists, concerned to identify their cause with the charisma of the Founding Fathers, contended that at the time of the Convention all public men expected slavery to die a natural death. This is far from the case. As Hildreth observed a century ago, the delegates from Georgia and South Carolina did not expect slavery to

[80] The 1779 and 1784 episodes are described by Alden, *South in the Revolution*, pp. 225-26, 345-46.

[81] *Constitutional and Political History*, I, 31.

[82] Jeffrey R. Brackett, "The Status of the Slave, 1775-1789," *Essays In The Constitutional History Of The United States In The Formative Period, 1775-1789*, ed. J. Franklin Jameson (Boston and New York, 1889), p. 311. The letter paraphrased was written to Lt. Col. John Laurens, July 10, 1782, and will be found in Washington's *Writings*, XXIV, 421.

end: "South Carolina and Georgia," Madison reported to Jefferson, "were inflexible on the point of slaves."[83] Nor is it safe to assume that the Upper South looked forward to emancipation. If so, why did every Southern delegation oppose Jefferson's 1784 proposal to prohibit slavery in the West? And if the South was rigid, the North gave way almost without protest. Gouverneur Morris, the delegate most outspoken against slavery in the Convention, was also the man who proposed the "bridge" (proportioning taxation to representation) that made possible the three-fifths compromise, and what he called a "bargain" between North and South on the question of slave importation. Farrand is perhaps a little hard on the delegates when he says that the majority "regarded slavery as an accepted institution, as a part of the established order."[84] It would be more accurate to say that almost without exception they felt that slavery was wrong; but that, inhibited by a concern to keep the Union together, by a predisposition to regard all property rights as sacred, and by an inability to imagine a society in which Negroes and whites could live together as citizens and brothers, they failed to grasp the nettle. Candid and forthright in so much else, the Fathers were evasive, ambivalent and indecisive in acting on slavery.

The upshot was that in the era of the Revolution the problem of slavery was recognized, was manageable, and was shirked. In Luther Martin's eloquent words, a Revolution

grounded upon the preservation of *those rights* to

[83] Hildreth, *Despotism in America*, p. 304; James Madison to Thomas Jefferson, October 24, 1787, *Records of the Convention*, III, 135. For confirming evidence as to the inflexible attitude of South Carolina and Georgia, see, e.g., *ibid.*, II, 95, 364, 371 and III, 378; *Debates in the State Conventions*, IV, 265. The Deep South attitude was one reason a Bill of Rights was omitted from the Constitution (*Records of the Convention*, II, 137 and III, 256).

[84] *The Fathers of the Constitution: A Chronicle of the Establishment of the Union* (New Haven, Toronto, London, 1921), p. 130.

which God and nature had entitled *us*, not in *particular*, but in *common* with *all the rest of mankind*,

ended by making a Constitution that was an

insult to that God . . . who views with equal eye the poor *African slave* and his *American master*.[85]

The abolitionists were right in seeing the American Revolution as a revolution betrayed.

[85] *Records of the Convention*, III, 211.

CHAPTER 11

ANTISLAVERY AND UTOPIA

BY JOHN L. THOMAS

THE century since the Civil War has slowly altered the portrait of the antislavery agitator until the utopian demeanor and perfectionist pose, softened by periodic restorations, has been nearly lost. The original likeness of the granite-jawed, misty-eyed millenarian, his opaque stare fixed on paradise anew, has been transformed by analytical studies and clinical findings into the displaced conservative in search of lost status. The antislavery gallery still offers many of its old exhibits—Elijah Lovejoy's press, the manacles of Anthony Burns, and John Brown's Address to the Jury—but they compete today with newer evidence of Federalist pedigrees, authoritarian profiles, and martyrdoms won in anguished protest against social change. Abolitionism itself seems less a museum than a mausoleum, less a monument to a militant minority than a record of social and political displacement capped by William Grayson's epitaph for "the Levite tribes of Christian love."

> These use the Negro, a convenient tool,
> That yields substantial gain or party rule.[1]

Yet Grayson's contemporaries in the Old South recognized in the abolitionist indictment something more dangerous than the hypocritical exposition of bogus gospel law. They peered beneath the surface of the antislavery

---

[1] William J. Grayson, "The Hireling and the Slave," *The Hireling and the Slave, Chicora, and Other Poems* (Charleston, S.C., 1856).

argument and discovered a millenarian expectation that seemed to threaten not merely slave institutions but all existing law and order. Calhoun was only the first of these Southern critics who saw the danger to American institutions in the abolitionist argument and accused them of fomenting a "war of religious and political fanaticism."[2] What seemed at first only an ill-conceived attack against slavery grew in the decade after 1840 into a full-fledged assault on all American political institutions, and to many Southerners it was clear that the abolitionists formed the vanguard of an unholy crusade against authority. George Fitzhugh, George Frederick Holmes, James Hammond, J. D. B. DeBow, and the other defenders of slavery called upon their fellow Southerners to stand firm for American liberties against the forces of change and not to "run hither and thither in search of all the absurd and degrading isms which have sprung up in the rank soil of infidelity."[3] Southerners, DeBow announced on the eve of secession, were true Americans, not Mormons or Spiritualists, Owenites, Fourierites, Agrarians, Socialists, Free-lovers or Millerites. "They are not for breaking down all forms of society and of religion and reconstructing them; but prefer law, order and existing institutions to the chaos which radicalism involves."[4]

The chaos which DeBow foresaw as the inevitable result of abolitionist agitation assumed two distinct forms in the Southern imagination. The first and more common figure was the omen of anarchy and a reign of ter-

[2] See, for example, Calhoun's speech in the Senate on the reception of antislavery petitions, February 6, 1837, *Congressional Globe*, 24 Cong., 2 sess., 168.

[3] James D. B. DeBow, "The Non-Slaveholders of the South," in DeBow *et al.*, *The Interest in Slavery of the Southern Non-Slaveholder. The Right of Peaceful Secession. Slavery in the Bible* (Charleston, 1860) as quoted in Eric L. McKitrick, ed. *Slavery Defended: The Views of the Old South* (Englewood Cliffs, N.J., 1963), pp. 173-74.

[4] *Ibid.*

ror. "From a thousand Jacobin clubs, here as in France," one Southern clergyman warned, "the decree has gone forth which strikes at God by striking at all subordination and law."[5] Others decried the disrespect for authority, both lay and clerical, preached by the abolitionists. One of the clearest expressions of this Southern dread of anarchy was George Frederick Holmes's impassioned review of *Uncle Tom's Cabin*. Holmes had read all of the outraged Southern responses to Mrs. Stowe's novel and was struck with their failure to expose the central flaw in the work, its transparently factitious quality. The novel, he argued, was pure fable, not so much untrue as utterly unreal, a tissue of moral absolutes woven with diabolical cleverness into successive syllogisms to prove that any institution not perfect ought to be destroyed. Mrs. Stowe's and the abolitionists' indictment struck at the heart of all community.

> If it was capable of proving anything at all, it would prove too much. It would demonstrate that all order, law, government, society was a flagrant and unjustifiable violation of the rights and mockery of the feelings of man and ought to be abated as a public nuisance. The hand of Ishmael would thus be raised against every man, and every man's against him. . . . The fundamental position, then, of these dangerous and dirty little volumes is a deadly blow to all the interests and duties of humanity, and is utterly impotent to show any inherent vice in the institution of slavery which does not also appertain to all other existing institutions whatever.[6]

[5] B. M. Palmer, *A Discourse. The South: Her Peril and Her Duty* (New Orleans, 1860), p. 10, as quoted in William Sumner Jenkins, *Pro-Slavery Thought in the Old South* (Chapel Hill, 1935), p. 240. Palmer was a Presbyterian minister and well-known Southern theologian.

[6] George Frederick Holmes, "Uncle Tom's Cabin," *Southern Literary Messenger*, XVIII (December 1852), as quoted in McKitrick, *Slavery Defended*, pp. 99-110.

In the years before the Civil War many Southerners came to agree with Holmes that the abolitionist argument would prove fatal to all human society, that "pandemonium itself would be paradise compared with what society would become, if this apparently simple and plausible position were tenable, and action regulated by it."[7] In their view the abolitionists were victims of an obsession with sin and guilt and a neurotic concern with perfection. Driven by a compulsion to find the perfect life, they had fashioned a garland of isms, and thus bedecked were leading the country down the path to chaos and ruin.

Other Southern critics of antislavery who actually studied the reform projects seemingly spawned by abolitionism concluded that the threat to American institutions lay not in an invitation to anarchy but in an open appeal to collectivism—to socialism, communism, or some other dangerous plan to control free Americans. Such an identification of abolitionism with European socialism came easily to a slaveholder like Jefferson Davis who found in both a principle of universal equality which would reduce all Americans to a dead level of conformity. "In fact," Davis complained, "the European Socialists, who, in wild radicalism . . . are the correspondents of the American abolitionists, maintain the same doctrine as to all property, that the abolitionists do as to slave property." *La proprieté, c'est le vol* served as the watchword of antislavery as well as of Proudhon's Parisian proletariat. "And the same precise theories of attack at the North on the slave property of the South would, if carried out to their legitimate and necessary logical consequences, and will, if successful in this, their first stage of action, superinduce attacks on all property, North and South."[8]

[7] *Ibid.*

[8] Jefferson Davis, "Speech, January 26, 1860," *Works*, IV, 183, as quoted in Jenkins, *Pro-Slavery Thought*, pp. 300-301.

It was just this discovery of the communitarian experiments of some of the abolitionists which George Fitzhugh turned against them, depicting them as refugees from a bankrupt free society and unknowing converts to the principle of slavery. "We think the opponents of practical, existing slavery, are estopped by their own admission; nay, that unconsciously, as socialists, they are the defenders and propagandists of slavery, and have furnished the only sound arguments on which its defense and justification can be rested."[9] Slavery, according to Fitzhugh, offered the only avenue of escape from the evils of free society. Alone among social systems it identified the interests of the strong with those of the weak. And those abolitionists who had branched out from antislavery and attempted to create social controls for unregulated competition were caught in a contradiction of their own making: they were trying to save in the name of freedom for the slave a crumbling capitalist order which the fact of their communal experiments proved bankrupt.

Thus Southerners, whether they identified abolitionism with anarchy or with un-American social control or

[9] George Fitzhugh, *Sociology for the South, or the Failure of Free Society* (Richmond, 1854), Ch. V. Defenders of slavery were not alone in identifying Northern religious reform with socialism. In his *History of American Socialisms* (Philadelphia, 1870) John Humphrey Noyes refers to revivals as a hope identical with the great hope of socialism. "And these movements—Revivalism and Socialism—opposed to each other as they may seem, and as they have been in the creeds of their partizans, are closely related in their essential nature and objects, and manifestly belong together in the scheme of Providence, as they do in the history of this nation. They are to each other as inner to outer—as soul to body—as life to its surroundings. . . .

"In fact, these two ideas, which in modern times are so wide apart, were present together in original Christianity. When the Spirit of truth pricked three thousand men to the heart and converted them on the day of Pentecost, its next effect was to resolve them into one family and introduce Communism of property. Thus the greatest of all Revivals was also the great inauguration of Socialism" (p. 26).

with an illogical combination of both, were agreed that the abolitionists were wild and dangerous radicals. Particularly disturbing was the suspicion that the sources of abolitionist heresy lay in an American tradition which they shared with the North, the growing conviction that the abolitionists had seized upon one part of this tradition and twisted it into a weapon to use against the South. In perverting the Christian gospel of love—in misappropriating the fruits of the Second Great Awakening—the abolitionists had committed their great crime. They had derived from simple Christian precepts a universal equality and a standard of perfection which made mockery of law and order. Implicit in the abolitionist reading of the American religious experience was a principle which, as one Southerner pointed out, was "tantamount to a repudiation of all authority." "Who is authorized to limit the application of this sweeping principle to the sole relation of slavery? It is as much the weapon of the socialist and the leveler as of the abolitionist."[10] Somewhere in the process of casting off Calvinism and adapting American Protestantism to democratic politics the abolitionists had hit upon a perfectionist egalitarian formula that now threatened to destroy the Union. What, Southerners asked themselves, had happened?

What had happened could best be called religious revolution, both a rapid and profound change in American theology and church polity and a subterranean shift in American thought. The revolution which accompanied the Second Great Awakening was the product of many forces: the deterioration of the fabric of a medieval determinism; the gradual decay of the ideal of church establishment; and egalitarian social forces unleashed by the American Revolution. In the beginning the effects of religious change on politics and society had been

---

[10] James Henley Thornwell, a Presbyterian minister and proslavery theorist, as quoted in Jenkins, *Pro-Slavery Thought*, p. 227.

chiefly conservative. American churchmen of every denomination, threatened with dispossession, hurried to bring a revitalized religious sentiment to the aid of sound politics and right conduct embodied in the Federalist party and Christian conservatism. The confessed aim of the benevolent societies which sprang up with the Second Great Awakening was social control. The American Bible Society, the Sunday School Union, the American Tract Society and all the other evangelical organizations saw their task as one of steering the country along a Christian track between the bogs of atheism and the wastes of infidelity. The American Colonization Society, by exporting inferior and unwanted Negroes, would return the country to Christian purity jeopardized by their presence. The Home Missionary Society aimed at fostering good behavior along with the gospel of love, and the Sabbath Union sought to forestall licentiousness by ensuring proper respect for the Lord's Day. The initial thrust of the great revival was conservative and traditional—toward the restoration of an older and largely imaginary Christian virtue.

But these moral reformers were also the legatees of a theological revolution the effect of which was to unleash the very egalitarian forces which Christian conservatives most feared. The significance of the new divinity lay in the abandonment of determinism and a new emphasis on human ability. The doctrine of free will, approximated in the sermons of Lyman Beecher and given full play in the preaching of Charles Grandison Finney, offered salvation to all. "He who will may come." Sin was equated with selfishness, and social wrong with the collective sins of unregenerate men who had only to live sinless lives and practice benevolence to win salvation and redeem the world at one stroke. Though not always openly acknowledged and constantly subjected to widely differing interpretations, the key doctrine of the moral reformers was perfectionism—the belief in the ultimate perfectibility of man and society. The spectrum of perfectionist thought in America ranged from the pale promises of final redemption in Oberlin theology through varying shades of conviction to the confident prophecies of immediate perfection of John Humphrey Noyes. In the reasoned sermons of Finney perfectionism could mean simply a striving for holiness. To the true believer it meant a practical goal to be achieved immediately. In its purest form, perfectionism, the doctrine of personal holiness, told men that they could become literally perfect by accepting Christ as their mentor and guide. When they stopped sinning and accepted Christ, they saved their souls and at the same time saved society. Perfectionism thus contained an anarchic appeal and a collectivist call, a command to shun evil and consult only conscience, and a mandate to join with the like-minded and look outward for perfect fellowship.

The perfectionist social ethic changed the whole course of the moral reform movement. Since social evils were only the collective sins of unregenerate citizens, the cure for them lay in an appeal to conscience, conviction of guilt, repentance, conversion, and finally rededication. Perfectionism was conservative insofar as it made every social problem a moral one and called for reform by example; but it was also potentially radical in that it offered a total solution and supplied the faithful with the will to seek it. It bred an uncompromising zeal and sense of urgency which transformed the various programs of moral reform. Originally the temperance movement had served as a conservative political device to defend the established order against "Sabbath-breakers, rum-sellers, tippling folk, infidels and ruff-scuff."[11] Its leaders preached moderation rather than total abstinence and were as much concerned with rampant democracy as with the

---

[11] Such was Lyman Beecher's description of the original purpose of the temperance movement. *Autobiography* (2d edn., 2 vols., New York, 1886), I, 35ff.

ravages of alcohol. Under the pressure of perfectionism, however, temperance societies became strictly prohibitionist and agitated for total abstinence in a cold-water campaign to redeem America. In the same way the American Peace Society, in its beginnings simply a forum for moderate-minded clergymen, was infiltrated and finally captured by Christian nonresistants who repudiated all use of force and preached pacifism as a total cure for the ills of American society.

By far the most radical change in the moral reform movement came with the rejection of the American Colonization Society by the abolitionists whose doctrine of immediate emancipation applied the perfectionist formula to slavery. Immediate emancipation provided a call for action if not an actual plan, a calculated appeal to guilt if not a workable program. As heirs of the Second Great Awakening the pioneer abolitionists proceeded from the assumption that all aspects of human behavior lay within the province of Christianity and that they themselves were God's agents for directing the great work of abolishing slavery. Because evil was one and all sins related, their Christian solution meant applying the rule of love, first to slavery, but eventually to all the evils of American society. "Practical Christianity," as they called it, would abolish slavery as a first step toward the millennium.

Southerners quickly discerned the spirit if not the fact of totality in the pioneer abolitionists' reform program. Most of the abolitionist veterans were professional reformers who brought to the cause a host of other interests in social betterment ranging from temperance and manual labor schools to nonresistance and dietary reforms. For them antislavery was simply the core of a complex of general reform. Furthermore, it was impossible, as Southern critics realized to their dismay, to discuss the doctrine of immediate emancipation in the accepted categories of radicalism and conservatism. For if immediate emancipation could be interpreted—as it often was intended—simply as a moral imperative, it could also serve in the mind of a zealot like John Brown as a call to revolution.

Immediately, therefore, the abolitionists encountered the organized opposition of church and state, and almost as quickly disillusionment set in. The clerical reaction against revivalism and reform after 1835 combined with a political reaction against antislavery agitation to block the avenues of institutional reform and turn the abolitionists back on their own resources. These resources in the case of a number of abolitionist pioneers were provided by their perfectionist ideal of purity. Faced by the growing hostility of unregenerate churches and of politicians who could not or would not attack slavery, these abolitionists promptly repudiated American institutions and plunged into the work of organizing perfect communities of their own along Practical Christian lines. The careers of three such abolitionists turned communitarians —Adin Ballou, John A. Collins, and George Benson— illustrate the progression of the perfectionist reformer from abolitionism to utopia and disclose the latent radicalism in the perfectionist ideal that so disturbed Southerners. More significantly, they also anticipated the disillusionment with utopia which affected the fate of the freedmen after the Civil War.

Adin Ballou was the thirty-four-year-old patriarch of a tiny Universalist sect in Mendon, Massachusetts, when he first discovered the antislavery cause in 1837. He was converted to abolition by one of William Lloyd Garrison's flying squads of agents covering the countryside in a determined drive for new recruits. Ballou accepted the ultra come-outer doctrines of the Garrisonians and agreed that slavery was utterly wicked "from its inception to its consummation." The Revolutionary generation had involved all Americans in a national vice; and church and state, though nominally separate, "were yet so far sympathetically and practically in harmony . . . to the slave power . . . as to demand withdrawal from both on the part of every enlightened, conscientious opponent of the gigantic crime."[12] Ballou soon realized the meaning of his new commitment. When he preached his first antislavery sermon on the text from Isaiah bidding the faithful loose the bands of wickedness, half of his congregation obeyed by walking out of the church. Undismayed, Ballou joined the Garrisonians on the lecture circuit, organized a local antislavery society, and published a pamphlet on immediate emancipation. He was wholly engrossed in a cause which, he admitted, "struck at what we all had been accustomed to deem venerable, sacred, and patriotic in our national life."

Then it dawned on Ballou that Practical Christianity, or "personal religion," as he called it, offered a solution not merely to the problem of slavery but to all the evils of an unregenerate world. True reform could flourish only in an environment of total dedication—"a righteousness starting at the utmost recesses of the individual soul and extending through the family and neighborhood into general society and seeking the holiness and happiness of all mankind."[13] Once assured of the possibility of perfection, true Christians could draw up a blueprint for utopia and proceed to build it as a working model for the nation. Ballou's own blueprint was "The Standard of Practical Christianity" which he drafted and presented to his Universalist flock in February 1839.

The Standard of Practical Christianity sounded a call to the faithful to renounce all earthly powers. "We cannot be governed by the will of man, however solemnly

[12] The two sources for Ballou's life and his Hopedale Community are *Autobiography of Adin Ballou* (Lowell, Mass., 1896) completed and edited by his son-in-law William S. Heywood, and Ballou's own *History of the Hopedale Community* (Lowell, Mass., 1897) also edited by Heywood. The quotation and the one following are from the *Autobiography*, pp. 279-80.

[13] Ballou, *Autobiography*, p. 296.

and formally declared, nor put our trust in an arm of flesh."[14] Practical Christians were exhorted to withdraw from the governments of the world, refuse to vote, hold office, bear arms, or obey unjust laws. As members of the perfect society they would not support a professional ministry, follow pernicious fashions, or join in the idle frivolities of the unregenerate. Instead, setting their sights on perfection and banishing sin from their daily lives, they should seek true social harmony and mark the way for the rest of mankind.

Hopedale (or Fraternal Community Number One), which Ballou founded in 1842 at nearby Milford, Massachusetts, as the first in a projected series of Practical Christian villages, lasted nearly fifteen years during which it grew from a single farmhouse housing twenty-eight communitarians into a model village of over one hundred and fifty inhabitants. In addition to publishing their own newspaper, the members founded their own antislavery auxiliary, legislated temperance within the confines of the community, experimented with spiritualism, Grahamism, phrenology, water cures, and mesmerism. The community served as a way-station for all of New England's reformers on their way to or from the endless succession of conventions and conferences for the improvement of American society. Along with George Ripley's Brook Farm and Bronson Alcott's ill-starred Fruitlands, Ballou's model village formed the matrix of utopian experimentation that so discomfited Southerners bent on protecting slavery with Christian conservatism. As a standing rebuke to corrupt proslavery America, Hopedale enjoyed a precarious but provocative existence before succumbing to the centrifugal forces of New England capitalism in 1856.

At the outset Ballou's opinions were those of a conservative who attributed social evils to the "heart of individual man." He explained his problem at Hopedale as

[14] "The Standard of Practical Christianity" is reprinted in full in the *Autobiography*, pp. 309-13.

one of navigation, steering between "the Scylla of threatening Communism" and "the Charybdis of selfish, un-
scrupulous, and hard-hearted Individualism."[15] For ten
years under Ballou's command Hopedale veered erratical-
ly between the poles of anarchism and collectivism. His
original scheme, a joint-stock enterprise in which members held shares, worked for wages, and paid rent, soon
succumbed to the criticism of the poorer disaffected members who proposed to abolish private property altogether. Ballou fought the radicals' plan as the "absolute
extinction" of individualism, and with a bare majority
defeated their proposal for reorganization, whereupon the
dissidents withdrew, taking with them little more than
the ill-will they bore the community.

But Ballou's communist critics left their mark on a
sensitive conscience: in 1844 he agreed to introduce
stricter industrial and social control over the "demon"
of selfishness. Hopedale was divided into producing Sections composed of workers' Bands, each in charge of
elected Monitors and Directors. Organizational tighten-
ing produced efficiency but even greater dissent. Net profits for the year 1845 totaled $1,200, but at the end of the
same year defections had nearly halved the working
force. Designed to put the "previously dominant individualism" under a ban, the social reconstruction of the
community along collectivist lines failed to achieve its
purpose. In 1847, admitting that collectivism had been
a "predetermined failure," the indefatigable Ballou
swung the pendulum back toward decentralization and
industrial autonomy by introducing a scheme for self-
regulating cooperatives.

Voluntary producers' cooperatives quickly yielded still
another unsatisfactory verdict. The revised system, though
managed with due care and tact, "interfered practically
so much with individual tastes, feelings, and wills, that
murmurs of dissatisfaction and even of revolt became at

[15] Ballou, *History of Hopedale*, p. 97.

length so frequent and so bitter as to embarrass and obstruct the orderly and efficient management of our business activities."[16] Rules and regulations, "the most indispensable requirements," created discord—"both managers and managed were annoyed, irritated, disgusted." Neither legislation nor the interposition of Ballou's executive authority could repair the broken apparatus. Accepting the inevitable, Ballou completely rewrote the constitution of Hopedale in the summer of 1847, eliminating the elaborate and complicated mechanism for social control and returning the community to the original joint-stock principle of relying "as little as possible on mere human constraint."[17]

Under a new relaxed regimen Hopedale seemingly prospered: new buildings were erected and new industries introduced. With all its improvements as proof of a revived spirit of private enterprise, the community's finances were not in a healthy state. Gradually all of the stock fell into the control of two sharp-eyed Yankee brothers who cared less for perfectionism than profits. As financial control slipped away from his followers, Ballou became more and more absorbed in a scheme for settling Western colonies on the Hopedale model and drew up an outline for a Practical Christian Republic. In his dream of a cooperative Christian America he saw entire towns and cities linked together in a federation of love, each working out its perfectionist destiny in its own way. Then, in 1852, he retired as president of Hopedale and began to devote his time to reviving the project of industrial communes, "wheels within the main wheel . . . responsible to the parent Community only in matters pertaining to fundamental principles, interests of universal concern, and the common organic policy which it had

[16] Ballou, *History of Hopedale*, pp. 160-61.
[17] Preamble to the revised constitution of Hopedale, *History of Hopedale*, pp. 165-68.

established."[18] Here was the key to perfect social organization—a self-regulating system of voluntary combinations which would provide "variety in unity," self-interest in obligation, and freedom in order.[19]

Hopedale's last attempt at perfection proved as abortive as earlier ventures. While members busied themselves with blueprints, creditors bought up the stock; and when they discovered in 1856 that their interest payments would not be forthcoming, they hastily withdrew their capital. Deprived of necessary funds, Hopedale collapsed within the year.

Ballou, chastened by his brush with entrepreneurial genius, accepted the result with true perfectionist forbearance but not without a measure of disillusionment. "From that time forward our beloved Hopedale village became gradually secularized and conformed to the habits, customs, and usages of similar boroughs elsewhere." The scepter of business enterprise was returned to the town, and the maxims of the unregenerate world ruled once again. All that was left to the community was moral power.[20]

In 1840 while Adin Ballou was still searching for a site for his community, another New England abolitionist, examining the appalling conditions in English industrial slums, also concluded that free society was a failure and that Negro slavery was simply one form of capitalist greed. John A. Collins was thirty years old and a relative newcomer to abolition when, in 1840, Garrison dispatched him to England on a fund-raising expedition. A graduate of Andover Theological Seminary, he had left the church during Garrison's war with the New England clergy and become a militant perfectionist preaching immediate emancipation and secession from corrupt "pro-slavery" churches. Since his conversion he

18 Ballou, *History of Hopedale*, p. 281.
19 *Ibid.*
20 Ballou, *History of Hopedale*, pp. 291-92.

had proved invaluable to Garrison by organizing local societies and directing the involved affairs of the Massachusetts Anti-Slavery Society. Just before he left for England he had arranged the passage to New York for the annual meeting of three hundred women delegates whose votes Garrison used to capture the national society. As a reward he was given the mission to England where he was expected to raise the money to save Garrison's bankrupt organization.

Collins' expedition failed conspicuously. Like Ballou, he was a true believer in perfectionism, but unlike the quiet though forceful Practical Christian, Collins was noisy and belligerent. Among English abolitionists he succeeded in raising only anti-Garrisonian resentment. Yet if he failed to promote good will or cash, Collins proved extraordinarily sensitive to the sufferings of the English working classes and the shocking living conditions in the cities. He attended Chartist lectures, held long talks with Robert Owen and studied the socialist tracts of English and French reformers. Soon he was convinced that slavery was no mere matter of color. "The English can condemn our prejudices against color over negro cars," he reported to Garrison, "while they are exercising the same prejudice against poverty, that we do against color."[21] British abolitionists were guilty of practicing a particularly inhuman kind of slavery which "gives to the poor the ostensible appearance of freedom the more successfully to grind him to powder." Collins arrived in England a Garrisonian perfectionist with all of the ultraist prejudices against institutions; he returned to America a year later a confirmed environmentalist anxious to try out his new ideas. These ideas were a curious combination of a perfectionist commitment to total freedom and a hazy belief in the power of a communist society to attain that freedom. Once back in the United States, Collins accepted the

[21] Manuscript letter, John A. Collins to William Lloyd Garrison, December 7, 1840, Garrison Papers, Boston Public Library.

job of General Agent of the American Anti-Slavery Society and in 1843 organized the One Hundred Conventions for the Garrisonians. Slavery, however, concerned him less now than the injustices of the profit system. "But upon deeper investigation," he explained to a puzzled critic, "we find that war, slavery, and intemperance, are but the effects of some cause lying further back. . . . May not then this question of the admitted right of individual ownership in the soil and its products be the great cause of all causes, which makes man practically an enemy to his species. . . ?"[22] At antislavery conventions Collins took a perfunctory part, scarcely concealing his impatience until the end of the meeting when he could announce that a socialist meeting followed at which the real and vital questions of the day would be discussed.

In June, 1843, Collins called a Property Convention (a "poverty convention" as conservative Bostonians called it) at the Chardon Street Chapel in Boston. Adin Ballou brought a contingent from Hopedale to debate the Owenite principle of "necessity" and left convinced that in repudiating private property Collins had side-tracked the search for perfection. Meanwhile Collins set out for Skaneateles in western New York where, in the autumn of 1843, he bought three hundred and fifty acres of rolling farmland complete with stone farmhouse and barns for $15,000, one-third down and a mortgage on the balance. On January 1, 1844, he published the first issue of his new paper, *The Communitist*, calling upon his neighbors to join his "Hunt of Harmony."

The antagonism between the principles of individualism and collectivism marked even the blueprint stage of Collins' project. The community was to be built on his "Articles of Belief and Disbelief," fundamentals which Collins deemed "essential to be assented to by every ap-

22 Manuscript letter, John A. Collins to Elizabeth Pease, February 2, 1843, Garrison Papers, Boston Public Library.

plicant for admission."[23] Emphasis lay on the negative—
"a disbelief in any special revelation of God to man,
touching his will, and thereby binding upon man as authority," rejection of the organized church, professional
clergy, the Bible, and miracles. As for government, Collins enjoined "a disbelief in the rightful existence of all
governments based on physical force . . . bands of banditti,
whose authority is to be disregarded." Members must also
disavow the right of property. Although they would remain strictly orthodox on the question of marriage, they
might be permissive as to divorce and, at any rate, would
give up all children to the community for indoctrination
in cold-water, vegetarian perfectionism.

All of the founder's proscriptions in turn were disavowed soon after the community was formed. A majority
of the new converts, who were every bit as enthusiastic as
Collins, disagreed as to the need for any articles of faith
whatever. They announced that as perfectionists and true
anarchists who believed in the undirected goodness of
men they could not agree to any regulation of conduct.
Faced with such determined opposition, Collins yielded,
and in the spring of 1844, just as the members were settling into their new quarters, he issued a second manifesto renouncing all creeds, sects, and parties.

> Our principles are as broad as the universe, and as
> liberal as the elements that surround us. They for-
> bid the adoption and maintenance of any creed, con-
> stitution, rules of faith, declarations of belief, touch-
> ing any or all subjects. . . . We estimate the man by
> his acts rather than by his peculiar belief. We say to
> him, Believe what you may, but act as well as you
> can.[24]

[23] The "Articles of Belief and Disbelief, and Creed prepared and
read by John A. Collins, November 19, 1843" is given in Noyes,
American Socialisms, pp. 163-67.

[24] Quoted in J. H. Noyes, *History of American Socialisms* (Philadelphia, 1870), p. 167.

Thus the issue between "No-God, No-Government, No-Money, No-Meat, No-Salt and Pepper" Collins and his more permissive followers was drawn at the outset. Collins was a propagandist and promoter; as a social planner and leader he fell far short. Although he had chosen his site well and in eight months managed to pay $4,000 on the mortgage, the atmosphere at Skaneateles was not conducive to harmony. "There was not much of the home-feeling there," one visitor recalled. "Every one seemed to be setting an example, and trying to bring others to it."[25] Some of the saints preferred the natural life, partaking of boiled mush in the privacy of some sylvan retreat, while others spiced their vegetarian meals at common table with pungent remarks on the appetites of their less dedicated fellows who ate "dead creatures." In an initial outburst of generosity Collins had deeded the property jointly to himself and his chief lieutenant whose view of universal reform differed widely from his own. Disputes ranged from the problems of industrial management to the procedure for admitting new members. Although Collins reserved to the community the right to expel unruly members, he refused to violate his nonresistance scruples by calling on the law. For several months the society remained heavily freighted with free-loading followers of the opposition party until Collins, at the cost of $3,000, succeeded in buying them off. His purge of the "restless, disappointed, jealous, indolent spirits" who had sought an anarchic haven from the world removed the resistance to Collins' collectivist rule but also reduced the community from its original ninety-one members to a token force of eleven men, eight women, and eleven children. With this hard core of veterans and some second thoughts on social planning Collins began again. "Our previous convictions have been confirmed

[25] "Recollections of E. L. Hatch," quoted in Noyes, *American Socialisms*, p. 177.

that all is not gold that glitters, that not all those who are most clamorous for reform are competent. . . ."[26]

The clearing of the "dark clouds" hovering over Collins' project unfortunately presaged no bright millennial noon. Free from the refractory but productive anarchist element, the Skaneateles search for perfection ended a short eight months later in the brambles of dissolution when the faithful, no longer sure of their direction, gave up and returned to their homes. Collins remained on the premises just long enough to give vent to a few observations on "dedicated" and "indolent" communitarians.

> Our enterprise, the most radical and reformatory in its profession, gathers these two extremes of character from motives diametrically opposite. When these are brought together, it is reasonable to expect that, like acid and alkali, they will effervesce, or, like the two opposite poles of a battery, they will repel each other. . . . Communities and Associations, in their commencement too heavily charged with an impracticable, inexperienced, self-sufficient, gaseous class of mind, have generally exploded before they were conscious of the combustible material they embraced, or had acquired strength or experience sufficient to guard themselves against those elements which threaten their destruction.[27]

The report marked the abandonment of his perfectionist hopes. A few years later he joined the trek to California where, a failure at prospecting for gold, he turned "brazen-faced" businessman, finally successful in the "denial of his earlier & better life."[28]

The year 1841 saw still a third attempt by a New Eng-

[26] *The Communitist*, September 18, 1845, as quoted in Noyes, *American Socialisms*, pp. 170-71.

[27] *Ibid.*

[28] Samuel J. May, Jr. to Richard D. Webb, July 12, 1864, May Papers, Boston Public Library, as quoted in Louis Filler, *The Crusade Against Slavery* (New York, 1960), p. 110n.

land abolitionist to found the perfect society. In February of that year George W. Benson sold his house and property in Brooklyn, Connecticut, to finance an experiment in true Christian living. As the brother-in-law of William Lloyd Garrison and the son of the patriarch of moral reform in New England, Benson had joined the abolitionists in 1831. Like most of the founders of the antislavery enterprise, he grew disillusioned at the refusal of the churches to take up the cause of the slave, and in his inflexibly righteous way he came to identify pro-slavery spirit with all religious and secular institutions. Viewed from the high plane of duty, the source of all evil appeared to be the sectarian prejudice of the American people. "Sectarianism," he told his fellow abolitionist Henry May, "is the hindrance to this peoples' advancement in Truth & holiness, man cannot be free while laboring to build up a sect or party, he must be left untrammeled to follow truth withersoever it may lead, before he can attain to a perfect man in Christ Jesus."[29]

His own search led Benson to the banks of the Connecticut River outside the town of Northampton where he and his abolitionist associates, David Mack, William Adam, and Samuel Hill, bought five hundred acres of meadowland and an abandoned factory as the site for their Northampton Association of Education and Industry. The associationists, or "Nothingarians," as they were called because they too repudiated all creeds and forms, followed the old manual-labor model of a self-sufficient community which produced its own food and manufactured goods for the market. Benson met the problem of social reorganization by limiting membership to professing perfectionists. The enterprise was divided into two separate concerns—a joint-stock company of subscribers who did not necessarily live in the community, and the industrial society itself composed of one hundred and

29 Manuscript letter, George W. Benson to William Lloyd Garrison, February 8, 1841, Garrison Papers, Boston Public Library.

twenty-five members who lived in common on the premises. True to their antisectarian principles, Benson and his associates prescribed no tests or articles of faith beyond a belief in perfectibility and a willingness to work. The center of the community was the four-story silk factory. There members worked and lived, all eating at a common table and receiving allotments of eighty cents a week for board, fuel, and light, twenty dollars a year for clothing.

The Northampton Association, unlike the Skaneateles community, did not flourish even in the beginning. Defections and a rapid turnover in personnel made industrial planning impossible, and there was a constant shortage of capital. Benson soon realized that the society needed a constitution and by-laws. Accordingly, at the first annual meeting the members adopted a Preamble and Articles of Association which tightened communal control by placing industrial management securely in the hands of elected trustees. This shift to centralization cost the community further losses in both money and manpower, and an urgent appeal for new funds proved unavailing. Within a year after its founding the Association stood on the verge of bankruptcy.

Business disagreements paled to insignificance compared to religious rifts and social squabbles within the community. One faction of Benson's free souls favored a minimum of restraint and a maximum of earthly pleasures like dancing and card-playing, while a group of more ascetically minded members condemned such profane habits as unbecoming a perfect society. Without capital and riddled with dissension, the Northampton Association expired in November 1846. The minutes of the last meeting tell the story with the economy of understatement.

> There being no business before the meeting, there was a general conversation among the members about

the prospects of the Association, and many were of the opinion that it was best to dissolve. . . . Some spoke of the want of harmony and brotherly feeling which were indispensable to the success of such an enterprise. Others spoke of the unwillingness to make sacrifices on the part of some of the members; also of the lack of industry and the right appropriation of time.[30]

Less than three years after its bold beginning the Northampton Association of Industry and Education had become simply Bensonville, its founder's utopian experiment reduced to a hydropathic spa where under Benson's benign direction the nature healer and escaped slave David Ruggles offered water-cures to ailing reformers.

There were other abolitionists besides Ballou, Collins, and Benson who attempted models of the good society. In Clinton County, Ohio, not far from Oberlin, the perfectionist Brooke brothers, manning the lone Garrisonian outpost in the West, tried their hand at communitarian reform in the Forties. Their no-money communist society of free-thinking "come-outers" lasted a single season before those with faith ran out of funds and those with funds ran out of faith. In New England, Bronson Alcott, another of Garrison's followers, encountered similar troubles at Fruitlands in attempting to translate perfectionism into a pilot project for social salvation.

Nor were all the converts to perfectionism part of the come-outer fringe of the antislavery movement. Theodore Weld, one of the soberest and most practical of the abolitionist agitators, joined a utopian venture at Raritan Bay, New Jersey, organized by the abolitionist Marcus Spring. Spring, a New York businessman with an inexplicable yen for perfection, had married the daughter of

[30] The minutes of the last meeting and a general account of the Northampion Association is given in Noyes, *American Socialisms*, pp. 154-60.

Arnold Buffum, one of the founders of the Massachusetts Anti-Slavery Society. Gradually Spring's antislavery creed broadened to include communitarian reform, in this case a plan for a nonsectarian "loving community" based on "the only law of life in God's kingdom."[31] When he established the Raritan Bay Union in 1852, Weld agreed to take charge of the educational department. Weld's school —Eagleswood—was a conspicuous success although Spring's joint-stock cooperative was not. Henry Stanton, by this time an active antislavery politician, sent his son to Eagleswood in the hope that Weld could make good his promise to provide "a freer, larger, more harmonious form of human existence." The Liberty party candidate and Free Soiler, Gerrit Smith enrolled his son, as did James Birney. One of the many curious visitors at Raritan Bay was Henry Thoreau who found the "queer place" redolent with the musty air of abolitionist perfectionism. "Imagine them sitting close to the wall, all around the hall, with old Quaker-looking men and women here and there. There sat Mrs. Weld [Angelina Grimké] and her sister, two elderly gray-headed ladies, the former in extreme Bloomer costume, which was what you may call remarkable; Mr. Arnold Buffum, with broad face and a great white beard, looking like a pier-head made of the cork-tree with the bark on, as if he could buffet a considerable wave; James G. Birney . . . with another particularly white head and beard; Edward Palmer, the anti-money man (for whom communities were made), with his ample beard somewhat grayish."[32] To Thoreau, as doubtless to other interlopers, Weld's collection resembled noth-

[31] Spring's description of the Raritan Bay Union is quoted in Benjamin P. Thomas, *Theodore Weld* (New Brunswick, N.J., 1950), p. 226.

[32] Henry David Thoreau to Sophia Thoreau, November 1, 1856, in Bradford Torrey, ed. *Journal of the Writings of Henry David Thoreau* (Boston, 1949), IX, 134-39; also quoted in Thomas, *Weld*, p. 233, and Henry Seidel Canby, *Thoreau* (Boston, 1958), 2d edn., pp. 410-11.

ing so much as a conclave of church elders awaiting the rule of the righteous and meanwhile contemplating the proper conduct of life.

The pull of Christian perfection on the abolitionists throughout the 1840's and early 1850's was only part of the greater magnetism which the idea of utopia exerted on all Americans. Many of the communities which sprang up in the wake of the Panic of 1837 were secular and European in conception—Fourier phalansteries, Owenite villages, and frontier Icarias. But utopia with its peculiarly American emphasis on right conduct held particular appeal for the moral suasion abolitionists who considered but rejected European ideas and tried, unsuccessfully, to adapt to their own perfectionist purposes the ideal of the organic society as the creator of the good life and the liberator of the individual. They could not accept the environmentalist assumptions of secular utopians like Albert Brisbane and Parke Godwin but held to the belief in the possibility of creating a perfect self-regulating society in which the moral priority of the individual would mysteriously harmonize with the needs and demands of the community. In a sense their failure was part of the failure of Emerson's generation to create a true sense of community out of the doctrine of self-reliance and to combine transcendental freedom with social obligation. Yet the perfectionists' working models, however ill-constructed and short-lived, did show ante-bellum Americans as much by their eventual failure as by their ephemeral accomplishments the possible uses of rational social control.

After 1850 abolitionism drifted from its utopian bearings toward involvement in the political crisis. Political antislavery—the Free Soil movement and the Republican party—was a popular response to the explosive questions of fugitive slaves and the status of slavery in the territories. The forces of politics swept aside the perfectionists and their utopian projects, leaving only the old sense of moral urgency which was now transferred to the problem of containing slavery. The risks of political antislavery, as it turned out, were great. Political parties gave power and a voice to free soilers who opposed the spread of slavery for purely selfish reasons. Northern politicians courted opinion which was anti-Negro as well as antislavery. They diffused the moral issues, fostered opportunism, cut the nerve of utopian vision, and ignored the possibilities of planning a racial democracy. In the long run it was this last failing—the Republican politicians' lack of a long-range plan—that proved their most serious liability. The Fugitive Slave Law, the Nebraska Act, the Dred Scott decision, and John Brown's Raid precipitated the political crisis over slavery but at the same time obscured the old ideals of the perfectionists. What the North needed in 1861 was the continuing ideal of the good society—both the dream and the kind of thinking and planning which the dream engendered. In order to abolish slavery, to raise the Negro to citizenship, and to build a racial democracy, the self-styled realism of the politicians was not enough.

The coincidence of the political crisis of the 1850's and the eclipse of utopianism was particularly significant in view of the failure of four years of war and twelve more of Reconstruction to produce a plan for a new equalitarian society. Southerners were correct in ascribing to the pioneer abolitionists a will to make the world over. Some of them had attempted just this task. Poorly conceived, hastily constructed, badly financed and as badly staffed, their pilot communities signally failed to harmonize the conflicting demands of the individual and the community. As working models they proved defective. Still, as experiments in controlled change they pointed in the right direction. The future of the Negro in America would depend on a renewed belief in perfectibility, social planning, and education—all the goals toward which the perfectionists had groped their way.

If the defenders of slavery correctly understood the nature of perfectionist antislavery, they were slow to realize how sharply the utopian habit had been checked by the failure of the communities and the rising political crisis of the 1850's. By the time of Lincoln's election all that remained of the original millennial spirit was a sense of emergency and an acute fear that the West would be lost to free institutions for all times.[33] Even the abolitionist communitarians no longer believed in their power to change the country by example. Adin Ballou spoke their general disillusionment when he confessed to Theodore Weld in 1856 that such communities as they had attempted were both impossible and undesirable.

> Few people [Ballou wrote] are near enough right in heart, head and habits to live in close social intimacy. . . . I concur with you in the opinion that we shall ere long find a way to carry our divine principles into social arrangements so as to secure all the good without the evils of Association as attempted in these unsuccessful experiments. We will unshackle and elevate the slave. We will raise woman to her destined sphere. We will educate the young. We will regenerate the public conscience, heart and opinion. We will do all in our power to make individuals and families what they ought to be,—and thus elevate society itself to the glorious state hoped for. . . .[34]

The collapse of the perfectionist communitarian ideal in the 1850's also coincided with the passing of secular utopianism. Despite their different assumptions about

[33] For an illuminating discussion of communitarian experiments, their importance for the West, and their connection with the problem of slavery expansion see Arthur E. Bestor, Jr., "Patent Office Models of the Good Society: Some Relationships Between Social Reform and Westward Expansion," *The American Historical Review*, LVIII (April 1953), 502-26.

[34] Adin Ballou to Theodore Weld, December 23, 1856, Weld Manuscripts, as quoted in Thomas, *Weld*, p. 229.

the nature of redeemed America the perfectionists and the secular communitarians had agreed on the importance of experimental models in achieving a general social reformation and on the dual role their communities would play in combining individual salvation with social redemption. The loss of this utopian dimension in the antislavery outlook affected not only the Garrisonian wing of the antislavery movement but also the political abolitionists who had never seriously considered the perfectionist program. When the secession crisis came the Garrisonians discarded their doctrine of Northern separation and accepted a war for the Union but not the social planning which that war made necessary. Their cry of "No Union with Slaveholders" rallied the North to the fight against slavery but not to the job of building a new social order for the freedmen. The political abolitionists were less directly but no less significantly affected by the eclipse of utopian thinking. Before the war they had rejected communitarian experiments as an evasion of the political question of abolishing slavery, but emancipation and Reconstruction brought new problems requiring social and economic controls, large-scale planning and a willingness to experiment with models. Now when the time came to consider the merits of planning, the perfectionists had already tested their ideas, found them wanting, and seemingly had proved what the antislavery politicians had suspected all along—that plans, controls, and models were of no use.

The failure of the utopian nerve narrowed the abolitionist vision by constricting social choices. For the contribution of the perfectionists lay precisely in their emphasis on planning as a bridge between improvement of the individual Negro slave, which had been their original concern, and the welfare of whole groups of Americans, black or white. With the Civil War this connection which a small but vital group of abolitionists had established was broken.

The result was an uncompleted social revolution: slavery was destroyed, but the new society of redeemed men which the perfectionists had promised was forgotten. The Freedmen's Bureau and its allied agencies did splendid work; philanthropists and educators poured money and effort into the South after the war. But belief in utopia had gone. For many of the abolitionists Reconstruction was a limited engagement fought for partial ends with a philosophy of adjustment. Such was the philosophy, for example, of the report of the United Freedmen's Inquiry Commission for 1863 written by the political abolitionist Samuel Gridley Howe. The Negro, Howe told the North, "does best when let alone, and . . . we must beware of all attempts to prolong his servitude even under the pretence of taking care of him. The white man has tried taking care of the Negro, by slavery, by apprenticeship, by colonization, and has failed disastrously in all; now let the negro try to take care of himself."[35]

Not all the abolitionists gave up so easily as Howe, and as the postwar years disclosed the increasing helplessness of the Negro to protect himself, many of them continued to work for the education and welfare of the freedmen. Yet Wendell Phillips was almost alone in constructing a plan for a new South built on confiscation and Northern capital. More common among abolitionists was Albion Tourgee's confession at the end of Reconstruction that his undirected humanitarianism had sent him on a "fool's errand." As for the perfectionists, now old and disenchanted, they had long ago given up the attempt to put their "divine principles" in action. In the years before the Civil War when a majority of abolitionists had been absorbed in the political problem of abolishing slavery, the perfectionists had moved beyond

[35] Samuel Gridley Howe *et al.*, *United States Freedmen's Inquiry Commission Report* (1863), quoted in Laura E. Richards, *Letters and Journals of Samuel Gridley Howe* (2 vols., Boston, 1909), II, 504.

the problem of containment to a consideration of the good society. Then when Reconstruction revealed an urgent need for planning and controls, these concepts stood discredited, even in the minds of the perfectionists themselves. They had spent an early summer in utopia and now were content to live out their time in the harsher climate of the Gilded Age.

CHAPTER 12

THE PSYCHOLOGY OF COMMITMENT:

THE CONSTRUCTIVE ROLE OF VIOLENCE AND SUFFERING FOR THE INDIVIDUAL AND FOR HIS SOCIETY

BY SILVAN S. TOMKINS

THIS is an essay in the psychology of commitment; why and how individuals and societies become committed to ideologies and to social movements. We will examine four abolitionists—Garrison, Phillips, Weld, and Birney as committed reformers. Why and how did each become attached to abolitionism? How did they influence others to become committed to abolitionism, or at the least to oppose the extension of slavery? It is our thesis that the same psychological dynamic underlies the commitment of the individual and the group. More particularly, we will argue that violence and suffering are critical in a democratic society, in heightening antipathy for violations of democratic values and in heightening sympathy for the victims of such violations. A radical magnification of negative feeling toward the oppressors and of positive feeling toward the oppressed is the major dynamic which powers the commitment first of the individual reformer and then of increasing numbers who are influenced by him.

The development of this thesis will require a preliminary presentation of my theory of motivation.[1] I have

[1] Silvan S. Tomkins, *Affect, Imagery, Consciousness*, Vols. I, II (New York, 1962, 1963). Vols. III, IV, in press. Vol. III will contain a more detailed account of the abolitionists.

argued that the primary motives of man are his eight innate "affects," or feelings. These are the positive affects of excitement, enjoyment, and surprise, and the negative affects of distress, anger, fear, shame, and contempt. These are innate. One does not learn to smile in enjoyment nor to cry in distress. However, the objects of each affect are *both* innate and learned. A baby does not learn the birth cry. It is an innate response to the excessive stimulation attendant upon being born. He will later cry when he is hungry or tired or exposed to too loud sounds. None of these are learned responses. But eventually he *will* learn to cry about many things about which he was initially unconcerned. He may learn to cry in sympathy when others are in distress and cry. But if the crying of others may be learned to evoke one's own distress cry, so may it also be learned to evoke contempt or shame rather than sympathy. There is nothing under the sun which some human beings have not learned to enjoy, to fear or hate, to be ashamed of, or to respond to with excitement or contempt or anger. This innate plasticity of the affect mechanism which permits the investment of any type of affect in any type of activity or object, makes possible the great varieties of human personalities and societies. Cultural diversity rests upon the biological plasticity of the affect system in man. "Puritanism," or negative affect about pleasure, and masochism, or positive affect about pain, are extreme examples of the possibilities of affect investment. The variety of possible affect investments are without limit. I may be very happy as a child and very sad as an adult, or conversely. I may be angry for a moment, for an hour, for a day, or always, or never. I may be frightened only occasionally or I may be anxious all my life. I may feel mildly ashamed of myself or deeply humiliated. I may feel ashamed because I have shown my feelings too publicly or because I was unable to show my feelings at all. In short, the object, the duration, the frequency, and the intensity of affect arousal and investment are without limit.

We will now introduce a corollary—the "density" of feeling and thought. "Low density" refers to those experiences which generate little or no feeling (affect) and little or no thinking (ideation), or, if the feeling and thought are intense, they do not last long. "High density" occurs whenever the individual has intense feelings and thoughts which continue at a high level over long periods of time. In such a case there is a monopolistic capture of the individual's awareness and concern. Low and high densities represent two ends of a continuum of organization of motive, thought, and behavior which are critical for the understanding of commitment. For brevity, we will hereafter arbitrarily refer to "low and high density organizations of feeling and thought" as "weak and strong affects."

There are two weak affect types, transitory and recurrent. Consider first the positive transitory case. Such would be the laughter in response to a joke. The experience might be extremely enjoyable but nonetheless of very low density, because it recruited no continuing ideation or affect beyond the momentary experience. An example of the negative transitory case would be a cut while shaving which occasioned a brief stab of pain and distress, but no further thought or feeling beyond this isolated experience. Each individual's lifetime contains thousands of such relatively trivial encounters. Collectively they may amount to a not inconsiderable segment of the life span. Nonetheless they constitute an aggregate of isolated components without substantial impact on the personality of the individual.

Recurrent weak affects characteristically begin with considerable intensity of feeling and thought but end with minimal involvement. Consider first the negative recurrent case. Everyone learns to cross streets with minimal affect and ideation. We learn to act *as if* we were afraid, but we do not in fact experience any fear once we have learned how to cope successfully with such contingencies. Despite the fact that we know that there is real danger involved daily in walking across intersections and that some pedestrians are in fact killed, we exercise normal caution with minimal attention and no fear. Street-crossing remains weak in its affect despite daily repetition over a lifetime. This is not to say that it was always so. The earliest such experiences may well have been high adventures for the daring child or they may have been the occasion of severe punishment at the hands of an anxious parent terrified at the sight of his toddler walking in front of a speeding automobile. Both the excitement and the pain or distress which might have been suffered at the hands of a parent do not long continue. Quickly all children learn some caution in this matter and it ceases to claim much attention. Such attenuation of feeling and thought necessarily depends upon the success of problem solutions. Paradoxically, human beings are least involved in what they can do best—when problems, once solved, remain solved. Man as a successful problem solver ceases to think and to feel about successful performance and turns ideation and affect to continuing or new, unsolved challenges.

This is so whether the original affect which powered problem solving was negative or positive. Just as we experience no terror in confronting traffic at the curb, so too in the positive, low density case, we experience no significant enjoyment or excitement in the daily recurrent performances which once delighted. As I finish my daily shaving I rarely puff with pride and think, "There, I've done it again."

What then of the strong affects? By definition they can be neither transitory nor recurrent but must be enduring. Whether predominantly positive or negative in tone, they must seize the individual's feelings and thoughts to the exclusion of almost all else. Consider first, negative monopolism of thought and feeling. If successful and *continuing* problem solution is the necessary condition of the weak affect, *temporary* problem solution is the necessary condition of strong affect. Consider our man on the curb. He is normally cautious but not overly concerned because his solution to the problem has always worked. But suppose that one day a passing motorist loses control of his car and seriously injures our hero. After his return from the hospital he is a bit more apprehensive than before, and now stands back a little farther from the edge of the curb than he used to. He may continue his somewhat excessive caution for some time, and (as he notes a car approaching with what appears a little too much speed) may even begin to wonder with occasional fear, whether such an accident might ever happen again. But if all goes well this increase in density of ideation and affect will pass and before long he will be indistinguishable from any other casual pedestrian.

But in our tragedy all does not go well. Uncannily a drunken driver pursues our hero and he is hit again. This time it is more serious and we see the beginnings of a phobia. Our hero stations himself inside of a building peering up and down the street before he will venture out to dare negotiate the crossing. By now his preoccupation with and fear of the deadly vehicle has grown to invade his consciousness even when he is far from the scene of potential danger. In the last act of this drama it is a bulldozer which penetrates his apparent fortress. What next? Will he be safe in the hospital? His ideation and affect have now reached a point of no return. He will henceforth generate possibilities which no reasonable man would entertain and these phantasies will evoke affects proportional to their extremity. Such strong affect is capable of providing a lifetime of suffering and of resisting reduction through new evidence. This happens if, and only if, there has occurred a sequence of events of this type: threat, successful defense, breakdown of defense and re-emergence of threat, second successful new defense, second breakdown of defense and re-emergence of threat, third successful new defense, third breakdown of defense and re-emergence of threat and so on, until an expectation is generated that no matter how successful a defense against a dread contingency may seem, it will prove unavailing and require yet another new defense, ad infinitum. Not only is there generated the conviction that successful defense can be successful only temporarily, but also, as new and more effective defenses are generated, the magnitude of the danger is inflated in the imagination of the "victim." This same process, we shall see, was involved in the polarization of North and South which culminated in the Civil War.

The continuing uncertainty of permanent problem solution is critical in monopolizing the individual's ideation and affect. Paradoxically it is just the fact that the individual is *not* entirely helpless in dealing with a given situation which continually magnifies both the apparent nature of the threat and his skill in coping with it. In this respect the individual may be likened to a tennis player who is first defeated by a poor opponent and who then practices sufficiently to defeat that opponent. But his triumph proves short-lived since the opponent now also improves and in turn defeats him. This then leads our hero further to improve his skill so that once again he defeats the adversary, only to have the tables turned yet once more when the latter improves his skill, and so on and on.

Let us now examine the structure of the strong positive affect case. Instead of increasing concern about warding off a threat as in the negative case, there is rather increasing concern about attaining a desired object, a concern which magnifies positive affect. Commitment is one type of strong positive affect. Let us consider two examples of commitment, one characteristically abortive commitment which ends either by transformation into a somewhat less intense positive affect, or ends in disenchantment; the other a commitment which extends over the entire life span. We refer in the first instance to romantic love and in the second to the committed artist or scientist.

Consider first the romantic lover who intends to commit himself for life to his beloved. We may distinguish him from two other types of lovers; first, the man who enjoys very much his contacts with his lady friend, but who does not miss her when he is otherwise occupied, and second, the man who does not miss his lady friend when all goes well, but who does turn to her for comfort when he becomes disturbed. In the second case, she does in fact always bring him tranquility; after being mothered back into peace of mind he is prepared again to pick up his life, and for the time being to forget his benefactress with gratitude but no regret. Not so with the romantic lover. He is *continually* aware of her absence and their enforced separation to which he responds with intense suffering and longing. Every time he is separated he dies a little and thereby, like the true mourner, comes to appreciate more and more his dependence upon the beloved, who grows increasingly desirable in her absence. Upon reunion with the beloved the intensity of his enjoyment and excitement is proportional to his prior suffering and there is now the beginning of a continual magnification. If the beloved becomes more valuable when she brings to an end the intolerable suffering and longing which precede reunion, so much the greater will the next suffering of separation become since the beloved has by now become even more wonderful than before. The beloved does not necessarily continue to support indefinite magnification of her magical qualities. Romantic love imposes separation and uncertainty which increase the period of time over which longing for the love object can occur, but with the transition to marriage and the honeymoon, prolonged intimacy and mutual exploration eventually produce a sufficient reduction in novelty and uncertainty so that excitement can no longer be indefinitely maintained. When under these conditions of continuing contact the beloved will no longer support the indefinite magnification of wonder and excitement, there may appear disenchantment or boredom, or intense excitement may be replaced by more moderate enjoyment of a familiar and deepening relationship. But the husband will no longer miss his wife throughout the working day even though he deeply enjoys his daily reunion with her at each day's end.

Consider next the varieties of committed scientists. Individual A enjoys tremendously both the discovery of truth, and the search for truth. He likes to putter around the laboratory. He likes to run experiments. He enjoys it when they succeed. But he is a nine-to-five scientist. When he goes home it is to another world. He does not take his scientific troubles home with him. Indeed he experiences a minimum of suffering in his role as scientist. He is in this respect like the person who enjoys the company of his lady friend, but who does not miss his enjoyment or suffer in the interim periods. Individual B, on the other hand, uses science as a sedative. Whenever he becomes depressed he turns to reading science or watching TV programs concerning the latest advances in science. However, as soon as his life becomes more rewarding, his interest in science flags, like the individual who sought out his lady friend to ease his suffering but once mothered back into peace of mind, forgot his benefactress.

A third kind of scientist is committed for a lifetime to the pursuit of truth. He is always aware of the absence of his longed-for ideal object—ultimate, permanent, Truth. Like individual A, he too enjoys the scientific way of life. He enjoys puttering with laboratory equipment, and with running experiments. But underlying all his enjoyment is a continuing unrest and suffering over the possibilities of error, and over the possibility of missing the main chance. When everything works as planned he is deeply excited and enjoys briefly the fruits of his labor. But his contact with truth is ordinarily as brief as it is sweet. Truth is a mistress who never gives herself completely or permanently. She will not tolerate a marriage no matter how committed her scientific lover. She must be wooed and won arduously and painfully in each encounter. With each encounter she deepens both the scientist's suffering and then his reward. It is a love affair which is never entirely and deeply consummated. Immediately following each conquest of Nature the victory is always discovered to have been less than it appeared and the investigation must be taken up again and pursued with more skill and more energy than before. As with the man who developed the phobia about street-crossing, the skill of this scientist must constantly be improved, and in both cases the effectiveness of achieved skill is only temporary. The difference between the two is that in the negative case of the street-crosser the individual is pursued by a threat, whereas in the positive commitment of the scientist he pursues an object of ever increasing attractiveness. In both cases an idealized object is created.

The magic of truth exists in such magnified form only in the mind of one who will pursue truth despite increasing suffering, so that each encounter becomes both more bitter and more sweet. In the romantic love affair there is a finite uncertainty which is almost entirely explored during the honeymoon. But in our third kind of scientific commitment there is sufficient continuing uncertainty so that there is endless magnification in the strength of the affects. It is a critical feature of high density commitment that there can be no *enduring* positive affect in having attained the pursued finite object. Rather the object is continuously redefined so that a newer version of the quest can be mounted. The same dynamic appears in the pursuit of money or power. These are also capable of committing the individual to an endless insatiable quest for an object which is put out of reach almost immediately after it is attained.

Let us turn to the interpretation of abolitionism in the light of our theory. We will now also examine more closely just how such strong affects are formed as well as the numerous ways in which they may fail to be sustained.

The commitment of Garrison, Phillips, Weld, and Birney to abolitionism proceeded in a series of steps consistent with our general theory of commitment. The critical role of adult experience in gradually deepening commitment is underlined by the differing early careers of these men and the diverse paths each took toward a common ultimate commitment to abolitionism. No one could have predicted with any confidence that these four young men would eventually provide leadership for the abolitionist movement. Garrison was first attracted to writing and to politics as a way of life. Phillips led the life typical of the Boston Brahmin of his time: attendance at Harvard College, Harvard Law School and then the opening of a law practice. Weld first gave a series of lectures on mnemonics, the art of improving the memory. Birney was twice suspended from Princeton for drinking, though he was each time readmitted and finally graduated with honors. He, like Phillips, became a gentleman lawyer, priming himself for a political career. After an early failure in politics he became a planter and lived the life of the young Southern aristocrat, drinking and gambling to excess. Paradoxically, of the four, he was the earliest to interest himself in the slaves, but the last to commit himself to their emancipation as his way of life.

It is essential to recognize that one cannot account for the abolitionist reformer on the assumption that his was a commitment such as that of "falling in love at first sight." None of these men knew at first that they were to commit their lives to the emancipation of the slave; three of the four were first attracted to a career in politics. But if there is a perennial danger of exaggerating the

continuity of human development, and especially the influence of the early years on the adult personality, there
is also the opposite danger of exaggerating the impact
of adult experience on crucial adult choices, and overlooking the contribution of the early years to choices
which on the surface appear to represent novelty in the
adult's experience. Our argument will stress both the
continuity and the discontinuity in the development
of Garrison, Phillips, Weld, and Birney in their growing
commitment to abolitionism.

All were early prepared and destined for leadership
of a special kind, for saving the self through saving
others. Each might have become a crusading politician,
writer, orator, or preacher. Indeed Birney did later run
as a crusading candidate for the Presidency of the United
States. Weld later, because of his failing speech, did become a writer for abolitionism instead of an orator. Phillips, after the Civil War, did continue crusading for
labor, for temperance, for Ireland against England, for
the American Indians, and for the abolition of capital
punishment. Garrison, too, after the Civil War, maintained his interest in women's rights and in temperance
reform, though with much less zeal than Phillips. Given
the continuity of their concern with salvation, the interest of these men in abolitionism was not wholly novel.
On the other hand, it would be a mistake to assume that
their concern with salvation *necessitated* their becoming
abolitionists.

Let us begin by examining the original "resonance"
which first attracted these and other men to abolitionism.
By resonance we mean the ability of any organized ideology or social movement to engage feeling and thought.
The fit between the individual's own, often loosely organized feelings and ideas, and the more tightly organized ideology or social movement, need not be a very
close one to induce resonance. Some men resonated to
abolitionism because slavery violated their Christian

faith, or because of a general sympathy for the underdog. Others resonated to the idea of abolition because of a belief in the perfectibility of man. Still others were attracted because of a belief in the democratic assertion of the equal rights of all men, or a belief in individualism. Some were originally attracted because their own salvation required that they save others. There were those who were attracted because they hated oppression and oppressors and some because they could not tolerate humiliation, even vicariously. The plight of the slave induced resonance for these and many other reasons.

The bases for the original resonance of Garrison, Phillips, Weld, and Birney to abolitionism contained common elements and also differences. All four were deeply Christian. Three of the four had conversion experiences. For Garrison, Phillips, and Weld their Christianity required that they save others if they would save themselves. Each of these three had been impressed by strong, pious Christian mothers that to be good meant to do good. The fourth, Birney, had been left motherless at the age of three, and his strongest relationship was with his father who believed not only in Christian good works, but more specifically had, along with *his* father, fought to make Kentucky a free state: though they lost this fight they continued to be active against slavery. In all four parents, moral and Christian zeal for the salvation of their children (and other sinners) was combined with great affection for the children. These parents provided the appropriate models for future reformers. The children were taught how to combine concern and contempt for the sinner with love for those sinners who would reform.[2]

Not only was there a strong Christian influence which

[2] For an extended discussion of the complexities of the impact of early socialization on the adult personality, and specifically on the personalities of the abolitionists, see Silvan Tomkins, *Affect, Imagery, Consciousness*, Vol. III (in press).

predisposed these men to resonate to abolitionism, but in addition their parents had also shown a pervasive concern with public service. Garrison's mother, who was the sole provider, nursed the sick. Birney's father was politically active in favor of emancipation. Phillips' father was mayor of Boston. Weld's father was a minister. All were concerned with service to others and provided a model which predisposed their sons to resonate to any movement based on public service.

Third, all four appeared to have been physically very active and extroverted as children. They had abundant energy which they translated into vigorous play and into fighting with their peers. This, too, contributed to their resonance to a movement which called for direct action and face to face confrontation before large groups.

Fourth, all were exposed to, influenced by, and modeled themselves after, the great orators of their day. As Perry Miller[3] has noted, one of the salient features of the puritan's reformation was the substitution of the sermon for the Mass. All four men were early exposed to the magic of the great orators of the day, both Christian and secular. All four as young men were fluent and articulate and gave evidence of being able to hold audiences by their speaking powers. The combination of great energy, extroversion, and the power to influence others by oratorical ability predisposed them to resonate to a movement which required those who could influence others in just such ways.

Fifth, all of them were physically courageous. They had all experienced and mastered the art of fighting with their peers, so that they had a zest for combat rather than a dread of it. No one who too much feared physical combat could afford to resonate to the defense of those held in bondage by the ever present threat of force. The overly timid cannot entertain a rescue phantasy.

[3] Perry Miller, *The New England Mind. The Seventeenth Century* (Boston, 1961), p. 298.

These are some of the characteristics which these four men shared and which originally attracted them to abolitionism. But there were also important differences between them. Phillips was first actively attracted to a defense of abolitionism by the murder of the abolitionist Lovejoy. As a patrician, he was outraged at the tyranny of the mob and its violation of civil liberties. He was also outraged that "gentlemen" of his own class, from his own beloved Boston, should form a mob and threaten the life of Garrison. He was attracted at first more by disgust at mob violence than by concern over slavery. In contrast, Garrison, Birney, and Weld were first attracted to the problem of slavery out of direct sympathy for the slave. Each resonated first not to abolitionism but to the program of the American Colonization Society of gradual emancipation with transportation of free American Negroes to Africa. Nor, for two of them, was even this interest salient from the outset. Although slavery interested Weld increasingly, temperance and manual labor education were his primary concerns for some time. Birney, due to his exposure to his father's and grandfather's political activity on behalf of emancipation, was earliest interested in the problem of slavery, but it was some time before he committed himself wholeheartedly to even the program of the American Colonization Society. It was to be several more years, when he was over forty, that he committed himself to abolitionism.

Garrison and Weld were soon to change the nature of their relationship to the problem of slavery. Garrison led the way with a frontal attack on the slaveholder and those who trafficked in slavery, and with a denunciation of the American Colonization Society. In this he was radically to influence others, including Weld, Phillips, and finally Birney. Added to sympathy for the slave was now contempt and anger both for the Southern sinners and for those Northerners who either cooperated with or were indifferent to Southern tyranny. Birney held back because he was not yet convinced that the Southern slaveholder could not be reached by reason, because he was temperamentally allergic to enthusiasm, and because he was at that time more interested in improving and preserving his beloved South than in destroying the slaveholder. Only painfully and reluctantly was he forced to leave the South and become an abolitionist.

Garrison, in contrast, had the greatest enthusiasm for nailing the sinner to the cross, while Phillips, disgusted more with his own class than with the Southern slaveholder, also resonated, as we have seen, to somewhat different aspects of abolitionism. Weld, in contrast both to Phillips and Garrison, was a shy "backwoodsman" as he described himself. He was indifferent to the political action which Birney espoused, disliked politicians and all sophisticates, was suspicious of too great a reliance on "reason," was greatly troubled by exhibitionism (in contrast to Garrison who thrived on it) and was much concerned about the general problem of sin. The resonance to abolitionism on the part of these four was prompted, then, by both the similarities and the differences we have here examined.

So much for the first stage in the development of commitment, the resonance by which the individual is initially attracted to the new ideology. The second stage occurs when risk is first ventured following this initial resonance. Not all who are attracted to an ideology will venture any risk on its behalf. Garrison was perhaps the boldest risk-taker, in part because he wanted so much "to be heard," as he said. To be heard he had not only to write but to speak in public. Early in his career he had been invited by the Congregational Societies in Boston to give the Fourth of July address at the Park Street Church. Garrison, in a letter to Jacob Horton, tells of his knees shaking in anticipation of the lecture, and a newspaper account reported that at first his voice was almost too faint to be heard; but eventually he overcame his stage fright and made a strong plea for the gradual emancipation of the slaves. Soon after this speech, however, he was to decide that immediate emancipation was required. Then he became more bold and accused a Northern ship captain and ship owner of trafficking in slaves. For this he spent seven weeks in jail. It cannot be said that this was altogether painful to Garrison. He appeared to enjoy both his martyrdom and the notoriety he gained, writing to everyone and conducting interviews from his cell. Although Garrison suffered least of the four abolitionists, and indeed appeared to enjoy combat, it would be a mistake, as his "shaking knees" tell us, to overlook the fear he sometimes experienced. Indeed all four men continually exposed themselves to physical and verbal opposition, and sometimes violent opposition. Each reacted somewhat differently. Garrison, though sometimes frightened, was more often delighted to be the center of attention. Phillips responded primarily with patrician contempt. Birney became depressed at the unreasonableness of his opposition, and Weld regarded his trials as tests by God of his mettle and worthiness.

This third stage, suffering in consequence of risk-taking, troubled each man in different ways. Phillips lost his status and former friends in Boston upper-class society. Weld was severely reprimanded by the Trustees and President of the Lane Seminary for his "monomania" in stirring the students to debate slavery. After joining the American Anti-Slavery Society he toured Ohio, converting thousands to the cause, but always facing angry mobs intent on attacking him and breaking up his meetings. He was hurt on numerous occasions. Indeed, he came to consider riots to be a test not only of his own mettle but of all his converts. Birney, too, met violence in response to his pro-Negro activity. He reacted with disappointment at the intransigency of the South, depression at the turning away of former friends and his loss of status, chagrin and surprise at the inability of "reason" to exert influence, considerable regret at having to leave his homeland and settle in the North, and not least, depression over the increasing alienation between his father and himself. Garrison clearly had least to lose and most to gain from assuming the risks of abolitionism though he, too, despite his zest for the fight and his love of being the center of attention, could on occasion become frightened and distressed. It should be noted that the same characteristics which prompted the initial resonance were also critical in creating the ability to tolerate the violence of the opposition and such negative affect as this ordinarily provokes. It was the combination of the general wish to save and reform coupled with energetic, articulate extroversion which diminished the sting of fear, of disappointment, and of depression at the loss of status and friends and the threat of physical injury and possible loss of life.

As a consequence of suffering, the fourth stage in the development of their commitment set in—an increase in their resonance to the movement, an increased identification with the oppressed Negro, an increased hostility toward the oppressor and toward those who remained uncommitted. This stage blends into later stages: an increased willingness to take still greater risks and to tolerate still greater suffering, with a proportionate increase in the intensity and duration of positive affect, until finally an irreversible commitment is reached. Thus Phillips now began to see for the first time, he said, the nobility and generosity of the Negro and of the lower classes in general. He began to compare their nobility invidiously with the smugness and corruption of upper-class society. He now found for the first time, he insisted, real and true friends. "Who are we that we should presume to rank ourselves with those that are marshalled in such a host? What have *we* done? Where is the sacrifice *we* have made? Where is the luxury *we* have surrendered?"[4]

---

[4] Irving H. Bartlett, *Wendell Phillips, Brahmin Radical* (Boston, 1961), p. 57.

In Weld's case, the continual violent opposition he faced while on his speaking tour served to deepen his commitment also: "God gird us to do all valiantly for the helpless and innocent. Blessed are they who die in the harness and are buried on the field or bleach there."[5]

Birney's initial response to the violence of the opposition was loneliness and depression. In 1834 he wrote to Weld: "I have not one helper—not one from whom I can draw sympathy, or impart joy, on this topic! . . . My nearest friends . . . think it is very silly in me to run against the world in a matter that cannot in any way do me any good. . . . Even my own children . . . appear careless and indifferent—if anything rather disposed to look upon my views as chimerical and visionary. . . . My nearest friends here are of the sort that are always crying out 'take care of yourself—don't meddle with other people's affairs—do nothing, say nothing, get along quietly—make money.' "[6] However, this seems to have increased Birney's determination again and again to confront both censure and the threat of physical violence, "believing that if ever there was a time, it is now come, when our republic, and with her the cause of universal freedom is in a strait, where everything that ought to be periled by the patriot should be freely hazarded for her relief." Men must "themselves die freemen [rather] than slaves, or our Country, glorious as has been her hope, is gone forever."[7]

Garrison, too, responded to opposition with increased defiance and with an increased identification with the Negro. In the first issue of *The Liberator* he flung his defiance in the face of the enemy:

> I am aware, that many object to the severity of my language; but is there not cause for severity? I

[5] Benjamin P. Thomas, *Theodore Weld. Crusader for Freedom* (New Brunswick, N.J., 1950), p. 116.

[6] Betty Fladeland, *James Gillespie Birney: Slaveholder to Abolitionist* (Ithaca, N.Y., 1955), p. 90.

[7] *Ibid.*, p. 146.

will be as harsh as truth, and as uncompromising as justice. On this subject, I do not wish to think, or speak, or write, with moderation. No! no! Tell a man, whose house is on fire, to give a moderate alarm; tell him to moderately rescue his wife from the hands of the ravisher; tell the mother to gradually extricate her babe from the fire into which it has fallen; but urge me not to use moderation in a cause like the present! I am in earnest. I will not equivocate—I will not excuse—I will not retreat a single inch—AND I WILL BE HEARD. The apathy of the people is enough to make every statue leap from its pedestal, and to hasten the resurrection of the dead.[8]

In an address to an audience of Negroes he said: "It is the lowness of your estate, in the estimation of the world, which exalts you in my eyes. It is the distance that separates you from the blessings and privileges of society, which brings you so closely to my affections. It is the unmerited scorn, reproach and persecution of your persons, by those whose complexion is colored like my own, which command for you my sympathy and respect. It is the fewness of your friends—the multitude of your enemies—that induces me to stand forth in your defense."[9]

It should not be assumed, however, that opposition did nothing but deepen early commitment. It also raised, at least temporarily, serious doubts and conflicts about the wisdom of such a commitment. As might have been expected it was Phillips and Birney, they who had most to lose in social position and privilege, who had the most serious and prolonged reservations before finally committing themselves. Phillips, almost thirty, traveled through Europe with his invalid wife. He knew that his mother and family expected that he would return

[8] Louis Ruchames, *The Abolitionists* (New York, 1963), p. 31.
[9] *Ibid.*, p. 39.

from his year abroad cleansed of his youthful enthusiasm for the radical movement. By the end of the year 1841, he had made a firm decision. He wrote to Garrison: "I will recognize in some degree the truth of the assertion that associations tend to destroy individual independence; and I have found difficulty in answering others, however clear my own mind might be, when charged with taking steps which the sober judgement of age would regret, . . . with being hurried recklessly forward by the enthusiasm of the moment and the excitement, though not I hope of all enthusiasm . . . upon the course we have taken for the last few years; and . . . I am rejoiced to say that every hour of such thought convinces me more and more of the overwhelming claims our cause has in the lifelong devotion of each of us."[10]

Birney's period of doubt and indecision, as we have seen, was prolonged. In 1828 he had written "It [is] hard to tell what one's duty [is] toward the poor creatures; but I have made up my mind to one thing . . . I will not allow them to be treated brutally."[11] He was always concerned lest he be seduced by feeling: "Fearing the reality as well as the imputation of enthusiasm . . . each ascent that my mind made to a higher and purer moral and intellectual region, I used as a standpoint to survey very deliberately all the tract that I had left. When I remember how calmly and dispassionately my mind has proceeded from truth to truth connected with this subject (i.e., slavery) to another still higher, I feel satisfied that my conclusions are not the fruits of enthusiasm."[12]

Even after Birney had apparently firmly committed himself to abolitionism he wrote to Gerrit Smith: "I am at times greatly perplexed. To have alienated from us

[10] Irving H. Bartlett, *Wendell Phillips, Brahmin Radical*, pp. 73, 74.

[11] William Birney, *James Birney and his times* . . . (New York, 1890), p. 12.

[12] William Birney, Letter on Colonization . . . (New York, 1834), p. 45.

those with whom we [went] up from Sabbath to Sabbath to the house of God—many of our near connections and relations estranged from us, and the whole community with but here and there an exception, looking upon you as an enemy to its peace, is no small trial."[13]

For Weld the only doubts which ever assailed him were doubts about his own worthiness, his ability to control himself and to tolerate trial by fire. To his beloved Angelina Grimké he had confessed: "You know something of my structure of mind—that I am *constitutionally*, as far as emotions are concerned, a quivering mass of intensities kept in subjection only by the *rod of iron* in the strong hand of conscience and reason and never laid aside for a moment with safety."[14] Whereas Phillips was concerned with the wisdom of his choice and Birney with the nature and consequences of his choice, Weld was concerned with his ability to tolerate the inevitable consequences of the morally necessary choice.

Only Garrison suffered no serious doubts once he had embarked on his voyage "against wind and tide." As he had written in an editorial on his twenty-fifth birthday, "I am now sailing up a mighty bay with a fresh breeze and a pleasant hope—the waves are rippling merrily, and the heavens are serenely bright. I have encountered many a storm of adversity—rough, and cruel, and sudden—but not a sail has been lost, nor a single leak sprung."[15] Later that year he was to spend seven weeks in jail. After this experience he wrote: "How do I bear up under my adversities? I answer—like the oak—like the Alps—unshaken, storm-proof. Opposition, and abuse, and slander, and prejudice, and judicial tyranny, are like oil to the flame of my zeal. I am not dismayed; but

[13] Betty Fladeland, *James Gillespie Birney: Slaveholder to Abolitionist*, p. 114.

[14] Benjamin P. Thomas, *Theodore Weld. Crusader for Freedom*, p. 154.

[15] Walter M. Merrill, *Against Wind and Tide* (Cambridge, Mass., 1963), p. 34.

bolder and more confident than ever. I say to my per-
secutors, 'I bid you defiance.' Let the courts condemn me
to fine and imprisonment for denouncing oppression:
Am I to be frightened by dungeons and chains? can they
humble my spirit? do I not remember that I am an
American citizen? and, as a citizen, a freeman, and what
is more, a being accountable to God? I will not hold my
peace on the subject of African oppression. If need be,
who would not die a martyr to such a cause?"[16]

In the deepening commitment of all four men there
was an increasing boldness in the risks they ventured and
in the felt righteousness of their cause. None regretted
having given his life to the struggle and each thought it
was appropriate that they and others had been prepared
to surrender their lives in defense of the struggle to free
the slaves. The continuing alternation between opposition, violence, and suffering, and the partial victories
with the deep, if brief, excitement and enjoyment they
brought, gradually made it appear to all of them that
this was what they had been born for.

The stages in the development of their commitment
to abolitionism can now be summarized. First, there is
a resonance to the general idea of the salvation of others;
second, risk is ventured on behalf of those who need to
be saved; third, as a consequence of the risk taken, there
is punishment and suffering; fourth, as a consequence of
such suffering resonance to the original idea of the necessity of salvation is deepened and identification with the
oppressed is increased, as is hostility toward the oppressor; fifth, as a result of increased strength of affect and
ideation, there will be an increased willingness to take
even greater risks and more possible punishment and
suffering; sixth, increased risk-taking does evoke still more
punishment and more suffering; seventh, there is a still
greater willingness to tolerate suffering concomitant with

[16] *Ibid.*, p. 39.

a proportionate increase in intensity and duration of positive affect and ideation in identification with the oppressed and with fellow abolitionists, and an increase in negative affect toward the enemy, whose apparent power and undesirability is magnified as the density of affect and ideation increases. The alternation between resonance and risk-taking—suffering and punishment— and the increased density of positive feeling and thought resulting in increased risk-taking endlessly repeated, cumulatively deepens commitment until it reaches a point of no return—of irreversibility at which point no other way of life seems possible to the committed reformer. It should be noted that the pathway from early resonance to final commitment is not necessarily without internal conflict. In the four men studied, each suffered doubt at some point whether to give himself completely to abolitionism as a way of life, though Garrison little.

The same dynamic violence and suffering which gradually deepened the commitment of these four men was also responsible for engaging the commitment of others to abolitionism or at least to resistance against the extension of slavery to free soil. The violence inflicted on the early abolitionists and the suffering they endured led others to take up their cause; it is here that we see the collective influence of these men on their society.

The murder of the abolitionist Lovejoy, and the mob action against Garrison which had excited the sympathy and indignation of Phillips and drawn him into the struggle, also excited the sympathies and indignation of others at the time. Dr. Henry Ingersoll Bowditch, a prominent physician became an abolitionist in response to the Garrison mob: "Then it has come to this that a man cannot speak on slavery within sight of Faneuil Hall." Seeing Samuel A. Eliot, a member of the city government, Bowditch offered to help him suppress the rioters. "Instead of sustaining the idea of free speech . . . he rather intimated that the authorities, while not wishing for a mob, rather sympathized with its object which was to forcibly suppress the abolitionists. I was completely disgusted and I vowed in my heart as I left him with utter loathing, 'I am an abolitionist from this very moment.' "[17]

Because the abolitionists were fearless, and again and again exposed themselves to the danger of physical violence, they evoked widespread sympathy and respect, and simultaneous indignation against those who hurt and threatened them.

The mob which destroyed Birney's press and threatened his life created widespread sympathy for both him and his cause. Salmon Chase, for one, was thenceforward ready to stand openly with the abolitionists; he was, in fact, to become the congressional representative of abolitionism. Chase later wrote that he "became an opponent of slavery and the slave Power while witnessing Birney's display of conviction and intelligence as he confronted the mobocrats."[18]

William T. Allan's indecision between preaching Christianity or becoming an abolitionist was resolved by the Cincinnati mob. Even Birney's own son, William, was converted to the movement by virtue of having faced this mob when it came after his father. Following that episode, in fact, letters of encouragement came to Birney from all over the country. Not the least of these was from the influential and widely respected New England minister, Dr. William Ellery Channing, who had previously stood aloof from the abolitionist movement:

> "I earnestly desire, my dear Sir that you and your associates will hold fast the right of free discussion by speech and the press, and, at the same time, that

[17] Lawrence Lader, *The Bold Brahmins* (New York, 1961), pp. 22, 23.

[18] Albert Bushnell Hart, *Salmon Portland Chase* (Boston, 1899), p. 51.

you will exercise it as Christians, and as friends of your race. That you, Sir, will not fail in these duties, I rejoice to believe. Accept my humble tribute of respect and admiration for your disinterestedness, for your faithfulness to your convictions, under the peculiar sacrifices to which you have been called. . . . I look with scorn on the most gifted and prosperous in the struggle for office and power, but I look with reverence on the obscurest man, who suffers for the right, who is true to a good but persecuted cause."[19]

Lewis Tappan expressed confidence that Birney would again publish his "Philanthropist." Daniel Henshaw, a Lynn, Massachusetts editor, called Birney "one of the noblest sons of the West" who had "dared to lift up his voice in favor of liberty when all around him seemed given over to corruption, to slavery, to moral destruction."[20] Even Alva Woods, whom Birney had once hired as president of the University of Alabama, in his baccalaureate address expressed his deep indignation at this action by the mob.

But it was not only Garrison, Phillips, Weld, and Birney who evoked violence, sympathy, and indignation. There were hundred of agents who were stoned, tarred and feathered, whipped, beaten, and, in some cases, killed. In Utica, New York, in 1835, delegates who had assembled to organize the New York State Anti-Slavery Society had been dispersed by a mob composed of "very respectable gentlemen." Gerrit Smith, the wealthy landowner who had been a colonizationist, was influenced by this demonstration to join the abolitionists; he invited the convention to meet at his estate at nearby Peterboro.

In addition to physical violence there was continual

[19] Betty Fladeland, *James Gillespie Birney: Slaveholder to Abolitionist*, p. 144.
[20] *Ibid.*, p. 145.

verbal abuse and threat of violence heaped publicly on
every abolitionist. In Garrison's case, a price was actually
placed on his head in the South. Indeed it seems clear
that without the exaggeration of Garrison's reputation
by the South, his influence could never have been as great
as it was.

We have argued that violence and suffering played a
central role in the commitment first of the abolitionist
and then in influencing general public opinion. At this
point I should clarify what I mean by violence and
suffering. By violence I refer to any negative affect inflicted with intent to hurt. This negative affect may be
an aggressive threat of physical violence or a verbal insult. By suffering, I refer to any negative affect produced in the victim as a result of violence, whether this
be a feeling of humiliation, helpless rage, terror, or distress. It is my argument that such violence and suffering
can, in a democratic society, arouse in outside observers
equally intense feeling. In hierarchically organized societies identification with the upper classes and castes
will radically attenuate empathy with the victims of
oppression. But in a democratic society, based on belief
in individualism and egalitarianism, it is possible to
arouse vicarious distress, shame, fear, or sympathy for a
victim and anger or contempt for an aggressor. As a by-
product, the ideas of the victim will then tend to become more influential than before such an attack. Most
men in a democratic society share its values to some extent and so even those who identify with the aggressor
will feel a certain amount of guilt at the challenge to
democratic values. Thus in the North, some of those who
had identified with slaveholders and been most hostile
to the abolitionists, joined in lionizing them after the
Civil War had ended; it is as if they were atoning for
having identified with the "antidemocratic" position. I
would argue that guilt over slavery was experienced in
the South, too, though there it was defended against by

exaggerating the villainy of the abolitionists and the evils of Northern "wage slavery."

In a recent investigation I conducted on the immediate impact of the assassination of the late President Kennedy I found a very general increase in sympathy and respect for the victim even among those who had previously been hostile toward him. A very small minority of Republican students ostentatiously played jazz records in their rooms to flaunt their hostility (they said) and to reduce their guilt (I think) for vicarious identification with the assassin. In all such cases the grounds for identification with the victim are numerous. First, the tendency to identify with any human being is general. Second, in a democratic society there is a taboo on inflicting hurt on anyone since it denies his equal right to life, liberty, and the pursuit of happiness. Third, to the extent to which there is also a tendency to identify with the aggressor, vicarious guilt is experienced and thereby increases sympathy for the victim as a secondary reaction. Fourth, insofar as the victim is defending others (including oneself) there is anger against the aggressor because the self is being vicariously attacked. Fifth, insofar as the victim is defending others (including oneself) there is guilt and sympathy for the victim who is "selflessly" fighting the battles of others (including one's own battles).

Because of heightened identification with the victim there results an increased polarization between the aggressor and the victim which magnifies the conflict and draws into the struggle thousands who would otherwise not have become involved. Quite apart from which side of the conflict gains the most converts, such polarization has the critical consequence of increasing the confrontation of the problem by the otherwise apathetic. One half of the battle of radical social change is to increase the density of affect and thought about the problem. To look steadily and hard at a social condition which violates the shared basic values of a society produces as much suffering for the society as a whole as does the condition itself for the segment of society primarily affected.

The Northern American citizen of the mid-nineteenth century was essentially ambivalent about slavery. He neither could approve it nor steadily disapprove it. He would have preferred to forget it. This is precisely what the abolitionists made more and more difficult. They were responsible for forcing confrontation and thereby radically increased the density of affect and ideation about the issue. Not all Northerners became maximally committed, but it is certain that the abolitionists greatly magnified the awareness and level of feeling of enemy and sympathizer alike and thereby exerted an amplified influence. The abolitionists did not permit Americans to look away from the ugly violation of the democratic ethos. In part they achieved this by provoking opposition and by offering themselves as victims. Thereby they evoked sympathy for themselves and their cause, and provoked anger and contempt for those who supported slavery.

By the 1850's it appeared to many, for the first time, that the abolitionists had not really exaggerated the moral iniquity of the South. In Boston, for example, many who at one time had regarded the abolitionists as the "lunatic fringe" were to have second thoughts when, in 1854, a former slave had to be taken by force from the city and shipped back to slavery as, ashamed and helpless, thousands were forced to look on. Gradually more and more Northerners came to experience the suffering of violence, at first vicariously and then more directly, until the climax at Fort Sumter. War is a special case of commitment and I would defend the position that a democratic society can commit itself to war only if it feels it has suffered violence upon itself directly or vicariously. It has therefore always been necessary for America to be attacked, before sufficiently intense and prolonged commitment can be generated to permit a defensive counterattack. This attack and counterattack, I have argued, is the way in which commitment to anti-slavery was first generated in the abolitionists, and finally, in more and more of the Northern citizenry.

PART V: COMPARISONS:

A. FOREIGN

B. DOMESTIC

CHAPTER 13

"A SACRED ANIMOSITY":

ABOLITIONISM IN CANADA

BY ROBIN W. WINKS

"WHEN I speak of the South, I mean south of Canada. The whole U.S. is the South."[1] So said Malcolm X, then leader of the Harlem Mosque of the Black Muslim movement in the United States, early in 1964. Perhaps unconsciously Malcolm X was accepting a common North American assumption: that Canada somehow had escaped involvement in the long Negro story, that neither slavery nor discrimination, neither Negro power nor Negro purpose were relevant to the Canadian scene or to Canadian history. Malcolm X was mistaken.

The Negro has been present on what today is Canadian soil for nearly as long as on American.[2] The Negro Canadian, like the Negro American, has experienced discrimination, vast uprootings, and the frustrating impotence of potential but badly used political power. Slavery was accepted in British North America long after most Northern states, by their constitutions, judicial decisions, or gradual-abolition acts had ended the practice.[3] Ironically,

[1] Marc Crawford, "The Ominous Malcolm X Exits from the Muslims," *Life*, LVI (March 20, 1964), 40A.

[2] The only general historical study of the Negro Canadian is Ida C. Greaves, "The Negro in Canada," *McGill University Economic Studies*, whole no. 16 (Orillia [1930]). The writer has near completion a manuscript on the Negro in Canada from slavery to the present time.

[3] Slavery was not formally abolished for British North America until 1833, and until 1800 slavery generally was accepted with little legislative restraint in all of the provinces (although gradual abolition had begun in Upper Canada). By the latter year Vermont,

between 1787 and 1800 fugitive slaves from Canada[4] fled south into New England and the Northwest Territory, reversing the popularly recognized direction of flow. In the last decade of the eighteenth and the first decade of the nineteenth centuries, British North Americans sought to limit or to abolish slavery within their borders, and a quiet, little known abolitionist movement, initially restricted within present-day Canada, experienced fruitful if limited victories. Later, in the 1830's and increasingly thereafter, Canadians took their place in the broader, continentally oriented abolitionist movement, the movement culminating in the American Civil War. It is primarily to the second of these two abolition movements in Canada, the international aspect of that "sacred animosity" between slavery and freedom of which Charles Sumner spoke in 1860,[5] that this essay addresses itself.

I

The first, or indigenous, Canadian abolitionist movement began almost immediately after the American Rev-

---

Pennsylvania, Massachusetts, Connecticut, Rhode Island, and New York had abolished slavery, and Ohio, New Jersey, New Hampshire, Indiana, and Illinois followed quickly. See Leon F. Litwack, *North of Slavery: The Negro in the Free States, 1790-1860* (Chicago, 1961), p. 3n.

[4] Technically the word "Canada" applied, before 1867, only to present-day Ontario and Quebec, which were known much earlier as Upper and Lower Canada and for the period 1841-67 as Canada West and Canada East or as "the United Canadas" or "the Canadas." The proper title to encompass these provinces (then colonies) together with Nova Scotia, New Brunswick, and Prince Edward Island (usually referred to collectively as the "Maritime Provinces") was "British North America." For the sake of convenience I shall nonetheless on occasion use the modern national term "Canada" to embrace the whole.

[5] "The Barbarism of Slavery," Sumner's speech before the Senate, June 4, 1860, in *The Works of Charles Sumner* (Boston, 1874), V, 124. The speech was given prominence in Canada West by the Toronto *Globe* (June 8, 1860) which attested to Canada's desire for a share in this "sacred animosity."

olution. Hardly a movement, in fact, so much as a sentiment, this local attack on slavery appeared at approximately the same time in Nova Scotia and in the Canadas.
Among the Loyalists there were many New Englanders
who had opposed slavery at home and who saw no good
reason to change their views in another setting. Many of
the older residents also resented the general ascendancy
of property which the arrival of slave-holding Loyalists represented. Religious attitudes joined with a quick
and sweeping anti-Americanism in some quarters to add
to the growing condemnation of slavery. The British
North American colonies should not, some thought, support an institution identified with the new Republic.

This locally created and locally expressed antislavery
sentiment did not result in total abolition of permissive
slave legislation, but it did issue within a decade and a
half in placing slave holders on the defensive and fore-
stalling further growth, first in the Canadas and later in
the Maritime Provinces. Slavery was abolished on a gradual basis for the entirety of the British Empire by an
Imperial act of 1833, an act which became fully effective
on August 1, 1838. Long before this, local action in the
British North American provinces virtually had halted
slavery in any case, even though the last Canadian born
into slavery lived to see all of North America free, dying
in Cornwall, Ontario, in 1871.

Thus British North Americans generally supported the
British antislavery drive of the early nineteenth century,
partially because it was British and partially because the
colonials either were hostile or indifferent to slavery. By
the 1830's and 1840's, however, the Canadas witnessed a
clear rise in anti-Negro sentiment. Hundreds and eventually thousands of Negroes poured north seeking freedom,
only to encounter prejudice in many forms. But in British
North America Negroes were at least free and generally
beyond the reach of pursuing masters or, after 1850, of
the Fugitive Slave Law. By 1860 there were thousands

of American Negroes on Canadian soil, most of them in Canada West.

The actual number of Negroes, fugitive and free, Canadian and American, in the provinces cannot be known. A popularly accepted estimate then and since was 60,000 to 75,000, with half this number said to have arrived after 1850.[6] This figure undoubtedly is too high but the official census for the Canadas, which cited 11,413 Negroes in 1860 and, at most, 8,000 in 1850, undoubtedly was too low, for the census was contradictory, inefficiently administered, and lacked any clear definition of the designations "colored" or "Negro."[7] Forced to choose between the rumors and guesses of unwary travelers,[8] the propaganda of abolitionists,[9] and the claims of South-

[6] Booker T. Washington, *The Story of the Negro: The Rise of the Race from Slavery* (New York, 1909), II, 240. Fred Landon, "The Negro Migration to Canada after the Passing of the Fugitive Slave Act," *Journal of Negro History*, V (January 1920), 22, accepts the figure of 60,000 but believes only 15-20,000 arrived in the last decade. A recent general study, John Bartlet Brebner, *Canada: A Modern History* (Ann Arbor, Mich., 1960), p. 227, refers to 40-50,000 Negroes. The London (Ont.) *Free Press*, January 12, 1958, mentions 60,000 "slaves" who escaped to "Canada" in the 1850's alone. Contemporary authority for the estimate of a total of 60,000 Negroes in the Canadas appears in "W.M.G.," "A Sabbath among the Runaway Negroes at Niagara," *Excelsior: Helps to Progress in Religion, Science, and Literature*, V (1856), 41.

[7] *Canada Census*, 1851, I, 37, cites 8,000 "coloreds," but p. 317 refers to 2,502 Negro males and 2,167 Negro females.

[8] Typically, Thomas Nye, a Montreal lawyer, recorded in his journal in 1837 that the "Africans . . . [were] said to be 10,000 at Wilberforce" alone, a patently ridiculous statement. One thousand is the figure best supported. See New York Historical Society, New York, Miscellaneous MSS: journal, p. 17, December 12.

[9] In 1851 Benjamin Drew estimated there were 30,000 fugitives in Canada West, and in the following year the Anti-Slavery Society of Canada, in its *First Annual Report* (Toronto, 1852), p. 17, accepted this figure. See Drew, *A North-Side View of Slavery* (Boston, 1856), p. 234. Most observers and subsequent historians have been annoyingly vague, unaware of British North America's earlier slave history and ignorant of the Negro population outside the Canadas. Nearly all assumed that every Negro seen was a fugitive.

erners who had good reason to exaggerate their losses,[10] one can do little better than to accept the conclusion of Samuel Gridley Howe, who traveled extensively in Canada West in 1863 to investigate the condition of Negro refugees. He, too, was imprecise in making distinctions between Canadian Negroes and American fugitives, but he estimated that up to 40,000 Negroes had entered the Canadas since 1800.[11] If the Negroes of Nova Scotia, New Brunswick, and Vancouver Island—on the West Coast, where a body of free blacks had moved from California in 1858-59—are added perhaps a total Negro population in 1860 of 60,000 may be accepted for the entirety of present-day Canada. But the figures cited by their originators were usually meant to apply to Canada West or, at the most, the United Canadas, and as such they represent a gross inflation.

The Negroes congregated in settlements to themselves, however, and where they did move they seemed to move in abundance, attracting attention and generating prejudice. This prejudice was manifested in the usual ways: in occasional acts of group violence directed against Negroes who attempted to rise too far or too fast, in public resentment of the Negro settlements, in bills to inhibit or prohibit Negro use of the franchise, in segregated schools, and in the subtle currency of daily speech. Terms like "nigger" were in general use, and "darkies," "sooties," and other epithets occur in private and public papers. In French Canada two imports, "odor" and "parfum d'Afrique," were employed by mid-century. Around York (ultimately Toronto) burning fallen trees into parts by placing small pieces of wood across them and then setting these on fire was known as "niggering." High

[10] See Larry Gara, *The Liberty Line: The Legend of the Underground Railroad* (Lexington, Ky., 1961), pp. 37-38.

[11] In his report to the Freedmen's Inquiry Commission (Boston, 1864), *The Refugees from Slavery in Canada West*.

compliment indeed was it to call a Negro "a colored man with a white soul," and as in the American Middle West by the 1860's generosity and honesty were summed up in the praise, "that was a white thing to do." Darky Lanes, Nigger Hills, Little Africas, and Black Halls were common.[12]

For the most part Negroes lived in their own segregated communities and small islands of blacks were spread throughout Canada West by 1860. In the 1820's Negroes formed a substantial body around Amherstburg, on the Canadian side of the Detroit River, where they made tobacco into a local staple.[13] They settled along the Canadian side of Niagara Falls where they farmed, were waiters in some of the hotels (until a growing influx of summer tourists from the Southern states led the hotel proprietors to relegate Negroes to less public places), and where they were used as guides in making the descent under the Falls.[14] Negroes worked on the roads, cleared land, dug canals, and in the cities were casual laborers, while a few were in commerce. Some were minstrels, several were schoolteachers or preachers to their brethren,

[12] See "A 'Canuck'" [Michael G. Scherck], *Pen Pictures of Early Pioneer Life in Upper Canada* (Toronto, 1905), p. 49; Etobicoke Historical Society, *Bulletin* no. 12 (July, 1961), p. 3; London *Free Press*, February 23, 1924; Public Archives of Canada [hereafter, PAC], Ottawa, Society for the Propagation of the Gospel papers [hereafter, SPG], microfilm: George Best, January 1, 1820. "Africville" appears on mid-century maps of Halifax in the Public Archives of Nova Scotia and the Yale University Library.

[13] *Genius of Universal Emancipation*, January 12, November 18, 1826, January 12, 1828; Joseph Pickering, *Inquiries of an Emigrant: being the Narrative of an English Farmer from the Year 1824 to 1830* . . . (4th edn., London, 1832), pp. 96-97.

[14] Library of Congress, Mrs. Basil Hall Letters: Mrs. Hall to "my dearest Jane," July 4 [finished July 15], 1827, p. 6; Columbia University Library, William J. Wilgus Papers: box III, sec. A, "Some Account of a Trip to the Falls of Niagara performed in the Month of May, 1836 by Thomas S. Woodcock," pp. 21-22; E. S. Abdy, *Journal of a Residence and Tour in the United States of North America, from April, 1833, to October, 1834* (London, 1835), I, 300-301.

and one won fame in Toronto as the singing "Black Swan."[15] But most Negroes, free and fugitive, were farmers.

They lived throughout British North America, from St. John's, Newfoundland, to Victoria, Vancouver Island, around Halifax and southwards, and near Guysborough and Amherst, in Nova Scotia, around Lake Otnabog in New Brunswick, and in Montreal. The largest body of Negroes undoubtedly lived in Canada West. There they clustered at Shanty Bay (or Oro) on Lake Simcoe, and in St. John's Ward in Toronto; near Guelph and Waterloo, Owen Sound, Amherstburg, Sandwich, and Sarnia; in St. Catharines, Hamilton, and Niagara Falls; at Dawn Mills, near Dresden, already known as "Nigger Hole," and most strikingly in their own provident communities.[16] These communities,[17] of which three were of importance,

[15] Fort Malden Museum: Fugitive Slave File; London, Ontario, Fred Landon Correspondence (in private possession of Professor Landon); Landon, ed. "The Proudfoot Papers," London and Middlesex Historical Society, *Transactions*, XI (1922), 87-88; William S. Fox, ed. *Letters of William Davies, Toronto, 1854-1861* (Toronto, 1945), p. 49: Davies to [brother] James, July 13, 1855; Toronto *Daily Patriot*, May 11, 1854; J. H. Hawkins, "Early Days in Brantford," Brant Historical Society, *Papers . . . 1908-1911*, p. 47.

[16] PAC, SPG: R. Rolph, July 1, 1829; Adam Fergusson, *Practical Notes made during a Tour in Canada, and a Portion of the United States, in MDCCCXXXI* (2d edn., Edinburgh, 1834), pp. 122-23, 127; Windsor, *Voice of the Fugitive*, December 1, 1851; Victor Lauriston, *Romantic Kent: More than Three Centuries of History, 1626-1952* (Chatham, n.d. [1953?]), pp. 382-83; E. C. Drury, "The Negro Settlement of Oro," typescript [often in error], November 2, 1959, in Orillia Public Library; and Orillia *Packet*, August 16, 1958.

[17] My general study of the Negro in Canada includes much material on these communities. After I had completed my research for this portion of the manuscript, William H. and Jane H. Pease published their *Black Utopia: Negro Communal Experiments in America* (Madison, Wis., 1963), which includes chapters on the three chief communities, Wilberforce, Dawn, and Elgin (Buxton). This is a thoroughly researched, thoughtful account from which I differ only on matters of detail. For exact locations of the Negro settlements, before they disappeared from the maps, consult H. F. Walling, ed., *Atlas of the Dominion of Canada* (Montreal, 1875), pp. 131, 151.

all in Canada West, attracted considerable unfavorable attention and, combined with the rising influx of destitute fugitives after 1850, did much to promote anti-Negro sentiment in the province.

The earliest of these colonies was Wilberforce, near Lucan, some twelve miles from London, where Negro refugees from Cincinnati settled in 1829. The original organizers of the colony, Israel Lewis and Thomas Cresap, had decided to purchase 4,000 acres of land in the Huron Tract for $6,000, and by reselling this land to new settlers for more capital, they hoped to buy up nearly a million acres. But Lewis and Cresap had no backing, and they soon found themselves unable to meet their commitments. The Quakers of Ohio and Indiana ultimately bought 800 acres for the settlement, and several hundred Negroes moved onto the land, but the seller, the Canada Company, refused to sell land to Negroes thereafter because the purchase fell far short of the original contract. The settlement was improvidently led and ill-organized, and the manual labor school and theological seminary which were to become the community's center never were founded. Reverend Nathaniel Paul and Israel Lewis solicited funds in England and the United States for the colony but apparently they never turned any money over to the community. Austin Steward, a fugitive slave who had been a grocer in Rochester, New York, provided a form of leadership from 1831 to 1837, but he then returned to the United States. With his departure Wilberforce virtually collapsed, although Negroes stayed on in the area. The Wilberforce experiment undoubtedly delayed further collective settlement in the Canadas, and the ignominious failure which followed upon the grandiose plan led many white Canadians to conclude that Negroes did, indeed, fulfill their stereotype: they were improvident, naïve, unable to plan, to prosper, or even to protest their fate effectively.[18]

[18] Wilberforce has attracted considerable attention and the rele-

The second Negro colony in Canada West was sponsored by the British-American Institute. The Canada Mission, an American group organized to establish schools in the Canadas, largely for Negroes, provided the initial stimulus. One of the founders of the Mission, Hiram Wilson, joined with Josiah Henson, a Negro preacher, and James Cannings Fuller, a Quaker philanthropist, to found a school of manual labor near London. The school opened in 1842, and a Negro community grew around it. Wilson and Henson proved to be ineffective administrators, and in 1850 the institute, heavily in debt, transferred its property to the Board of the American Baptist Free Mission Society. Two years later John Scoble, who had won fame as the Secretary to the British and Foreign Anti-Slavery Society, became manager. He quarreled with Henson, Wilson, and some of the members of the Canadian Anti-Slavery Society, and his leadership ultimately proved as ineffective as that of the founders. Scoble, an English moderate, also swept Dawn, as the colony was known, into the growing dispute between the Garrisonians and the moderate wings of abolitionism, and he used his office as a political forum, taking an active part in Clear Grit (or reform) politics from 1857 to 1861. Henson, who had often seemed on shaky moral ground in the past, was convicted of fraud on a charge placed by Scoble, and the leaders of the experimental utopia ultimately destroyed Dawn by feuding among themselves and by drawing upon Dawn attacks

---

vant literature is large. Steward wrote an autobiography, *Twenty-two Years a Slave, and Forty a Freeman: Embracing a Correspondence of Several Years, while President of Wilberforce Colony, London, Canada West* (Rochester, N.Y., 1857). Benjamin Lundy, early Quaker abolitionist, visited the settlement in 1832 and kept a journal which he published serially in the *Genius of Universal Emancipation* beginning with volume XII (April 1832). It is reprinted in Fred Landon, ed. "The Diary of Benjamin Lundy Written during his Journey through Upper Canada, January, 1832," Ontario Historical Society, *Papers and Records*, XIX (1922), 110-33.

from Garrisonian, antireform, and Negrophobic quarters. In 1868 the community was abandoned.

The third effort to reach utopia in Canada was more successful. William King, an Irishman of good education, who was a missionary in Canada West for the Free Presbyterian Church of Scotland, founded the Elgin Association with the moral support of the Toronto synod of his church in 1849. The Elgin community, near Chatham, was to combine secular education and practical training with Christian instruction. King benefited from the mistakes made at Wilberforce and Dawn, and he also planned carefully before occupying land. He founded two organizations, in fact: the first, the Buxton Mission, was the ecclesiastical arm of Elgin, and it stood, physically and spiritually, at the center of the settlement. The second, the Association, was the secular arm, and it promoted a message of self-help, hard work, and thrift. King helped develop small industry at Elgin, craftsmen, a hotel and general store, and self-sustaining vegetable supplies. His school system was remarkably successful, concentrating as it did on immediate and practical needs at the primary level. Despite heavy attacks from local conservative politicians and from anti-Negro whites, Elgin thrived. Crop failures and an ill-advised attempt to engage in lumbering, as well as internal dissension, harmed the settlement, but King was able to counter these problems through the force of his own paternalistic and intelligent leadership. Elgin became the one reasonably successful Negro communitarian experiment in British North America. By the time the Association was dissolved in 1873, it had sent out into the Canadas and the United States a number of educated, self-supporting Negroes. Not self-consciously devoted to the antislavery campaign, but inextricably bound up with that movement through its efforts to raise the freeman and to succor the fugitive, Elgin and its leader King achieved the kind of success which Negro leaders of the twentieth century might well

condemn but which seemed, in the coming age of Booker
T. Washington, forward looking, rational, and fundamentally Christian.[19]

The major thrust in the Canadian contribution to
world-wide abolitionism came not from the mission
boards, the self-segregated, self-help communities, the
begging ministers, or the isolated Negroes of the Maritime Provinces, however. These groups were interested in
helping the Negroes who were citizens in British North
America and welcoming those who were fugitives. But
as organizations and collective bodies they did not attack slavery directly. Certainly individual members of
some of the communities helped flay slavery through the
press or hoped to weaken it by journeys south of the
border to guide fugitives toward freedom.[20] Certainly,
too, many reasoned that any aid given to fugitives in

[19] Material on Elgin is abundant. King left a manuscript autobiography and considerable correspondence (PAC, King Papers). The
Association issued regular reports, some of which are available, as
are those of the Buxton Mission, which appeared in the *Ecclesiastical and Missionary Record*. King's biography has been written by
Annie Straith Jamieson, *William King, Friend and Champion of
Slaves* (Toronto, 1925), and the early settlement has been analyzed
by William H. and Jane H. Pease in "Opposition to the Founding of
the Elgin Settlement," *Canadian Historical Review*, XXXVIII (September 1957), 202-18. A useful obituary of King appears in the Boston *Herald*, January 7, 1895.

[20] The most effective of the white Canadians who actually traveled
into the South was Alexander Milton Ross, a "red-hot abolitionist"
who took time from his interests as a doctor and an ornithologist to
aid many fugitives in their search for freedom. See Fred Landon,
"A Daring Canadian Abolitionist," *Michigan History Magazine*, V
(October 1921), 364-73; T. E. Champion, "The Underground Railway
and One of Its Operators," *Canadian Magazine*, V (May 1895), 9-16;
and Ross's two books, *Memoires of a Reformer (1832-1892)* (Toronto,
1893), and *Recollections and Experiences of an Abolitionist* (Toronto, 1875). Ross's work can also be traced through his correspondence
at Rhodes House, Oxford, in the Papers of the British and Foreign
Anti-Slavery and Aborigines Protection Society [hereafter, "Anti-
Slavery Papers"]; in the Edith Rossiter Bevan Autograph Collection
at the Library of Congress; in the Ralph Waldo Emerson Papers at
Harvard University's Houghton Library; and in Cornell University,
Olin Library: Ross to B. G. Wilder, March 24, 1877.

British North America made the provinces additionally attractive, and that by creating a magnet for runaway slaves, they were helping to sap the strength of the institution. But abolitionism in Canada was expressed more precisely and more directly (although not always with more effect) through attempts to subdue prejudice within the provinces and to lend vocal and moral support, and limited financial aid, to the more exposed but also far more effective abolitionist groups in the United States.

II

There is an abundance of evidence that Negroes generally were tolerated but unwelcome in Canada, particularly in Canada West. They were considered "dangerous customers,"[21] to be shunned and kept at a distance. The foundress of the Ursuline community at Chatham felt they were thieves; "Canadians are tired of them . . . ," she wrote. Travelers' accounts tended to agree that whites viewed the Negroes "with no small disfavor." There were, as the Chatham *Journal* discovered, certain "Nigger peculiarities" which made them unassimilable. Helpless and dependent, often unable to find work, the fugitive slaves in particular led Canadians to an ambivalent attitude. That Negroes should wish to escape to Canada was visible testimony to the greater freedom of Canadian life but once present they competed with local labor for jobs in an area where, except for brief periods of time, the labor market was more restrictive than in the United States. Still, when a fugitive fled from Canada West to rejoin her master, the Toronto *Globe*, the province's most influential newspaper, charged the "ignorant negro" with shrinking "from the responsibilities of freedom."

The free Canadian Negroes also were a problem, for they were bolder and under no fear of extradition.[22] As

[21] W. L. Smith, *Pioneers of Old Ontario* (Toronto, 1923), pp. 306-7.

[22] On extradition, see in particular Roman J. Zorn, "Criminal Ex-

one daughter of Robert Baldwin, Canada West's distinguished and liberal political leader of the 1840's, wrote of her pioneer life, "One great misery . . . was the unpleasantness of being obliged to sit at table with one's servants, a black one sometimes being amongst them." Violence of thought sometimes gave rise to violence of action: Negro houses in Dresden, at Dawn, and at Sandwich were burned, as were Negro clubs in St. Catharines and Hamilton. In 1863 a race riot in Detroit spilled over into Windsor, and at the close of the Civil War in 1865 a group of Quebec volunteers for the Federal army, who had enlisted ostensibly to "fight slavery," celebrated their arrival at the border by raiding a Negro church in Windsor on a Sunday evening.[23]

The first major Canadian antislavery society was created to combat not such individual expressions of fear and disdain but rather to meet growing evidence of organized, group prejudice. Two events in particular—a

---

tradition Menaces the Canadian Haven for Fugitive Slaves, 1841-1861," *Canadian Historical Review*, XXXVIII (December 1957), 284-94; and Alexander L. Murray, "Canada and the Anglo-American Anti-Slavery Movement: A Study in International Philanthropy," unpubl. Ph.D. diss. (Univ. Pennsylvania, 1960).

[23] Fort Malden Museum: Assessment rolls for 1849 for the Township of Colchester; "W.M.G.," "A Sabbath among the Runaway Negroes," pp. 40-43; Landon Correspondence: Mother M. Xavier, Chatham, n. d.; Fox, ed. *Davies*, p. 39: William to James Davies, January 28, 1855; Isaac Fidler, *Observations on Professions, Literature, Manners, and Emigration in the United States and Canada, Made during a Residence there in 1832* (London, 1833), pp. 380-82; Catherine F. Lefroy, "Recollections of Mary Warren Breckenridge, of Clarke Township," Ontario Historical Society, *Papers and Records*, III (1901), 110-13, and reprinted in Women's Canadian Historical Society of Toronto, *Transactions*, no. 3 (1902), pp. 1-4; "Two Brothers," *The United States and Canada, as Seen by Two Brothers in 1858 and 1861* (London, 1862), p. 107; *A Thrilling Narrative from the Lips of the Sufferers of the Late Detroit Riot, March 6, 1863 . . .* (Detroit, 1863), and reprinted in *Heartman's Historical Series*, whole no. 72 (Hattiesburg, Miss., 1945); Toronto *Globe*, December 23, 1859; Toronto *Leader*, May 5, 1865; Detroit *Free Press*, March 7, 1863; New York *Daily Tribune*, March 9, 1863.

local election and a public petition relating to segregated schools—prepared the ground for the new society. The injection of "the Negro question" into local politics probably was most prominent but the school issue was more important.

Negroes and whites had been taught in the same classrooms early in the century but by the 1830's most Negroes were attending separate schools. In many cases they had wanted such schools, for often fugitive slaves were unable to do the regular work set by the Education Department.[24] Moreover, some schools had grown out of, or remained a part of, Christian mission systems in the Canadas which assumed separation. Then, too, Dawn had been founded to support a separate vocational school. Nonetheless, many Negroes paid taxes and wished access to the public schools. In 1843 the Negro residents of Hamilton petitioned the Governor General to confirm their right to public schooling, and the President of the Board of Police in Hamilton replied to the Governor General's query that white parents would take their children out of the schools if they were forced to attend with Negroes.

The provincial legislature passed a Separate Schools Act in 1850 (which was to remain on Ontario's books until the 1960's, although the last separate school under the act closed in 1891) which permitted any group of five Negro families to ask local public school trustees to establish a separate school for them. The act was intended to be permissive but as a considerable body of correspondence in the papers of Egerton Ryerson, long Superintendent of Schools in Canada West, shows, the effect of the bill was to give whites a weapon to force

[24] However, an examination of the books used in the King Street School in Amherstburg in 1833-43 indicates that this school, at least, used texts of difficulty equal to those used in other schools. Mr. Alvin McCurdy of Amherstburg kindly permitted the writer to consult six of the standard texts of the period from his private collection on local Negro history.

Negroes into applying for such schools. In the act's first year of operation, the Negro inhabitants of Simcoe petitioned Ryerson for aid in getting their children into the public school, and he replied that it was a "deplorable calamity" that children of a group so depressed in the United States should also be abused in Canada. To another petition he noted that blacks attended schools in Toronto, for the residents of that city had "too much good sense, and Christian and British feeling to make the slightest objection." Ryerson urged that Negroes who were denied access to public schools should prosecute for damages, but few did so, from fear, ignorance of the law, lack of funds, or weary indifference. In 1855 a Negro plaintiff in Simcoe won a verdict for damages and costs, but since the defendants had no property, the plaintiff had to pay costs himself and was forced to sell his farm in order to do so. By 1859 the decision in this trial, Washington v. Trustees of Charlotteville, was being interpreted to mean that where no separate school was established for Negroes, they had the right to attend the common school, but Ryerson was also arguing that Boards of School Trustees could establish any kind of schools they felt "best adapted to the social condition of their respective communities," and that children could not claim admission to any schools other than those established for them. The effect of such a view was local option on separated schools, and while Toronto and Hamilton retained mixed schools, St. Catharines, Dresden, Simcoe, Chatham, Sandwich, Malden, Anderdon, and other communities had fully segregated school systems. Such schools were common in Nova Scotia as well—where three still were operating on a segregated basis in 1964.[25] All of the separate Negro schools were Protestant or secular, and when in 1861 the Ursuline nuns attempted to establish a school for Catholic Negroes, white Catholics protested.

[25] *Canada Week*, I (May 11, 1964), 2.

In 1862 even London, the center of antislavery sentiment in southwestern Canada West, decided to establish segregated schools "when financially practicable." With staggering originality the Toronto *Leader*, a conservative daily, praised this decision and asked, "Where is the white man or woman in this city who would wish to see his daughter married to a black man?"[26]

A second means of mass expression of contempt and fear of Negroes was by public resolution and political action. In 1831 the Upper Canadian Assembly had passed a resolution of alarm at the intention of the Canada Company to sell tracts of land to the Wilberforce Negroes and had opposed any "large influx" of blacks. The Assembly received petitions from residents of several communities in the 1830's and 1840's against permitting Negroes to enter and against mission societies that hoped to aid colonization. The Elgin Association in particular met major opposition from various groups in Chatham when it successfully petitioned for an act of incorporation in 1850. In the following year the citizens of Chatham were given an opportunity to express themselves unequivocally on the issue, for in June a local Tory, Edwin Larwill, mounted a petition to discourage further Negro immigra-

[26] *Friend of Man*, March 7, 1838; Amherstburg *Courier*, June 2, 1849; Toronto *Globe*, July 1, 1851, January 19, 1859; Chatham *Gleaner*, January 9, 1848; Toronto *Leader*, January 5, 1863; Chatham *Daily News*, February 11, 1949; Ontario Provincial Archives [hereafter OPA], Toronto: Hodgins Papers, Egerton Ryerson to W. H. Draper, April 12, 1847; *ibid.*, Education Department Papers, Incoming Correspondence and Letters Outward [Ryerson Papers], contains petitions to the Governor General and to Ryerson, October 15, 1843, December 12, 1851, January 13, August 9, 1856, February 26, 1857, March 2, 1859, and March 17, 18, 1862, as well as eleven letters dealing with segregated schools. See also Drew, *North-Side View of Slavery*, pp. 94-96; Mother M. Mercedes, "The History of the Ursulines in Ontario," unpubl. M.A. thesis (Univ. Western Ontario, 1937), pp. 38-40; C. B. Edward, "London Public Schools, 1848-1871," London and Middlesex Historical Society, *Transactions*, V (1914), 20-21; *Revised Statutes of Ontario, 1950* . . . (Toronto, 1950), IV, 643-80: ch. 356, pt. i, sec. 2, on "Protestant and Coloured Separate Schools."

tion, and in December he ran for the House of Assembly on the basis of the petition. He was defeated for re-election by his opponent, Colonel John Prince, who received an almost solid Negro vote.

Larwill ran again in 1854, this time from outer Kent County, and won. His victory was brief, for his tactics and speech were so like those of many Southern American senators as to be an embarrassment to Canadians. Almost at once Larwill proposed a poll tax on Negroes and asked for legal restrictions on abolitionist groups. He mixed his racist harangues in the Assembly with placatory appeals to the United States in order to win a more favorable reciprocal trade treaty, and apparently those who were not disturbed by his racism were offended by his desire to appease the Republic. In January 1858, he was soundly defeated by Archibald McKellar, a lawyer from Chatham and a friend of William King. But the Negroes, who had voted solidly Conservative since 1848, when they had rallied behind Colonel Prince, now were faced with a former friend turned enemy, for in 1858 Prince denounced all Negroes as "animals," declared that the majority were criminals,[27] and echoed another original charge: "They might as well try to change the spots of the leopard, as to make the black a good citizen." The effect of Larwill's campaign and of Prince's defection from the cause of the fugitive slave was to embroil the Negro in Canada West in a province-wide political dispute.[28]

[27] There is much conflicting evidence and advice on the question of the Negro criminal rate in Canada West. The best source, the Reports of Penitentiary Inspectors, did tend to emphasize the high percentage of Negroes in jails but the same reports also noted that fugitives educated only to slavery were more prone to crime. See, for example, the Inspectors' Reports in the Appendices to the *Journal of the House of Assembly of Upper Canada*, 1837-38, and the *Journals of the Legislative Assembly of the Province of Canada*, 1841-43.

[28] On the Negro issue in politics see *African Repository and Colonial Journal*, VI (1831), 27-29; *Voice of the Fugitive*, February 26, December 17, 1851, February 12, 1852; Chatham *Gleaner*, January

The undisputed provincial leader of the reform opposition to the Tories and to separate schools, George Brown, was editor of the Toronto *Globe*. In a few short years he and his "Clear Grits" would help father the Canadian Confederation. He also was one of the most important members of the Anti-Slavery Society of Canada, which he helped found in 1851, and he used his newspaper to espouse ,the antislavery cause. His father Peter, also a journalist, had championed the cause early, and George had taken an interest in the condition of the Negro in Canada from the inception of the *Globe* in 1844. He, his brother Gordon, his father Peter, and his sister Isabella formed the nucleus of an antislavery society in Toronto, and Isabella's husband, Thomas Henning, was the first secretary of the Canadian Anti-Slavery Society.[29] This group, together with radical politicians like the Reverend John Rolph, polemicist Charles Stuart, and the Reverend Michael Willis provided the moving force behind the Canadian abolitionist movement of the 1850's. They were strengthened by itinerant whites—Benjamin Lundy, John Scoble, or John Brown—and by local Negroes and members of the international community of black opposition to slavery—Samuel Ringgold Ward, Henry Bibb, J. W. Loguen, Paola Brown, Peter Gallego, and others. The Browns' *Globe* was Canada West's most powerful voice for abolition. Far more restrained than Garrison's

---

4, 11, 18, 25, 1848; Montreal *Witness*, July 19, September 6, 27, 1854; Toronto *Globe*, May 28, October 30, 1856, February 13, 1857, January 2, 5, November 5, 16, 1858; January 1, 1864; Toronto Public Library, Robert Baldwin Papers: Adam Wilson to Baldwin, July 12, 1843; *Journals of the Legislative Assembly of the Province of Canada . . . 1849*, p. 138; *. . . 1850*, pp. 37, 69, 77, 108, 110, 127, 170, 220, 284; *. . . 1854*, pp. 82, 101; *. . . 1852-53*, p. 897; W. G. Brownlow and Abram Pryne, *Ought American Slavery be Perpetuated? A Debate . . .* (Philadelphia, 1858), pp. 46, 103, 107-8, 237-38; Pease and Pease, *Black Utopia*, pp. 103-7.

[29] J.M.S. Careless, *Brown of the Globe*, I: *The Voice of Upper Canada, 1818-1859* (Toronto, 1959), pp. 102-3.

The Liberator and far more powerful than the lesser abolition sheets, it provided the group with a forum for political and social reform. In the *Globe* George Brown attacked Henry Clay, the Fugitive Slave Law of 1850, the New York *Herald*, Larwill, Prince, and separate schools with equal force.[30]

The Toronto society was able to ground its work in previously established channels of communication. In 1827 Samuel E. Cornish and a Quebec-educated Jamaican, John B. Russwurm, editors of *Freedom's Journal*, which they published in New York for two years, sent agents into Canada to solicit support.[31] Negroes in Windsor established a short-lived antislavery society there, and Canadians, led by Rolph, attended a temperance convention in Saratoga Springs in 1837 which brought them into contact with many American abolitionists.[32] Scoble's efforts at Dawn, Josiah Henson's willingness to exploit the fact that he apparently was the inspiration for Uncle Tom in Harriet Beecher Stowe's work, and direct aid given to the Negro settlement by Arthur and Lewis Tappan and Gerrit Smith were well-known and widely discussed developments on both sides of the border. The Negro communitarian experiments served to interest many in the plight of the Negro, and Elgin in particular, which under King attracted many touring abolitionist lecturers from England and the United States, was intertwined with the movement.

One clearly abolitionist group established on behalf of the Negroes—The Refugee Home Society—persisted into the 1850's, providing yet another tie between the Toronto

[30] See, for example, editorials of February 7, March 19, May 28, August 10, September 19, October 5, November 9, 1850, February 22, March 6, 27, April 3, 12, 18, May 10, 13, June 20, September 18, 25, November 27, December 18, 1851, and March 24, 1852.

[31] Herbert Aptheker, *The Negro in the Abolition Movement* (New York, 1941), p. 33; Washington, *Story of the Negro*, II, 292-93.

[32] M. A. Garland, "Some Frontier and American Influences in Upper Canada prior to 1837," London and Middlesex Historical Society, *Transactions*, XIII (1929), 26-27.

society and the fugitive slaves. This society arose from a convention of Negroes held in Windsor in 1846. Led by Isaac Rice, leader of Windsor's Negro community, and the Reverend T. Willis, a Negro Methodist preacher, the Negroes established the Sandwich Mission to buy land along the Detroit frontier for fugitives. Henson, Bibb, and other Canadian and American abolitionists soon were involved. Ultimately this society failed as Wilberforce and Dawn failed, but the society served better than any other (with the possible exception of Elgin) to relate the Negro Canadian communitarian movement to the greater whole of abolitionism.[33]

Indeed, by the 1850's the Canadas could not prevent being a part of the larger whole, for reasons more geographical than ideological. Sharing a common environment with the United States, ethnically and religiously similar, populated in part by descendants of former American colonists, and living near a long, often artificial, and little-patrolled border, Canadians inevitably found themselves involved in continental problems. Fugitive slaves fled to where freedom was. Their destinations changed with the times, and the times changed with European diplomacy, the rise of evangelical and dissenting sects, or fluctuations in the cotton market. Canada West acquired an almost mythical quality for many who sought freedom "under the paw of the British Lion," for while British North America itself had been free of slavery for less than two decades, and while many British North Americans patently disliked Negroes, the fugitive slave

[33] On the Refugee Home Society see Pease and Pease, *Black Utopia*, pp. 109-22, and Murray, "Canada and the Anglo-American Anti-Slavery Movement." Murray also has written on "American Slavery as a Disruptive Factor in Canadian-American Church Relations," unpubl. paper read at the Canadian Historical Association meetings, Montreal, 1961. Murray's thesis—that the issue of slavery disrupted cross-border Protestant church relations—was challenged by William H. Pease in an unpublished commentary following the address. Pease suggested that doctrinal issues, or politico-economic problems, led to the break in American fellowshipping patterns.

did enjoy complete legal freedom in the provinces. This may have meant only the freedom to starve but if so, the Negroes starved on their own and not their masters' time. After 1850, when law enforcement agencies in the free states were compelled by the Fugitive Slave Law of that year to aid in recapturing slaves who fled North, British North America took on a more attractive aspect; especially so, since British and Canadian courts had so interpreted the extradition clause of the Webster-Ashburton Treaty as to make recovery of fugitive slaves under it difficult.

From the fugitive's point of view, Canada West was a logical destination. Canada East was alien because of the French language, and the Maritime Provinces were too distant, and perhaps too maritime, for many of the Negroes who escaped from the old Southwest after 1850 knew little of the sea. In Canada West winters were less formidable, the people spoke English, the laws were British, the entire area rested on an agricultural base not unlike the upper South and the Middle West, and some of the major religious denominations—notably the Baptists, the Wesleyan Methodists, the Congregational Union of Canada, and the Free Church Presbyterians—had taken antislavery positions. True, as the supply of cheap land dwindled, prejudice against newly arrived Negroes increased, and more and more the fugitives had to seek employment in the unfamiliar cities. True, the idea of equality of opportunity through education was confused by the separate schools act. True, Negroes generally lacked political solidarity in Canada West, except around Chatham and in St. John's Ward in Toronto, so that their vote brought them fewer benefits than their numbers might have provided. True, too, that the Negroes did not assimilate happily, for they did not, after all, come to Canada because it was Canada: they came to escape from slavery. They were propelled, not attracted. But these negative conditions received, from 1851 onward, serious antislavery attention in

Canada West, and at least one could say that nearly all Canadians were opposed to legalized slavery.[34]

Earlier antislavery societies had been ephemeral in the extreme,[35] but the growing plight of the Negro in Canada West, attacked by politicians and the conservative press, under pressure to ask for separate schools he often did not want, and under the new constraints of the Fugitive Slave Law, brought forth the one long-term British North American antislavery society. In 1850 a meeting was held "on behalf of slaves" coming to Canada West, in the Mechanics' Institute in Toronto,[36] and during the year that followed, the Browns worked through the *Globe* to create additional interest. In 1851 Torontonians were given frequent opportunities for public debate. Between February and May the *Globe* editorially chastised its journalist opposition for being soft on slavery, while under the collective name "Common Sense" a substantial group publicly protested Canadian support for the antislavery movement in the United States. Frederick Douglass delivered a heated oration in St. Lawrence Hall and Paola Brown, a remarkably large-lunged young woman, shouted to audiences throughout Canada West: "Slaveholders, I call God, I call Angels, I call Men, to witness, that your destruction is at hand, and will be speedily consummated, unless you repent."[37] In September a North American

---

[34] Abolitionist leaders in the United States knew the Canadian scene reasonably well. Garrison (whose father had been a Canadian) lectured in Canada, as did Gerrit Smith, who maintained a voluminous correspondence with Canadian abolitionists (see the Gerrit Smith Miller Papers at the Syracuse University library). Arthur and Lewis Tappan had been in business briefly in Montreal. John Brown, of course, staged his most famous conference in Chatham.

[35] A short-lived antislavery society was formed in Toronto in 1837 by the Reverend Ephraim Evans, a Wesleyan Methodist and editor of the *Christian Guardian*, and it grew to claim 106 members but did not last out the decade. See Toronto *Constitution*, November 16, 1837. A complete file of the *Guardian* may be consulted in the Victoria University Archives, Toronto.

[36] Toronto *Globe*, August 10, 1850.

[37] *Ibid.*, March 6, 8, 1851; Jesse E. Middleton, *The Municipality of*

Colored Convention met in Toronto, and its fifty delegates asked Henry Bibb, Negro journalist from Windsor, and T. F. Fisher and J. D. Tinsley of Toronto, to prepare an appeal to Negro residents in Canada to found an agricultural league similar to the defunct land societies.[38] Acting independently, William Lloyd Garrison wrote to a Toronto friend, Mrs. Caroline H. Dall, and asked her to organize a supplementary relief fund for fugitives there, which she did. Also in 1851 Harriet Tubman moved to St. Catharines to begin seven years of Canadian residence, during which time she guided fugitives into the province. This also was the year of Larwill's campaign on racist lines in Chatham and of the petition from the Negroes of Simcoe against separate schools.[39] Clearly, something larger, more dedicated to principle, better organized, than these individual actions was needed to deal with the growing ferment.

The Anti-Slavery Society of Canada filled this need. It was organized "to aid in the extinction of Slavery all over the world" by all lawful and peaceful means. On February 26, 1851, a public meeting at city hall, with the mayor in the chair, launched the new organization. A committee was appointed to correspond with antislavery societies in the United States and Britain, and a constitution and by-

Toronto: A History (Toronto, 1923), I, 247; Fred Landon, "The Anti-Slavery Society of Canada," *Journal of Negro History*, IV (January 1919), 33-40; Brown, *Address intended to be Delivered in the City Hall, Hamilton, February 7, 1851, on the Subject of Slavery* (Hamilton, 1851), p. 49.

[38] Bibb printed the address in his newspaper, and the following year a constitution was adopted for "The American Continental and West India League" which was to promote settlement throughout the New World.

[39] Houghton Library: Siebert Collection, I, Mrs. Caroline H. Dall, August 25, 1889; Smith College library: W. L. Garrison II Collection, funeral address on occasion of death of Lewis Hayden, April 11, 1889; Earl Conrad, *Harriet Tubman* (Washington, 1943), pp. 45-72, 115-18; Sarah Bradford, *Harriet Tubman: The Moses of Her People* (2d ed., Auburn, N.Y., 1886), pp. 39-53.

laws were prepared. The new society elected Reverend Michael Willis President, Thomas Henning Secretary, and Andrew Hamilton Treasurer. Fourteen local Vice-Presidents were named to the Executive Committee, including two Negroes and most of the better known abolitionists in Canada West. George Brown, John Rolph, and Samuel Ringgold Ward also were included on the Committee. Henning was instructed to solicit advice from John Scoble, then still Secretary of the British and Foreign Anti-Slavery Society, Lewis Tappan, Secretary of the American and Foreign Anti-Slavery Society, and Sydney H. Gay of the American Anti-Slavery Society.[40]

The new President, Reverend Michael Willis, was a Scot who had come to Canada in the 1840's. In 1847 he became Professor of Theology in Knox College, Toronto, where he was the voice of the local Free Church Presbyterian community. From an early interest in the poor he had moved on to slavery, and he had gained a local reputation as a debater of much skill on the subject. Known for his energy and his "earnest and nervous style" of speech, Willis was ideally suited for his position. He lost no time in contacting Sydney Gay to let him know of his own group's purposes, and as a result Willis was one of the speakers at the Eleventh Annual Meeting of the American Society in May of 1851.[41]

Secretary Henning had been an early abolitionist, and in 1836 he had publicly charged the churches with harboring slavery.[42] He proved an indefatigable correspondent,

[40] Anti-Slavery Society of Canada, *First Annual Report*, pp. 9-12.

[41] See obituary notices on Willis, who died in Scotland in 1879, in *Acts and Proceedings of the Sixth General Assembly of the Presbyterian Church in Canada* (Toronto, 1880), p. 59; and Toronto *Weekly Globe*, August 29, 1879. See also Toronto *Globe*, November 27, 1851; Willis, *Death Made Tributary to the Glory of God . . .* (Toronto, 1869), pp. 25-35; and Historical Society of Pennsylvania, Philadelphia, Simon Gratz Autograph Collection: Willis to Robert Burns, May 5, 1842.

[42] See Henning, *Slavery in the Churches, Religious Societies, etc.:*

and he maintained contacts with such American abolitionist friends as Gerrit Smith well into the 1870's. Immediately after the Canadian society was established Henning wrote to Scoble, Tappan, and Gay, and he and the society subscribed to all of the antislavery organs they could. The society clearly hoped to avoid entanglements in the many divisive arguments that had so damaged the antislavery cause elsewhere, for as Henning wrote to Gay in 1852, his group wanted to cooperate with all societies. But although Henning's carefully worded letters helped the society avoid clear commitment to issues it considered tangential, his strong views on several issues that ultimately proved crucial to the abolitionist movement were to bring the Canadian society directly into the arena of major controversy.[43]

In the first year the society limited itself to playing Lady Blessington, gathering information, and seeking to define its position. A Ladies' Association for the Relief of Destitute Colored Fugitives cooperating with the men provided over a hundred fugitives with money and clothes. The Anti-Slavery Society itself went on record as having no confidence in the American Colonization Society or in any plans to transport Negroes to the West Indies and so advised the Governor General when he inquired, adding that the members of the society rejoiced in Canada's ability to shelter fugitives. The members operated an adult evening school to train fugitives in agricultural pursuits, endorsed Dawn and the Refugee Home Society, surveyed the Negro population of Canada West, fed fugitives, sponsored speakers, fought extradition, and held annual *soirées*

A Review, with Prefatory Remarks by J.J.E. Linton (Toronto, 1836). Linton had settled at Stratford in 1833 and was to become well known through his pamphlets for new settlers.

[43] Columbia University Library: Sydney Howard Gay Papers, Henning to Gay, October 25, 1851; Miller Papers: Henning to Smith, December 7, 1874.

to raise funds. By the second year Willis was able to tell Scoble that the society wished to move on from its emphasis on relief to a more direct expression of abolitionist sentiment, and he proposed sending Samuel Ringgold Ward throughout the province on a speaking tour.[44]

Henning, Willis, and the Browns guided the society until the Civil War. It seldom had enough money, or enough followers, or enough direct contact with the daily routine of the antislavery crusade, to have any real influence outside Canada West. Indeed, Canadian abolitionists in general seemed cut off from the mainstream, and except for Henning and Rolph, who corresponded extensively, most were content to await what might come to them to do. Ultimately the society suffered from the same divisive influences that operated in Britain and the United States: religious dissension, "the women question," unreliable agents, inept leadership, and increased attention to unrelated local political problems. Most important, however, was the fact that the abolitionist movement in Canada could gather little strength from the chief political preoccupations of the leaders of society, for it was not related organically to a political party as it was in the United States. While local by-elections involved "the Negro question," provincial elections never did, and no Canadian political party ever championed the Negro, then or since. The Negroes had little influence themselves except locally; in Toronto they voted for the Clear Grits but in Chatham they followed the Tories, and thus divided they were unlikely to acquire any power.[45]

[44] Anti-Slavery Society of Canada, *First Annual Report*, pp. v-vi, 12-18, 22-24; Rhodes House, Anti-Slavery Papers: C23/26, Willis to Scoble, February 12, 1852; *ibid.*, E2/8, Minute Book of the British and Foreign Anti-Slavery Society, entries of March 5, 1852, October 3, 1856.

[45] Even George Brown momentarily wavered during the Civil War, when he feared a Federal invasion of the Canadas in retaliation for anti-Northern sentiment as expressed in his newspaper. His brother Gordon held the *Globe* to a staunch antislavery line even then, and it was Gordon, not George, who received a gold watch from the pro-

The society did what it could from its shaky base. The aged Thomas Clarkson, who had been responsible for the transfer of a large body of Negroes from Nova Scotia to Sierra Leone in 1791-92, was added to the Executive Committee, as was William McClure, an Irish Methodist who worked on behalf of Negroes around London, C. W.[46] A resolution in praise of *Uncle Tom's Cabin* was passed, 1,500 copies of the first annual report were distributed, and auxiliary societies were formed in Kingston, Hamilton, London, Windsor, and Grey County; Willis lectured on behalf of the society while in Scotland and Ireland; and 14,000 signatures were gathered in support of an anti-slavery manifesto. In 1853 the society took a firm stand for immediate emancipation but by 1857 it had retreated to its initial position of being a fugitive slave relief organization and an opponent of "colour-phobia" in the Canadas. The society could, in truth, do little more.[47]

There were other means of supporting the cause of abolition, of course. One could prepare antislavery addresses quite independently of the societies, especially outside Canada West, where there were no such organizations. In Nova Scotia the Reverend William Sommerville, a Reformed Presbyterian from Cornwallis, attacked slavery repeatedly. One could also found refugee settlements

---

Northern American community in Toronto at the end of the war. See Fred Landon, "The Canadian Anti-Slavery Group," *The University Magazine*, XVII (December 1917), 546.

[46] Boston Public Library [hereafter BPL], W. L. Garrison Papers: XXXVI, 55, 61, McClure to R. D. Webb, October 23, December 3, 1868; Anti-Slavery Society of Canada, *Second Annual Report* (Toronto, 1853), p. iii. For an obituary of McClure, see *Minutes of the Forty-third Annual Conference of the Methodist New Connexion Church of Canada held at Owen Sound, Ontario . . .* (London, Ont., 1871), pp. 10-11.

[47] Anti-Slavery Society of Canada, *Second Annual Report*, pp. vi, 7-12, 28; Miller Papers: Henning to Smith, January 9, 22, February 2, 13, 16, 1861, deals with the Anderson fugitive slave extradition case. See also August 11, 1862, October 12, 1863, and Toronto *Globe*, January 1, 1864.

or contribute to mission aid societies. One could, when the Civil War broke out, enlist in the Union army and fight against the slaveholders, as some 18,000 Canadians did.[48] Or one could support one or more of the many British and American, or few Canadian, newspapers that served a specifically abolitionist purpose. In Canada the *Globe* and the Montreal *Gazette* seldom missed an opportunity to present the abolitionist point of view, and there were four antislavery newspapers as well. The chief of these were Henry Bibb's *Voice of the Fugitive*, which he issued in Windsor from 1851 to 1853, and its competitor, Mary Shadd's *Provincial Freeman* published in Toronto and after 1855 in Chatham.[49] In 1856 J.J.E. Linton began free distribution in Stratford of *The Voice of the Bondsman*, and in 1860 the Reverend A. R. Green launched *The True Royalist and Weekly Intelligencer* in Windsor. Both papers disappeared quickly.

These newspapers are symptomatic of the many problems that prevented any single antislavery endeavor in British North America from being an unqualified success: the papers were quarrelsome, vindictive, naive, and fre-

[48] Sommerville, *Southern Slavery not Founded on Scripture Warrant: A Lecture* (Saint John, 1864); OPA, Canniff Family Papers: package 13, MS. speech and MS. article; University of Toronto library, John Charlton Papers: MS. autobiography, pp. 137-38; and Fred Landon, "Abolitionist Interest in Upper Canada," *Ontario History*, XLIV (October 1952), 165-72. On enlistments, see Robin W. Winks, "The Creation of a Myth: 'Canadian' Enlistments in the Northern Armies during the American Civil War," *Canadian Historical Review*, XXXIX (March 1958), 24-40.

[49] *The Voice of the Fugitive* is readily available on microfilm. *The Provincial Freeman* may be consulted at the University of Pennsylvania; on it, see Alexander L. Murray, "*The Provincial Freeman*: A New Source for the History of the Negro in Canada and the United States," *Journal of Negro History*, XLIV (April 1959), 123-35. There are two numbers of *The True Royalist* at the Fort Malden Museum and one number of *The Voice of the Bondsman* at the Lawson Memorial Library of the University of Western Ontario, London. A copy of *The Provincial Freeman* may also be seen in the Smith College Library, and a microfilm is available in the Yale University Library.

quently unintelligent. *The True Royalist*, founded as the organ of the British Methodist Episcopal Church of British North America, with Green as a self-proclaimed bishop, in opposition to an older Negro church, the British Methodist Episcopal Church in Canada, served only a schismatic purpose. Henry Bibb and Mary Shadd refused to cooperate to further the Negro cause and used their presses to attack each other. Ultimately an incredible variety of sensitivities, distractions, foolish quarrels, prideful hurts, and personal ambitions held the antislavery groups back far more than in the United States, where manifestations of the same petty spirit were overridden by men and forces of much greater power.[50]

The chief supporters of the antislavery cause in Canada West were ministers, and dissension between them also crippled the society. Willis, Henning, and Brown held the organization together, and all were Presbyterians. Where a denomination was not shared, doctrinal differences were added to others. Some strongly opposed the begging ministers, mostly Negro, who toured the Canadas ostensibly collecting funds to support the Negro communities, while others pointed out that begging was a proper part of the Christian tradition. Some accused the churches as a whole of harboring slavery, and at the 1857 annual meeting of the Canadian Anti-Slavery Society the Reverend Robert Dick referred to the sects as the bulwark of slavery. When a Toronto religious paper, *The Church*, suggested that Canadians should welcome fugitives but not denounce slavery, the *Globe* lashed out angrily. As in the United States, the American Board of Commissioners for Foreign Missions, the American Tract Society, the American Home Missionary Society, and the American Sunday

[50] Thomas Clarkson's wife offered a lock of her husband's hair for sale at an antislavery fair, and the lock eventually made its way to Canada West, from which she received at least four letters demanding that she attest to its authenticity. Thomas Henning broke with James Scoble because the latter failed to send a (deserved) letter of thanks for lodgings.

School Union were charged with proslavery bias. The last two bodies were well known in Canada through their periodicals and by occasional Canadian-directed activities. In 1856 J.J.E. Linton was joined by none other than Thomas Henning in protesting that Canadian churches were fellowshipping with proslavery groups in the United States and that the Methodist Episcopal Church's *Canada Sunday School Advocate* was a proslavery reprint of its New York equivalent. In Canada East the Grand Ligne Mission fellowshipped with proslavery Southern Baptists, and the Presbyterians and Methodists were said to be equally guilty. Only the Methodist New Connection group, which had no American fellowship, the Unitarians, and the Young Men's Christian Associations of Montreal, Kingston, and Halifax, which had broken from the parent YMCA, were free of blame. These charges were as unjust as they were disruptive, for both the Canadian Presbyterians and Baptists had worked on behalf of antislavery, and as early as 1841 the latter had declared that they should help cleanse the Baptists of the Southern United States.[51]

Linton's and Henning's attacks on fellowshipping were tinged with a more generalized anti-Americanism which limited the effectiveness of the abolition movement in Canada. Dislike for the United States as a whole often found its most effective expression in denunciations of

[51] On Linton see his pamphlet, *Slavery Question: Report of the New York General Association, 26th August, 1855* (Stratford, C.W., 1855), pp. 1-7, and his paid advertisement in the Toronto *Globe*, May 29, September 25, 1857, and June 4, November 23, 1858, denouncing the American Tract Society. Linton was best known for his crusade in 1856 against American traveling circuses, which he felt fostered proslavery feelings through their Negro dialect songs. On Dick, see the *Globe*, May 2, 1857. On Henning's attack, see his pamphlet, *Slavery in the Churches*, pp. 4-5, 8, 21, 28-29. The early Baptist stand appears in *The Canadian Baptist Magazine*, I (February 1838), 205, and IV (April 1841), 239, 243; and *The Gospel Tribune and Christian Communionist*, III (June 1856), 57. On the YMCA see *Canadian Evangelist*, III (1853), 58-59.

slavery and of the Federal government, and even Northern travelers in the Canadas were referred to by otherwise intelligent Canadians as slaveholders. As John
Charlton, a young abolitionist, noted, prejudice against
the United States around Simcoe was so strong that American maps were not allowed in class rooms. Canadians
considered themselves well informed on American matters but there were those who could ask whether Buffalo
was in the state of New Orleans. The *Globe* argued that
Canadians had the "duty of preserving the honour of the
continent" against slavery. From its founding in 1846 the
Montreal *Witness*, a "weekly review and family newspaper," attacked the United States and slavery as synony-
mous. In the first volume alone, no fewer than twenty
articles, poems, and editorials were devoted to antislavery.
A typical article related how a young slave girl was
hanged in New Orleans for striking her mistress, remarked that the religious press of the North had been
silent on the incident, and concluded that the affair was
"a hideous offshoot of American Republicanism and
American Christianity." The highly emotional description, representative of this form of popular Victorian por-
nography, told in detail how the victim, "a young and
beautiful girl," had been ravished by her master and, her
infant torn from her arms, had died on the gallows, "the
rope around her delicate neck . . . [while] swinging there
alive for nearly half an hour—a spectacle for fiends, in
the shape of humanity." The story was not compromised
for its readers by its assumption that New Orleans was in
Mississippi or that the editor of the *Witness* apparently
saw "beneath that dark skin a *white* soul wrung by mortal
agony."[52]

The Canadian abolitionist movement, like the Ameri-

[52] Charlton Papers, MS. autobiography, p. 167; *Witness*, January
5, May 18, July 6, 20, 27, August 3, 10, September 21, October 12,
November 16, December 12, 21, 1846 (the quotations are from June
8, p. 190, and June 22, p. 206, italics added), and March 24, 1852.

can, was in fact several movements which from time to time seemed to confuse lesser issues with the greater. In 1832 William Lloyd Garrison had published a pamphlet, *Thoughts on African Colonization*, in which he denounced for what they were plans to remove the Negro to Africa, Haiti, or the British West Indies—plans which accepted the basic proslavery argument that the Negro was innately inferior. Five years later, in 1837, a schism within the ranks of the abolitionist movement began when a group of antislavery men from Andover Theological Seminary attacked Garrison's outspoken language, his willingness to give women a place on the lecture platform, and his denunciation of the apparent indifference of organized religion to slavery. In 1840 Garrison succeeded in having a woman elected to the business committee of the American Anti-Slavery Society, and several members, led by the society's president, Lewis Tappan, bolted the meeting to form the American and Foreign Anti-Slavery Society. Another schism issued from Garrison's decision, made clear in 1844, that the American Constitution was a protector of slavery and that if necessary the Union itself should be dissolved to achieve abolitionist ends.

These schisms were felt in British North America as well. The question of American disunion was not central to Canadian thought, although there were those who argued that a fragmented American Union would restore to Britain control of the balance of power in the Americas, a balance lost following the Clayton-Bulwer Treaty.[53] But the "women question" loomed large, as did concern for "good taste" in fighting slavery. The Canadian Anti-Slavery Society cooperated with women's organizations but included no women on its programs, and Henning continued to correspond with Garrisonians and anti-Garrisonians alike. In the United States the "mute suasion-

[53] Robin W. Winks, "A Nineteenth-Century Cold War," *The Dalhousie Review*, XXXIX (Winter 1960), 464-70.

ists," as Garrisonian Frances H. Drake wrote, divided their time between promoting migration to Canada and opposing those who wanted immediate abolition.[54] Because many of the Northern antislavery spokesmen who toured British North America were opposed to Garrison's views, Canadians were well informed on the nature of the schisms.

Charles Stuart represented the problems which these issues, compounded by distance and anti-Americanism, posed for Canadian abolitionists. Captain Stuart had lived in both England and the United States, where he had helped bring Theodore Dwight Weld into the antislavery movement, and he had resided in Amherstburg between 1817 and 1822. There he had aided Negroes in establishing themselves on the land. In 1850 he settled at Lora Bay, in Canada West, and became a member of the new Canadian Anti-Slavery Society. His attacks on the American government were couched in Garrisonian prose: he emphasized "the deep filth of sin in which [the United States] is now proudly wallowing" and found that he could not "dutifully expose my wife and myself to the outrages of of [sic] a power so ferocious, so hypocritical, and so base as [America's] present, de facto, government." The American people too, he said, were "democratical-demagogical. . . ." He was torn by religious doubts which resolved themselves in religious dogmatism, and he wrote with "a confused medley of polemical theology, whining cant and complementary bombast" that wearied his correspondents.[55] When Weld became a Unitarian, Stuart stopped writing to him, convinced that they could not meet in the next world. He wrote incessantly to Gerrit Smith, sometimes about their common interest in the Negro but more often to persuade Smith that Christ was

[54] BPL, Weston Papers: XIX, Drake to Maria Weston Chapman, October 31, 1843.

[55] Miller Papers: Stuart to Smith, January 8, 1853, April 16, 1855, September 26, 1857; Edward A. Talbot, *Five Years Residence in the Canadas* (London, 1824), I, vi.

God. Stuart had joined Tappan's antifeminist group in 1840, and he asserted that the idea that "whatever is morally right for a *man* to do is morally right for a *woman* to do" was an "insane innovation . . . [to be] vigorously resisted." Whenever he could, Stuart blocked contributions to the Garrisonians, for the money would support "a pernicious party" rather than abolition. Opposition to women's participation, he concluded, was "the cause of liberty and love."[56] He forbade the use of any products of slave labor and would not permit sugar or cotton in his home, and his wife, whom he held to a most rigorous religious orthodoxy, had to find substitutes. Stuart's opposition to slavery once had been effective, for he had helped the Amherstburg fugitives, drawn Weld and others into the movement, and represented Jamaica at the 1840 world antislavery convention in London. But when his help could have mattered most he was pursued by the Hound of Heaven while himself pursuing the hares of mid-Victorian masculinity. Unfortunately, Stuart is all too representative of many of the Canadian abolitionists who, neither more nor less human than their American counterparts, became preoccupied with important but unrelated issues.[57]

[56] Garrison Papers: XI, circular, Stuart to R. Wardlaw, 1841; *ibid.*: X, Stuart to J. A. Collins, November 4, 6, 7, 1840; *ibid.*: III, circular, Stuart to the Friends of Religion and Humanity, November 1, 1833.

[57] The sources on Stuart are widely scattered. See Fred Landon, "Captain Charles Stuart, Abolitionist," *Western Ontario History Nuggets*, no. 24 (1956), pp. 1-19; on Stuart's Amherstburg years consult John J. Bigsby, *The Shoe and Canoe, or Pictures of Travel in the Canadas* . . . (London, 1850), I, 263-66, and his own *The Emigrant's Guide to Upper Canada* . . . (London, 1820). Stuart's second period in Canada may be traced through his and his wife's correspondence with Gerrit Smith (the Miller Papers contains 99 letters from or concerning Stuart), and in the James G. Birney, Theodore D. Weld, Angelina Grimké Weld, and Sarah Grimké collections in the Clements Library at the University of Michigan. The intermediate years in New York, Ohio, New Jersey, Michigan, Jamaica, and England can be pieced together from letters in the following collections: Houghton Library, Charles Sumner Papers,

Finally, the Canadian Anti-Slavery movement also suffered from cupidity, false ambition, inefficiency, and dishonesty. In ten short years several of the early heroes of the Canadian movement had lost their effectiveness through one or more of these human failings. Among those who fell from favor were Samuel Ringgold Ward, Hiram Wilson, Josiah Henson, and James Scoble. In 1851 Henning had been a strong supporter of Ward, and "the original nigger" (so-called because, as Wendell Phillips said, he was so black one could not see Ward when he shut his eyes) had addressed enthusiastic audiences in Congregational and Methodist New Connection churches throughout Canada West. By 1853, however, Ward was editing the *Provincial Freeman* for Mary Shadd and attacking the Refugee Home Society, the *Voice of the Fugitive*, and Henry Bibb, who was one of the Vice-Presidents of the Canadian Anti-Slavery Society. Ward argued that Negroes who bought land from the Refugee Home Society paid more than if they bought directly from the government, and he took a Garrisonian stand against all such self-segregated communities. Michael Willis defended Bibb, and Ward broke with the Anti-Slavery Society and left for England and then Jamaica, with letters from Henning trailing behind denouncing him as a swindler.[58]

Few of these men seemed provident enough to prevent contracting debts they could not pay, and this too was an embarrassment to the Society. Hiram Wilson borrowed heavily, "trusting in the Lord to find means of paying,"

XXXI; BPL, Phelps Papers, XII; Historical Society of Pennsylvania, Simon Gratz Autograph Collection; Rhodes House, Anti-Slavery Papers, C22 and E 2/6; New York Historical Society, Hawks Manuscripts; Fort Malden Museum, Amherstburg Deeds. See also Stuart's *The West India Question* (New Haven, 1833).

[58] Oscar Sherwin, *Prophet of Liberty: The Life and Times of Wendell Phillips* (New York, 1958), p. 212; Gay Papers: Henning to Gay, October 25, 1851; Pease and Pease, *Black Utopia*, pp. 116-17; Rhodes House, Anti-Slavery Papers: C32, Henning to S. A. Chamerovzow, December 10, 1855, January 17, 1856.

and when the good Lord did not pay, antislavery philanthropists in the United States or Britain had to do so for
Him. Josiah Henson was frequently in trouble over financial matters, and although he made some ineffectual attempts to meet his obligations, ultimately a generous English group had to pay his major debts. Scoble's personal
ambition, and his desire to have Dawn removed from the
American Baptist Free Mission Society's supervision and
placed under the British and Foreign Anti-Slavery Society, also produced constant and sometimes expensive
friction. While more circumspect financially, Scoble remained a controversial and divisive figure.[59]

III

The significance for Canada of the international phase
of abolitionism is rather different than students of the
abolitionist movement have been inclined to think. The
chief importance credited to Canada has been twofold:
as a haven for fugitive slaves, Canada was said to be a
stronghold of freedom for the Negro in an alien North
American environment, and at the time of the Civil War,
Canada was expected to provide pro-Northern moral support against the slaveocracy. Both of these traditional interpretations of Canada's rôle in the antislavery crusade

[59] Syracuse University Library, Gerrit Smith Calendar, p. 129:
Wilson to Smith, December 18, 1839; Weston Papers, XXV: Edwin
Mathews to Mary A. Estlin, April 30, 1852, and E. Sturge to Maria
Weston Chapman, December 22, 1851; *ibid.*, XXVI: Mary to Caro-
line Weston, December 29, 1851; *ibid.*, XXIX: Eliza Weston to John
Bishop Estlin, May 14, 1851; Anti-Slavery Papers, C113/83A:
Mathews to Thomas Sturge, November 15, 1851; *ibid.*, C160/19:
John Roaf to Scoble, December 31, 1851; Gay Papers: Samuel May,
Jr., to Gay, March 28, 1853; Massachusetts Historical Society, Amos
A. Lawrence Papers: Lawrence to Samuel Morley, November 30, to
J. E. Thayer, October 22, 1852, to Henson, April 19, August 21,
1850, and October 11, 1852, to Garrison, February 16, 1851, and to
Roaf, December 22, 1852, and *ibid.*, Morley to Lawrence, October 5,
1852; *ibid.*, George Ellis Papers: Henson to Ellis, March 16, 1846;
ibid., Edmund Quincy Papers: Quincy to Elizabeth N. Gay, November 2, 1851.

have been seriously overemphasized[60] and as a result the true significance of Canada's place in this phase of the long story of the Negro's quest for freedom has been mistaken.

Much of Canada's participation in the abolition movement resulted from geographical proximity rather than from ideological affinity. Negroes fled to Canada, as we have seen, for negative rather than positive reasons, and once there they encountered race and color prejudice not unlike what they found in Massachusetts or Ohio. Free they were but equal they were not. Indeed, the position of the Negro in Canada was not to differ radically from his position in the post-Civil War United States, and America's deferred commitment to equality was deferred continentally rather than nationally.

British North America could not avoid an issue so likely to convulse the continent. But surprise lies not in the extent of the Canadian involvement so much as in the general ineffectiveness of that involvement. While there were short-lived antislavery societies in Toronto, such societies could be formed easily and without any necessary financial or genuinely moral commitment. When the society of 1837 was founded in Toronto, there were 1,006 antislavery societies in the United States, 213 in Ohio alone, and 33 in Maine. That John Brown should have held his pre-Harpers Ferry meeting in Canada West may seem obvious for ideological reasons, especially since Canada as a goal of the Underground Railroad has been numerically exaggerated, but Brown had equally obvious geographical reasons for meeting in Chatham: trace his

[60] For typical examples of these points of view, see Wilbur H. Siebert, *The Underground Railroad from Slavery to Freedom* (New York, 1899); Alice Felt Tyler, *Freedom's Ferment: Phases of American Social History from the Colonial Period to the Outbreak of the Civil War* (Minneapolis, 1944); and Henrietta Buckmaster, *Let My People Go: The Story of the Underground Railroad and the Growth of the Abolition Movement* (New York, 1941).

route from Kansas through Nebraska, Iowa, Illinois, and Michigan, and it strikes like an arrow into Canada West. Rather than consciously choosing Canada, Brown would consciously have had to avoid it on his way to upper New York.

The Civil War was a shared experience but not in the way abolitionists expected. It was to contribute its major part to the formulation of a Canadian confederation in 1867 and to the nature of the Canadian constitution, the British North America Act of that year. Canadians fought in both Northern and Southern armies, and Confederates in particular ultimately were to abuse Canadian neutrality by staging raids upon Federal territory from Canadian soil. Abolitionists in the United States had been misled by their Canadian counterparts to assume that the provinces would stand behind the North in the Civil War. As Samuel Gridley Howe wrote to Theodore Parker in 1860, "I look with the more interest upon Canada, because it seems to me she is to be the great and reliable ally of the Northern States. . . . When the lines are fairly drawn what an immense moral aid it will be to the North to have such a population as that of Canada . . . at her back!"[61] But when the lines were fairly drawn, British North Americans proved to be anti-Northern, opposed to a war fought to preserve the Union, rather inclined to the Southern position once they saw that Lincoln was not fighting to end slavery. The outcome of the Civil War did not please the Canadian abolitionists, for they shared the general Canadian postwar fear that the Federal triumph had intensified the dangers of annexation by an avaricious Republic bent on continentalism.[62]

[61] L. E. Richards, ed. *Letters and Journals of Samuel Gridley Howe* (Boston, 1906-1909), II, 447, March 25, 1860.

[62] Robin W. Winks, *Canada and the United States: The Civil War Years* (Baltimore, 1960), pp. 206-43.

Nor, ironically, did the Canadian abolitionist movement lead to any fundamental improvement in the condition of the Negro in Canada, even though this was the most consistent goal of the Canadian Anti-Slavery Society. In the United States the abolitionist movement helped bring on a Civil War which added yet another dimension to the commonly shared Negro American story. Today the Negro American may, on the whole, assume himself to be the product of a common historical experience with slavery, war, and reconstruction, and as he wages his civil rights campaign, he does so with at least some sense of historical continuity and of ethnic unity. But in Canada the Negro's position was different from the outset, and the Negro Canadian who emerged from the period of abolitionism and Civil War differed even more markedly than before the war from the Negro American.[63]

The general Canadian response to environment, to immigration, and to cultural pluralism has differed in two important respects from the response in the United States, and as a result the Negro Canadian has come to occupy a rather different position in Canadian society than the Negro does in American society. The first difference arises from the tendency of many Canadians, especially in the nineteenth century, to think of themselves as transplanted Europeans. While the American consistently asked Crèvecoeur's question, "What then is the American, this new man," assuming by it that the American had become, in fact, a new man, many Canadians continued to assert with equal vigor that they were representatives of European man and of European civilization. Given this feeling, the Negro in their midst was related by them to his origins, as the MacGregor, the O'Farrell, or the Thomas related themselves to their Scots, Irish, and Welsh origins. To white Canadians the

[63] Robin W. Winks, "The Position of the Negro in the Maritime Provinces," Canadian Historical Association, *Annual Report* (1964).

Negro was and is an African, as they are Europeans, and as such he is a sport, an exotic in a commonly shared but mutually alien environment. In short, while in the United States the Negro became an object of enslavement, discrimination, ánd even hatred, he came to be viewed (colonizationists aside) as a natural part of the new American landscape, while in Canada the Negro may ultimately have achieved a measure of equality but he nonetheless was deemed foreign to the landscape, equal but alien.

Related to the tendency of many Canadians to seek no new man in the New World was a second cultural response of white Canadians to their environment which influenced the Negro Canadian as well. One goal of newly arrived immigrants to the United States traditionally was to shed the old world and its ethnic badges of identity as quickly as possible. Immigrants to Canada have been far less eager to assimilate into some amorphous, anonymous North Americanism or even Canadianism. A bi-cultural society of English and French-speaking settlers encouraged what was to become a highly plural society, in which each group, and most strikingly the French Canadian, has fought to guard its separate identity. Since most Canadians retain a justifiable pride in their own ethnic and past national heritages, they assume that the Negro Canadian should do so as well, that it is natural that he should be left alone, self-segregated to his own communities. But while the white British North American could take pride in his national heritage, march as an Orangeman, thrill to the skirl of the pipes or to tales of Dollard des Ormeaux at the Long Sault, the Negro Canadian had no national heritage to fall back upon for self-identification. He was alone.

The enslaved American Negro was, in a very real sense, as Stanley Elkins has demonstrated, also alone.[64]

[64] Stanley M. Elkins, *Slavery: A Problem in American Institutional and Intellectual Life* (Chicago, 1959).

But he did have the common unity of a shared North American experience, and following the Civil War this common unity was carried forward into new expressions of self-awareness, ethnic identification, and eventually pride. The Negro Canadian remained divided, withdrawn, without a substantial body of shared historical experience. Even today Negro Canadians refuse to unite as a group, for they are stratified by class lines of their own creation. The descendants of the Negro slaves brought to Nova Scotia and the Canadas by the Loyalists at the end of the American Revolution think of themselves as among the founders of the nation. The descendants of the Black Refugees of the War of 1812 who were transported to Nova Scotia by the British, as well as the descendants of the Jamaican Maroons (most but not all of whom ultimately moved on to Sierra Leone) in the Maritimes, feel they have little in common. The descendants of the fugitive slaves who fled to British North America during the ferment of abolitionism are viewed by the line of Loyalist slaves as outlanders; the fugitive line in Ontario, in turn, looks down upon the Nova Scotian Negroes who were aided in their escape by the British government, having not to fear the breath of pursuit from Simon Legree and Mrs. Stowe's mythical hounds when Eliza carried the Negro race northward with her to freedom. Subsequent Negro migrations to Canada—West Coast Negro businessmen who entered British Columbia, dry land Negro farmers from Oklahoma who moved onto the Canadian plains in 1909-19, Harlem Negroes who sought out the gayer lights of Montreal during the period of America's experiment with prohibition, and the post-World War II migration of West Indians into Canada—have even less in common with these earlier groups.

Widely dispersed nationally, if clustered locally, and brought to Canada in differing waves of immigration, both pre- and post-Civil War, waves which provided little common experience, and well aware that they would best avoid discrimination by attracting as little attention to themselves as possible, Negro Canadians not only failed to unite, they viewed Negro unity as a too visible danger. Abolitionism in the United States may not have led to Negro equality but it did provide a link between the liberal white community and the Negro leadership, and today it remains a reservoir of fact and emotion upon which those engaged in the battle for Negro equality may draw. Abolitionism in British North America united neither whites nor Negroes, and myths arising from the period when Canadians succored fugitive slaves have served to help Canadians obscure their own need for subsequent legislation in the area of civil rights. Jean Genêt might well have been speaking to those who barely hear this muffled voice of Canadian abolitionism when he wrote, in *The Blacks*,

> . . . In order that you may remain comfortably settled in your seats in the presence of the drama that is already unfolding here, in order that you be assured that there is no danger of such a drama's worming its way into your precious lives, we shall even have the decency . . . to make communication impossible. We shall increase the distance that separates us . . . everything here . . . will take place in the delicate world of reprobation.

CHAPTER 14

BRITISH AND AMERICAN
ABOLITIONISTS COMPARED

BY HOWARD R. TEMPERLEY

THE American abolitionists have not enjoyed a good press. Except in the avowedly partisan works of the post–Civil War period, mostly written by the abolitionists themselves or their descendants, their activities have been regarded with less than average indulgence. In standard textbooks they are still commonly presented, along with Southern fire-eaters, as a group whose main contribution to history lay in weakening the bonds binding the Union together. Even those most sympathetic to their cause have felt peculiarly constrained to apologize for what are still regarded as their embarrassing excesses. Nor has modern scholarship done much to raise their reputations. To the familiar charges of fanaticism, self-righteousness, and political irresponsibility have now been added a number of new and no less damaging criticisms. What motivated the abolitionists, it has been variously suggested, was not their hatred of slavery but their search for a surrogate religion, their desire to buttress their declining social positions and their morbid obsession with martyrdom.[1] However wrong American slavery may have been—and virtually all commentators are nowadays agreed that it was wrong—very little credit, it would appear, should

[1] See, for example, Gilbert H. Barnes, *The Antislavery Impulse* (2d edn., Gloucester, Mass., 1955); "Toward a Reconsideration of the Abolitionists" in David Donald's *Lincoln Reconsidered* (New York, 1956); and Hazel Catherine Wolf, *On Freedom's Altar: The Martyr Complex in the Abolition Movement* (Madison, Wis., 1952).

be given to those who took the lead in drawing attention to this fact.

This stern attitude toward the American abolitionists is the more puzzling when compared to the very different treatment afforded their British counterparts. So long as the antislavery controversy lasted, British abolitionists were subjected to much the same criticisms as the Americans. But the immediate struggles once over, such charges were either forgotten or remembered only as historical curiosities. As the victors of the antislavery crusade, the British antislavery leaders stood in their own day high in the popular esteem, and their reputations have remained high ever since. Few British heroes are regarded with more veneration than Wilberforce, Clarkson, and Buxton, or are believed to have acted from worthier motives.[2] Even those who have felt obliged to reject the popular image of these leaders as earthly saints, pointing out that the sympathy they afforded the slaves did not always extend to oppressed groups nearer home, have found remarkably little fault with their antislavery policies. Not only is it taken for granted that they were right to embrace the aims they did, it is also assumed that in doing so they showed more foresight and wisdom than other public figures of the day. Thus, during the reactionary period of the 1790's, it is Wilberforce rather than the more cautious Pitt who is credited with having shown the better judgment, just as, during the 1820's, it was the Anti-Slavery Society and not the reluctant Tory ministry that is characterized as having possessed the firmer grasp of realities. Far from being the unworldly visionaries and irresponsible meddlers which their opponents claimed, the British anti-

[2] Typical examples of this pious attitude of historians toward the British abolitionists are R. Coupland, *Wilberforce: A Narrative* (Oxford, 1923); Earl Leslie Griggs, *Thomas Clarkson: The Friend of Slaves* (London, 1936); and R. H. Mottram, *Buxton the Liberator* (London, 1946).

slavery leaders have long been accepted as men of more than average courage, foresight, and good sense.

Such disparity in attitude need not, of course, involve any contradiction. It is arguable that both accounts are warranted: that the behavior of the Americans merits relatively severe treatment and that the conduct of the British was every bit as praiseworthy as has generally been supposed. But, warranted or not, the matter is obviously one that calls for some explanation.

In the first place, it is clear that, whatever distinction may be made between the two movements, it does not concern the fundamental nature of the practices against which both protested. No one has argued that the slave trade in which American vessels were involved was any more or any less reprehensible than the slave trade—which, in any case, was largely the same slave trade—in which British vessels were involved. Both contributed to the spread of violence within Africa itself, both committed their victims to the agonies of the middle passage and to the hardships of the seasoning period that followed. Similarly, though practices undoubtedly varied, there would not seem to be any case for drawing a moral distinction between slavery as it existed in the American Southern states and as it existed in the British sugar colonies. If the one aroused in some Englishmen a sense of moral indignation, it is hardly surprising that the other should have aroused similar feelings in some Americans.

In the second place, the two movements undoubtedly had close emotional and intellectual affinities, both deriving their inspiration from essentially the same sources —Enlightenment liberalism stemming from the natural rights philosophies of the eighteenth century and evangelical religion based on the teachings of the New Testament. While it would be wrong to claim that these two elements had achieved at any given time precisely the same blend on the two sides of the Atlantic, it is still evident that there was a good deal of similarity in the way in which they interacted. This was particularly apparent during the early period when the institutional and personal ties linking the two movements together were unusually close. Beginning with the Quakers in the first half of the eighteenth century but broadening out to include members of other denominations also, there had developed by the 1780's what was virtually a single trans-Atlantic antislavery community, based on the exchange not only of ideas but also of personnel.[3] During the early nineteenth century these ties became more tenuous, though as David B. Davis has shown in a recent article, antislavery thought on the two sides of the Atlantic continued to develop along roughly parallel lines.[4] In each case the failure of the antislavery forces to make headway against the stubborn opposition of planting interests weakened their initial commitment to gradualist measures and contributed to the emergence, around 1830, of a new militancy. After 1830, as will be shown later, the movements continued to show similar ideological tendencies and once again developed close personal and institutional links.

In the third place, the question arises as to how far any distinction can be made between the movements on the basis of the weight of individual talent deployed on their behalf. Here, of course, one is on dubious ground since attributes such as talent are difficult enough to define and certainly do not lend themselves to measurement on a quantitative basis. But accepting that such comparisons must necessarily be of a rough and ready nature and involve a large measure of subjective judgment, it may still be worth while considering whether the British

[3] Michael Kraus, "Slavery Reform in the Eighteenth Century: An Aspect of Transatlantic Intellectual Co-operation," *The Pennsylvania Magazine of History and Biography*, 60 (1936), pp. 53-66.

[4] "The Emergence of Immediatism in British and American Antislavery Thought," *Mississippi Valley Historical Review*, 49 (1962-63), pp. 209-30.

were, as a group, conspicuously more able than their American counterparts. After all, if it could be shown that the American movement attracted only men of inferior intellect and mediocre ability this would go far toward explaining their relatively low reputations. But, in fact, this does not seem to have been the case. In neither instance, it would appear, were the movements able to elicit the exclusive services of the most able men in the country, though such men as Franklin, Jefferson, and John Quincy Adams in the United States and Pitt, Brougham, and O'Connell in Britain did provide essential support. Among those who became the leaders of the two movements, the qualities essential for effective action included dedication, a capacity for hard work, the ability to marshal arguments and to write and speak effectively. Were the British leaders better endowed in these respects than the Americans? The answer is by no means self-evident. Whatever defects of character may be attributed to the Americans it would be difficult to accuse them either of a lack of dedication or of an aversion to hard work. Similarly, there is no reason to assume that the Americans were any less effective in marshalling or expounding arguments than their British counterparts. As speakers Theodore Weld and Wendell Phillips were at least the equals and probably the superiors of any of the British antislavery orators. Nor, for that matter, would one be justified in supposing that the literary talents displayed by the British were superior to those of the Americans. Clarkson may have been a better pamphleteer than Weld, but the British movement never produced a journalist to compare with Garrison or an individual work of propaganda that was the equal of *Uncle Tom's Cabin*.

Granting, then, that there was a similarity in the basic objects and philosophies of the antislavery leaders and, further, that in their basic talents they were not, as groups, unequally matched, one is left to consider whether their very different treatment at the hands of historians has not been due rather to the political and social contexts in which the two groups were obliged to operate. It is generally accepted that what may be praiseworthy behavior in one situation may be vicious or antisocial in another. Was there, therefore, something inherent in the differing logic of the two situations which, regardless of aim, ideology, or talent, has made one group appear benevolent heroes and the other, if not exactly villains, at least morally and politically suspect?

In the case of the early agitation against the slave trade, the problem appears to be not why the American movement failed to produce national leaders of the eminence of Wilberforce and Clarkson but why it failed to produce any national leaders at all. Prominent political figures, such as Franklin and Jefferson, did, it is true, give the movement encouragement, as did Pitt and Fox in Great Britain, but no specifically antislavery leaders at this time took it upon themselves to focus public attention in the way in which Wilberforce and Clarkson did in Britain and Garrison and Weld were to do at a later date in the United States.

Here, certainly, the explanation would seem to lie in the particular circumstances in which the struggles were conducted. In the United States, the late eighteenth and early nineteenth centuries were a period of ferment and change which saw far-reaching innovations in many fields. In Britain, on the other hand, this was a reactionary period and one which saw comparatively few changes, particularly of a humanitarian variety. Thus, although Britain and the United States both outlawed the trade in 1808, the British Act stands out in a way in which the American Act does not, as one of the few innovations of the time and possibly the only one to which posterity can give its unqualified approval. The British measure, moreover, had been the result of a campaign extending over a period of some twenty years and carried on in such a way as to attract maximum attention to the issues involved. Societies had been organized, petitions circulated; year after year the whole matter had been debated exhaustively in Parliament and given widespread coverage in the press. The campaign was, in fact, also notable as the first organized attempt to mobilize public opinion in Britain and so provoked interest among contemporaries as much on account of the novelty of its techniques—the establishment of a network of local societies, for example, and the mass reproduction of the Anti-Slavery Society's seal on coins and brooches—as because of the peculiar virtues of its aims.[5] This goes a long way toward explaining the attention which Wilberforce and his colleagues received during their own lifetimes, for, as the sponsors and agents of such a campaign, they inevitably drew attention to themselves as well as to their cause.

The outlawing of the trade by the United States was, by contrast, an oddly piecemeal affair. Restrictions on the importation of slaves had been imposed by individual colonies from time to time during the colonial period though less for humanitarian reasons than because of the feeling within slaveholding communities that too large a population of Negroes exposed them to the danger of insurrection. Such considerations, to which was presently added an infusion of democratic idealism, continued to influence policies during and after the Revolution, especially during the period immediately following the uprising in Haiti, thus giving the movement toward abolition a peculiarly hybrid character. By 1800, feeling against slavery, often of a vague and nondogmatic variety, was fairly widespread, though the antislavery societies as such—as might be expected in a country so recently and as yet so loosely united—still lacked both a national

[5] E. M. Hunt "The North of England Agitation for the Abolition of the Slave Trade, 1780-1800" (M.A. thesis, University of Manchester, 1959).

organization and organs for giving national expression to their views. In this latter respect the situation in the United States was very different from that in Britain where the national society had predated the local organizations, the great majority of which had, indeed, been created through its sponsorship.[6] Since most of the American agitation was confined to the local and state levels it attracted relatively less attention.

There were also political reasons why Americans—who, in spite of the less centralized character of their government, were no strangers to nation-wide publicity campaigns—were in this instance slower than the British to resort to such expedients. Among leaders, at the national level especially, there was an awareness that deference to Southern sensibilities was a price that had to be paid for Southern participation in the Union and a consequent reluctance to force issues that were likely to cause the South offense. Jefferson's deletion of all mention of slavery and the slave trade from his original draft of the Declaration of Independence and the caution with which the same issues were handled by the delegates at the Constitutional Convention are telling evidence of the need for restraint which responsible leaders felt when they approached such sensitive areas. Making deals with the South or even attempting, tactfully, to manipulate Southern opinion was one thing; but launching a campaign after the British fashion was quite another and likely, it was felt, to do more to hinder than to advance the cause, besides bringing other troubles in its train. Thus, while the British in their situation had every reason to adopt the methods they did, the Americans had cause to choose a less direct approach.

These facts at least help to explain why America at this time failed to produce any antislavery leaders of note.

[6] "Minute Books of the Society for the Abolition of the Slave Trade," British Museum Additional Manuscripts 21254-21256. Entry for June 10, 1788.

Whether, had the advocates of the trade put up a more stubborn resistance, this would have continued to be the case is open to question. In the event, the trade was abolished at the first legal opportunity permitted under the Constitution. The American and British acts, in fact, both took effect within a matter of months. Of the two, the British measure was the more significant as Britain had up to that time been the world's leading carrier of slaves and also because the Act itself was more conscientiously enforced. There is little evidence of direct British participation in the trade after 1808 whereas Americans—and not Southerners only—continued to be actively engaged in it up to the Civil War.[7] Most of this trade, however, was not to the United States but to Latin America, principally Cuba and Brazil. Insofar as the American Act succeeded, as it unquestionably did, in cutting down the number of slaves imported into the Southern states, it was certainly a notable measure.

In a sense, the antislavery forces in both countries had been luckier than might have been expected, since in each instance economic change had played into their hands. In the case of the British—a fact which is often overlooked—the movement had been aided by the relative decline in the economic importance of the trade due to the rise of new forms of commerce. Important assistance had also come from the planters in the older sugar islands who already had all the slaves they wanted and were anxious to deny their rivals in the newly acquired colonies of Trinidad and British Guiana the opportunity to build up adequate labor forces.[8] The Americans, similarly, had profited from the economic decadence of the tobacco system and the belief, general after the Revolu-

[7] W.E.B. DuBois, *The Suppression of the African Slave Trade to the United States, 1638-1870* (New York, 1904), pp. 109-12 and Warren S. Howard, *American Slavers and the Federal Law, 1837-1862* (Berkeley and Los Angeles, 1963), *passim*.

[8] Eric Williams, *Capitalism and Slavery* (Chapel Hill, 1944), pp. 149-50.

tion, that slavery as an economic institution was doomed.

After 1808, the antislavery leaders were less fortunate. While the struggle against the trade was in progress, British leaders, reluctant even at that time to ignore the evils of slavery itself, had persuaded themselves that once importation ceased, the institution of slavery would wither away.[9] Since there had never been a slave system which was not nourished by a trade, it was easy to exaggerate the effects which the abolition of the trade would have. As British antislavery leaders saw it, the effect of cutting off imports would be to raise the price of slaves. This, in turn, would oblige slaveholders to treat their slaves more humanely, until, the institution becoming progressively less repressive, even the most hardened slaveholders would realize that an entirely free system would be more efficient. So, by the operation of benevolent economic forces, the entire structure would be swept away. All the antislavery leaders needed to do was wait.

In the United States, too, there was a belief that economic forces would provide a solution. There, however, there was a social difficulty which had first to be overcome. It was clear that the problem of absorbing a large free Negro element into the population would, irrespective of economic advantage, act as a brake on any general movement toward manumission. It was to find a solution for this social difficulty by devising means of getting rid of the emancipated Negroes that the opponents of slavery in America now turned to colonization. The results were dispiriting. By 1830, a mere 1,420 Negroes had been settled in the new colony of Liberia[10] and there was little prospect of greater success in other areas.

In both instances the opponents of slavery had miscalculated. The British had not made allowance for the

[9] R. Coupland, *The British Anti-Slavery Movement* (London, 1933), p. 112.

[10] E. L. Fox, *The American Colonization Society, 1817-1840* (Baltimore, 1919), p. 89.

resilience of the slave system or for the fact that the economic rivalry of Brazil and Cuba—still profiting from an unrestricted trade in slaves from Africa—would make the British sugar producers more than ever anxious to cling to such slaves as they already had. Similarly, the Americans had not reckoned on the advent of cotton as a large-scale commercial crop or on the opening up of new Western lands, both of which helped to rejuvenate the slave system and caused slave prices to soar higher than ever before. Thus, on the two sides of the Atlantic the opponents of slavery were brought almost simultaneously to the conclusion that there was no alternative but to undertake what they had so far avoided—a frontal attack upon the institution of slavery itself.

In the case of the British, this was a perfectly feasible proposition. There was no strong opposition to abolition except from the planting interests and these represented only a tiny minority of the population and one whose political influence, once considerable, was now much diminished. The population at large, while it had little to gain from emancipation, had correspondingly little to lose. There was no domestic concern, as there was in the United States, over what to do with the freed Negroes. Above all, there was no doubt that Parliament had the power to do what the abolitionists wanted. West Indians might talk of the sovereignty of their own assemblies, of seceding from the Empire and having themselves annexed to the United States, but no one seriously doubted that if once Parliament decided to abolish slavery it had the power to see its decision carried through. There was nothing that the planters could do, legally or illegally, to stop it.

Thus, the primary task facing the British abolitionists was that of persuading Parliament to act. This could be done in two principal ways: one was to work directly through Parliament itself and appeal to the humanity and good sense of its members; the other was to influence Parliament indirectly by appealing to the sympathies of the population at large. The Anti-Slavery Society, established in 1823, employed both methods, though, especially during its early years, the emphasis was mainly on the first. Committed only to "the mitigation and gradual abolition of slavery" there seemed a fair chance that the Society would obtain the necessary action without needing to employ outside pressures. Parliament was not unamenable. Although reluctant to do what the Society demanded with respect to abolition, it was quite prepared to attempt some mitigation of the system by passing regulatory codes.[11] What finally inclined the British movement toward radicalism was not so much the slowness of Parliament to act—though that was part of it—as the deliberate refusal of the sugar planters to observe the regulations which Parliament laid down. Since mitigation was proving impossible, the idea of immediate emancipation became increasingly attractive and in 1831 the Society officially accepted the immediatist view.[12] Simultaneously, the younger and more radical elements in the movement launched, through the Agency Committee, an offshoot of the Society, a national campaign of the type with which Americans were later to become familiar, denouncing slavery as a sin and demanding its immediate extirpation.[13]

What effect this campaign had is not easy to measure, though there seems little doubt that it helped to give urgency to the issue. That at all events it did not alienate support is clear enough from the fact that within two years Parliament had passed a bill abolishing slavery

[11] Accounts of this phase of the struggle will be found in F. J. Klingberg's *The Anti-Slavery Movement in England* (New Haven, 1926), pp. 182-272; R. Coupland's *The British Anti-Slavery Movement* (London, 1933), pp. 118-34; and W. L. Mathieson's *British Slavery and its Abolition, 1828-1838* (London, 1926), pp. 115-95.

[12] David B. Davis, "The Emergence of Immediatism in British and American Antislavery Thought," *Mississippi Valley Historical Review*, 49 (1962-63), 219-22.

[13] Sir George Stephen, *Anti-Slavery Recollections: In a Series of Letters to Harriet Beecher Stowe* (London, 1854), pp. 138, 160-61.

throughout the dominions, replacing it with a system of apprenticeship to be followed by complete freedom after eight years. Some of the more radical abolitionists attacked the Act on the grounds that freedom was not to be immediate and also on account of the £20,000,000 granted to the slaveholders as compensation, which, they argued, constituted an official recognition of the right of masters to hold property in slaves.[14] But such opposition was not widespread, most abolitionists being content to accept the Act as it stood.

Meanwhile, the obstacles facing the antislavery forces in the United States were proving of an altogether more formidable nature. Slavery, always a more integral part of the American than of the British economy, was, now that cotton had become the principal American export, proving itself more profitable than ever. There was also the continuing problem of what to do with the Negroes supposing they were emancipated—a problem to which neither the American Colonization Society nor the abolitionists seemed able to provide a satisfactory answer. But most important of all, there simply was no way in which, without the consent of the slaveholding states— an improbable eventuality—slavery could constitutionally be abolished except by—another improbable eventuality—the use of the presidential fiat in time of war. Abolition by constitutional amendment was out of the question since that would have required ratification by three-quarters of the states and between a half and a third of the states (12 out of 24 in 1830, 15 out of 33 in 1860) held slaves and were therefore unlikely to consent. Wherever they turned American abolitionists were faced by the fact that there was no effective machinery for coming to grips with the essential problem—slavery as it existed within the individual states. There were, as it

14 *Ibid.*, p. 191; W. L. Burn, *Emancipation and Apprenticeship in the British West Indies* (London, 1937), p. 117; *Hansard's Parliamentary Debates*, Third Series, Vol. 18, pp. 582-99.

turned out, some issues which fell within the field of normal political discussion, such as the right to petition, the existence of slavery in the District of Columbia and in the territories and the right of the South to recapture runaways. But these were marginal issues. On the central issue of slavery within the individual states the position of the South was constitutionally impregnable.

Thus, compared with the British abolitionists, the Americans found themselves in a frustrating position. While they had quite as much reason as the British for wanting to abolish slavery, they were effectively denied the means for doing so. It was as if, in the British controversy, the West Indians had been allowed the right to veto any measure which seemed to be to their disadvantage. That radicals among the American abolitionists should have been provoked to the extent of denouncing the Constitution as a proslavery document, is hardly surprising. What is perhaps more surprising is that a greater number of Americans did not share their view.

But here one is confronted by another major difference between the two movements which is that whereas the British issue was throughout a peripheral matter so far as most British people were concerned, the American issue menaced the very basis of the society which Americans had labored to build up. How potentially disrupting they believed the issue to be is suggested by the following exchange which occurred in 1835 between a leading British abolitionist, Richard Robert Madden, and Andrew Jackson. Dr. Madden, visiting Washington on his way home from the West Indies, had been the President's guest at a dinner given at the White House. Taking advantage of Jackson's evident good humor, he observed:

> "The sooner, General, you adopt a similar measure in the United States the better. It would be a fitting finale to a great career like yours to connect it with

such an act of emancipation." The President was standing with his back to the fire when I said this. He burst out laughing and addressing his guests on either side, said, "This gentleman has just come from the West Indies, where the British have been emancipating their slaves. He recommends me to make myself famous by following their example. Come here Donelson" (turning round to his private secretary), "put the poker in the fire, bring in a barrel of gunpowder, and when I am placed on it give the red poker to the Doctor, and he shall make me famous in the twinkling of an eye. . . ."[15]

Jackson, as it happened, was himself a slaveholder, but Americans did not have to be slaveholders to believe that the issue was explosive and therefore best left alone. Most Northern politicians would have sympathized with Jackson's attitude. Even John Quincy Adams, who, as his diary reveals, believed as early as the time of the Missouri Compromise that "A life devoted to it [abolition] would be nobly spent or sacrificed," was so appalled by the dangers inherent in the issue that he waited fifteen years before publicly committing himself and even then declined to be directly associated with the abolitionists.[16]

Americans, in short, found themselves in a torturing dilemma. Either they could deny their ideals by keeping quiet or they could place them in jeopardy by expressing their views. In either event the consequences were likely to be formidable. How formidable, it was of course impossible to say. Adams foresaw, more clearly probably than any other man of the time, the possibility of war. But even if Americans looked no further than to the future effectiveness of the national government—or, in the case of politicians, to their own future effectiveness

[15] Richard Robert Madden, *Memoirs, Chiefly Autobiographical from 1798 to 1886*, ed. T. M. Madden (London, 1891), p. 96.

[16] Samuel Flagg Bemis, *John Quincy Adams and the Union* (New York, 1956), pp. 327-71.

as national leaders—it was evident enough that the agitation of the slavery question would involve sacrifices. And to what purpose if the issues so raised were insoluble? Why imperil a system which was conferring very real benefits on the American people over issues which for the most part allowed of no practical solution?

Even if the American abolitionists had shown themselves saints in all other respects they would still, in raising the slavery issue, have been open to charges of political irresponsibility. Such charges were widely voiced at the time and modern historians, conscious of the terrible price which Americans were to pay in the Civil War, have had an additional reason for finding the charges plausible. Yet, in a society which prided itself, as American society did, on its ability to arrive at satisfactory policies through free discussion, it is questionable how much blame can fairly be attached to those whose principal fault lay in speaking out against an institution so clearly at odds with America's political and religious traditions. After all, what made the abolitionists significant was not simply what they said but the fact that it struck an answering chord in so many other Americans.

More perhaps than has been generally realized, the American abolitionists were the products of an impossible situation. Attention has often been drawn to the bitter internecine quarrels which from the 1830's onward plagued the American movement as evidence of its essentially factious and irresponsible character. What has not been pointed out is the extent to which such behavior sprang naturally from the circumstances in which it was obliged to operate. Denied viable means of achieving their goals, the abolitionists were left with a series of alternative programs each one, from the practical point of view, as futile as the last. What, therefore, were they to do? Should they attempt to organize themselves into a political movement? Should they concentrate instead on stirring the consciences of Southern slaveholders? Or should they simply exercise their prerogative to denounce the slaveholders as frequently and as vociferously as possible? If the abolitionists often failed to agree it was partly because there was so little on which to agree.

That the factiousness and extremism associated with the American movement were the product of the frustrations of the American situation is further suggested by the fate of the British movement after 1838. Up to this time, British abolitionists had found their task, if not easy, at least comparatively straightforward, in that there had never been any doubt as to where ultimate authority lay or as to where they should apply for redress. The British political system, with its constitutional principle of parliamentary supremacy had made abolition a practical undertaking. After 1838, this was no longer the case. With the termination of apprenticeship, the last remaining vestige of slavery in Britain's sugar colonies, the abolitionists were no longer primarily concerned with conditions existing within the Empire but with slavery as it existed in the world at large, over which, of course, Parliament had no authority. Like their American counterparts, they were seeking to achieve reforms in areas where their influence could carry little weight and where there was absolutely no prospect of an early victory or of the attainment of results by direct action. British abolitionists, in fact, were in very much the same position with respect to what happened to slavery in Brazil or Tunis as American abolitionists were with respect to what happened to it in Mississippi or South Carolina. They could attempt to exert pressure through the British government in much the same way that American abolitionists sought to exert pressure through the Federal government; they could stir up public opinion in Britain just as American abolitionists could stir up public opinion in the North; they could send out lecturers, distribute pamphlets, dispatch formal addresses, harangue visiting clergymen, and write articles for newspapers. In short, they could adopt any one of a number of techniques familiar to their American counterparts, none of which held out much hope of altering the basic situation. Thus, after 1838, the British movement was exposed to many of the same frustrations which had already characterized the American movement. It is highly significant, therefore, that at this same time it should also have experienced similar internal stresses and conflicts and even developed an antipolitical Garrisonian wing.[17] As with the American movement, quarrels arose, factionalism spread, groups divided; old policies were rejected as ineffective; new and equally ineffective policies were suggested; practical politicians remained quietly in the wings while "extremists" stepped boldly forward into the center of the stage. "Its first concern," observes Gilbert H. Barnes, speaking of the American movement, "was not the abolition of slavery; it was 'the duty of rebuke which every inhabitant of the Free States owes to every slaveholder.' Denunciation of the evil came first; reform of the evil was incidental to that primary obligation."[18] The same might be said of the later British movement also, though it should be remembered that in both cases, this choice of policy was not altogether a voluntary one. If the abolitionists did little more than denounce slavery, it was because there was little else they could do.

Compared with the British, the American abolitionists never had a chance. In their own day the odds against them were too great and the Civil War has helped further to blacken their reputations. Whether, in another context they would have displayed the qualities expected of practical reformers as distinct from "agitators," there is no way of knowing. Judged by the strictest standards of what constitutes political responsibility, the American abolitionists are vulnerable, but so too are the Jacksons

17 Howard R. Temperley, "The British and Foreign Anti-Slavery Society, 1839-1868" (Ph.D. Thesis, Yale University, 1960), pp. 303-15.
18 Gilbert H. Barnes, *The Anti-Slavery Impulse*, p. 25.

and the Websters and the other political leaders who, for too long, failed to grapple with the issues raised. So also are the moderate, respectable citizens, North and South, who deplored the excesses of the extremists but failed to cooperate in achieving a solution short of war. In the last resort, the failure was not that of any particular group. It was the failure of a whole society.

CHAPTER 15

AMBIGUITIES IN THE ANTISLAVERY
CRUSADE OF THE REPUBLICAN PARTY

BY ROBERT F. DURDEN

NINETEENTH-CENTURY Americans confronted the problem of what to do about the presence of a large and growing Negro minority living amidst a majority that grew increasingly conscious of belonging to the Caucasian or "Anglo-Saxon" race. In 1860 approximately four million slaves, or 90 per cent of all the Negroes in the nation, were in the South, as were some 250,000 free Negroes, a bit over half of all the free Negroes in the nation. The South attempted to solve or, actually, to escape the problem of racial adjustment by denying its existence. Repudiating an earlier Jeffersonian tradition of skepticism about slavery, the South from the 1820's on increasingly froze in a fanatic defense of the "peculiar institution." It came to be hailed as a "positive good," the blessed cornerstone of an allegedly superior "Southern way of life." In their tragically stubborn refusal to consider the possibility of any change in their racial arrangements, ante-bellum Southerners tortured and twisted not only their political heritage but also their professed belief in the fatherhood of God and brotherhood of Man. Surely a large portion of the ultimate responsibility for the catastrophe that began in 1861 must rest with all those Southerners, both the leaders and the led, who attempted to flee into a never-never land of proslavery perfection.

The greatest open question concerning responsibility for the war does not have to do with the slaveholding South, however, but rather with the Northern political party, the Republicans, whose presidential victory in 1860 precipitated secession. Vociferously opposed to the extension of slavery from their birth in 1854, the Republicans eventually led the nation during the war to the abolition of the institution. That they were antislavery is indisputable. Just *why* they were, however, is a much more complicated matter than many historians have been willing to admit.

The thesis of this essay is that the Republican party, as a party, had no more "moral" solution in 1860 to the problem of racial adjustment in America than did the benighted South. In fact, the Republicans ignored the racial problem as much as they possibly could and concentrated their fire in fierce attacks on the institution of slavery and on the slaveholders. When Republicans had to speak to the racial aspect of slavery they usually combined their opposition to the institution with a profound and avowed antipathy toward the enslaved race. Some of them were clearly antislavery partly because they were as scornful of the Negro as they were of the political power which the Southern minority had gained through counting three-fifths of the slaves as population for Federal purposes. Racists themselves, some Republicans participated in their great sectional crusade for reasons that were highly ambiguous if not clearly immoral. There can be surprise that the entire nation had to grapple with the problem of racial adjustment in the mid-twentieth century only because myths and errors have encrusted the record of the era of the Civil War and Reconstruction.

That a large portion of the Northern population before the Civil War intensely disliked having Negroes anywhere near them should by now be a truism; and a bit less than 5 per cent of the nation's Negroes were to be found in the free states in 1860. As early as 1835, Alexis de Tocqueville, himself a profound libertarian and perhaps the most detached and penetrating of all observers of the

American scene, commented: "Whoever has inhabited the United States must have perceived that in those parts of the Union in which the Negroes are no longer slaves they have in no wise drawn nearer to the whites. On the contrary, the prejudice of race appears to be stronger in the states that have abolished slavery than in those where it still exists; and nowhere is it so intolerant as in those states where servitude has never been known." More recently, Professor Leon F. Litwack's study of the plight of the free Negroes in the North has but confirmed and documented in detailed and scholarly fashion the report of the famed French traveler of the 1830's.[1]

Horace Greeley, the brilliantly partisan editor of what was perhaps the most influential Republican paper of the Civil War era, the New York *Tribune*, liked to blame Northern race riots and Jim Crow laws on Irish Catholics and other "doughface" Democrats. And it was true that many Northern Democrats in the ante-bellum era resorted to a crude, unbridled Negrophobia in their appeal to popular prejudices. But the striking fact is that the *Tribune* itself, the sectional oracle that linked abolitionists with anti-extensionists and New Englanders with Midwesterners in the Republican crusade, revealed unmistakable signs of the very racism which led Southerners to their pathetic defense of slavery as the greatest of all goods.

The Northern blind were still some four months away from the war with the Southern blind when the *Tribune* undertook to explain "The Republican Position" to a North made fearful and apprehensive by the imminent secession of South Carolina. Mincing no words, the antislavery spokesman declared that the Republican party's stand was, in substance, "that all the unoccupied territory of the United States, and such as they may hereafter

[1] Alexis de Tocqueville, *Democracy in America*, ed. Phillips Bradley (2 vols., New York, 1945), I, 373; Leon F. Litwack, *North of Slavery: The Negro in the Free States, 1790-1860* (Chicago, 1961).

acquire, shall be reserved for the benefit and occupation of the white Caucasian race—a thing which cannot be except by the exclusion of Slavery." In which class of states, free or slave, the *Tribune* asked, did the white race occupy the more enviable position? "Is it not notorious that the existence of Slavery in a State tends to keep and to drive the white race out of it, both by closing up a thousand avenues to profitable employment which might otherwise successively spring into existence, and by affixing to all manual labor a certain badge of degradation? . . . Could anything be more in the interest of the men of the white Caucasian race, than to secure to them the quiet possession of the new Territories, and thus to put an end to that dogging of their steps by gangs of negro slaves by which they have been pursued and driven from one new State to another?"[2]

Side by side with this candidly racial justification for the Republican party's great unifying denominator and "moral principle" of anti-extension, another *Tribune* editorial reiterated the theme of the right of peaceful secession, a theme that many other Republican spokesmen strangely endorsed and repeated during the early months of the 1860-61 winter of secession. Although Greeley was later to emphasize all sorts of qualifications attached to the doctrine of peaceful secession, the *Tribune's* meaning was fairly clear in the forthright statement that if seven or eight of the cotton states of the deep South sent "agents to Washington to say 'We want to get out of the Union,' we shall feel constrained by our devotion to Human Liberty to say, Let them go! And we do not see how we could take the other side without coming in direct conflict with those Rights of Man which we hold paramount to all political arrangements, however convenient and advantageous."[3]

[2] New York *Daily Tribune*, December 17, 1860. All references are to the *Daily Tribune*.
[3] *Ibid.*

Since Republicans in April 1861 began their leadership of the North in a war to preserve the Union, the ostensible willingness of some leading Republican spokesmen to accept peaceful secession in December 1860 and January 1861 has puzzled historians as much as it must have baffled many observers at the time. Professor David Potter has quite correctly pointed out that much of the alleged willingness of Republicans to separate peacefully from the South was essentially a roundabout way of calming Northern opinion and of strengthening the Republican party in its stand of refusing to accept any compromise that dealt with the issue of slavery in the territories.[4] This was certainly part of the story in the *Tribune's* case; when the proposals identified with Senator John J. Crittenden of Kentucky and his distinguished committee began to be discussed as the most realistic possibility for compromise in the tradition of 1820 and 1850, no Republican voice was louder in opposition than the *Tribune's*. Yet the unwillingness to compromise on the central partisan principle of the Republicans concerning the territories was only a part of the motivation behind the newspaper's talk of peaceful secession.

Compromise along other lines, and specifically along the line of allowing the Negro-filled states of the deep South to separate from the rest of the nation, was a possibility that the *Tribune* kept before its readers during the early stages of the secession crisis and gave up reluctantly only when forced to do so by geographical complications and the all-important need for the Republican party to stand unitedly against all talk of compromise of any kind.

"If the slaveholders of the Gulf States would be reasonable," a *Tribune* editorial explained on January 31, 1861, "they might perhaps eventually get away peaceably. . . . The slaveholding territory east of the Mississippi and south of the Potomac can be spared by the nation with-

---

[4] *Lincoln and His Party in the Secession Crisis* (New Haven, 1942), pp. 51-57.

out great detriment. But the approaches to the Gulf, the country north of the Potomac, and that west of the Mississippi River, and the control of the mouths of that river, cannot be spared." Related to this idea was a proposal which *Tribune* editorials hailed first as "A Reasonable Compromise" and then as "The Only Possible Compromise." This project, reportedly being seriously discussed in Washington, looked to gradual, compensated emancipation and subsequent colonization in Liberia of the approximately 600,000 slaves in the states of Delaware, Maryland, Missouri, Arkansas, Texas, and Louisiana. Such a move would, the *Tribune* declared, "secure to Freedom the States north of the Potomac and west of the Mississippi" and, at an estimated cost of not more than $100,000,000, "would be cheap in comparison to the money cost of civil war, to say nothing of the other than pecuniary losses which war involves." When a New York legislator introduced a resolution endorsing such a plan in the state assembly, the *Tribune* insisted that this scheme of ridding the border states of both slavery and the Negroes would in time rid the North, at least, "of an odious and formidable evil, the ultimate result of which, if some remedy be not soon applied, will be to Africanize one-half of the continent. . . ."[5]

The *Tribune* editorials refrained from saying in so many plain words that the states south of the Potomac and east of the Mississippi could go their own, Africanized way. But that was what they meant, and James Shepherd Pike, the *Tribune's* special correspondent in Washington, said precisely that and more in his bold and frank dispatches. Pike, then famous for his journalistic assaults on slavery and slaveholders, affords the clearest possible example of the moral ambiguity that clearly characterized the antislavery views of many Republicans.[6]

[5] January 16, 19, 1861.

[6] Just who wrote the aforementioned editorials is not known. Greeley's temporary advocacy of the right of peaceful secession for

Dropped from his job as Washington correspondent for the Boston *Courier* because of his fierce attacks on Daniel Webster and the Compromise of 1850, Pike, a native of Calais, Maine, accepted in April 1850 Greeley's invitation to write for the *Tribune*. His columns from the capital, always signed with "J.S.P.," soon became well known in the politico-journalistic world, and Pike helped to make the *Tribune's* Washington coverage "the best showcase for high-minded reporting" in the nation and to earn Greeley's paper the record of having "the most brilliant staff any American newspaper had yet assembled."[7]

As the *Tribune's* special Washington correspondent and an associate of rising Republican leaders such as Benjamin Wade, Salmon P. Chase, and William Pitt Fessenden, Pike quickly established his reputation as one of the most articulate Northern sectionalists. In response to Stephen A. Douglas's Kansas-Nebraska Act in 1854, Pike called on the "whole North" to unite in a new, anti-slavery coalition because a "solid phalanx of aggression rears its black head everywhere south of the Mason and Dixon line, banded for the propagation of Slavery all over the continent."[8] Rather than see Douglas' bill pass,

the cotton states is familiar, however, and the late Professor Jeter A. Isely pointed out in *Horace Greeley and the Republican Party, 1853-1861* (Princeton, 1947), p. 299, that the editor believed that American Negroes would eventually gravitate toward and live alone in the Gulf states. Although the New York newspaper was known, North and South, as "Greeley's *Tribune*" it was in fact the property of a company in which the editor owned considerably less than half the stock. Pike became one of the ten associate editors as well as a stockholder earlier in the 1850's. Glyndon G. Van Deusen, *Horace Greeley: Nineteenth Century Crusader* (Philadelphia, 1953), p. 132.

[7] Bernard A. Weisberger, *Reporters for the Union* (Boston, 1953), p. 17; Frank L. Mott, *American Journalism: A History of Newspapers in the United States through 260 Years: 1690 to 1950* (New York, 1950), p. 262.

[8] *Tribune* editorial, February 25, 1854. Pike's authorship is shown by internal evidence and the editorial's inclusion in his scrapbooks in the Pike MSS, Calais Free Library, Calais, Maine.

Pike declared in a dispatch from Washington that it would be better that "confusion should ensue—better that discord should reign in the National Councils—better that Congress should break up in wild disorder—nay, better that the Capitol itself should blaze by the torch of the incendiary . . . than that this perfidy and wrong should be finally accomplished."[9]

In the presidential election year of 1856, Pike's moral passion and antislavery rhetoric reached new heights. Concerning "bleeding Kansas," the Downeaster declared that there had been enough argument and logic about Kansas; what the North wanted was "*preachers*, with tongues of fire, and a leader holy, rapt, and mystical as a seraph." Where was "the Master" who would seize the "great harp of liberty" and rouse all Northerners? And after Congressman Preston Brooks assaulted Senator Charles Sumner, Pike proclaimed that unless "the Northern and Southern civilizations can be harmonized, become positively assimilated, a long union of the two is impossible."[10]

Greeley first sent word through Charles A. Dana, the managing editor and Pike's close friend, that such disunionist talk would harm the Republican cause, and if Pike felt he had to write such extreme letters he should send them to New England papers where they would not lose votes for the Republican candidate. Willfully refusing to heed the admonition, Pike soon came forth in the *Tribune* with a strong restatement of his views. "Personally, I have no doubt that the Free and Slave States ought to separate," he declared. But since the idea of separation was "not now palatable" and "not generally shared by our people," Northerners should at least send more and better warriors to Congress. "Persuasion and argument are good," Pike concluded, "but there always

[9] May 18, 1854.
[10] *Tribune*, datelined from Washington, April 24 and May 28, 1856.

comes a time when steel and gunpowder are better." He thought that time had now come for the United States, since "a collision is at hand."[11]

Greeley himself immediately wrote the obdurate associate editor and urged him to stay away from such speculation. "My objection to your Disunion articles is not that I am for or against Disunion; or do or don't believe it is coming," the editor explained, "but that I know its proposition from our side would injure the Republican cause and drive back thousands into Union saving." He believed that if New York City voters were given a choice of disunion with Kansas as a free-soil state or union with Kansas as a slave state, the latter choice would prevail by a majority of thirty thousand in the city and would also carry the state. "Now if you really want Disunion," Greeley continued, "keep still and let events ripen. I don't want it; for I believe the same spirit and resolution on our part which are required to dissolve the Union would suffice to rule it, rescuing it from the rule of the Slave-drivers." He concluded that rather than disunion, he preferred the "ascendancy of Liberty" with the slave states remaining in the fold. But "if they choose to go, let them go."[12]

Even this personal plea from Greeley failed to persuade Pike to keep quiet, but the remainder of his disunion letters were kept out of print during the presidential campaign, presumably on the orders of Greeley and Dana. With the election over, however, and while Washington political circles were anticipating the forthcoming Dred Scott decision, Pike reasserted his views in the *Tribune*: "If we cannot, as a nation, agree to go back to the position of the founders of the Government, and regard Slavery as an exceptional institution, and administer the Government in the interest of universal Freedom; or, if we will not agree upon any fixed compromise in respect

11 Dana to Pike, May 30, 1856, Pike MSS; *Tribune*, June 3, 1856.
12 Greeley to Pike, June 5, 1856, Pike MSS.

to the institution of Slavery, the longer continuance of the existing Union is a political impossibility." Subsequently Pike explained that the slaveholder's program for perpetual bondage meant that "an Ethiopia in the South is inevitable." That, however, would merely be "retribution" for the crimes of slavery. The slaveholders possessed four million Negroes now and would, he predicted, eventually hold ten millions. "This mass of barbarism will enforce its own expulsion from our system as a matter of necessity," Pike concluded.[13]

Although Greeley realized that outright abolitionism and disunionism were major political liabilities, Pike for a long time stubbornly ignored the fact, and his apparent reconciliation to a disruption of the existing Union gave him an important link with the disunionists of New England. Thomas Wentworth Higginson, one of the Massachusetts abolitionist fire-eaters, recognized a kindred spirit in the *Tribune's* Washington correspondent and sent encouragement. Higginson did not know whether Pike had any interest in the "Massachusetts disunion movement" but his "powerful letters in the *Tribune*" suggested that he was not "so blind as most people to the real tendencies of the time." "All the laws of nature work for disunion," the zealous minister added; "there is a mine beneath us, and the South will cram in powder quite as fast as we can touch it off."[14]

Despite the applause of Higginson and other avowed disunionists, Pike gradually toned down his public writings. By 1860, when the Republican party needed more than ever to repudiate the charge against it of dangerous radicalism, Pike devoted his journalistic talents to denunciations of the "slavocracy" and assurances that the slaveholders' threats of secession were just "so much gasconade." The future for the nation never looked brighter; in fact, there "is no nation in existence whose disorders

[13] *Tribune*, datelined December 18, 1856, and January 30, 1857.
[14] Higginson to Pike, February 9, 1857, Pike MSS.

are so trivial as our own."[15] While busy alleviating the fears of Northern voters about Republican intentions, Pike also undertook to speak candidly about a matter that most Republicans, whether moderate or extreme, usually preferred to avoid, and that was the party's stand on the racial, as distinct from the slavery, question. Discussion of slavery among Republicans rarely dealt with this purely racial aspect of the problem; it was usually the Southern proslavery apologists who insisted that the institution be considered first and foremost in its racial context. Pike, however, openly declared the racial beliefs which underlay the thinking of himself and other Republicans and which furnish a vital clue to what much of Northern disunionism was all about.

"What We Shall Do with the Negro" was the title of his essay, and Pike premised his argument upon the assertion that the only way the Negro could be eliminated as the center of all national controversies was to remove him altogether from the scene by "a separation of the White and Black races." He believed that nothing could be more "certain than that a great democratic republic cannot forever submit to the anomaly of negro Slavery in its bosom." But even with the hated institution extinguished, "the ignorant and servile race will not and cannot be emancipated and raised to the enjoyment of equal civil rights with the dominant and intelligent race; they will be driven out." Such action might be a "cruel and unchristian process, but it is natural," and the "only solution the question of African Slavery admits of among us."

Already anticipating some of the difficulties that he and other Republicans would later face, Pike declared that the peculiar problem in treating abolition, under the democratic process, arose from the "necessity of conferring political power by the act of liberation." The slaveholder feared "nothing but the blind forces of the enslaved mass, or the great storms of political action,

15 *Tribune*, January 31, February 1, 1860.

breaking from prescribed boundaries, and acting with whirlwind force, threatening Slavery and society alike with sure and overwhelming destruction."

But the "battles of Freedom against Slavery" were not to be viewed only from the slaveholders' viewpoint. The "white laboring classes" had also to be considered, since the Negro, whether free or slave, stood in their way too. "The slaveholder is claiming to spread the negro everywhere," Pike continued, "and the Popular-Sovereignty man stands coolly by, and says, 'Let him do it wherever he can.' We say the Free States should say, confine the negro to the smallest possible areas. Hem him in. Coop him up. Slough him off. Preserve just so much of North America as is possible to the white man, and to free institutions. We shall get none too much any way. We are likely to get far too little."

Senator Benjamin Wade, Republican from Ohio and one of Pike's friends, had recently suggested colonizing the free Negroes of the North somewhere on the southwestern border of the nation. Pike endorsed this notion but quickly added that the free blacks were but "the mere twigs and branches torn from the great forest of Negro Slavery." The four million slaves were the important class, and the Republicans should make it clear that once the extension of slavery had been stopped their next aim would necessarily be "to get rid of the negro population entirely, by massing it within its present limits." The party could not, certainly, deal with all of the minor "details" of the matter without encountering opposition that would hinder the progress of their "great conceptions and duties." But at least Republicans should "assail the whole body of evil, so far as we can do it within constitutional limits, and leave its accidents and its fragmentary aspects, like those we have commented on, to individual action."[16]

[16] *Tribune*, March 13, 1860. Concerning Senator Wade's colonization scheme, it is worth noting that one of his supporters wrote him

Three days after his frank article explaining how the Republicans would "coop up" and then "slough off" the Negroes, Pike returned to a theme that was much more congenial for a party of high-minded crusaders. The Republicans, he explained, were "after something real and substantial." "The rights of man are as tangible and real as the everlasting laws of the Universe," he expounded. "In upholding them and defending them from all their enemies, high and low, we do a noble and a glorious work. We may even say that in doing this, we do not much care whether we go according to law or against law. Every man is at liberty, in virtue of that liberty wherewith God has made him free, to act according to his convictions, whether those convictions are in accordance with law or in opposition to law." The Republican party, at any rate, could "only compact its power by building itself firmly around principle." If it kept "the virtue to contend steadily and faithfully for fundamental truths, and to hold fast to a lofty integrity in shaping measures of administration," then surely a glorious future would unroll before it.[17]

Many of Pike's and his fellow Republicans' ideas about "fundamental truths" and the Negro's future were clearly at cross purposes, but there came a showdown in the winter of 1860-61 when disunionism was no longer an empty threat from slaveholders or from abolitionists but a fast-spreading, terrible reality in the deep South. One

---

as follows: "You are right upon every issue which will be likely to agitate the country in this campaign. And I like this new touch of colonizing the Niggers. I believe practically it is a d—n humbug. But it will take with the people. Our creed runs into what the French call a *Cul de sac*, which I take to be a Road with the end chopped off. If we are to have no more slave states what the devil are we to do with the surplus niggers? Your plan will help us out on this point. But practically I have not much faith in it. You could not raise twenty five cents from a Yankee to transport a Nigger to South America. . . ." Dan Tilden to B. F. Wade, Wade MSS; furnished through the courtesy of Mr. Thomas Clark, Roanoke Rapids, N.C.

17 *Tribune*, March 16, 1860.

reason the eminent *Tribune* correspondent had joined the Northern disunionists and abolitionists in the mid-1850's was his sincere belief that the Negro could not and should not be incorporated into the American democratic system. Even in the early 1850's he had stated in the *Tribune* his belief that the Gulf states would inevitably be "Africanized" and surrendered to the Negroes. In the secession crisis of 1860-61 this idea still lingered in his mind, and he desired emancipation in the states north of the Potomac and west of the Mississippi, by Federal mandate if necessary, and then the separation of the rest of the nation from the "Africanized" states of the southeast, or as he later described it, the "negro pen." During the war, especially about 1863-64, when Northern armies faltered and Federal financing became difficult, Pike reverted to this idea of "fighting for a boundary" rather than for the preservation of the old union. That is, he urged a compromise peace which would leave the Negroes and their masters in their own, separate, Africanized nation.

That is one half of the complex network of ideas that Pike and some other Republicans entertained. But it is not the whole story. Pike's writings from the early 1840's on show that he and other "Conscience" Whigs and then Republicans regarded slavery as an abomination and the alleged domination of the Federal government by the "slavocracy" and their "doughface" allies as an intolerable situation that had to be ended regardless of the costs. There must be, he thought, no more compromising with the South, and Northern threats of disunionism had been one counteragent to the more familiar Southern cries for secession. In other words, disunionism in Pike's case, and probably in many others, meant, on the one hand, that he wanted no more compromise with the "slavocracy." On the other hand, however, his disunionism also meant that if the Union should disintegrate, there might be a good chance of getting rid of the slaveholders and their Negroes by shoving them into a "negro pen." As long as he had the choice Pike possibly preferred the Union as it was, if it could be had without compromise and with Republican domination of the Federal government. But his alternate choice, in 1860-61 and later, looked to separation from the Negro-filled states of the deep South. The convolutions in his thinking, which closely paralleled many of the erratic positions of the *Tribune* as well as of some other prominent Republican spokesmen, may be clearly traced in the newsletters that Pike sent from Washington during the secession crisis.

Pike wrote his first letter about the crisis on the day that the crucial lame-duck session of Congress convened, December 4, 1860. His first stand, and the one to which he, as well as the *Tribune*, ultimately reverted after a great deal of twisting and turning, presented the Republican as patriot and lover of the Union. Overlooking the earlier talk about disunionism and the God-given liberty to rise above laws and constitutions when principle demanded, Pike asserted that the Federal government's first duty was clearly to maintain the Union. The causes of the threatening "embarrassments" had nothing to do with the secession issue, nor was it a party question. Men had to take sides "for or against the Government, not for or against a party, or its principles or notions."[18]

Four days after writing his plea for the maintenance of the Union, Pike coolly declared in the *Tribune*, "We seem about to surrender the Gulf States to the Black race, and the Whites who as yet rule that race." He did not view the prospect with the hostility that some entertained, but then they simply had not "reflected upon it as one of the ultimate, inevitable necessities of our political condition." Since it was "the destiny of American Slavery to Africanize the Gulf States" and "to dissever them from the great body of the Republic," whether that was done

18 *Tribune*, December 6, 1860; datelined Washington, December 4.

"one or two generations sooner or later" was hardly a matter of great consequence in the long run.

Pike felt certain that there would be a "peaceable issue" of the complications that threatened from the South. There was surely "no cause for any physical conflict in the readjustment of our political relations. . . ." "If we are to have any separation at all," he argued, "it is for the interest of all to have it a peaceful separation, and it will be a national disgrace, if, in its incipient stages, it takes on any other form." The areas north of the Potomac and west of the Mississippi would, however, be required for the future development of the United States even if the lower South should "peaceably" separate itself.[19]

Both Pike, and the *Tribune* in its editorial policies, had now begun the business of preserving the Union in one breath and advocating peaceable secession for the southeastern states in the other. Although Pike admitted before the year ended that the policy of the "excision" of the cotton states had not found general favor in Republican circles, *Tribune* editorials, as mentioned earlier, continued to allude to the scheme throughout the month of January. Pike's main theme in his despatches, however, became the necessity for Republicans to cling to their principles, and particularly anti-extension, in the face of the would-be compromisers. He also began to allude to drastic steps that the new administration might have to take. He reminded his readers that Senator Wade, in a speech just before the presidential election, had declared that the "act of secession is an edict of emancipation." "Who can fail to feel the awful truth of this enunciation?" Pike asked. "The North to-day is a sleeping volcano. And when its fires shall be agitated by the breath of popular passion roused to fury against the great crim-

[19] *Ibid.*, December 10, 1860. For letters to the editor from readers who supported Northern separation from the slave states, see *ibid.*, December 10 and December 12, 1860.

inals who would destroy a Government like this, who shall set bounds to its action?"[20]

Even in his Union-saving posture, however, Pike managed to strike a racist note. "The whole question involved," he explained, "is whether this Government shall control Slavery, or whether Slavery shall control the Government." One would think that the compromisers could see the issue. When the slaveholders asserted "their royal prerogative to govern this country by declaring that Cotton is King," Pike thought that was "only a modest way they have of asserting that the Negro is King" and it was now simply a question of "whether he shall be deposed, and the White Man take his place." The people had decreed the change, and the compromisers "had better step aside and let events progress in their natural order."[21]

As secession spread from South Carolina across the lower South, the *Tribune* correspondent lashed out at any mention of compromise along the lines proposed by Senator Crittenden. Even as the upper South and border states clearly hesitated to secede, Pike joined the ultras who insisted that the Federal government take strong and positive action. Since secession, according to him, proved that the Southerners really wanted to spread and secure slavery, it was clear that secession meant war. Emancipation loomed as the best Federal weapon against the seceders, for "if the Free States are driven into war," they would surely strike at the "root of the conflict." The administration of President Buchanan he violently excoriated, declaring that "imbecile hands" had the levers of control and "eunuchs" led affairs. "What is needed

[20] *Tribune*, December 28, 1860.

[21] *Tribune*, January 1, 1861. In his dispatches on January 3 and January 9, Pike reverted to "the policy of the excision of the Gulf States as being the most natural policy of the United States Government to free itself from the Slavery question." Although editorials supporting the idea appeared as late as January 31, 1861, Pike in his dispatches increasingly turned to ideas that are more traditionally associated with the Radical wing of the Republican party.

here is wine, and bark, and iron, and sulphur, and steel,"
he suggested. "Such another pack of Miss Nancies [as
Buchanan, *et al.*] to oppose treason and bullying, the
world never saw."[22]

By late January 1861, Pike had moved to the position
that all of the slaveholding states of the border and upper
South, except perhaps Delaware, would try to secede and
that the government might as well prepare to try to prevent it. Republicans in Congress had been content to
follow a policy of "masterly inactivity" but now "events
crowd upon them so fast, that they begin to perceive the
necessity of adopting, at no distant day, an affirmative
policy which shall furnish new safeguards for Freedom."
As for the Gulf states, it was clear that the Republican
Administration's policy would be to blockade their ports
"if they refuse to pay Federal revenue."

But in the border states where slaves were not numerous, Pike thought it clear that even bolder Federal action
was in order. "Emancipation and compensation might be
very bad policy in States where the Africanization was
rapidly going on, or where for other causes it might be
deemed unsuitable." But Republicans were increasingly
convinced, he reported, that in the border states those
might be "the very weapons with which to battle Secession." Pike's idea was stark in its simplicity: "If Revolution can be stayed in no other way, it must be met by

[22] *Tribune*, January 4, 5, 11, 12, 13, 1861. Ironically enough, in
view of their growing militancy, Pike's dispatches as well as *Tribune*
editorials also developed the theme that business and prosperity
were already improving in the North and were destined to grow
even better, not "from bloody wars, but from the peaceful operations of the laws of trade." The secession movement was going to be
"one of the most advantageous things that ever happened to this
Government, and to the cause of Freedom." Like a "refreshing storm
in the political atmosphere," it would "give us clear and settled
weather and a joyous and enduring sunshine over the whole land."
The editorial of January 22 concluded that all would "live to rejoice
that [they] were spared to see the day that this negro question in
this country was brought to a head. And this too, with less disturbance to material interests than was ever thought to be possible."

revolution. Certainly the revolutionist could not expect to be exempt from incurring the dangers of the weapons he himself has forged. All extensive conflagrations have to be arrested by extraordinary and often destructive methods. The authorities blow up a small district to save a large one. How, then, could Maryland or Missouri complain at having Slavery suddenly overset within their limits, if the act was one demanded by high considerations of national safety?"[23]

Two and a half months before the war had even begun, the Downeaster had foreshadowed the critical issue which would soon divide President Lincoln from the Radical wing of his own party. While Senator William H. Seward and his powerful ally in New York state, Thurlow Weed, concentrated on protecting and strengthening the strained ties which held the states of the upper South in the Union, Pike openly advocated the very policy which would have been most likely to have driven those states immediately into the arms of the Confederacy. Temporarily ignoring the Constitution on which even "higher-law" Republicans were now supposed to be standing firm, Pike had moved to the advanced position that the threat of secession in the upper South should be answered by a Federal emancipation policy.

Pike's last contributions to the *Tribune*, before he secured in March a long-sought diplomatic appointment as Lincoln's minister to The Hague, were primarily assaults on Seward and all the friends of compromise who threatened "to lose us the hard-won fruits of a victory won in behalf of civilization and humanity, and to reinaugurate the Slave Power in the Union, and enthrone it on the enduring basis of the Constitution itself." In February, as Seward's moderating influence in Washington increased, the *Tribune* spokesman openly expressed doubts as to Lincoln's policy. Would the President-elect follow the Weed-Seward "compromisers" or would he fol-

23 *Tribune*, January 31, 1861.

low what Pike considered the "main body" of Republicans, the faction that would become known in history as the Radicals? Pike feared that the Lincoln administration would not be "anything above average height of public sentiment in regard to the present emergency" and would probably therefore be in favor of a weak, conciliatory program. Not until the day following Lincoln's inauguration in early March 1861 could Pike happily confess his belief that the "back of compromise" had been broken once and for all. And now that there were to be no concessions he demanded full exercise of the "legitimate powers of the Government in the direct line" of Republican principles. That is, he urged an emancipation policy which the border states could take or leave as they liked.[24]

Not until September 1862 and the issuance of his preliminary emancipation proclamation did the troubled President catch up with the Radical demand for an emancipation program. Even then Lincoln's cautious approach to the gigantic problem of slavery in the states lacked the directness and scope that Pike and many other Radicals would have preferred. When that step came, however, Pike could only look on and growl his doubts about Lincoln and Federal policy in letters from The Hague, where the Downeaster remained until mid-1866.[25]

With the departure of Pike as associate editor and special Washington correspondent, the *Tribune* lost one of its most forceful and vivid, as well as most frankly racist, spokesmen. No one person on the staff of what was then the nation's most powerful Republican newspaper could quite take the place of James S. Pike. Yet the racial am-

[24] *Ibid.*, February 15, 18, 23, March 1, 5, 7, 1861. *Tribune* editorials attacked Seward and the moderate Republicans' efforts for compromise during this same period.

[25] For Pike's diplomatic career and postwar role as a journalistic spokesman first for the program of Radical Reconstruction and then for the Liberal Republican, anti-Radical movement of 1872, the reader is referred to this writer's book on Pike (Durham, N.C., 1957).

biguities in the *Tribune's* vehement antislavery stand continued to be quite apparent even with Pike gone. The fast-changing exigencies and circumstances of the desperate war did apparently push Greeley himself, as they did Lincoln too for that matter, in the direction at least of what a later generation would recognize as genuine liberalism on the racial question; but even then, as is suggested below, the general racism, prejudice, and fear in the North were of such proportions as to frustrate and prevent any progress toward steps that might have helped to make possible genuine racial adjustment in the nation.

One of the most constantly discussed subjects in Republican political and journalistic circles in 1862 was the colonization of the Negroes. Radical demand for a Federal emancipation policy grew steadily more urgent in the face of Federal military reversals and the increasingly clear and painful fact that the war was to be a long and bloody ordeal. The Northern public, however, would require some idea of a Republican policy concerning racial adjustment before there could be even partial acceptance of the military necessity of emancipation. This is where the colonization idea, which Lincoln himself advanced in early 1862 and long supported, gained its political utility, despite the fact that it had since the early 1820's been shown to be an impractical and morally dubious panacea for the race problem.[26]

Although the *Tribune* opposed any notion of involuntary or forced colonization, it declared unequivocally that "our conviction is strong that the blending in one great community of races so diverse as the European and the African is unnatural, enforced by Slavery, and that Liberty will gradually dissociate them in such manner as

[26] Litwack, *North of Slavery*, pp. 272-73, describes the colonization plans advanced in 1858 by such Republicans as Senator James Doolittle of Wisconsin, Francis P. Blair, Jr., and Edward Bates of Missouri, and Montgomery Blair of Maryland; Litwack notes that various "Republican and abolitionist spokesmen enthusiastically indorsed the Blair-Doolittle proposals."

shall most conduce to their own good and the well-being of mankind. Let there be Liberty and all good will naturally follow." When Senator Doolittle of Wisconsin in the spring of 1862 advanced his plan for colonizing Negroes in the West Indies or Central America, the *Tribune* reiterated its approval for voluntary separation of the races. It dissented, however, from the Senator's further propositions that "the Rebellion was caused, and that Slavery is upheld, from a fear of what is called Negro Equality; and that ample provision for the expatriation of Blacks would soften Rebel hate of the North and of Universal Freedom."

Still, the New York journal agreed that "a separation of the White and Black races in our country is desirable, and will prove advantageous to both." The *Tribune* did suggest that there was hardly any need to talk about colonization in foreign countries. "We have an area large enough for Five Hundred Millions of People, not one-tenth of which has ever felt the point of a plow . . . ," the editorial continued, "and it is simple wisdom, it is naked common sense, to retain as many honest workers as possible. Let Florida, or Western Texas, or both, be conceded to the Blacks, not to the exclusion of any Whites who might choose to live among them but as a region to be colonized, improved, cultivated, and governed by them subject to the Constitution and laws of the Union."[27]

All the talk of colonization was but a prelude, of course, to the Radical Republicans' increasingly vehement insistence on a war of abolition. *Tribune* editorials began to be especially forceful and explicit on the subject around May 1862: "Let us work and wait. By-and-by, when Money grows scarce, and Credit droops, and Recruiting goes hard, and Southern Fevers decimate our armies, it will

[27] April 22, May 2, 1862. See also March 21, 1862, where the *Tribune* elaborated its thesis that only slavery had produced the unnatural "commingling" of the races whereas "liberty may be trusted to separate them."

crawl through the hair matting of the very thickest skulls that we cannot afford to make the Rebels a present of Four Millions of People, who only wait to be civilly asked to help us rather than serve our enemies. Then the supreme absurdity, the preposterous folly, of voting to confiscate the other property of the Rebels and leave them their slaves, will be manifest even to the dullest and dimmest vision. . . . Never mind. The American People are under treatment. They need to be cured of their malignant hate and scorn of Four Millions of their fellow country-men, hitherto held in a worse than Egyptian bondage. The disease is chronic and deep-seated; but the treatment is heroic, and must ultimately prevail. Have faith, be patient, and on with the War for the Union!"[28]

The military necessities of 1862 had obviously given the *Tribune* itself some of the "heroic treatment" it mentioned, for it was at least now able to admit that Northerners in general, and not just Irishmen or Democrats, suffered from a chronic, deep-seated racial prejudice. Yet in almost the same breath that the New York newspaper cried that the nation's "scorn and hate" for Negroes might be responsible for the possible loss of the war, it turned around to limit the nation's problem to slavery. "A Radical is one who wishes to go to the root of the matter," the *Tribune* explained. "The root of this Rebellion is Slavery. Not only is [the Rebellion] confined absolutely to Slave States, but its vitality is greatest in the most intensely slaveholding sections of those states. . . ." Nothing could conceal the fact it was "Slavery, and nothing but Slavery, that now seeks and menaces the permanent division and destruction of the American Union."[29]

Arguing not only for emancipation but also for a Federal policy of arming the Negroes, the *Tribune* pointed out that "not one of that race, who know as well as we that the war hinges upon them, is allowed to shed his

28 May 29, 1862; see also May 3, 1862.
29 June 27, July 2, 1862.

blood in this quarrel." "Why is this dark blood cherished so royally among us?" the editorial asked. "There is a black somebody under the heel of the power which is aiming at the nation's life," a subsequent issue declared, "and it is generally conceded that a sharp twinge in that heel just now would be highly salutary to the nation."[30]

The question of arming the freedmen who came within Federal jurisdiction in various parts of the South became a major issue in 1863. The position of many Republicans was probably not too different from that of the Unionist fugitive from Bedford county in middle Tennessee, whose letter to the *Tribune* received editorial commendation and deserves to be quoted at some length: "I am often asked up here, 'will the nigger fight?' As many are interested in the question, I will answer. I am more puzzled over the nigger questions after twenty years' study of them than I was at the beginning. The nigger, like the spirit-rapper, seems to have made fools of the wisest men of the land. But I am proud to say that I have never in all my life said one good word for Slavery, for, as I have

[30] July 10, August 2, 1862. See also July 11, 17, 1862. Early in 1863, after Lincoln's Emancipation Proclamation, the Radical demand was for arming not just Northern Negroes but freedmen in the South. The *Tribune's* correspondent in Norfolk, Virginia, reported that some 10,000 able-bodied Negroes at the "contraband station" near there were eager to fight for the Union. "A low rate of pay only ought to be given to these recruits," the correspondent urged. ". . . They ought not to be paid as much as white men— nor in any way placed on an equality with them. The negroes themselves do not desire or expect this. If they are well clothed, well armed, paid at the rate of $6 per month and a ration, and led by white officers, they will be content, and more than content." To the alleged "Doughface" cry that if white men could not save the country it was not worth saving, this newsman responded: "Well, we can save it by white men, and if necessary will do it. But as white men, on the average, are worth a little more than black ones, let us save the country and save all the white men who are worth saving by the aid of a few thousand blacks. We cannot see any objection to this, except such as have always existed in the minds of the 'nigger worshippers.' They count white men very cheap—but negroes are too valuable to be shot or bayoneted." February 10, 1863.

seen it, I have never known a good thing of it. That the nigger is a curse to all people he mingles with, I am fully convinced. He is as a slave a natural born slink and a coward. But the Southern nigger has a great deal of pride in him; if you can rouse that feeling, and inspire him with the clear hope of being free, I believe he will make a good soldier,—a very desperate soldier. The experiment is to be tried. None of us know. As a Southern man, I could wish the nigger might not appear in this war; but if it will aid in putting down the Rebellion (as it will), and save the effusion of blood less interested in the questions at issue than his, why, you may arm niggers, mules, or whatever else can be effective, and welcome, so far as I feel concerned. Arming the niggers is touching the galled jade exactly at the spot to make her wince most. It is retaliative and retributive justice."[31]

This "retaliative and retributive justice" in hitting the South "at the spot to make her wince most" was an obvious and admitted motive behind the *Tribune's* successful demands for a policy of emancipation and arming of Negroes. But there was also a curious hope held out to the North that the abolition of slavery would rid the North of its own relative handful of Negroes. Though now in a new context and stripped of an earlier connection with the idea of peaceful secession of the Gulf states, the *Tribune's* prediction of the voluntary segregation of the freedmen in the South was obviously consistent with and derived from its prewar notions about an Africanized zone. In the days immediately preceding Greeley's famed "Prayer of Twenty Millions" to Lincoln, demanding an emancipation policy, the *Tribune* attempted to calm Northern fears that such a policy would bring Negroes northward by asserting that, "Nothing ever drove the negro away from his genial South but Slavery, and the overthrow of Slavery will fix his residence where his welfare and his tenacious local attach-

[31] May 9, 1863.

ments prompt him to stay." Besides, "the laboring white men" of the North, whether native or foreign, had the least cause of all to hate the Negro since he removed "from them the discredit of the lowest social place, and does offices which leave [the white man] free to compete for the highest rewards of industry." The very day before Greeley's "Prayer" appeared, the *Tribune* again assured its readers: "In due season, the Blacks will freely and naturally gravitate toward some tropical region, being replaced by Whites at least in all the Border-State region. But this matter will regulate itself if well let alone."[32]

This idea that racial adjustment would be a matter of concern only in the South, provided slavery were abolished, did not derive its authority solely from editorial pronouncements of the *Tribune*. No less a personage than General David Hunter, an early hero of abolitionists after Lincoln revoked his order freeing slaves in his department, sent word from Port Royal, South Carolina, that nothing was more absurd in the North "than the bugbear of 'a general migration of negroes to the North,' as a necessary sequence of emancipation. So far is this from being a fact," Hunter continued, "that although it is well known that I give passes North to all negroes asking them, not more than a dozen have applied to me for such passes since my arrival here, their local attachments being apparently much stronger than with the white race. My experience leads me to believe that the exact reverse of the received opinion on this subject would form the rule, and that nearly if not quite all the negroes

[32] August 8, 19, 1862. When certain citizens of Syracuse, New York, had earlier petitioned the state legislature for a law prohibiting Negro immigration into the state (similar to laws already existing in Indiana, Illinois, and some other Northern states), the *Tribune* had opposed the idea by arguing that when slavery was abolished "the fifty thousand [Negroes] we now have will soon dwindle to thirty, twenty, and ultimately to ten thousand or less, without the help of proscriptive legislation." April 23, 1862. The same idea was repeated more forcibly early in 1863, when Lincoln's Emancipation Proclamation was still new. *Ibid.*, January 12, 1863.

of the North would migrate South whenever they shall be at liberty to do so without fear of the auction-block."[33]

In explaining the alleged preference of the Negro for Southern parts, the *Tribune* liked to emphasize "genial climate," "warm blood," and similar matters. Its own columns, however, furnished more substantial clues to explain whatever truth the idea had. The bloody race riots that occurred in New York and other Northern cities in 1863 still lay in the future when a *Tribune* correspondent who had been traveling among slaveholders in Arkansas and Tennessee declared: "The hatred of the negro at the South is far less prevalent than in the Northern States. . . . In childhood they have mingled together . . . so that the prejudice against the *complexion* of the negroes at the South scarcely exists. With the Southern people it is simply a prejudice against their becoming free." Once they had become free, however, the correspondent believed that the Southern whites would "find the whole race alike useful and essential to them as hired servants and laborers." The Negroes would become a "useful peasantry," the benevolent paternalism of the whites would reassert itself, and with "Nature and Providence" taking care of things "the great problem of emancipation will be solved" throughout the South. A more tough-minded correspondent in New Orleans, who had no inclination to gloss over racial difficulties in the South,

[33] *Tribune*, August 4, 1862. The Democratic New York *Herald* pounced on Hunter's statement as an argument against arming Negroes. They might turn their guns on Northern soldiers, the *Herald* suggested, since the "mutual antipathy between the Northern man and the negro has ever been far greater than between the Southern man and the black race." Quoted in *Tribune*, August 7, 1862. Writing on the "Contrabands in Washington," a *Tribune* correspondent reported that the superintendent of the large camp for Negroes north of the city had made a special check about the Negro's alleged desire to go North and found that "of the 3,500 who have passed under his charge during the four months of his possession of the office, not 35 were found who were willing to go farther North." *Ibid.*, November 7, 1862.

put the matter more bluntly when he confessed his conclusions: " 'Between the devil and the deep sea' is a
nautical conception of a dilemma. Between Jeff. Davis's
threats of hanging [Negro soldiers] and the wicked prejudice, hatred, contempt, and ill usage experienced at our
hands, the poor Africans are evilly entreated."[34]

Confronted by vigorous attempts in both Pennsylvania and New Jersey to secure laws prohibiting Negro
immigration, the *Tribune* finally faced up to the truth
in its editorials. "The Blacks, even in the Free States,"
it avowed, "are yet a despised, buffeted, ill-used race. In
the vulgar estimate, the 'Jim Crow' of the cheap theaters
and singing saloons—a low, ignorant, sensual trifler and
buffoon—is their typical representative. Loyal Whites
have generally become willing that they should fight, but
the great majority have no faith that they will really do
so." The *Tribune* had confessed the true bleakness of the
racial situation in the North, yet it also showed clearly
that it at least had made progress in the direction
of genuine liberalism: "We make no pretense, and never
did make any, to special friendship for the Blacks. Believing justice to each to be every man's true interest,
we would gladly see our constitutions, laws, our public
opinion and social usages, so modified that every human
being should be treated according to his worth, in utter
disregard of his race or color." And for the sake of all
more than just for the sake of the Negroes, the *Tribune*
hoped to see a "general response to the call for Afric-
American Volunteers to put down the Rebellion."[35]

There was indeed truth in the *Tribune's* confession in
October 1862 that "Sixteen months of active war have
instructed, tamed, and sobered us." Grim military necessities were obviously the best teachers of the time, but
the *Tribune*, like many Republican spokesmen, had always had a penchant for the loftier and more abstract

[34] *Tribune*, December 5, 1862, February 21, 1863.
[35] May 1, 1863.

principles. As the war progressed the New York newspaper increasingly applied these principles to the whole question of the Negro. A newspaper in Portland, Maine, attacked the emancipation policy as merely a first step in an "unnatural and unwise" interference in "God's immutable laws" which had designed the "inferior race" to be subordinated to white men. "Call this order slavery as at the South, or degradation as at the North," the Maine spokesman declared, "and you won't alter the nature of it, nor make the negro any less a negro, nor his natural servitude any less obvious and severe." To this blast the *Tribune* responded, both clearly and cogently, that if God had made Negroes inferior "no constitution or statute can possibly countervail that decree, nor does it require the aid of either to insure its execution." More positively, and in a manner reminiscent of Thomas Jefferson, the *Tribune* added: "The controlling consideration in the premises is that *Human Rights do not depend on the equality of Man or Races*, but are wholly independent of them."[36]

Principle did, however, need buttressing by practical considerations, and the *Tribune* warned that the North should "beware of persistence in injustice and prejudice against the negro, lest we have him against us." An early counterproclamation of emancipation by the Confederate government might "bring thousands of blacks into the field against our soldiers." For after all, the editorial concluded, the "slaves know their masters; in many instances they trust them; us they have hitherto beheld through a distorted medium, nor has our general behavior toward them been of a character to correct their early impressions." Soon reverting to the principle of the matter, the *Tribune* declared in one of its most prophetic moments, that the nation was "destined to be saved, 'yet so as by fire.'" "We are to be saved, because experience, trial, suffering, are slowly teaching us to be humane and

[36] October 6, 7, 1862. Italicized in original.

just, even to the despised 'niggers.' If we are too tardy in mastering this lesson, we shall temporarily fail, and History will inscribe on our tomb, 'Here lies a people who would not be just to their humblest caste, and, by thus trampling on the rights of others, they justly forfeited and sacrificed their own.' "[37]

The *Tribune* had, in truth, finally found its moral footing with reference to the problem of racial adjustment. The urgent necessities of the Civil War itself had made that possible. Yet neither the *Tribune* nor any other Republican spokesman had come upon any real solution other than the abolition of slavery itself. That done, all else would take care of itself. The shallow optimism and superficial thinking of many antislavery Republicans might be epitomized in the *Tribune's* assertion, made while it was still demanding an emancipation policy: "What a good time is coming when the negro questions shall all have been legislated upon, and when the African race will no longer be a bone of contention in our legislative halls!" Then when the President finally issued his preliminary proclamation, Greeley's journal exulted, "By a word the President transforms a State sunk in the semi-barbarism of a medieval age to the light and civilization of the Nineteenth Christian Century."[38]

Republicans favored policies that gave Federal tariff protection to manufacturers, public lands to railway companies, and national banks to businessmen and financiers. Yet liberty and laissez faire were, for a considerable period, the magic words for any problem of racial adjustment that the South might face. "Give the negro liberty, not license," a *Tribune* correspondent wrote from Hilton Head, South Carolina, "and we need not be very solicitous about his temporal welfare. He will provide for himself much better than we can provide for him." Underscoring the same view, a *Tribune* editorial de-

[37] October 17, November 25, 1862.
[38] April 25, September 24, 1862.

clared that "Freedom will speedily and surely renovate" the devastated South. Many freedmen would be eager to buy land (the editorial did not say what they would buy it with), and the South would provide such a vast market for manufactures that the "artisans of the whole world will be gainers." Why, with a peace that preserved the Union and destroyed slavery the "South will soon forget the bitterness of defeat in the consciousness of new-born security, of new hope; while Christendom will heartily congratulate us that the black cloud which threatened us with destruction has given place to the gladdest and most genial sunshine." From the "furnace of affliction" the nation would have "emerged fairer and stronger than ever."[39]

Such rosy optimism could not last long in the stubborn persistence of bitterly divided feelings about the race question, even in the North. In the spring of 1864 when the Senate refused to pass a bill equalizing the pay of white and Negro soldiers and to move against the Jim Crow system on the District of Columbia's streetcars, the *Tribune* confessed its weariness of the whole matter: "We deprecate the introduction in Congress of many bills relating to Slavery or Negroes. We wish it were possible forthwith to carry a very brief Constitutional Amendment prohibiting Slavery evermore on every acre of North American soil, and there stop. We would gladly obtain this by compact whereby all further allusion to Slavery or Negroes in Congress should be forbidden evermore." Then when certain Democratic editors chortled over the failure of one of the colonization ventures that Lincoln had encouraged, the *Tribune* bitterly and ironically suggested that if a simple solution of "this Black Problem" were all that was required, "without any consideration of good faith, brotherhood or benevolence," then the thing to do was simply to "slit the weasands of all colored people, without distinction of age or sex.

[39] March 10, March 28, 1863.

Official butchers might be appointed to superintend this humane slaughter, and if the salaries were made large enough, we believe the offices would be filled without any delay or difficulty."[40]

The *Tribune* obviously did not have much success in persuading the Northern public at large to consider the matter of racial adjustment in a philosophic, calm manner. The last half of 1864 found Greeley's newspaper comparatively quiet on the whole subject, except for a steady insistence on the complete abolition of slavery as the grand panacea for the nation's problems. On the very last day of the year an editorial reminded Northern readers who were still apprehensive about the effects of emancipation on their communities that only the institution of slavery drove Negroes northward, and once that was gone "they will have no inducement to migrate hitherward."

By the time the nightmare of the war ended in the spring of 1865, the New York *Tribune*, the nation's most powerful and prestigious Republican newspaper, had traveled some distance from the "principles" of keeping the West for white men and allowing the "mass of barbarism" in the deep South peacefully to separate itself from the rest of the nation. The sectional and party oracle had more or less backed into the belief that in the matter of racial adjustment in the United States human rights did not "depend on the equality of Man or Races, but are wholly independent of them." This kind of principle of equal rights was one that the majority of Americans in the mid-twentieth century would not only accept but try honestly to give substance to in legislation and judicial rulings affecting most if not all of the vital areas of the nation's life. There is no evidence, however, that the majority of the Republican party, much less of the Northern people as a whole, had truly come to accept the principle in 1865. On the contrary, the evi-

[40] February 29, March 25, 1864.

dence suggests that most Northerners were victims of the same racist convictions that held sway in the South. Professor C. Vann Woodward has suggested quite correctly that after the war the Radicals committed the country to a third great war aim, an aim in addition to Union and emancipation, and that was "a guarantee of equality" that popular convictions were not prepared to sustain. In the Fourteenth and Fifteenth Amendments the nation made legal commitments that had "overreached moral persuasion."[41]

Historians who yet insist on interpreting the Civil War as a moral crusade by righteous Republicans and Northerners against a wicked Southern slavocracy are but parrotting the empty, partisan shibboleths of a century ago. Perhaps it would be a closer approximation to the impossibly complicated truth if we recognized, once and for all, that neither North nor South of a century ago had exclusive title to tragically narrow vision and deficient morality.

[41] "Equality: The Deferred Commitment," in *The Burden of Southern History* (Baton Rouge, 1960), p. 83.

CHAPTER 16

THE NORTHERN
RESPONSE TO SLAVERY

BY MARTIN DUBERMAN

THE abolitionist movement never became the major channel of Northern antislavery sentiment. It remained in 1860 what it had been in 1830: the small but not still voice of radical reform. An important analytical problem thus arises: why did most Northerners who disapproved of slavery become "nonextensionists" rather than abolitionists? Why did they prefer to attack slavery indirectly, by limiting its spread, rather than directly, by seeking to destroy it wherever it existed?

On a broad level, the answer involves certain traits in the national character. In our society of abundance, prosperity has been the actual condition—or the plausible aspiration—of the majority. Most Americans have been too absorbed in the enjoyment or pursuit of possessions to take much notice of the exactions of the system. Even when inequalities have become too pronounced or too inclusive any longer to be comfortably ignored, efforts at relief have usually been of a partial and halfhearted kind. Any radical attack on social problems would compromise the national optimism; it would suggest fundamental defects, rather than occasional malfunctions. And so the majority has generally found it necessary to label "extreme" any measures which call for large-scale readjustment. No one reasonably contented welcomes extensive dislocation; what seems peculiarly American is the disbelief, under *all* circumstances, in the necessity of such dislocation.

Our traditional recoil from "extremism" can be defended. Complex problems, it might be said, require complex solutions; or, to be more precise, complex problems have no solutions—at best, they can be but partially adjusted. If even this much is to be possible, the approach must be flexible, piecemeal, pragmatic. The clear-cut blueprint for reform, with its utopian demand for total solution, intensifies rather than ameliorates disorder.

There is much to be said for this defense of the American way—in the abstract. The trouble is that the theory of gradualism and the practice of it have not been the same. Too often Americans have used the gradualist argument as a technique of evasion rather than as a tool for change, not as a way of dealing with difficult problems slowly and carefully, but as an excuse for not dealing with them at all. We do not want time for working out our problems—we do not want problems, and we will use the argument of time as a way of not facing them. As a chosen people, we are meant only to have problems which are self-liquidating. All of which is symptomatic of our conviction that history is the story of inevitable progress, that every day in every way we *will* get better and better even though we make no positive efforts towards that end.

Before 1845, the Northern attitude toward slavery rested on this comfortable belief in the benevolence of history. Earlier, during the 1830's, the abolitionists had managed to excite a certain amount of uneasiness about the institution by invoking the authority of the Bible and the Declaration of Independence against it. Alarm spread still further when mobs began to prevent abolitionists from speaking their minds or publishing their opinions, and when the national government interfered with the mails and the right of petition. Was it possible, men began to ask, that the abolitionists were right in contending that slavery, if left alone, would not die out but expand, would become more not less vital to the country's interests? Was it possible that slavery might even end by infecting free institutions themselves?

The apathetic majority was shaken, but not yet profoundly aroused; the groundwork for widespread antislavery protest was laid, but its flowering awaited further developments. The real watershed came in 1845, when Texas was annexed to the Union, and war with Mexico followed. The prospect now loomed of a whole series of new slave states. It finally seemed clear that the mere passage of time would not bring a solution; if slavery was ever to be destroyed, more active resistance would be necessary. For the first time large numbers of Northerners prepared to challenge the dogma that slavery was a local matter in which the free states had no concern. A new era of widespread, positive resistance to slavery had opened.

Yet such new resolve as had been found was not channeled into a heightened demand for the abolition of the institution, but only into a demand that its further extension be prevented. By 1845 Northerners may have lost partial, but not total confidence in "Natural Benevolence"; they were now wiser Americans perhaps, but Americans nonetheless. More positive action against slavery, they seemed to be saying, was indeed required, but nothing too positive. Containing the institution would, in the long run, be tantamount to destroying it; a more direct assault was unnecessary. In this sense, the doctrine of nonextension was but a more sophisticated version of the standard faith in "time."[1]

One need not question the sincerity of those who believed that nonextension would ultimately destroy slavery,

[1] Arresting slavery's further spread, Lincoln said, would "place it where the public mind shall rest in the belief that it is in course of ultimate extinction. . ." ("House Divided" speech, June 16, 1858, Roy P. Basler, ed. *The Collected Works of Abraham Lincoln*, New Brunswick, 1953, II, 461.)

in order to recognize that such a belief partook of wishful thinking. Even if slavery was contained, there remained large areas in the Southern states into which the institution could still expand; even without further expansion, there was no guarantee that slavery would cease to be profitable; and finally, even should slavery cease to be profitable, there was no certainty that the South, psychologically, would feel able to abandon it. Non-extension, in short, was hardly a fool-proof formula. Yet many Northerners chose to so regard it. And thus the question remains: why did not an aroused antislavery conscience turn to more certain measures and demand more unequivocal action?

To have adopted the path of direct abolition, first of all, might have meant risking individual respectability. The unsavory reputation of those already associated with abolitionism was not likely to encourage converts to it. Still, if that doctrine had been really appealing, the disrepute of its earlier adherents could not alone have kept men from embracing it. Association with the "fanatics" could have been smoothed simply by rehabilitating their reputations; their notoriety, it could have been said, had earlier been exaggerated—it had been the convenient invention of an apathetic majority to justify its own indifference to slavery. When, after 1861, public opinion did finally demand a new image of the abolitionists, it was readily enough produced. The mere reputation of abolitionism, therefore, would not have been sufficient to repel men from joining its ranks. Hostility to the movement had to be grounded in a deeper source—fear of the doctrine of "immediatism" itself.

Immediatism challenged the Northern hierarchy of values. To many, a direct assault on slavery meant a direct assault on private property and the Union as well. Fear for these values clearly inhibited antislavery fervor (though possibly a reverse trend operated as well—concern for property and Union may have been stressed in order to justify the convenience of "going slow" on slavery).

As devout Lockians, Americans did believe that the sanctity of private property constituted the essential cornerstone for all other liberties. If property could not be protected in a nation, neither could life nor liberty. And the Constitution, so many felt, had upheld the legitimacy of holding property in men. True, the Constitution had not mentioned slavery by name, and had not overtly declared in its favor, but in giving the institution certain indirect guarantees (the three-fifths clause; noninterference for twenty-one years with the slave trade; the fugitive slave proviso), the Constitution had seemed to sanction it. At any rate no one could be sure. The intentions of the Founding Father remained uncertain, and one of the standing debates of the ante-bellum generation was whether the Constitution had been meant by them to be a pro- or an antislavery document.[2] Since the issue was unresolved, Northerners remained uneasy, uncertain how far they could go in attacking slavery without at the same time attacking property.

Fear for property rights was underscored by fear for the Union. The South had many times warned that if her rights and interests were not heeded, she would leave the Union and form a separate confederation. The tocsin had been sounded with enough regularity so that to some it had begun to sound like hollow bluster. But there was always the chance that if the South felt sufficiently provoked she might yet carry out the threat.

It is difficult today fully to appreciate the horror with which most Northerners regarded the potential breakup

[2] For a sample pamphlet exchange, see Lysander Spooner, *Unconstitutionality of Slavery* (Boston, 1845), and Wendell Phillips, *Review of Lysander Spooner's Essays on the Unconstitutionality of Slavery* (Boston, 1845).

of the Union. The mystical qualities which surrounded "Union" were no less real for being in part irrational. Lincoln struck a deep chord for his generation when he spoke of the Union as the "last best hope of earth"; that the American experiment was thought the "best" hope may have been arrogant, a hope at all, naïve, but such it was to the average American, convinced of his own superiority and the possibility of the world learning by example. Today, more concerned with survival than improvement, we are bemused (when we are not cynical) about "standing examples for mankind," and having seen the ghastly deeds done in the name of patriotism, we are impatient at signs of national fervor. But 100 years ago, the world saw less danger in nationalism, and Americans, enamored with their own extraordinary success story, were especially prone to look on love of country as one of the noblest of human sentiments. Even those Southerners who had ceased to love the Union had not ceased to love the idea of nationhood; they merely wished to transfer allegiance to a more worthy object.

Those who wanted to preserve the old Union acted from a variety of motives: the Lincolns, who seem primarily to have valued its spiritual potential, were joined by those more concerned with maintaining its power potential; the Union was symbol of man's quest for a benevolent society—and for dominion. But if Northerners valued their government for differing reasons, they generally agreed on the necessity for preserving it. Even so, their devotion to the Union had its oscillations. In 1861 Lincoln and his party, in rejecting the Crittenden Compromise, seemed willing to jeopardize Union rather than risk the further expansion of slavery (perhaps because they never believed secession would really follow, though this complacency, in turn, might only have been a way of convincing themselves that a strong antislavery stand would not necessarily destroy the Union). After war broke out the value stress once more shifted: Lincoln's party now loudly insisted that the war was indeed being fought to preserve the Union, not to free the slaves. Thus did the coexisting values of Union and antislavery tear the Northern mind and confuse its allegiance.

The tension was compounded by the North's ambivalent attitude toward the Negro. The Northern majority, unlike most of the abolitionists, did not believe in the equality of races. The Bible (and the new science of anthropology) seemed to suggest that the Negro had been a separate, inferior creation meant for a position of servitude.[3] Where there was doubt on the doctrine of racial equality, its advocacy by the distrusted abolitionists helped to settle the matter in the negative.

It was possible, of course, to disbelieve in Negro equality, and yet disapprove of Negro slavery. Negroes were obviously men, even if an inferior sort, and as men they could not in conscience (the Christian-Democratic version) be denied the right to control their own souls and bodies. But if anti-Negro and antislavery sentiments were not actually incompatible, they were not mutually supportive either. Doubt of the Negro's capacity for citizenship continually blunted the edge of antislavery fervor. If God had intended the Negro for some subordinate role in society, perhaps a kind of benevolent slavery was, after all, the most suitable arrangement; so long as there was uncertainty, it might be better to await the slow unfolding of His intentions in His good time.

And so the average Northerner, even after he came actively to disapprove of slavery, continued to be hamstrung in his opposition to it by the competitive pull of other values. Should prime consideration be given to freeing the slaves, even though in the process the rights

[3] On this point see W. S. Jenkins, *Pro-Slavery Thought in the Old South* (Chapel Hill, 1935), and William Stanton, *The Leopard's Spots* (Chicago, 1960).

of property and the preservation of the Union were threatened? Should the future of the superior race be endangered in order to improve the lot of a people seemingly marked by Nature for a degraded station? Ideally, the North would have liked to satisfy its conscience about slavery and at the same time preserve the rest of its value system intact—to free the Negro and yet do so without threatening property rights or dislocating the Union. This struggle to achieve the best of all possible worlds runs like a forlorn hope throughout the ante-bellum period—the sad, almost plaintive quest by the American Adam for the perfect world he considered his birthright.

The formula of nonextension did seem, for a time, the perfect device for balancing these multiple needs. Non-extension would put slavery in the course of ultimate extinction without producing excessive dislocation; since slavery would not be attacked directly, nor its existence immediately threatened, the South would not be unduly fearful for her property rights, the Union would not be needlessly jeopardized, and a mass of free Negroes would not be precipitously thrust upon an unprepared public. Nonextension, in short, seemed a panacea, a formula which promised in time to do everything while for the present risking nothing. But like all panaceas, it ignored certain hard realities: would containment really lead to the extinction of slavery? would the South accept even a gradual dissolution of her peculiar institution? would it be right to sacrifice two or three more generations of Negroes in the name of uncertain future possibilities? Alas for the American Adam, so soon to be expelled from Eden.

The abolitionists, unlike most Northerners, were not willing to rely on future intangibles. Though often called impractical romantics, they were in some ways the most tough-minded of Americans. They had no easy faith in the benevolent workings of time or in the inevitable triumphs of gradualism. If change was to come, they argued, it would be the result of man's effort to produce it;

patience and inactivity had never yet helped the world's ills. Persistently, sometimes harshly, the abolitionists denounced delay and those who advocated it; they were tired, they said, of men using the councils of moderation to perpetuate injustice.

In their own day, and ever since, the abolitionists have faced a hostile majority; their policies have been ridiculed, their personalities reviled. Yet ridicule, like its opposite, adoration, is usually not the result of analysis but a substitute for it. Historians have for so long been absorbed in denouncing the abolitionists, that they have had scant energy left over for understanding them. The result is that we still know surprisingly little about the movement, and certainly not enough to warrant the general assumptions so long current in the historical profession.

Historians have assumed that the abolitionists were unified in their advocacy of certain broad policies—immediate emancipation, without compensation—and also unified in refusing to spell out details for implementing these policies. To some extent this traditional view is warranted. The abolitionists did agree almost unanimously (Gerrit Smith was one of the few exceptions) that slaveholders must not be compensated. One does not pay a man, they argued, for ceasing to commit a sin. Besides, the slaveholder had already been paid many times over in labor for which he had never given wages. Defensible though this position may have been in logic or morals, the abolitionists should perhaps have realized that public opinion would never support the confiscation of property, and should have modified their stand accordingly. But they saw themselves as prophets, not politicians; they were concerned with what was "right," not with what was possible, though they hoped that if men were once made aware of the right, they would find some practical way of implementing it.[4]

[4] See, for example, L. Maria Child, *The Right Way the Safe Way* (New York, 1860). After the Civil War began, the abolitionists modified their stand on compensation—thus showing that "pragmatic

The abolitionists were far less united on the doctrine of immediate emancipation—at least in the 1830's, before Southern intransigence and British experience in the West Indies, convinced almost all of them that gradualism was hopeless. But during the 1830's, there was a considerable spectrum of opinion as to when and how to emancipate the slave. Contrary to common myth, some of the abolitionists did advocate a period of prior education and training before the granting of full freedom. Men like Weld, Birney, and the Tappans, stressing the debasing experience of slavery, insisted only that gradual emancipation be immediately begun, not that emancipation itself be at once achieved.[5] This range of opinion has never been fully appreciated. It has been convenient, then and now, to believe that all abolitionists always advocated instantaneous freedom, for it thus became possible to denounce any call for emancipation as "patently impractical."

By 1840, however, most abolitionists had become im-

---

flexibility" of which they were supposedly devoid. In the winter of 1861, Garrison got up a petition to compensate loyal slaveholders, and in 1862, most abolitionists gave enthusiastic approval to plans for compensated emancipation in the District of Columbia.

[5] For sample abolitionist writings advocating gradual freedom, after apprenticeship, see L. Maria Child, *Anti-Slavery Catechism* (Newburyport, 1836), pp. 18-19; J. A. Thome and J. W. Alvord to T. Weld, February 9, 1836, *Letters of Theodore Dwight Weld, Angelina Grimké Weld, and Sarah Grimké, 1822-1844*, eds. G. H. Barnes and D. L. Dumond (New York, 1934), I, 257; C. K. Whipple, "The Abolitionists' Plan," *The Liberty Bell* (1845). Even Garrison was at first willing to hold newly freed slaves in "the benevolent restraint of guardianship" (*Thoughts on African Colonization* [Boston, 1832], pp. 79-80). Donald Mathews has pointed out to me that Benjamin Lundy in *The Genius of Universal Emancipation* printed many plans for gradual freedom (e.g., in the issues of September 5, 12, 15, 1825), but, discouraged by the lack of response, Lundy finally discontinued doing so. Thus it might be well to ask whether the abolitionists, in moving steadily toward "immediatism" (a shift largely completed by 1840), had not been driven to that position by the intransigence of their society in the preceding decade, rather than by any inherent "extremism" in their own temperaments.

mediatists, and that position, "practical" or not, did have a compelling moral urgency. Men learned how to be free, the immediatists argued, only by being free; slavery, no matter how attenuated, was by its very nature incapable of preparing men for those independent decisions necessary to adult responsibility. Besides, they insisted, the Negro, though perhaps debased by slavery, was no more incapacitated for citizenship than were many poor whites, whose rights no one seriously suggested curtailing.

The immediatist position was not free of contradiction. If slavery had been as horrendous as the abolitionists claimed, it was logical to expect that its victims would bear deep personality scars—greater than any disabilities borne by a poor white, no matter how degraded his position. Either slavery had not been this deadly, or, if it had, those recently freed from its toils could not be expected to move at once into the responsibilities of freedom. This contradiction was apparent to some immediatists, but there was reason for refusing to resolve it. Ordinarily, they said, a system of apprenticeship might be desirable, but if conditions to emancipation were once established, they could be used as a standing rationale for postponement; the Negro could be kept in a condition of semislavery by the self-perpetuating argument that he was not yet ready for his freedom.[6]

Moreover, any intermediary stage before full freedom would require the spelling out of precise "plans," and these would give the enemies of emancipation an opportunity to pick away at the impracticality of this or that detail. They would have an excuse for disavowing the broader policy under the guise of disagreeing with the specific means for achieving it. Better to concentrate on the larger issue and force men to take sides on that alone, the abolitionists argued, than to give them a chance to

[6] See, for example, James A. Thome and J. Horace Kimball, *Emancipation in the West Indies* (New York, 1838), pp. 83, 85, 108.

hide their opposition behind some supposed disapproval of detail.[7] Wendell Phillips, for one, saw the abolitionists' role as exclusively that of agitating the broader question. Their primary job, Phillips insisted, was to arouse the country's conscience rather than to spell out to it precise plans and formulas. *After* that conscience had been aroused, it would be time to talk of specific proposals; let the moral urgency of the problem be recognized, let the country be brought to a determination to rid itself of slavery, and ways and means to accomplish that purpose would be readily enough found.[8]

No tactical position could really have saved the abolitionists from the denunciation of those hostile to their basic goal. If the abolitionists spelled out a program for emancipation, their enemies would have a chance to pick at details; if they did not spell out a program, they could then be accused of vagueness and impracticality. Hostility can always find its own justification.[9]

A second mode of attack on the abolitionists has centered on their personalities rather than their policies. The stereotype which has long had currency sees the abolitionist as a disturbed fanatic, a man self-righteous and self-deceived, motivated not by concern for the Negro, as he may have believed, but by an unconscious drive to gratify certain needs of his own. Seeking to discharge

[7] For sample awareness of the dilemma inherent in "plans," see William Jay, *An Inquiry into . . . the American Colonization, and Anti-Slavery Societies* (New York, 1835), p. 197; "Instructions of the American Anti-Slavery Society to Theodore Weld," February 20, 1834, in Barnes and Dumond, *Weld-Grimké Letters*, I, 126.

[8] See, for example, his speech "Daniel O'Connell" in Wendell Phillips, *Speeches, Lectures, and Letters* (Boston, 1891), Second Series, pp. 384-420.

[9] I am not suggesting that all those who opposed immediatism were necessarily opposed to emancipation; no doubt some of those in opposition objected only to the means, not the end. I know of no way, though, to measure accurately the proportionate strength of the two groups, nor, more complicated still, the degree to which each actually understood its position.

either individual anxieties or those frustrations which came from membership in a "displaced élite," his anti-slavery protest was, in any case, a mere disguise for personal anguish.[10]

A broad assumption underlies this analysis which has never been made explicit—namely, that strong protest by an individual against social injustice is ipso facto proof of his disturbance. Injustice itself, in this view, is apparently never sufficient to arouse unusual ire in "normal" men, for normal men, so goes the canon, are always cautious, discreet, circumspect. Those who hold to this model of human behavior seem rarely to suspect that it may tell us more about their hierarchy of values than about the reform impulse it pretends to describe. Argued in another context, the inadequacies of the stereotype become more apparent: if normal people do not protest

[10] In pointing out what seems to me certain inadequacies in this stereotype, I do not mean to imply that no psychological or sociological explanation of the abolitionists is possible. Wide personality variations among individual abolitionists is not incompatible with their sharing a few traits in common—these traits being the crucial ones in explaining their "reform motivation." But if so, these common traits have not, in my view, yet been delineated. Which is not to say that they did not exist, nor that they may not be successfully isolated in the future. There could, for example, be some point in examining the "sociological truism" that "when family integration weakens, the individual becomes more available for participation in some kinds of collective behavior" (Leonard Broom and Philip Selznick, *Sociology*, New York, 1957, p. 406), or the suggestion by Seward Hiltner that "the person who is vociferous and diligent on behalf of minority groups may be impelled by unsolved authority problems" ("Psychology and Morality," *Princeton Alumni Weekly*, September 22, 1964). Then there is the possibility, first suggested to me in conversation with Silvan Tomkins, of a connection between "being good to others" and an unfulfilled (because frightening) need to get close to people; by expressing concern for the unfortunate it becomes possible to discharge safely (because impersonally), some of the pent-up need for warmth and affection. Needless to say, all the cautions I try to outline in this essay against current psycho-social interpretations of the abolitionists, would apply to any future interpretations as well.

"excessively" against injustice, then we should be forced to condemn as neurotic all those who protested with passion against the Nazi persecution of the Jews.

Some of the abolitionists, it is true, *were* palpable neurotics, men who were not comfortable within themselves and therefore not comfortable with others, men whose "reality-testing" was poor, whose life styles were pronouncedly compulsive, whose relationships were unusual compounds of demand and phantasy. Such neurotics *were* in the abolitionist movement—the Parker Pillsburys, Stephen Fosters, Abby Folsoms. Yet even here we must be cautious, for our diagnostic accuracy can be blurred if the life style under evaluation is sharply different from our own. Many of the traits of the abolitionists which today "put us off" were not peculiar to them, but rather to their age—the declamatory style, the abstraction and idealization of issues, the tone of righteous certainty, the religious context of argumentation. Thus the evangelical rhetoric of the movement, with its thunderous emphasis on sin and retribution, can sound downright "queer" (and thus "neurotic") to the 20th century skeptic, though in its day common enough to abolitionists and nonabolitionists alike.

Then, too, even when dealing with the "obvious" neurotics, we must be careful in the link we establish between their pathology and their protest activity. It is one thing to demonstrate an individual's "disturbance" and quite another then to explain all of his behavior in terms of it. Let us suppose, for example, that Mr. Jones is a reformer; he is also demonstrably "insecure." It does not necessarily follow that he is a reformer *because* he is insecure. The two may seem logically related (that is, if one's mind automatically links "protest" with "neurosis"), but we all know that many things can be logical without being true.

Even if we establish the neurotic behavior of certain

members of a group, we have not, thereby, established the neurotic behavior of *all* members of that group. The tendency to leap from the particular to the general is always tempting, but because we have caught one benighted monsignor with a boy scout does not mean we have conclusively proved that all priests are pederasts. Some members of every group are disturbed; put the local police force, the Medal of Honor winners, or the faculty of a university under the Freudian microscope, and the number of cases of "palpable disturbance" would probably be disconcertingly high. But what *precisely* does their disturbance tell us about the common activities of the group to which they belong—let alone about the activities of the disturbed individuals themselves?

Actually, behavioral patterns for many abolitionists do *not* seem notably eccentric. Men like Birney, Weld, Lowell, Quincy—abolitionists all—formed good relationships, saw themselves in perspective, played and worked with zest and spontaneity, developed their talents, were aware of worlds beyond their own private horizons. They all had their tics and their traumas—as who does not—but the evidence of health is abundant and predominant. Yet most historians have preferred to ignore such men when discussing the abolitionist movement. And the reason, I believe, is that such men conform less well than do the Garrisons to the assumption that those who become deeply involved in social protest are necessarily those who are deeply disturbed.

To evaluate this assumption further, some effort must be made to understand current findings in the theory of human motivation. This is difficult terrain for the historian, not made more inviting by the sharp disagreements which exist among psychologists themselves (though these disagreements do help to make us aware of the complexities involved). Recent motivational research, though not conclusive, throws some useful new perspectives on "reformers."[11]

A reaction has currently set in among psychologists against the older behaviorist model of human conduct. The behaviorists told us that men's actions were determined by the nature of the stimulus exerted upon them, and that their actions always pointed towards the goal of "tension reduction." There was little room in behaviorist theory for freedom of choice, for rationality, or for complex motives involving abstract ideas as well as instinctive drives.

Without denying the tension-reducing motives of certain kinds of human behavior, a number of psychologists are now insisting on making room for another order of motivation, involving more than the mere "restoration of equilibrium." Mature people, they believe—that is, those who have a realistic sense of self—*can* act with deliberation and *can* exercise control over their actions. This new view presumes an active intellect, an intellect capable of interpreting sensory data in a purposive way. The power of reflection, of self-objectification, makes possible a dynamic as opposed to a merely instinctive life. Men, in short, need not be wholly driven by habit and reflex; they need not be mere automatons who respond in predictable ways to given stimuli. Rather, they can be reasoning organisms capable of decision and choice. Among the rational choices mature men may make is to commit themselves to a certain set of ethical values. They are not necessarily forced to such a commitment by personal or social tensions (of which they are usually unaware), but may come to that commitment deliberately, after reflective consideration.

11 For recent discussions, see R. S. Peters, *The Concept of Motivation* (London, 1958); Gardner Lindzey, ed. *Assessment of Human Motives* (New York, 1958); Robert C. Birney and Richard C. Teevan, eds. *Measuring Human Motivation* (New York, 1962); Erich Fromm, "The Revolutionary Character" in *The Dogma of Christ* (New York, 1963).

The new psychology goes even one step further. It suggests that the very definition of maturity may be the ability to commit oneself to abstract ideals, to get beyond the selfish, egocentric world of children. This does not mean that every man who reaches outward does so from mature motives; external involvement may also be a way of acting out sick phantasies. The point is only that "commitment" need not be a symptom of personality disturbance. It is just as likely to be a symptom of maturity and health.

It does not follow, of course, that all abolitionists protested against slavery out of mature motives; some may have been, indeed were, "childish neurotics." But if we agree that slavery was a fearful injustice, and if motivational theory now suggests that injustice will bring forth protest from mature men, it seems reasonable to conclude that at least some of those who protested strongly against slavery must have done so from "healthy" motives.

The hostile critic will say that the abolitionists protested *too* strongly to have been maturely motivated. But when is a protest *too* strong? For a defender of the status quo, the answer (though never stated in these terms) would be: when it succeeds. For those not dedicated to the current status, the answer is likely to be: a protest is too strong when it is out of all proportion to the injustice it indicts. Could any verbal protest have been too strong against holding fellow human beings as property? From a moral point of view, certainly not, though from a practical point of view, perhaps. That is, the abolitionist protest might have been *too* strong if it somehow jeopardized the very goal it sought to achieve—the destruction of human slavery. But no one has yet shown this to have been the case.[12]

---

[12] In this regard, there has been a persistent confusion of two separate indictments against the abolitionists: first, that they disrupted the peace, and second (in the classic formulation given by Daniel Webster), that they "bound more firmly than before" the

At any rate, current findings in motivational theory suggest that at the very least we must cease dealing in blanket indictments, in simple-minded categorizing and elementary stereotyping. Such exercises may satisfy our present-day hostility to "reformers," but they do not satisfy the complex demands of historical truth. We need an awareness of the wide variety of human beings who became involved in the abolitionist movement, and an awareness of the complexity of human motivation sufficient to save us from summing up men and movements in two or three unexamined adjectives.

Surely there is now evidence enough to suggest that commitment and concern need not be aberrations; they may represent the profoundest elements of our humanity. Surely there are grounds for believing that those who protested strongly against slavery were not all misguided fanatics or frustrated neurotics—though by so believing it becomes easier to ignore the injustice against which they protested. Perhaps it is time to ask whether the abolitionists, in insisting that slavery be ended, were indeed those men of their generation furthest

---

bonds of the slave. It is undeniably true that the abolitionists contributed to the polarization of public opinion, and to that extent, to the "disturbance of the peace" (which is not the same as war). But it does not follow that because they stirred up passions, they made freeing the slaves more difficult. This would be true only if it could be shown that the slaves could have been freed *without* first arousing and polarizing opinion. The evidence does not seem to support such a position. In all the long years before the abolitionists began their campaign, the North had managed to remain indifferent to the institution, and the South had done almost nothing, even in the most gradual way, toward ameliorating it. Had the abolitionists not aroused public debate on slavery, there is no guarantee that anyone else would have; and without such a debate it seems unlikely that measures against the institution would have been taken. The fact that the debate became heated, moreover, cannot wholly be explained by the terms in which the abolitionists raised it; what must also be taken into account is the fact that the South, with some possible exceptions in the border area, reacted intransigently to *any* criticism of the institution, however mild the tone or gradual the suggestions.

removed from reality, or whether that description should be reserved for those Northerners who remained indifferent to the institution, and those Southerners who defended it as a "positive good." From the point of view of these men, the abolitionists were indeed mad, but it is time we questioned the sanity of the point of view.

Those Northerners who were not indifferent to slavery—a large number after 1845—were nonetheless prone to view the abolitionist protest as "excessive," for it threatened the cherished values of private property and Union. The average Northerner may have found slavery disturbing, but convinced as he was that the Negro was an inferior, he did not find slavery monstrous. Certainly he did not think it an evil sufficiently profound to risk, by "precipitous action," the nation's present wealth or its future power. The abolitionists were willing to risk both. They thought it tragic that men should weigh human lives in the *same* scale as material possessions and abstractions of government. It is no less tragic that we continue to do so.

PART VI: CONCLUDING

CHAPTER 17

ABOLITIONISTS, FREEDOM-RIDERS, AND

THE TACTICS OF AGITATION

BY HOWARD ZINN

FEW groups in American history have taken as much abuse from professional historians as that mixed crew of editors, orators, run-away slaves, free Negro militants, and gun-toting preachers known as the abolitionists. Many laymen sympathetic to the Negro have been inspired by Garrison, Phillips, Douglass, and the rest. Scholars, on the other hand (with a few exceptions), have scolded the abolitionists for their immoderation, berated them for their emotionalism, denounced them for bringing on the Civil War, or psychoanalyzed them as emotional deviates in need of recognition.

It is tempting to join the psychological game and try to understand what it is about the lives of academic scholars which keeps them at arm's length from the moral fervor of one of history's most magnificent crusades. Instead, I want to examine in fact the actions of the abolitionists, to connect them with later agitators against racial exclusiveness, and try to assess the value of "extremists," "radicals," and "agitators" in the bringing of desired social change.

At issue are a number of claims advanced by liberal-minded people who profess purposes similar to the radical reformers, but urge more moderate methods. To argue a case too heatedly, they point out, provokes the opponent to retaliation. To urge measures too extreme alienates possible allies. To ask for too much too soon results in getting nothing. To use vituperative language arouses emotions to a pitch which precludes rational consideration. To be dogmatic and inflexible prevents adjustment to rapidly changing situations. To set up a clash of extremes precipitates sharp conflict and violence.

All of these tactical sins, adding up to immoderation, extremism, impracticality, have been charged, at different times, by different people, to the American abolitionists. But the charges have not been carefully weighed or closely scrutinized as part of a discussion of preferable tactics for reform. I am claiming here only to initiate such a discussion.

Twentieth century man is marking the transition from chaotic and quite spontaneous renovation of the social fabric to purposeful and planned social change. In this transition, the tactics of such change need much more careful consideration than they have been given.

The Abolitionists

There is no denying the anger, the bitterness, the irascibility of the abolitionists. William Lloyd Garrison, dean of them all, wrote in blood in the columns of the *Liberator* and breathed fire from speakers' platforms all over New England. He shocked people: "I am ashamed of my country." He spoke abroad in brutal criticism of America: "I accuse the land of my nativity of insulting the majesty of Heaven with the greatest mockery that was ever exhibited to man." He burned the Constitution before several thousand witnesses on the lawn at Framingham, calling it "source and parent of all other atrocities—a covenant with death and an agreement with hell" and spurred the crowd to echo "Amen!"[1]

He provoked his opponents outrageously, and the South became apoplectic at the mention of his name.

[1] I have not given citations for the more familiar of Garrison's and Phillips' statements, and a few other quotations which are easily found in the better-known studies of the leading abolitionists, in biographies of Lincoln, and in standard works on the pre-Civil War period.

South Carolina offered $1,500 for conviction of any white person circulating the *Liberator*, and the Georgia legislature offered $500 for the arrest and conviction of Garrison. Garrison's wife feared constantly that reward-seekers would lie in wait for her husband on his way back from a meeting and snatch him off to Georgia.

Wendell Phillips, richer, and from a distinguished Boston family, was no softer. "Don't shilly-shally, Wendell," his wife whispered to him as he mounted the speakers' platform, and he never did. The anger that rose in him one day in 1835 as he watched Boston bluebloods drag Garrison through the streets never left him, and it remained focused on what he considered America's unbearable evil—slavery. "The South is one great brothel," he proclaimed.

Gradualism was not for Phillips. "No sir, we may not trifle or dally. . . . Revolution is the only thing, the only power, that ever worked out freedom for any people." The piety of New England did not intimidate him: "The American church—what is it? A synagogue of Satan." He scorned patriotic pride: "They sell a little image of us in the markets of Mexico, with a bowie knife in one side of the girdle, and a Colt's revolver in the other, a huge loaf of bread in the left hand, and a slave whip in the right. That is America!"

Phillips did not use the language of nonresistance as did Garrison. On that same green where Garrison burned the Constitution, Phillips said: "We are very small in numbers; we have got no wealth; we have got no public opinion behind us; the only thing that we can do is, like the eagle, simply to fly at our enemy, and pick out his eyes." And: "I want no man for President of these States . . . who has not got his hand half clenched, and means to close it on the jugular vein of the slave system the moment he reaches it, and has a double-edged dagger in the other hand, in case there is any missing in the strangulation."

But even Garrison and Phillips seem moderate against the figure of John Brown, lean and lusty, with two wives and twenty children, filled with enough anger for a regiment of agitators, declaring personal war on the institution of slavery. Speeches and articles were for others. The old man studied military strategy, pored over maps of the Southern terrain, raised money for arms, and planned the forcible liberation of slaves through rebellion and guerrilla warfare. On Pottowattomie Creek in the bleeding Kansas of 1856, on the Sabbath, he had struck one night at an encampment of proslavery men, killing five with a cold ferocity. On his way to the gallows, after the raid on the Harpers Ferry arsenal in Virginia in the fall of 1859, he wrote: "I John Brown am now quite certain that the crimes of this guilty land will never be purged away; but with Blood."

The Negro abolitionist, Frederick Douglass, newly freed from slavery himself, and long a believer in "moral suasion" to free others, talked with John Brown at his home in 1847 and came away impressed by his arguments. Two years later, Douglass told a Boston audience: "I should welcome the intelligence tomorrow, should it come, that the slaves had risen in the South, and that the sable arms which had been engaged in beautifying and adorning the South, were engaged in spreading death and devastation." He thought the Harpers Ferry plan wild, and would not go along; yet, to the end, he maintained that John Brown at Harpers Ferry began the war that ended slavery. "Until this blow was struck, the prospect for freedom was dim, shadowy, and uncertain. . . . When John Brown stretched forth his arm the sky was cleared."

These are the extremists. Did they hurt or help the cause of freedom? Or did they, if helping this cause, destroy some other value, like human life, lost in huge numbers in the Civil War? To put it another way, were they a hindrance rather than a help in abolishing slavery? Did their activities bring a solution at too great a cost? If we answer these questions, and others, we may throw light on the uses or disuses of modern-day agitators and immoderates, whose cries, if not as shrill as Garrison's, are as unpleasant to some ears, and whose actions, if not as violent as John Brown's, are just as distasteful to those who urge caution and moderation.

What is Extremism?

The first four pages of a well-known book on Civil War politics (T. Harry Williams, *Lincoln and the Radicals*) refers to abolitionists, individually and collectively, in the following terms: "radical . . . zealous . . . fiery . . . scornful . . . revolutionary . . . spirit of fanaticism . . . hasty . . . Jacobins . . . aggressive . . . vindictive . . . narrowly sectional . . . bitter . . . sputtering . . . fanatical . . . impractical . . . extreme."[2] Such words, in different degrees of concentration, are used by many historians in describing the abolitionists. Like other words of judgment frequently used in historical accounts, they have not been carefully dissected and analyzed, so that while they serve as useful approximations of a general attitude held by the writer (and transferred without question to the reader) they fail to make the kinds of distinctions necessary to move historical narrative closer to the area of social science. The word "extremist," used perhaps more often than any other in connection with the abolitionists, might serve as subject for inspection.

"Extremist" carries a psychological burden when attached to political movements, which it does not bear in other situations. A woman who is extremely beautiful, a man who is extremely kind, a mechanic who is extremely skillful, a child who is extremely healthy—these represent laudable ideals. In politics, however, the label "extremist" carries unfavorable implications. It may

[2] T. Harry Williams, *Lincoln and the Radicals* (Madison, Wis., 1941), pp. 3-6.

mean that the person desires a change in the status quo which is more sweeping than that requested by most people. For instance, in a period when most people are willing to free the slaves, but not to enfranchise them, one wanting to give them equal rights would be considered an extremist. Or it may mean someone who urges a more drastic action to attain a goal shared by most people; that is, someone who advocates slave revolts (like John Brown) rather than compensated emancipation followed by colonization abroad (like Lincoln).

Yet, in any given political situation, there is a very large number of possible alternatives, both in desired goals and in the means of achieving them. The actual alternatives put forward in any one situation are usually much fewer than the total range of possibilities. And the most extreme suggestion put forward at the time will be labeled "extremist" even though it may be far less sweeping than other possible courses of action.

For instance, William Lloyd Garrison, looked upon both by his antagonists and by modern historians as an "extremist," did not seek goals as far-reaching as he might have. He explained, around 1830, his stand for "immediate abolition" as follows: "Immediate abolition does not mean that the slaves shall immediately exercise the right of suffrage, or be eligible to any office, or be emancipated from law, or be free from the benevolent restraints of guardianship." Yet the ideas of suffrage and office-holding were not too much for Thaddeus Stevens and Charles Sumner—nor for Garrison—in 1865, when actual freedom had come for the slaves.

Wendell Phillips, another "extremist," opposed the use of violence to free the slaves. He said, in 1852: "On that point, I am willing to wait. I can be patient. . . . The cause of three millions of slaves, the destruction of a great national institution, must proceed slowly, and like every other change in public sentiment, we must wait patiently for it." John Brown was not as patient.

Charles Sumner, the "radical" Republican in the Senate, did not urge going beyond the Constitution, which gave Southern states the right to maintain slavery if they chose. Garrison, burning the Constitution, was less restrained. The Anti-Slavery Society announced that "we will not operate on the existing relations of society by other than peaceful and lawful means, and that we will give no countenance to violence or insurrection." Yet, the Society was denounced as a hotbed of extremism, the public memory of Nat Turner's violent insurrection having been dimmed by just a few years of time.

The point is, that we are not precise in our standards for measuring "extremism." We do not take into account all possible alternatives, in either goal or method, which may be more extreme than the one we are so labeling. This leads writers to call "extreme" any proposal more drastic than that favored by the majority of articulate people at the time (or by the writer). In a society where the word "extreme" has a bad connotation, in a literate community enamored of the Aristotelian golden mean, we often hurl that word unjustifiably at some proposal which is extreme only in a context of limited alternatives.

Consider how movements denounced as radical begin to look moderate as soon as still more radical movements appear. The NAACP, denounced all over the South as virtually Communist, began to look respectable and legalistic when the sit-inners and Freedom Riders moved into mass, extra-legal action in 1960 and 1961. And the White Citizens Councils of the South could lay claim to being "moderate" segregationists so long as the KKK was around. (The *deliberate* creation of a new extremist group to make an old one more palatable is not yet a major tactic by either right or left; McCarthyism could have been, though it probably was not, the clever offspring of someone who wanted to make "normal" Communist-hunting in this country seem mild.)

With the criterion for extremism so flexible, with the limits constantly shifting, how can we decide the value or wrongness of a position by whether it is "extreme" or "moderate"? We accept these labels because they afford us a test simple enough to avoid mental strain. Also, it is easy and comfortable—especially for intellectuals who do not share the piercing problems of the hungry or helplessly diseased of the world (who, in other words, face no *extreme* problems)—to presume always that the "moderate" solution is the best.

To jump to the cry "extremism" at the first glimpse of the unfamiliar is like a boy with his little telescope peering into the heavens and announcing that the star he dimly perceives at his edge of vision is the farthest object in the universe. It was James Russell Lowell who said: ". . . there is no cant more foolish or more common than theirs who under the mask of discretion, moderation, statesmanship, and what not, would fain convict of fanaticism all that transcends their own limits. . . . From the zoophyte upward everything is *ultra* to something else. . . ."[3]

If the notion of "extremism" is too nebulous to sustain a firm judgment on a goal or a tactic, how do we judge? One point of reference might be the nature and severity of the problem. Even that moderate, Lao Tzu, said you use a boat for a stream and a litter for a mountain path; you adapt your means to your problem. While more modest evils might be dislodged by a few sharp words, the elimination of slavery clearly required more drastic action. The abolitionists did not deceive themselves that they were gentle and temperate; they quite consciously measured their words to the enormity of the evil.

Garrison said in 1833: "How, then, ought I to feel and speak and write, in view of a system which is red with innocent blood drawn from the bodies of millions of my

[3] James Russell Lowell, *The Anti-Slavery Papers of James Russell Lowell* (Boston, 1902), II, 82-83.

countrymen by the scourge of brutal drivers. . . . My soul should be, as it is, on fire. I should thunder, I should lighten, I should blow the trumpet of alarm long and loud. I should use just such language as is most descriptive of the crime."

How evil was slavery? It was a complex phenomenon, different in every individual instance, with the treatment of slaves varying widely. But the whole range of variation was in a general framework of unspeakable inhumanity. Even at its "best," slavery was a ferocious attack on man's dignity. It was described matter-of-factly by a supporter of the system, Judge Edmund Ruffin of North Carolina: "Such services can only be expected from one who has no will of his own; who surrenders his will in implicit obedience to another. Such obedience is the consequence only of uncontrolled authority over the body. There is no remedy. This discipline belongs to the state of slavery. . . . It constitutes the curse of slavery to both the bond and the free portion of our population. But it is inherent in the relation of master and slave."[4]

And at its worst, slavery was, as Allan Nevins has said: ". . . the greatest misery, the greatest wrong, the greatest curse to white and black alike that America has ever known."[5] Ads for fugitive slaves in the Southern press (5,400 advertisements a year) contained descriptions like the following to aid apprehension: ". . . Stamped N.E. on the breast and having both small toes cut off. . . . Has some scars on his back that show above the skin, caused by the whip. . . . Has an iron band around his neck. . . . Has a ring of iron on his left foot. . . . Has on a large neck iron, with a huge pair of horns and a large bar or band of iron on his left leg. . . . Branded on the left cheek, thus 'R', and a piece is taken off her left ear on the same side; the same letter is branded on the inside of both legs." One plantation diary read: ". . . whipped

---

[4] Ralph Korngold, *Two Friends of Man* (Boston, 1950), p. 85.
[5] Allan Nevins, *Ordeal of the Union* (New York, 1947), I, 461.

every field hand this evening."[6] A Natchez slave who attacked a white man was chained to a tree and burned alive.

Against this, how mild Garrison's words seem.

Emotionalism and Irrationality

In the 1820's, G. F. Milton wrote, in *The Eve of Conflict*, "a new and rival spirit welled up from the West . . . an emotional democracy, bottoming itself on Rousseau's mystic claims of innate rights, looking on Liberty as a spontaneous creation and asserting rights unconnected with responsibilities, among these the universal manhood competence for self-government. . . . The Abolition movement . . . was a manifestation of emotional democracy." Milton talks further of "deep-seated passions" and "the emotional flood . . . psychic forces clamoring for expression . . . a drive for reform, change, agitation, which boded ill for any arbitrament of intelligence." Thoreau, Parker, and other reformers, he says, "showed a remarkably keen insight into latent mass emotions and did not hesitate to employ appropriate devices to mobilize the mob mind."[7]

Fanaticism, irrationality, emotionalism—these are the qualities attributed again and again, in a mood of sharp criticism, to the abolitionists; and, indeed, to radical reformers in general. How valid is the criticism?

If being "emotional" means creating a state of excitement, both for oneself and for others, which intensifies the forms of already existent behavior, or creates new, more energetic behavior patterns, then we need not argue. The abolitionists were all, in varying degrees, emotional in their response to situations and in the stimuli they projected into the atmosphere. What *is* arguable is the notion that this "emotionalism" is to be deplored.

[6] Korngold, *loc.cit.*
[7] George F. Milton, *The Eve of Conflict* (Boston, 1934), p. 156.

The intellectual is taken aback by emotional display. It appears to him an attack on that which he most reveres—reason. One of his favorite terms of praise is "dispassionate." The words "calm . . . judicious . . . reasonable" seem to belong together. He points to evil rousers of emotion: the Hitlers, the Southern demagogues of racism, the religious charlatans, and faith healers. And yet, sitting in a Negro Baptist Church in the deep South during the desegregation movement of the 1960's, and listening to the crowd sing "We shall overcome . . . we shall overcome . . ." and hearing it cry "Freedom! Freedom!" the intellectual may well feel a surge of joy and love, damped only slightly by a twinge of uneasiness at his spontaneous display of feeling.

He is uneasy, I would suggest, because of a failure to recognize several things: that emotion is a *morally neutral* instrument for a wide variety of ends; that it serves a positive purpose when linked to laudable goals; that it is not "irrational" but "nonrational" because, being merely an instrument, its rationality is derived only from the value with which it is linked.

When, at a high moment of tension in the battle over slavery, William Lloyd Garrison first heard the freed Negro Frederick Douglass speak, at a crowded meeting in Nantucket, he rose and cried out: "Have we been listening to a man—or a thing?" The audience stirred. In this flash of words and transferred emotion, a group of New England men and women, far removed from the plantation and its daily reminders of human debasement, were confronted with an experience from which they were normally separated by space and social status. By this confrontation, they became more ready to act against an evil which existed just as crassly before Garrison's words were spoken, but whose meaning now flooded in on them for the first time.

The Horst Wessel Song drove Nazi myrmidons forward, but the Battle Hymn of the Republic inspired antislavery fighters. Like music and poetry, whose essence is the enlargement of sensuous experience, and whose potency can be focused in any ethical direction—or in none —the agitation of emotions by words or actions is an art. And as such, it is an instrument of whatever moral camp employs it.

What needs to be said, finally, to assuage the embarrassment of the emotionally aroused intellectual, is that there is no necessary connection between emotionalism and irrationality. A lie may be calmly uttered, and a truth may be charged with emotion. Emotion can be used to make more rational decisions, if by that we mean decisions based on greater knowledge, for greater knowledge involves not only extension but intensity. Who "knows" more about slavery—the man who has in his head all the available information (how many Negroes are enslaved, how much money is spent by the plantation for their upkeep, how many run away, how many revolt, how many are whipped and how many are given special privileges) and calmly goes about his business, or the man who has less data, but is moved by a book (Harriet Beecher Stowe's) or by an orator (Wendell Phillips) to *feel* the reality of slavery so intensely that he will set up a station on the underground railroad? Rationality is limited by time, space, and status, which intervene between the individual and the truth. Emotion can liberate it.

Does the Agitator Distort the Facts?

Abolitionist reformers, and those who supported them, historian Avery Craven wrote in *The Coming of the Civil War*, spread thousands of distortions about the South. The American people, he said, "permitted their shortsighted politicians, their overzealous editors, and their pious reformers to emotionalize real and potential differences and to conjure up distorted impressions of those who dwelt in other parts of the nation. For more than two decades, these molders of public opinion steadily created the fiction of two distinct peoples contending for the right to preserve and expand their sacred cultures. . . . In time, a people came to believe . . . that the issues were between right and wrong; good and evil."[8] Craven's thesis is that the war was repressible, but abolitionist (and slaveholder) exaggerations brought it about.

A similar charge is made by T. Harry Williams in *Lincoln and the Radicals*: "Thirty years of abolitionist preachings had instilled in the popular mind definite thought patterns and reactions regarding the Southern people and their social system. It was widely believed that slavery had brutalized the Southern character, that the owner of human chattels was a dour, repulsive fiend, animated by feelings of savage hatred toward Negroes and Northern whites."[9]

Because the reformist agitator is so often charged with distortion and exaggeration, and because thinkers with an abiding concern for the truth are often led by such charges to keep a safe distance from such agitators, it is essential to discuss this point.

Distinctions ought first to be made between outright misstatements of fact and personal slander on the one hand, and on the other, exaggerations of the truth, and the singling out of those aspects of a complex truth which support the viewpoint of the reformer. It needs to be acknowledged that false statements have at times been made by radical reformers, and this is unpardonable, for if the reformer speaks the truth, then material exists on all hands to support him, and he needs no falsification of the evidence to back his case. As for character-denigration, it is not only repugnant to truth-seekers, but makes explanation embarrassing when the attacked person is revealed as something different. Witness Phillips' angry assault on Lincoln: "Who is this huckster in politics? Who

[8] Avery Craven, *The Coming of the Civil War* (N.Y., 1942), 2.
[9] Williams, *op.cit.*, p. 285.

is this county court advocate?" And during the war: "... if he had been a traitor, he could not have worked better to strengthen one side, and hazard the success of the other." And again, in a *Liberator* article, Phillips' headline: "Abraham Lincoln, the Slave-Hound of Illinois."

More serious, and more frequent, however, are charges of exaggeration and distortion, leveled at the radicals. At the root of this problem is that once we get past simple factual statements ("On March 3, 1851, field hand .... was whipped by his master.") and begin to deal with general characterizations of social institutions (like Nevins' statement about slavery being "the greatest misery, the greatest curse. . . .") we are in a realm where words like "true" and "false" cannot be applied so simply. Slavery was a complex institution, and no one statement can describe it fully. Slave-master relationships varied from kindness to cruelty and also defy generalization. We are here in that philosophical realm dealing with the theory of knowledge, a field in which historians play all the time, without paying any attention to the rules, while the philosophers sit in their studies discussing the rules and rarely look out the window to see how the game is played.

There is an answer to the problem of how to state simply a complex truth—but this requires an activist outlook rare among scholars. It means deciding from a particular ethical base what is the action-need of the moment, and to concentrate on that aspect of the truth-complex which fulfills that need. If we start from the ethical assumption that it is fundamentally wrong to hold in bondage—whether kindly or cruelly—another human being, and that the freeing of such persons requires penetrating the moral sensibilities of a nation, then it is justifiable to focus on those aspects of the complexity which support this goal. When you teach a child to be careful crossing the street, and say, "You can be killed by an

automobile," you are singling out of the totality of automobile behaviors that small percentage of incidents in
which people are killed. You are not telling the whole
truth about automobiles and traffic. But you are emphasizing that portion of the truth which supports a morally
desirable action.

The complaint by T. Harry Williams that as a result
of abolitionist agitation, "It was widely believed that
slavery had brutalized the Southern character. . . ." takes
note of an abolitionist emphasis which does not photo-
graphically depict total reality. Not every white Southerner was brutalized by slavery. And yet, some were, and
many others were affected—by the simple fact of learning
to accept such a system without protest. These effects are
so various and complicated that the word "brutalized"
does not exactly fit, nor does any other word. But the
focusing on this fact of brutalization points to a crucial
aspect of slavery, and the recognition of that aspect
may be decisive in overthrowing a terrible system.
The scholar who accepts no harsh judgment because
it does not do justice to the entire complex truth, can
really accept no judgments about society, because all are
simplifications of the complex. The result is scholarly detachment from the profound ethical conflicts of society,
and from that human concern without which scholarship
becomes a pretentious game.

Historical Perspective and the Radical

It is paradoxical that the historian, who is presumably
blessed with historical perspective, should judge the radical from within the narrow moral base of the radical's
period of activity, while the radical assesses his immediate
society from the vantage point of some future, better era.
If progress is desirable, and if escape from the bonds of
the immediate is healthy, whose perspective is more accurate—that of the agitator, or that of the scolding historian?

James Russell Lowell wrote in 1849: ". . . the simple fact undoubtedly is that were the Abolitionists to go back to the position from which they started, they would find themselves less fanatical than a very respectable minority of the people. The public follows them step by step, occupying the positions they have successively fortified and quitted, and it is necessary that they should keep in advance in order that people may not be shocked by waking up and finding themselves Abolitionists."[10]

Garrison himself took note of the profound change in the nation by 1860, thirty years from the time he had started his tiny, maligned newspaper. He spoke to the Massachusetts Anti-Slavery Society, shortly after John Brown's execution, which had brought shock and indignation throughout the North: "Whereas, ten years since, there were thousands who could not endure my lightest rebuke of the South, they can now swallow John Brown whole, and his rifle into the bargain."

The historian too often moves back a hundred years into a moral framework barbarian by modern standards and thinks inside it, while the radical shakes the rafters of this framework at the risk of his life. Wendell Phillips, speaking affectionately of the abolitionist leader Angelina Grimké, said: "Were I to single out the moral and intellectual trait which most won me, it was her serene indifference to the judgement of those about her." That kind of indifference (David Riesman calls it inner directedness) is hard to find in contemporary scholarship.

Compromise

The argument over the wisdom of radical agitation in the tactics of social reform was aptly expressed in Boston in pre-Civil War years by two leading figures. Samuel May, speaking of Garrison, said: ". . . he will shake our nation to its center, but he will shake slavery out of it." Reverend Lyman Beecher said: "True wisdom consists

10 Lowell, op.cit., p. 53.

in advocating a cause only so far as the community will sustain the reformer." The agitator, declare the moderate reformers, shakes so hard that he makes compromise impossible, alienates friends, and delays rather than speeds the coming of reform.

Compromise was not disdained by the abolitionists; they were fully conscious of the fact that the outcome of any social struggle is almost always some form of compromise. But they were also aware of that which every intelligent radical knows: that to compromise in advance is to vitiate at the outset that power for progress which only the radical propels into the debate. Lowell put this most vividly, declaring that the abolitionists "are looked upon as peculiarly ungrateful and impracticable if they do not devote their entire energies to soliciting nothing, and express a thankfulness amounting almost to rapture when they get it."[11]

The abolitionist took an advanced position so that even if pushed back by compromise, substantial progress would result. Garrison wrote: "Urge immediate abolition as earnestly as we may, it will be gradual abolition in the end." And Phillips said: "If we would get half a loaf, we must demand the whole of it." The Emancipation Proclamation itself was a compromise, the tortured product of a long battle between radicals and moderates in and out of the Lincoln administration, and only the compelling force of the abolitionist intransigeants made it come as soon as it did.

Two factors demand recognition by moderates who disdain "extreme" positions on the ground that compromise is necessary. One is the above-mentioned point that the early projection of an advanced position ensures a compromise on more favorable terms than would be the case where the timorous reformer compromises at the start (in which case the result is a compromise upon a compromise, since he will be forced to retreat even from his re-

[11] *Ibid.*, p. 80.

treat after all the forces are calculated at the social weigh-ing-in). The other is that there is a huge difference be-tween the passive wisher-for-change who quietly adds up the vectors and makes a decision as to which is the com-posite of all existing forces, and the active reformer who pushes so hard *in the course of adding-up* that the com-posite itself is changed. The latter—the radical—is view-ing compromise as a dynamic process, in which his own actions are part of the total force being calculated. He bases his estimate of what is possible on a graph in which his own action and its consequences are calculated from the first.

Moderation as a Tactic

Does the agitator alienate potential allies by the ex-tremism of his demands, or the harshness of his language? Lewis Tappan, the wealthy New Yorker who financed many abolitionist activities, wrote anxiously to George Thompson, the British abolitionist: "The fact need not be concealed from you that several emancipationists so disapprove of the harsh, and, as they think, the unchris-tian language of *The Liberator*, that they do not feel justified in upholding it." This, in general, was the feel-ing of the Executive Committee of the American Anti-Slavery Society in the early years of the movement. Un-doubtedly, the Society itself was not diverted from its aim of abolishing slavery because of Garrison's immoderation; they were concerned lest others be alienated.

But who? The slaveholder? The slave? The moderate reformer? The open-minded conservative? It needs to be acknowledged that different sections of the population will respond differently to the same appeal, and in judg-ing the effect of bold words upon the population, this population must be broken up into parts, based on the varying degrees of receptivity to the ideas of the reformer. Why should the radical soften his language or his pro-gram to please that element of the population which cannot possibly be pleased by anything short of total surrender of principle, whose self-interest in fact dictates rejection of any reform? Lowell wrote: "The slaveholder, when Mr. Greeley would politely request him to state what method would be most consonant to his feelings, would answer, as did the . . . boy whose mother asked him what he would like for breakfast, 'Just what you ain't gut!' "[12]

Only the hypothesis of common interest for the entire population can justify an appeal to the opponent on the basis of reason, asking him to perceive his interest more accurately. But if in fact there is a diversity of interest, then the lighting up of the truth can only bring out more sharply that conflict which stands in the way of agreement. The slaveholders themselves pointed to the impossibility of their being won over by moderate overtures. In 1854, the editor of the Richmond *Enquirer*, wrote: "That man must be a veritable verdigreen who dreams of pleasing slaveholders, either in church or state, by any method but that of letting slavery alone."[13] William Ellery Channing tried such appeal and failed. One of his brochures against slavery was so mild that some described it as putting people to sleep, but he was abused so harshly it might as well have been one of Garrison's flame-breathing *Liberator* editorials.

With a population of diversified interests, tactics must be adapted and focused specially for each group, and for the group most inimical to reform, it is doubtful that moderation is effective. With the intransigeants, it may be only the most powerful action that impels change. It was Nat Turner's violent slave revolt in Virginia in 1831 that led the Virginia legislature into its famous series of discussions about the abolition of slavery. "For a while indeed," Ralph Korngold writes, "it seemed that what years of propaganda by the Quakers had failed to ac-

[12] *Ibid.*, pp. 88-89.
[13] Korngold, *op.cit.*, p. 89.

complish would come as a result of Turner's blood-letting."[14]

When friends of the reformers rail against harsh words or strong action (as the American Anti-Slavery Society did against Garrison) it is clear that they themselves will not be put off from reform because of it, but fear the effects on others. And if neither extreme opposition nor hard-and-fast friends can be moved by tactics of moderation, this leaves, as a decisive group, that large part of the population which is at neither end of the ideological spectrum, which moves back and forth across the center line, depending on circumstances.

Garrison was quite aware that most of the American population to which he was appealing was not sympathetic with his views, and he was completely conscious of how distant were his own fiery convictions from those of the average American. But he was persuaded, as were Phillips and other leading abolitionists (John Brown felt it, and acted it, if he did not express it intellectually) that only powerful surges of words and feelings could move white people from their complacency about the slave question. He said once in Philadelphia: "Sir, slavery will not be overthrown without excitement, a most tremendous excitement." He must lash with words, he felt, those Americans who had never felt the whip of a slaveowner. To his friend Samuel May, who urged him to keep more cool, saying: "Why, you are all on fire," Garrison replied: "Brother May, I have need to be all on fire, for I have mountains of ice about me to melt."

We have the historical record as a check on whether the vituperative language of Garrison, the intemperate appeals of Wendell Phillips, hurt or advanced the popular sentiment against slavery. In the 1830's a handful of men cried out against slavery and were beaten, stoned, and shot to death by their Northern compatriots. By 1849, antislavery sentiment was clearly increasing, and some of

[14] *Ibid.*, p. 54.

the greatest minds and voices in America were speaking out for abolition. Lowell asked curtly of those who charged the abolitionists with retarding the movement: ". . . has there really been a change of public opinion for the worse, either at the North or the South, since the *Liberator* came into existence eighteen years ago?"[15] And by 1860, with millions of Americans convinced that slavery was an evil, open insurrection by John Brown brought more public support than had the mere words of Garrison thirty years before.

This is not to say that extremists may not drive possible allies from their movement. But this is generally not because of the ferocity of their attack on an institution which is the object of general dislike, but because of their insertion of other issues which do not touch public sensibilities as much. Theodore Weld, an effective Midwestern abolitionist, who was marvelous at organizing abolitionist societies in Ohio, criticized Garrison for his violent attacks on the clergy, for his anarchist utterances against government in general, and for his insistence on bringing many other issues—women's rights, pacifism, etc.—into the antislavery fight. For marginal supporters, such side issues may bring alienation. Whether such estrangement would be significant enough to offset the general social value of having one important issue ride on the back of another, is another question.

The Agitator and the Politician

The politician is annoyed and angry at the pushing of the radical reformer, and the moderate observer thinks the radical unfair and injudicious in making extreme demands of the man in office, but both critics fail to distinguish between the social role of the politician and that of the agitator. In general, this distinction is perceived more clearly by reformers than by office-holders. Wendell Phillips put it neatly: "The reformer is careless of num-

15 Lowell, *op.cit.*, p. 50.

bers, disregards popularity, and deals only with ideas, conscience, and common sense. . . . He neither expects nor is overanxious for immediate success. The politician dwells in an everlasting now. . . . His office is not to instruct public opinion but to represent it."

James Russell Lowell expressed the idea in another way: "The Reformer must expect comparative isolation, and he must be strong enough to bear it. He cannot look for the sympathy and cooperation of popular majorities. Yet these are the tools of the politician. . . . All true Reformers are incendiaries. But it is the hearts, brains, and souls of their fellow-men which they set on fire, and in so doing they perform the function appropriated to them in the wise order of Providence."[16] The observer who is critical of the radical may be subconsciously conjuring the picture of a world peopled only with radicals, a world of incessant shouting, lamenting, and denunciation. But it would be good for him to also imagine a world without *any* radicals—a placid, static, and evil-ridden world with victims of injustice left to their own devices, a world with the downtrodden friendless. In all ages, it has been first the radical, and only later the moderate, who has held out a hand to men knocked to the ground by the social order.

The moderate, whose sensitive ears are offended by the wild language of the radical, needs to consider the necessary division of labor in a world full of evil, a division in which agitators for reform play an indispensable role. When Horace Greeley charged Garrison with fanaticism, Lowell retorted: "Why God sent him into the world with that special mission and none other. . . . It is that which will make his name a part of our American history. We would not have all men fanatics, but let us be devoutly thankful for as many of that kind as we can get. They are by no means too common as yet."[17]

In Abraham Lincoln we have the prototype of the political man in power, with views so moderate as to require

[16] *Ibid.*, pp. 88-89.   [17] *Ibid.*, pp. 82-83.

the pressure of radicals to stimulate action. The politician, by the very nature of the electoral process, is a compromiser and a trimmer, who sets his sails by the prevailing breezes, and without the hard blowing of the radical reformer would either drift actionless or sail along with existing injustice. It is hard to find a set of statements more clearly expressive of the politician's ambivalence than those which Lincoln made during his 1858 race for the Senate against Douglass. At that time he told a Chicago audience in July: "Let us discard this quibbling about this man and the other man, this race and the other race being inferior, and therefore they must be placed in an inferior position." But in September, he told an audience in southern Illinois:

> "I am not, nor ever have been, in favor of bringing about in any way the social or political equality of the white and black races. I am not nor ever have been in favor of making voters of the free negroes, or jurors, or qualifying them to hold office, or having them marry with white people. I will say in addition that there is a physical difference between the white and black races which, I suppose, will forever forbid the two races living together upon terms of social and political equality; and in as much as they cannot so live, that while they do remain together, there must be the position of the superiors and the inferiors; and that I, as much as any other man, am in favor of the superior being assigned to the white man."

The most shocking statement about Lincoln—and all the more shocking when we realize its essential truth— was made by Frederick Douglass in 1876 at the unveiling of the Freedmen's Monument in Washington:

> "To protect, defend, and perpetuate slavery in the United States where it existed Abraham Lincoln was

not less ready than any other President to draw the sword of the nation. He was ready to execute all the supposed constitutional guarantees of the United States Constitution in favor of the slave system anywhere inside the slave states. He was willing to pursue, recapture, and send back the fugitive slave to his master, and to suppress a slave rising for liberty, though his guilty master were already in arms against the Government. The race to which we belong were not the special objects of his consideration. Knowing this, I concede to you, my white fellow citizens, a pre-eminence in his worship at once full and supreme. First, midst, and last, you and yours were the objects of his deepest affection and his most earnest solicitude. You are the children of Abraham Lincoln. We are at best only his stepchildren, children by adoption, children by force of circumstances and necessity."

In the fascinating dialogue—sometimes articulated, sometimes unspoken—between Abraham Lincoln and the abolitionists, we have the classic situation of the politician vis-à-vis the radical reformer. It would be wrong to say that Lincoln was completely a politician—his fundamental humanitarianism did not allow that—and wrong to say that some of the abolitionists did not occasionally play politics—but on both sides the aberrations were slight, and they played their respective roles to perfection.

Albert Beveridge, in his biography of Lincoln, emphasized the fact that despite the influence of Herndon, his abolitionist law partner, Lincoln's early environment was powerfully affected by the Southern viewpoint. This accounted for "his speeches, his letters, his silence, his patience and mildness, his seeming hesitations, his immortal inaugural, his plans for reconstruction."[18] Bev-

18 Albert Beveridge, *Abraham Lincoln* (Boston, 1928), III, 32.

eridge saw Lincoln as a man who "almost perfectly reflected public opinion" in his stands. Lincoln opposed repeal of the Fugitive Slave Law, was silent on the violence in Kansas and the beating of Sumner, and followed the tactic of saying nothing except on issues most people agreed on—like stopping the extension of slavery.

During the secession crisis, and through most of the war, Lincoln's stand on slavery was so ambiguous and cautious as to make the British abolitionist George Thompson tell Garrison: "You know how impossible it is at this moment to vindicate, as one would wish, the course of Mr. Lincoln. In no one of his utterances is there an assertion of a great principle—no appeal to right or justice. In everything he does and says, affecting the slave, there is the alloy of expediency."[19] Lincoln made no move against slavery in those border states siding with the Union, except to offer them money as an inducement for gradual abolition, and when General David Hunter and John Fremont acted to free slaves under their command Lincoln revoked their orders. His position was quite clear (as both abolitionist-minded Ralph Korngold and conservative-minded Harry Williams agree in their historical studies); Lincoln's first desire was to save the Union; abolition was secondary and he would sacrifice it, if necessary, to maintain Republican rule over the entire nation.

While Lincoln kept reading the meter of public opinion, the abolitionists assaulted in massive ideological waves both the public and the meter-reader. In the winter of 1861-62, fifty thousand persons heard Wendell Phillips speak. Millions read his speeches. Petitions and delegations besieged Lincoln at the White House. Garrison went easy on Lincoln, but his own writings had created an army of impatients. Samuel Bowles, editor of the *Springfield Republican*, wrote that "a new crop of Rad-

[19] Korngold, *op.cit.*, p. 285.

icals has sprung up, who are resisting the President and making mischief."[20]

Evidence is that Lincoln, who had reflected public opinion well enough in 1860 to win the election, was not abreast of it in 1861 and 1862, on the issue of slavery. And this points to something with huge significance: that while both the politician and the agitator have their own specific roles to play in that fitful march toward utopia, which involves both surge and consolidation, the politician meter-reader is plagued by an inherent defect. His reading is a static one, not taking into account the going and imminent actions of the reformers, which change the balance of forces even while he is making the decision. The tendency, therefore, is for all political decisions to be conservative. Most of all, the politician is so preoccupied with evaluation of the existing forces that he leaves out of the account his own power, which is expended on *reading* public opinion rather than on *changing* it.

Where presidents have been more than reflectors of a static consensus, the exertion of their force into the balance of power has usually been in pursuit of nationalistic goals rather than reformist ones. The carrying out of any war requires the conscious shifting of the balance of public sentiment in support of the war, which is not likely to have enthusiastic and overwhelming support before its inception. (Even the supposed mass clamor for war in 1898 was an exaggerated image created in a rather placid pond by the heavy stones of Hearst and Pulitzer.) Lincoln, Wilson, Roosevelt, and Truman worked hard to create popular support for the wars they administered.

Andrew Jackson's dynamic action on the bank was a creator rather than a reflector of public opinion; but historians and economists are still puzzled over whether his policy was designed genuinely to broaden economic democracy to reach the lowest societal levels, or was on be-

20 *Ibid.*

half of disgruntled small bankers and entrepreneurs hearkening for a laissez-faire which would increase their own share of national profit-taking. The reforms of Teddy Roosevelt and Wilson were largely diluted toasts to Populist and Progressive protest. Franklin D. Roosevelt's New Deal comes closest to a dynamic effort to push through a reform program, while creating the sentiment to support it. Since Roosevelt, we have had no such phenomenon.

In the area of racial equality, from Lincoln to Kennedy, the man at the pinnacle of national political power has chosen to play the cautious game of responding, inch by inch, to the powerful push of "extremists," "troublemakers," and "radicals." For Lincoln it was the abolitionists; for Kennedy the sit-inners and Freedom Riders. The man sitting in the White House has the inner mechanism of the public opinion meter in his lap; he can, by a direct manipulation of its gears, bring a transformation that otherwise requires a thousand times more energy directed from the outside by protest and outcry. So far, no one with presidential power has played such a dynamic role in the area of racial exclusiveness.

Agitators and War

A Tulane University professor of history wrote in the May 1962 issue of the Journal of Southern History:[21]

> "Eventually, however, the abolitionists reached a large Northern audience and thus brought on the bloodiest war in American history. Convinced that they had an exclusive line to God they determined to force their brand of morality on their Southern brethren. It is not surprising that many Southerners still regard this assumption of moral superiority by the New England Puritans—and by their pharisaical heirs the latter-day abolitionists—as obnoxious."

[21] Gerald M. Capers, *Journal of Southern History* (May 1962), p. 249.

One of the standard arguments against the agitator is that his proddings and shoutings, his emotional denunciations, lead to violent conflict—that, in the case of the Civil War, it was the abolitionists who played a crucial role in bringing about the terrible bloodbath. Avery Craven, in *The Coming of the Civil War*, blames "short-sighted politicians . . . over-zealous editors . . . pious reformers" for emotionalizing and exaggerating sectional differences, for bringing people to believe the issue was between good and evil, and thus creating mythical devils to be fought. It was, Craven says, a repressible conflict, made irrepressible by these forces.

It is clear that we cannot ascribe to the abolitionists the power to push moderates into action and at the same time deny that their words and actions have the effect of sharpening conflict over the social issue which concerns them. But the distinction between social conflict and war is overwhelmingly important. Agitators have the power to heighten feelings and tensions, but they are outside of the decision-making machinery which produces a war. It is strange that a society and a culture which are so resentful of "determinist" theories gave great credence to the idea that the Civil War was irrepressible, once given the conflict of ideas represented by slaveholders and abolitionists. This clash, however, existed in sharp form for thirty years without producing war. War became inevitable only with the simultaneous emergence of two factors: the determination of leading Southerners, holding state power, to create a separate nation; and the insistence of the Republicans, in possession of the national government, that no such separate nation must be permitted to exist. It was this issue which brought war, because only this, the issue of national sovereignty, constituted a direct attack on that group which ran the country and had the power to make war.

The institution of slavery did lie at the root of the economic and social schism between the sections. However, it was not the antihuman, immoral aspect of the institution which brought all the weight of national power against it; it was the antitariff, antibank, anticapitalist, antinational aspect of slavery which aroused the united opposition of the only groups in the country with power to make war: the national political leaders and the controllers of the national economy. Jefferson Davis' speech, April 29, 1861, before a special session of the Confederate Congress, saw the Northern motives not as humanitarian, but as based on a desire to control the Union.

The conflict between the slave states and the Northern politicians existed independently of the battle between slaveholders and abolitionists. The latter by itself could not lead to war because the abolitionists were not in charge of war-making machinery (and in fact, did not advocate war as a method of solving their problem). The former conflict by itself could have brought war and did bring it precisely because it brought into collision two forces in both sections of the country with the power to make war. What the abolitionists contributed to this conflict was that they gave Lincoln and the North a moral issue to sanctify and ennoble what was for many Republican leaders a struggle for national power and economic control. They could have waged war without such a moral issue, for politicians have shown the ability to create moral issues on the flimsiest of bases—witness Woodrow Wilson in 1917—but it was helpful to have one at hand.

What the abolitionists did was not to precipitate the war, nor even to cause the basic conflict which led to war—but to ensure, by their kind of agitation, that in the course of the war, some social reform would take place. That this reform was drastically limited is shown by the feeble character of the Emancipation Proclamation (of which Richard Hofstadter has said: "It had all the moral grandeur of a bill of lading").[22]

The Radical Reconstruction period rode along on a zooming moral momentum created by the Civil War, but crass political desires were in control; when these desires could no longer be filled by Negro suffrage, the Negro was sacrificed and Radical Reconstruction consigned to the ash heap. The abolitionists were not responsible for the war—they were responsible for sowing the seeds—with the Thirteenth, Fourteenth, and Fifteenth amendments—of an equalitarian society, seeds which their generation was unwilling to nurture, but which were to come to life after a century.

Agitators Today: The Sit-Inners of the South

There is no point—except for that abstract delight which accompanies historical study—in probing the role of the agitator in the historical process, unless we can learn something from it which is of use today. We have, after a hundred years, a successor to the abolitionist: the sit-in agitator, the boycotter, the Freedom Rider of the 1960's. Every objection—and every defense—applicable to the abolitionist is pertinent to his modern-day counterpart.

When the sit-in movement erupted through the South in the spring of 1960, it seemed a radical, extreme departure from the slow, law-court tactics of the NAACP, which had produced favorable court decisions but few real changes in the deep South. And it upset Southern white liberals sympathetic to the Negro and friendly to the 1954 Supreme Court school decision. This, they felt, was going too far. But the fact that "extremism" is a relative term, and the additional fact that the passage of time and the advance of social change make a formerly radical step seem less radical, became clear within a year.

[22] Richard Hofstadter, *The American Political Tradition* (New York, 1954), p. 132.

For one thing, the increased frequency and widespread character of the sit-ins got people accustomed to them and they began to look less outrageously revolutionary. But more important, the advent of the Freedom Rides in 1961—busloads of integrated Northerners riding through the most backward areas of the deep South in direct and shocking violation of local law and custom—made the sit-ins seem a rather moderate affair. And, at the same time, the emergence of the Black Muslims as antiwhite militants, with their claim of black superiority, put the integrationist advocates of nonviolence in the position of being more radical than the NAACP, but less so than the Black Muslims. Nonviolence itself, the accepted tactic of the sit-in and Freedom Ride people, was a rather moderate tactic in a century of violent upheaval throughout the world.

The old argument of Garrison that his radicalism was pitched to the level of the evil he was fighting is directly applicable to the new young radicals of the American South. Is sitting at a lunch counter in a white restaurant, and refusing to leave, really a very extreme measure in relation to the evil of segregation? Is insisting on the right to sit side by side, regardless of race, in a bus or train or waiting room, a terribly radical move—in the face of a century of deep humiliation for one-tenth of the nation? By 1960 the NAACP, denounced in 1954 and 1955 as radical and Communistic, seemed remarkably mild next to the sit-in students. By 1961 the sit-in students seemed moderate against the Freedom Riders, and the Riders themselves even timid compared to the Muslims.

The element of emotionalism, present in any mass movement, has a special place in the movement for racial equality in the 1960's. Every important demonstration and action has been accompanied by church-meetings, singing, fiery oratory. But all of this has been an instrument designed to heighten a most rational objective: the securing in fact as well as in theory the basic principles of the Declaration of Independence and the Fourteenth Amendment to the Constitution. The leadership of Martin Luther King, Jr. represents that new blending of emotional religion and intellectual sophistication which marks the current equal rights campaign. King plays upon the emotions and religious feelings of his people, but contains this within a controlled rationality which drives towards carefully defined goals.

Does the race agitator in the South today exaggerate the truth about conditions in that part of the country? "Don't believe all those stories you hear about us," a soft-voiced woman from South Carolina told me once. "We're not all that bad to our colored people." She was right, and wrong. The South is far better than most agitated Northerners imagine; and much worse than any white Northerner believes. It is a complexity of swift progress and deep-rooted evil. Dramatic and publicized progress in race relations is still only a thin veneer on a deep crust of degradation. To be a Negro in the South has, for most Negroes, most of the time, no drastic consequences like beatings or lynchings. But it has, for all Negroes in the South, all of the time, a fundamental hurt which cannot be put into words or statistics. No Negro, even in that minority of wealth and position, can escape the fact that he is a special person, that wherever he goes, whatever he does, he must be conscious of this fact, that his children will bear a special burden on their emotions from the moment they begin to make contact with the outside world. For the majority, their entire way of life is conditioned by it, the fact that the women must be office cleaners rather than stenographers, that the men must be porters rather than foremen; their children may have it better, but their own generation, their own lives, constitute a sacrifice offered to the future.

And for a certain minority of Negroes, there is police brutality, courtroom injustice, horrible conditions in Southern jails and work-gangs, the simple fact that capital punishment is much more likely to be invoked for a Negro criminal than for a white. The South is not one mad orgy of lynchings and brutality, as Communist propaganda might have it. But there is a kind of permanent brutality in the atmosphere, which nobody's propaganda has quite accurately described. Because of this, no accusation directed against the South is much of an exaggeration. Any emphasis upon the evil aspects of Southern life is a valuable prod to the movement for equality.

As for the moderate exhortation to compromise, the angry but cool Negro students in the South have learned that this is best left as the very last act in the succession of moves toward settlement of any issue. Department stores, before the sit-ins, were willing to compromise by adding more segregated eating facilities for Negroes. After the sit-ins, the only compromise which the students had to accept was to wait a few months in some cases, or to leave some restaurants out of the settlement, or to put up with inaction on connected issues like employment rights; but the lunch counters were fully integrated. The lesson has been well learned by now: throw the full weight of attack into the fray despite demands for prior concessions; then the final compromise will be at the highest possible level.

"You'll alienate the merchants if you sit-in, and they'll never agree to integrate," the students were told when they began their movement. But they knew, through some semiconscious perception rather than by complex rational analysis, that certain antagonists in a social struggle cannot be won over by gentleness, only by pressure. The merchants were alienated, not only from the students, but from their customers. It was the latter effect which was most striking, and it led to their capitulation and the integration of lunch counters in leading Southern cities. On the other hand, students were careful to try not to alienate the ordinary Southern white, the customer, the observer. They were scrupulously polite, nonviolent, and impressive in their intelligence and deportment. With a precise instinct, they singled out of the complex of opponents which ones would have to be irritated, and which would need to be cajoled.

In spite of some fearful murmurs immediately after the 1954 Supreme Court Decision, there is no prospect of civil war in the United States over desegregation. And this points up the fact that the total collision between two power groups which is called war cannot come about through the action of radical reformers, who stand outside these power groupings. The movement for desegregation today has all the elements of the abolition movement: its moral fervor and excitement, its small group of martyrs and mass of passive supporters, its occasional explosions in mob scenes and violence. But there will be no war because there are no issues between the real power groups in society serious enough, deep enough, to necessitate war as a solution. War remains the instrument of the state. All that reformers can do is put some moral baggage on its train.

The role of the politician vis-à-vis the agitator was revealed as clearly in the Kennedy Administration as in was under Lincoln. Like Lincoln, Kennedy read the meter of public concern and reacted to it, but never exerted the full force of his office to change the reading drastically. He too had a deeply ingrained humanitarianism, but it took the shock of Birmingham to bring from him his first clear moral appeal against segregation and his first move for civil rights legislation (the Civil Rights Act of 1964). Lyndon Johnson, holding to the level created by the agitation of that Birmingham summer, still hesitated—even while modern-day abolitionists were being murdered in Mississippi—to revoke the Compromise of 1877 and decisively enforce federal law in that state.

Behind every one of the national government's moves toward racial equality lies the sweat and effort of boycotts, picketing, beatings, sit-ins, and mass demonstrations. All of our recent administrations have constituted a funnel into which gargantuan human effort—organized by radical agitators like Martin Luther King, Jr. and the young professional militants of the Student Non-Violent Coordinating Committee—is poured, only to emerge at the other end in slow dribbles of social progress. No American President, from Lincoln to Johnson, was able to see the immense possibilities for social change that lie in a *dynamic* reading of public opinion. Progress toward racial equality in the United States is certain, but this is because agitators, radicals, and "extremists"— black and white together—are giving the United States its only living reminder that it was once a revolutionary nation.

INDEX